PRIVILEGE, PERSECUTION, AND PROPHECY

Privilege, Persecution, and Prophecy

The Catholic Church in Spain
1875–1975

FRANCES LANNON

For my valued colleague Matt Kelly, with very best wishes,
Frances Lannon
29.09.2003

CLARENDON PRESS · OXFORD

This book has been printed digitally and produced in a standard specification in order to ensure its continuing availability

OXFORD
UNIVERSITY PRESS

Great Clarendon Street, Oxford OX2 6DP

Oxford University Press is a department of the University of Oxford.
It furthers the University's objective of excellence in research, scholarship,
and education by publishing worldwide in

Oxford New York

Auckland Bangkok Buenos Aires Cape Town Chennai
Dar es Salaam Delhi Hong Kong Istanbul Karachi Kolkata
Kuala Lumpur Madrid Melbourne Mexico City Mumbai Nairobi
São Paulo Shanghai Singapore Taipei Tokyo Toronto

with an associated company in Berlin

Oxford is a registered trade mark of Oxford University Press
in the UK and in certain other countries

Published in the United States
by Oxford University Press Inc., New York

© Frances Lannon 1987

The moral rights of the author have been asserted
Database right Oxford University Press (maker)

Reprinted 2002

All rights reserved. No part of this publication may be reproduced,
stored in a retrieval system, or transmitted, in any form or by any means,
without the prior permission in writing of Oxford University Press,
or as expressly permitted by law, or under terms agreed with the appropriate
reprographics rights organization. Enquiries concerning reproduction
outside the scope of the above should be sent to the Rights Department,
Oxford University Press, at the address above

You must not circulate this book in any other binding or cover
and you must impose this same condition on any acquirer

ISBN 0-19-821923-7

Jacket photograph: Republican militiamen 'execute' a statue of the Sacred Heart at the Cerro de los Angeles near Madrid, 1936. Associated Press.

Preface

ALL dates chosen to delimit periods of historical research are arbitrary, but more than the attractions of formal symmetry led to the decision to begin this book with the restoration of the Bourbon monarchy in 1875 and end it with a further monarchical restoration exactly one hundred years later. Just as the beginning of Alfonso XIII's reign gave the Spanish Church a decisive opportunity of recuperation after decades of damage, so Franco's death in 1975 left the Church at an equally crucial turning-point as Spain for the first time created a democratic regime based on general if not universal agreement. Catholic experience and values, Catholic institutions and controversies form an essential part of the social and political history of Spain in the turbulent intervening decades. Without taking them into account, it is not possible to understand Spanish social structure or political mobilization or ideological conflict, or the eventual emergence of a consensus on the need for democratic pluralism. So far, however, no comprehensive account of Catholic life and politics in this period, such as this book seeks to provide, has been attempted. The enterprise is only possible at all now because of the numerous valuable studies published in recent years by historians, sociologists, and anthropologists, on subjects as diverse as Catholic peasant and labour organizations, religious practice, religious festivals, and Church–state relations.

My chief aim in writing this book has been to explore the Spanish Catholic world and to trace its impact on Spanish culture, society, and politics. I have not paid detailed attention to purely institutional ecclesiastical matters, like the internal subdivisions of dioceses; and at the other extreme, I have dealt only briefly with the motives and aspirations of the Church's enemies. The reader will find here no sustained history of anti-clericalism, even though that would have helped explain more fully the defensive mentality so prevalent in ecclesiastical circles, nor any proper description of the Franco regime's use of repression and torture, although that was largely responsible for the bitter opposition to the dictatorship demonstrated by many priests and lay people in the 1960s and 1970s. To analyse Catholicism in Spain in this period is already, perhaps, an over-ambitious venture: to analyse in equal depth all the events and influences that impinged on it would require another book. Because of my interest in the internal structures and tensions of Catholic attitudes and values, I have relied mainly on Catholic and ecclesiastical sources. Both popular religion and the Church—like everything else Spanish—varied enormously from one area to another. I have therefore tried to avoid ever giving the impression that Madrid—or the primatial see of Toledo—was Spain, and have drawn heavily on local materials elsewhere, including Andalusia, Catalonia, and the Basque country.

The book is divided into two sections, the first on religious practice and Catholic culture, the second on Catholic politics. This is not because I believe these categories are in any way mutually exclusive. On the contrary, at every step the political and the pastoral are interdependent. The analysis of Social Catholicism presented in Chapter 6, or of the Mondragón co-operatives in Chapter 9, belong as much with pastoral and devotional life as with politics, while the alienation of many priests from Franco's dictatorship traced in Chapter 4 on the clergy is an essential part of the political history of the end of the period. Everything in Part I is relevant to Catholic politics, and the implicit definition of politics in Part II cannot and does not exclude consideration of theological and pastoral trends. The rather spurious division has allowed me, however, to adopt different chronologies. Changes in religious practice and mentality, or in the expression of religious commitment, occur at a pace quite different from the rapid movements of political controversy. In the first section of the book each chapter ranges through the whole period, providing—or such is the intention—a view of Catholic life in Spain within which the second section can then make sense as something more satisfactory than just a narrative of political actions and reactions. In Part II, both Chapters 5 and 6 cover the period 1875–1923, and subsequent chapters proceed more or less chronologically from 1923 up to 1975. I have not attempted to document or evaluate the Church's responses to the establishment of democracy since 1975—which merits another, different study—but I hope this book will cast some light on both the extent and the limits of the embrace that the Spanish Church could offer to pluralism and modernity.

It is pleasant to have the opportunity, at last, formally to thank the many people and institutions whose support has brought this project to completion. I gratefully acknowledge research grants from the British Academy and the Modern History Faculty Board, Oxford, and the earlier postgraduate award from the Department of Education and Science, all

Preface

of which enabled me to work in Spanish archives. Without the sabbatical leave generously given by Oxford University and Lady Margaret Hall, this book would have taken much longer even than it has done, to materialize. I owe a very special debt of gratitude to the Society of the Sacred Heart and to many of its communities and individual members in Spain and England. During most of the preparation of the book I was a member of this religious congregation. Directly and indirectly it helped fund my research; many of its members took a lively interest in the book's progress; and in Spain, more often than not, its communities not only gave me hospitality but also, invaluably, helped me find my way round the local ecclesiastical world. Many other religious and priests gave me information, assistance, and access to diocesan, seminary, convent, congregational, and school archives. My debt to them is evident, and is sometimes specified in footnotes to the text. At no stage did any of them make the availability of information dependent on the interpretation I would give it. If they find errors or things to disagree with in this work, I hope they will also recognize a sincere attempt to make truthful sense of what I saw. I must especially thank Fr. Ander Manterola, librarian of the seminary at Derio, for help on many occasions, and for access to his own collection of material on Church affairs in the Basque area. I also profited from the superb research facilities and the hospitality of the Benedictine Abbey of Montserrat, and from conversations there with Fr. Hilari Raguer and Fr. Josep Massot. I thank the publishers of *Social Compass—International Review of Socio-Religious Studies*, for permission to reproduce the map on page 11 and the table on page 91. Drafts of this book were read by Raymond Carr, Paul Preston, Mary Vincent, and Tom Buchanan: I greatly appreciated their criticisms and have tried to act on them. Tempting though it is to cast round for ways of evading full responsibility for the finished product, that responsibility is, of course, mine. Should the text prove clear and readable, however, I shall gladly acknowledge the influence of Charles Wenden, who generously read and criticized it. If rambling sentences and a gorgeous superabundance of adjectives have anywhere survived, that, too, is my responsibility. Finally, I have to thank Claire Lewis, who got me computerized at the crucial moment, thereby ensuring that writing and revising this book proved less daunting than they would otherwise have done.

F.L.

Contents

Abbreviations	xi
Privilege, Persecution, and Prophecy	1
PART I: THE CATHOLIC WORLD	7
1. Religious Practice and Piety	9
2. Cultural Values	36
3. The Professionals I: Religious Communities	59
4. The Professionals II: Diocesan Priests	89
PART II: CATHOLIC POLITICS	117
5. The Politics of Restoration	119
6. Catholic Action and Social Catholicism	146
7. Dictatorship and Republic	170
8. War and Victory	198
9. Towards Modernity	224
Sources and Select Bibliography	258
Index	269

Abbreviations

ACNP	Asociación Católica Nacional de Propagandistas. Catholic male lay association founded 1909 by Fr. Angel Ayala, SJ, and particularly interested in social questions. Dominant lay leader was Ángel Herrera.
AP	Acción Popular. Originally called National Action. AP was a Catholic conservative party founded in 1931 and committed to the protection of religion and property. Emerged from ACNP circles and formed nucleus of later mass party CEDA.
ASP	Acción Social Popular. Founded in Barcelona in 1907 by Fr. Gabriel Palau, SJ, to propagate Catholic social teaching and encourage Catholic syndicates called Professional Unions.
BEAS	*Boletin eclesiástico del arzobispado de Sevilla*
BEOB	*Boletín eclesiástico del obispado de Bilbao*
BEOSS	*Boletín eclesiástico del obispado de San Sebastián*
BEOV	*Boletín eclesiástico del obispado de Vitoria*
CEAS	Comisión Episcopal del Apostolado Seglar. Committee of Spanish bishops founded 1966 to oversee lay Catholic Action groups.
CEDA	Confederación Española de Derechas Autónomas. Mass, conservative Catholic party founded 1933, led by José María Gil Robles.
CEE	Conferencia Episcopal Española. Organization of all Spanish bishops, founded 1966 as a result of the Second Vatican Council, to give hierarchy a national rather than just diocesan voice.
CNCA	Confederación Nacional Católica Agraria. Founded 1917 as agrarian parallel to Catholic industrial syndicates, and part of official lay Catholic Action. Closely connected to ACNP.
CNCCO	Consejo Nacional de Corporaciones Católicas Obreras. Association of Catholic workers' groups founded 1896 with Fr. Antonio Vicent, SJ, chaplain, and the Marquis

	of Comillas the dominant figure. Virtually the official industrial sector of Catholic Action. In 1919, became the CNSOC.
CNSCL	Confederación Nacional de Sindicatos Católicos-Libres. Founded 1916 from Catholic syndicates that originated from the work of Fr. Pedro Gerard, OP, in Jerez. Free syndicates in the sense of both having no non-worker members, and of not requiring religious tests. Clearly Catholic, even though not formally confessional, and often called Free-Catholic rather than simply Free, to distinguish them from the CNSL.
CNSL	Confederación Nacional de Sindicatos Libres. Founded 1924 from syndicates that originated in Traditionalist circles in Barcelona. Militant and sometimes violent, they should not be confused with the CNSCL. The Barcelona Free syndicates were not only non-confessional, but also highly independent of the Church.
CNSOC	Confederación Nacional de Sindicatos Obreros Católicos. A new name given in 1919 to what had been the CNCCO, to give expression to the new workers-only policy of membership. 'Syndicate' replaced 'circle' or 'corporation' to mark the change.
CNT	Confederación Nacional del Trabajo. Anarchist union federation founded in 1911.
CSIC	Consejo Superior de Investigaciones Científicas. State-funded research institute founded 1939 to promote intellectual culture in keeping with the values of the civil war victors.
DHEE	*Diccionario de Historia Eclesiástica de España.*
DSCC	*Diario de Sesiones de las Cortes Constituyentes de la República Española.*
ETA	Euzkadi ta Askatasuna. Basque Land and Liberty, a separatist organization founded 1959 that embarked on assassination policies in 1968.
FJC	Federació de Jovens Cristians. Catholic Catalan youth association active in the 1930s.
HOAC	Hermandades Obreras de Acción Católica. Catholic workers' associations, developed first in the early 1940s, recognized in 1946 by the hierarchy as an official, specialized part of Catholic Action.
ILE	Institución Libre de Enseñanza.

Abbreviations

JAP	Juventudes de Acción Popular. Youth section of AP then CEDA.
JARC	Juventud Agraria Rural Católica. The agrarian equivalent of JOC.
JOC	Juventud Obrera Católica. Young Catholic workers' association, growing in late 1940s and 1950s, and at peak of its vitality in mid 1960s. Recognized as youth branch of Catholic Action in industry 1956. Like HOAC, primarily a grass-roots organization rather than a creation of the hierarchy.
PNV	Partido Nacionalista Vasca. Basque Nationalist Party, Catholic, founded 1891.
Propagandist.	Member of the ACNP.
PSP	Partido Social Popular. Catholic party founded only months before Primo de Rivera's coup dispensed with political parties in September 1923.
RyF	Razon y Fe.
SOV	Solidaridad de Obreros Vascos. Basque Catholic Unions, associated with the PNV, founded 1911. Also called STV, Solidaridad de Trabajadores Vascos.
SVP	Society of St. Vincent de Paul.
UGT	Unión General de Trabajadores. Socialist Unions affiliated to the Spanish Socialist Party.

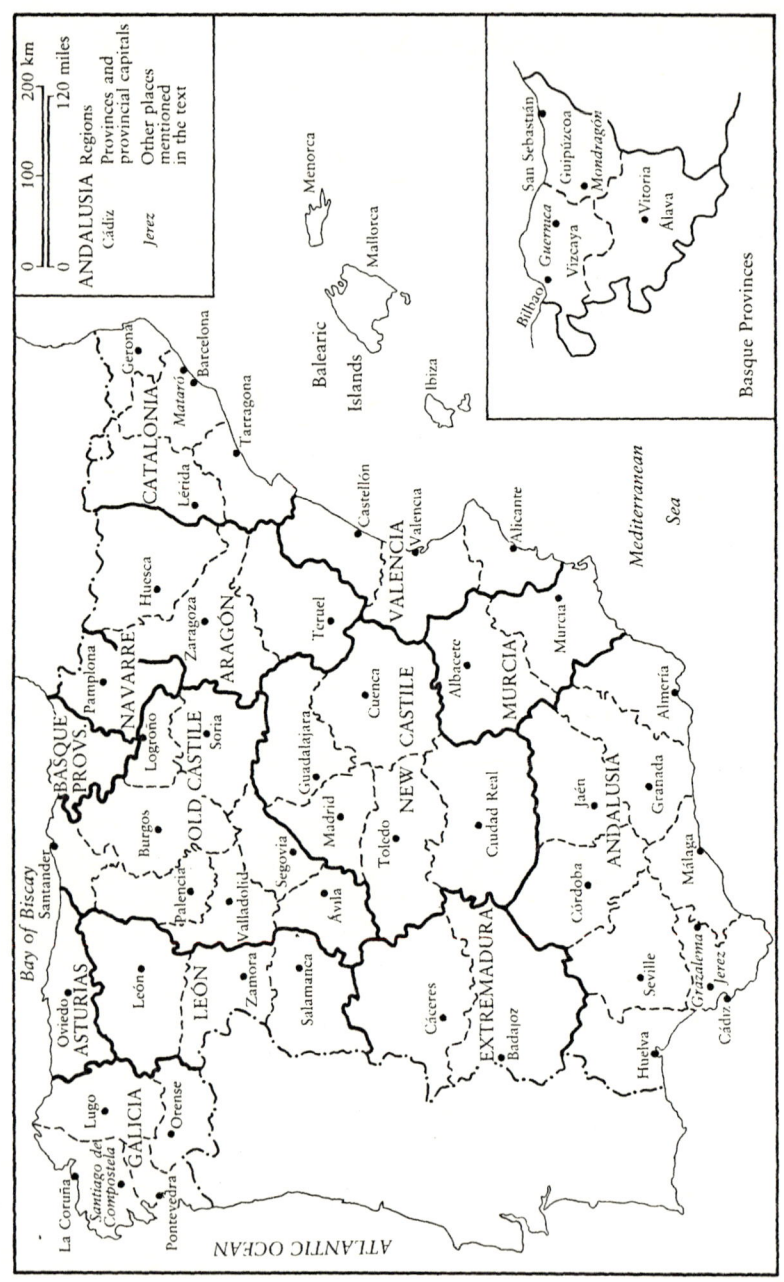

Map 1. General map of Spain

Privilege, Persecution, and Prophecy

IN 1875, the Catholic Church in Spain looked expectantly if a little sceptically to the newly restored Bourbon monarchy for its own restoration. So far, neither institution had fared well in the nineteenth century. Since the 1830s two distinct branches of the Bourbon family had competed for the throne, and a second dynastic war in forty years was still being fought in the north of Spain. Nor had the experience of the successful line in Queen Isabel II vindicated the hopes of those who had supported her against the Carlist alternative. As a disputed claimant of only three years old she succeeded her father Ferdinand in 1833, but was eventually forced off the throne into exile in 1868. Between the 1868 revolution and the proclamation of her eighteen-year-old son Alfonso as king, Spain had experimented briefly with an imported monarch in the form of Amadeo of Savoy (November 1870 to February 1873), and then even more briefly with a highly volatile republic. When General Martínez Campos 'pronounced' in favour of Alfonso XII on 29 December 1874, he was following a well-established nineteenth-century pattern of initiating constitutional change by military means, but earlier precedents suggested it was easier to introduce a new regime than to consolidate it.

The survival of the restored Bourbon monarchy under Alfonso and then his son Alfonso XIII until 1931 is largely attributable to the fact that although Martínez Campos 'pronounced' in time-honoured fashion, the form of the restoration monarchy had actually been planned intelligently and with political subtlety by Antonio Cánovas del Castillo. This conservative politician from Málaga set out to create a political structure which, by ensuring the alternation in power of two major parties, the Conservatives and the Liberals, would eliminate the need for military intervention while incorporating into Spanish political life all but convinced republicans at one extreme and irreconcilable Carlists at the other. Alfonso came into a turbulent inheritance in 1875, but with a warm welcome from a political class exhausted and troubled by a bewildering decade of discontent and constitutional instability, and determined to halt somewhere in the middle the violent pendulum swings that had characterized Spanish political life for generations. A constitutional monarchy, an army dedicated to fighting Spain's enemies instead of overseeing its public life, and a parliament outwardly on the English model with two chambers and two major alternating parties, looked promising.

As the Church considered its position, it too surveyed a desolate recent history. Throughout the century it had frequently suffered persecution, including outbreaks of popular anti-clerical violence in the fearful massacre of the monks in 1834 and 1835, the expropriation and sale of Church property by liberal or progressive governments, and the suppression of male religious communities in 1837. Furthermore, the promulgation of religious liberty in the short-lived constitution of 1869 seemed to many Catholics an act of national apostasy, a scandalous opening to error and corruption threatening the essential Catholic identity of Spain and of Spaniards.[1] Much greater damage had been done, however, by the expropriation of Church property by progressive governments in the 1830s and 1850s in fruitless efforts to balance the budget. Between 1836 and 1845, 83% of properties belonging to religious communities and 40% of those owned by diocesan clergy were sold. In the second, much more protracted sale after 1855, it was the turn of the secular priests to be the prime target, and their losses comprised 75% of total ecclesiastical property confiscated.[2] The male religious orders virtually disappeared, and although the actual residences of bishops and priests were exempt from sale, and their own pastoral function acknowledged, dioceses were impoverished by the loss of tens of thousands of large and small rural properties and their income.

There is no doubt that by the 1870s the Church was in dire need of institutional restoration. Religious communities were again managing to establish themselves in small numbers, but the male religious, particularly, constituted only a fraction of what they had been early in the century, and the number of diocesan priests had also dropped. Even more serious in the long term, because more difficult to remedy, was the definitive loss in the two bouts of *desamortización* of financial solidity and independence. The Church retained many priceless but unsaleable

---

[1] For the Church earlier in the nineteenth century, see W. J. Callahan, *Church, Politics, and Society in Spain, 1750–1874* (Harvard, 1984). For the debates on religion in the 1869 constituent Cortes, see S. Petschen, *Iglesia–estado un cambio político. Las constituyentes de 1869* (Madrid, 1974).

[2] The best survey of the *desamortización* is F. Simón Segura, *La desamortización española del siglo XIX* (Madrid, 1973). The indispensable source for Church resources and personnel is J. Sáez Marín, *Datos sobre la iglesia española contemporánea 1768–1868* (Madrid, 1975).

treasures, many magnificent cathedrals, but it had become entirely dependent upon state funding for the maintenance of its clergy and its buildings, and inevitably dependent upon rich private benefactors for new pastoral foundations in the shape of schools, or hospitals, or orphanages. The ancient estates that had been the basis of much of the Church's charitable and pastoral work had gone. The remaining problem was how to do without them, and how to accept benefactions from the propertied classes without becoming identified with their interests and provoking the sort of popular alienation that led sooner or later to further persecution. It was a problem to which the Church of the restoration monarchy found no solution.

Cánovas's constitution could not return expropriated ecclesiastical property. Nor did it re-establish perfect Catholic unity. Religious liberty was restricted to the private practice of religions other than Catholicism, but was still entirely unacceptable to Church leaders. To devoutly Catholic Carlists, it afforded yet further proof of the ungodliness of Isabel and her heirs. But there were enormous attractions for the Church in a new order that recognized Catholicism as the religion of state, stipulated that all education in Spain should be in accordance with Catholic doctrine, and took responsibility for the upkeep of the diocesan clergy and Church buildings. Here was hope of stability, orthodoxy, and influence. Many politicians feared Cánovas was making too many concessions, and showering the Church with privileges. But ecclesiastical definitions of privilege were as narrow as the definitions of persecution were wide. In the Church's view, state funding, state protection, and virtual ideological hegemony for Catholicism were no more than it needed and had a right to expect in order to fulfil its divine mission of propagating the truth that it, and it alone, could teach.

The restoration settlement enabled the Church to get on with its task of evangelization in the nine archdioceses and forty-seven dioceses of Spain. This duty was urgent because of the years of disruption, and the urban growth and patchy industrialization that were producing insanitary suburbs full of displaced families but often devoid of churches, priests, and schools. The unchurched urban poor had their counterpart among poor rural wage labourers in the south for whom church-going was not, and probably never had been at any point since the expulsion of the Moors, a regular part of life as it was for northern peasant smallholders. Since the Church's institutional resources in both buildings and personnel were very unevenly distributed in the north's favour, and its potential benefactors would inevitably attract new ecclesiastical foundations to their own desirable parts of the expanding towns, the most difficult challenge for the Church was how to make the religious restoration promised by the Alfonsine monarchy reach beyond the traditionally devout north and the conservative bourgeoisie to the southern countryside and the urban working classes.

Contemporary clerical observers, statistical analyses, and increasing political and popular anti-clericalism all combined to show that it failed. The Catholic revival was strong in areas of traditional religious practice, and among the new bourgeoisie to whom it offered a potent theoretical bulwark against radicalism. It never succeeded as a missionary force beyond these areas and groups. For all its ardour, and the state resources behind it, the Church found itself on the defensive against unfavourable demographic, sociological, and intellectual trends. Just as it failed to inoculate the urban working classes against a dreaded socialism by convincing them it could and would promote their interests effectively, so it was unable to stop the intellectual élite abandoning its doctrines and discipline for an imported humanistic rationalism. It preached mainly to the converted, and no matter how loud its voice or strident its tone, the message did not carry any further. The Catholic revival soon became a movement of consolidation and defence rather than of confident, proselytizing expansion. Defensive dogmatism and disapproval marked ecclesiastical attitudes to the heterodox, the negligent, and the sceptics. The Church militant was drawn up in battle array against Spaniards whom it considered, and who considered themselves, its enemies.

At the same time, however, Catholicism was traditionally the religion of Spaniards, and ecclesiastical leaders were convinced that the state had a duty to protect it and impose its teachings. Between the promulgation of Cánovas's constitution in 1876, and the military coup that ended the parliamentary regime in 1923, the state generally fulfilled that role, although with far more second thoughts and limitations than the Church thought proper. Primo de Rivera's coup then produced something much more congenial, a dictatorship under the king, utterly committed to the Church's view of a national Catholic culture that eschewed political and ideological pluralism. Unfortunately for the Church, the dictatorship did not last very long, and in 1931 the least corrupt elections to date ushered in the Second Republic. Not only had the Church lost its supreme defender, the king; it was faced with a republican constitution that reduced it to a cultural institution without special status or state funding. Worse, the constitution permitted civil marriage and divorce, and forbade members of religious orders to teach in Spain, thereby threatening the vast network of Catholic schools that formed the greatest achievement of the revival. Privilege had given way to what many Catholics regarded as outright persecution.

When a group of generals 'pronounced' against the republic in July 1936, most bishops were far from sorry and hastened to acclaim the military rising as a blow for Catholic civilization against communism and ungodliness. The war was an agrarian war, and a class war, and a war between centralizers and federalists. It was also an armed conflict between, in general, defenders of the Church and its opponents. Thousands of priests and religious died in the first months of the war in a ferocious religious persecution. But Franco's victory brought the Catholic Church the most substantial privileges it has enjoyed in modern times—state funding, control of the entire education system, ideological monopoly, and legislative embodiment of its moral values. Furthermore, it gradually became apparent that this Catholic dictatorship would last much longer than Primo's, and even restore the monarchy.

Here, however, the oscillation between privilege and persecution ceased. When Franco died in 1975, his successor as head of state, Alfonso XIII's grandson Juan Carlos, encouraged the careful dismantling of the regime to create a democratic, pluralist, constitutional monarchy. The Church survived the radical transformation of the political world because it had distanced itself from the dictatorship more and more earnestly during its final decade. Prophecy was the biblical term in vogue in ecclesiastical circles to describe that distancing process. Prophecy meant, on the Old Testament model of Jeremiah or—best of all—Amos, denouncing injustice and corruption among the rulers in order to defend the poor, the oppressed, the powerless, the elect of Yahweh. The conversion of radical lay activists and priests, and then eventually the Church hierarchy to this prophetic mode contributed powerfully to the destruction of the dictatorship from within. By delegitimizing the regime, the Church earned its entry in peace into the new democratic world. There was no question of persecution: no political group wanted to try again the provocative policies of the Second Republic—the Church had learnt for its part to restrain its definition of persecution and to accept political pluralism.

On privilege, however, the ecclesiastical dictionary remained adamant. Although the democratic, secular state was urged to go on financing clergy and churches, respecting Church teaching on moral issues including divorce and abortion, and subsidizing Church schools, none of this qualified as privilege. It was, the bishops argued, simply recognizing the reality of Spain's Catholic tradition, and the Church's contribution to its national culture. The Church was successful in most of its claims, and where it was not, did not hesitate to unleash the enormous resources under its control to campaign vehemently, relentlessly, for what it regarded as right and just. Must not the prophetic voice be raised in season and out, argued clerical and lay leaders. Must it not resound in democracy as well as dictatorship? But in pluralism, as in an authoritarian system, the Church's task was to win not just the political battle, but also, and much more difficult, the hearts and minds of the Spanish people.

PART I
The Catholic World

I

Religious Practice and Piety

THE Counter Reformation ensured that Spain would not be Protestant. That it must therefore be Catholic was a truism made inevitable by the religious division of Europe in the sixteenth century. The modern Spanish state was forged in the fires of orthodoxy—burning out the Moors, sending the flame of true religion to the new world, and consuming the disbelievers and deviants at home. It was 'the hammer of heretics, torchbearer of Trent, sword of Rome, cradle of St Ignatius'.[1] With empire, orthodoxy, and the unity of the state so inextricably connected in its great age of expansion and conquest, it is not surprising that Spain has so often been regarded as necessarily and essentially Catholic, and that the notion of a non-confessional state has become generally acceptable only very recently, with the constitution of 1978.

At the level of religious practice rather than formal definition, however, Catholic identity has not been such a seamless robe. Even the Council of Trent and its Spanish enthusiasts could not cut away all ignorance, doubt, and pagan traditions, and Catholicism inevitably coexisted with alternative cosmologies, private scepticism, and garbled versions of itself, as official religions have always done everywhere. Easier to observe than these pervasive nonconformities have been more recent influences which have given to Catholic practice in Spain a sharply defined geographical and sociological outline. Although the exact chronology has yet to be established, it seems clear that in the course of the nineteenth century the combined effects of the Church's loss of its traditional rural base with the nationalization of monastic estates and other Church properties, the emergence of a bitterly divisive agrarian system in the south in which the Church came to be seen by landless labourers as an ally of the great *latifundio* landlords, the spread of socialist and anarchist ideas inimical to religious belief and institutions, and the classic de-churching influences of urbanization on the

---

[1] M. Menéndez y Pelayo, *Historia de los Heterodoxos Españoles*. 8 vols. (Buenos Aires, 1945), vii, 558; originally published in 3 vols. (1880–2).

new working classes—all created a Spain conspicuously Catholic in some areas and social strata and hardly Catholic at all in others.[2]

From a plethora of studies made in the 1960s and 1970s we now have a reasonably clear idea of recent Catholic practice in Spain measured by the conventional though inadequate tests of attendance at Sunday Mass and fulfilment of the traditional 'Easter duty' of receiving holy communion at least once a year. Although information for earlier decades is much more sparse, there is enough of it to suggest broad lines of continuity through the late nineteenth and twentieth centuries. Catholic practice was affected by the following factors: region, size of settlement, the ownership of property, occupation, age, and sex. Formal religiosity has been highest among women, among property-owning families, among northerners, among people who were not manual wage-labourers, and among the inhabitants of small settlements, although there are interesting modifications to be noted in all of these. Catholic practice has not been exclusively the preserve of the affluent, nor has it provided a compensatory 'heart of a heartless world', as classical Marxism thought it might, for the most insecure and destitute.

In 1965 Rogelio Duocastella produced the first map of religious practice in Spain, based on Sunday Mass attendance, in the tradition of Gabriel Le Bras's sociology of religion.[3] The statistics were gathered from disparate studies of scattered dioceses or parishes over a period of more than ten years, and the map was far from complete. Nevertheless, neither its detail, nor the assumptions made about its gaps have been substantially challenged by subsequent studies. The general pattern is a simple one of high levels of practice throughout much of the north and low levels in the south. Highest attendance figures at Mass were registered in the diocese of Pamplona, covering the province of Navarre, with a breathtaking 90%. At the other extreme, a semi-rural parish in Seville diocese would have found such crowded churches unimaginable, since a 13% turnout was more usual there. Statistics for the Basque provinces, and the more northerly parts of Old Castile, approximated to the Pamplona results; Extremaduran and Andalusian samples were much closer to those of the parish in Seville; in between, a band of territory cutting across the centre of Spain from Ciudad Rodrigo and

[2] For a comprehensive survey of the 19th century Spanish Church before the restoration of the monarchy, see Callahan, *Church, Politics, and Society*.

[3] Originally published in *Social Compass*, xii (Dec. 1965), 281, then in R. Duocastella, J. Marcos, and J. M. Díaz-Mózaz, *Análisis sociológico del catolicismo español* (Barcelona, 1967), 47.

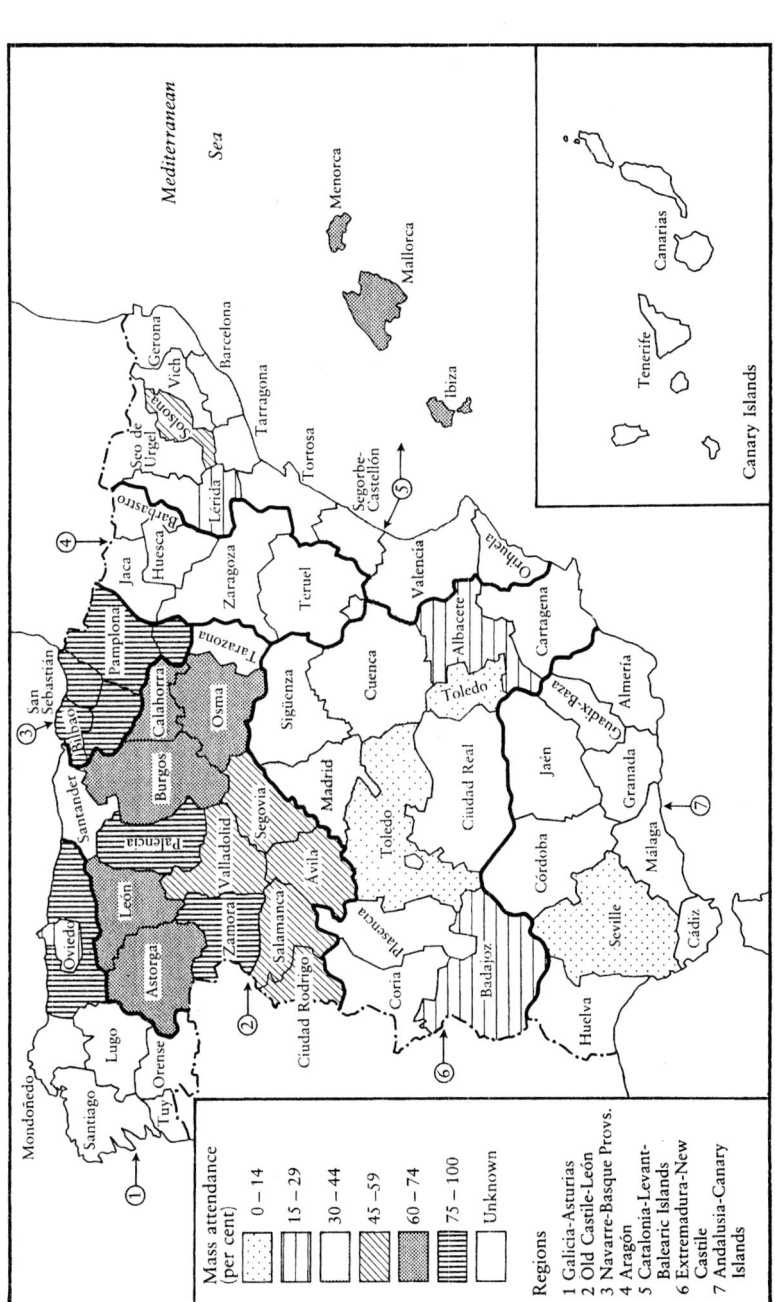

Map 2. Sunday Mass attendance in Spanish dioceses, from surveys conducted 1950–64. From R. Duocastella, 'Géographie de la Pratique Religieuse en Espagne', *Social Compass*, xii (Dec. 1965). 281.

Salamanca in the west to Valencia in the east held an intermediate position, with its more northerly western end recording attendances of 45% to 60% and its more southerly eastern end, 30% to 45%. These bare, albeit partial statistics are important in showing immediately that the regional variations in formal religiosity have been so great as to belong to contrasting and antithetical cultural worlds. The image of the church, the place of religion in everyday life, the actual experience of church-going, and attitudes to the religious professionals—the priests and the religious communities—had very little in common between, say, Avila and Almería, or Alava and Huelva. In Old Castile or the Basque provinces, church-going was part of the weekly routine for most people, and the daily routine for a substantial minority; almost everyone had at least one relative who was a priest or religious; and parish activities provided a focus for social life. In Extremadura and Andalusia the contrast was, in some areas, overwhelming. It is not surprising that preachers intent on the evangelization of the south felt themselves to be in an alien and hostile world, and there are reports from the end of the nineteenth century of occasions when they had to take to their heels to avoid stones thrown by angry peasants.[4]

The geographical extremes are best illustrated, perhaps, by two examples that also illuminate the influence of occupation, sex, and rural or urban environment. In the 1960s the northern province of Alava was still largely rural, and traditional mixed smallholdings remained prevalent: the provincial capital of Vitoria, however, had become an industrial centre pulling immigrants not only from the surrounding countryside but from much further south. As one would expect, Sunday Mass attendance was higher in the countryside than in the city, the figures being nearly 90%, and 60% respectively.[5] More striking is the fact that one in three country dwellers in the province actually went to Mass every day. But the most interesting feature of religious behaviour was that there were in some parishes more men than women attending Sunday Mass, and often nearly as many men as women at daily Mass. Even weekday religion was not a specifically female phenomenon, therefore, and Sunday religion was a matter for the whole family rather than primarily for women and children, as was often the case where the level

[4] Callahan, *Church, Politics, and Society*, 241 on Fr Tarín; *BEAS*, xxxii (1899) 402. For the observations of Ramón Sarrabia, a Redemptorist preacher in north and south Spain in the first half of the 20th century, see W.J. Callahan, 'Was Spain Catholic?', *Revista Canadiense de Estudios Hispánicos*, viii (1984), 159–82.

[5] Information on Alava from R. Duocastella, J. Lorca, and S. Misser, *Sociología y pastoral. Estudio de sociología religiosa de la diócesis de Vitoria* (Barcelona, 1965).

of practice was low. Catholic practice was sex-specific where it was weakest, but not where it was strongest, and to understand the vigour of Spanish Catholicism in its heartlands one must recognize its immersion in the ordinary routine not just of individuals but also of families. For those in agriculture, it had traditionally been part of the work routine as well, with—as an anthropological study of a small rural town in Aragón has shown—religious feasts marking the major events of planting and reaping, hiring farmhands, and renewing tenancies or making contracts, even though by the middle of the twentieth century 'the religious aura which surrounded the agricultural tasks is gradually disappearing. The month, the week, the day and the hour are replacing the ancient conventional divisions of time.'[6] In the city of Vitoria manual workers were much less keen on going to Mass than were their bosses or white-collar workers, but here too the variations are instructive. While 52% of skilled workers fulfilled the obligation to hear Sunday Mass, the figure for unskilled workers, frequently immigrants from the south, was only 29%. Occupation, class, and regional derivation all combined in the final pattern where local, better trained, and better paid people were much more likely to go to church than poorer immigrants in non-prestigious jobs.

It would be wrong to generalize from the Alava example and assume a practising countryside round a less devout town as the norm. The poor province of Huelva was as far removed from the religious culture of Alava as it was physically distant from it at the south-west extremity of Spain, bordering both Portugal and the Atlantic. When Cardinal Ilundain prepared a report on it for his *ad limina* visit to the pope in 1932 it was notorious both for its concentration of *latifundio* estates, with their inevitable concomitant of landless labourers, and for its Riotinto mines. The information Ilundain received from the local parish clergy was not encouraging. In Neva, a settlement of 18,000 people in the Riotinto belt, only 300 attended Sunday Mass and most of those were women. The agricultural villages were no better: only three out of every thousand were church-goers in the rural parish of El Rosal de la Frontera. In another frontier parish, Palos, the unfortunate incumbent put male non-attendance at Mass at 100%, female at 95%.[7] While

---

[6] C. Lisón-Tolosana, *Belmonte de los Caballeros* (Oxford, 1966), 24–36.

[7] Archivists in the archiepiscopal palace in Seville were unable to produce this *ad limina* report for me, but it is quoted very extensively in J. Ordóñez Márquez, *La apostasía de las masas y la persecución religiosa en la provincia de Huelva 1931–6* (Madrid, 1968), especially 26–222. For Neva, see 161–2; El Rosal, 172; Palos, 90.

peasant smallholders in the north were devout, landless peasant labourers in the far south were equally conspicuous by their neglect. Religion was clearly not regarded as an acceptable compensation for poverty and extreme insecurity. In the countryside, practice tended to coincide with property holding and also with literacy or semi-literacy. Where there were few peasant plots and virtually no schools, churches were empty except for some women. What comfort they found there they were obviously unable to communicate either to their husbands and sons or to the majority of the other women in their localities. Priests reported to Ilundain that things were getting worse rather than better, and that hostility to themselves and the Church was sharpening with the spread of anarchist and socialist organizations and propaganda, but much of Andalusia and Extremadura bear all the marks of areas never brought into regular church-going habits rather than recently experiencing a rapid and dramatic 'secularization'. The very regions of the celebrated final expulsion of the Moors and Catholic reconquest in the fifteenth century seem never to have been truly conquered for the Church in that or any subsequent campaign. Certainly the Catholic revival of the late nineteenth century did not achieve in the southern countryside that quite dense institutional presence it achieved further north, and in some parts of all major towns and cities.

Some notion of what the unchurched reality of the south was like can be gained from the correspondence between priests and their archbishop in the diocese of Seville in those years when the usual protective cover of state patronage was lifted. Article 26 of the republican constitution of 1931 committed the Spanish government to phasing out state funding of clergy stipends—one of various measures to secularize the state and reduce ecclesiastical power. Accordingly, in January 1932 Cardinal Ilundain wrote to his 260 parish priests instructing them to set up committees of laymen in their parishes to raise money for the maintenance of their own clergy. Members, he wrote, were to be adult, male, practising Catholics of good moral character and some local standing. These requirements provoked some sardonic comments as twenty-three priests reported that in their parishes few or no such people existed, and that parochial self-financing was out of the question.[8] Some set up a committee of some kind, but warned the archbishop that in fact its members were not practising Catholics.[9] The parish priest of

---

[8] Archivo diocesano de Sevilla, Parroquial 1932, Legajos 1–4. E.g. Cala, Fuente Palmera, Palomares (parishes ordered alphabetically).
[9] Ibid., e.g. La Roda.

El Berrocal, probably exasperated that Ilundain had not accepted his assertion that men in his area only came to church to get married, wrote a second letter making the novel suggestion that the committee in El Berrocal might be composed of women instead—a proposal not at all to the cardinal's liking. The membership of the committees that were set up and duly reported is instructive; apart from the very occasional craftsman or smallholder, members were lawyers, notaries, chemists, doctors, landowners, industrialists, and state school teachers. This raised numerous difficulties quite apart from the obvious one of class alignment. As the priest in Tribujena, Cádiz province, pointed out, the four devout men of his parish were the chemist and three state primary school teachers, but all four lived in the area only because they had been appointed to posts there, and as non-natives they had little influence and could not be expected to be very effective.

Other correspondence reinforces the desolate impression given in these letters. Thirteen incidents of arson or explosions in churches were reported; various priests gave details of confrontations with newly elected anti-clerical local authorities determined to stop religious rituals such as bell-ringing, processions, weddings, baptisms, and funerals; there were very many complaints that statues and crosses had been destroyed by local people or removed by order of the new socialist and anarchist local councils. The priest at Coripe said it was quite impossible for him to visit again the little village of La Muela in his parish because the 200 inhabitants were entirely without religion or culture, were anarchists, and had threatened him with stoning and death; moreover, on recent occasions when he had celebrated Mass there his congregation had consisted of just one person. Various priests related their experiences of imprisonment—usually for conducting religious ceremonies that local councillors wanted to ban—and of receiving threats of violence and actually suffering violence. Many were weary and disillusioned, while seven begged permission to leave the area, at least temporarily, because of their terror of anti-clerical attacks. No one reading this grim correspondence could doubt that the lack of formal religious practice in the south was an indicator not merely of indifference, but often of hatred and determined opposition to the Church. The mantle of the Catholic state covered and often hid from view a rural southern society in which, when bereft of that covering, the Church shuddered and worried about its survival.

In some settlements, of course, and in the more affluent areas of the towns, the situation was not so bleak. Ilundain's 1932 report to the

Vatican included villages like Valverde del Camino—with a population of 10,000 occupied in craft industries like woodwork and shoe making as well as agriculture—where 30% to 40% of the men and 70% to 80% of the women were regular church-goers. In two of the three parishes in Huelva town one quarter of the population attended Sunday Mass, although in the third parish, Sagrado Corazón de Jesús, which covered the poorest areas, the incumbent reported a total of ninety people at most out of a parish of 8,000. But the overall averages were low: in his summing up Ilundain gave an estimate of 20% of women and 6% of men attending church in the archdiocese as a whole, which comprised Huelva and Seville provinces, and part of the provinces of Córdoba, Málaga, and Cádiz.[10] In the same diocese thirty years later, notwithstanding the political and social pressures towards Catholic conformity in Franco's dictatorship, still only about one third of the population could be regarded as practising. For the city of Seville the proportion was not a third but a quarter.[11]

Geographical position, then, was itself an immensely important factor in religious practice, with the north-east and the south-west providing extremely sharp contrasts. Its effects were modified by the autonomous factors of property and occupation. Rural life did not necessarily promote religious conformity, as the archdiocese of Seville amply demonstrates, while Vitoria retained very high levels of practice even in urban, industrial conditions. It is, however, true that the discouraging effects of the industrial town on religious practice common elsewhere in nineteenth and twentieth-century Europe was strong in Spain. It was noted in Barcelona by clerical observers in the 1850s, and was painfully apparent in the sprawling, undermanned working-class parishes of Madrid at the beginning of this century.[12] By the 1930s it was widely recognized, not least by worried Catholic commentators, that the urban proletariat of Madrid, or Barcelona, or Bilbao, or Valencia, or Seville, or the mining centres of Asturias, rarely entered a church and lived in almost complete ignorance of Catholic doctrine and ritual. The Church and its affairs were simply alien to urban working-class culture. One of the best known contemporary accounts—that of Fr. Francisco Peiró, Jesuit priest of San Ramón parish in the Vallecas quarter of Madrid—described the situation in 1935 in depressing detail. Peiró had an unimaginable total of 80,000

---

[10] J. Ordóñez Márquez, op. cit., 148–9, 31, 219–22.
[11] Figures in a publication of the Diocesan Synod of Seville, *La iglesia y su servicio a la realidad humana* (Seville, 1973), 24, 29.
[12] Callahan, *Church, Politics, and Society*, 241, and 'Was Spain Catholic?' 170–1.

Religious Practice and Piety 17

parishioners, of whom only 7% attended Sunday Mass—less than 7% in real terms, since that figure included the children in the parish schools. Fewer still made their Easter duty. While only one in ten died with the Church's sacraments, one in four was not even baptized and many could not recite the 'Our Father'. Statistics for the comparable parish of San Millán were much the same.[13] Two short studies were published in 1935 by priests concerned about similar situations in Vizcaya, the first on Portugalete, a densely populated industrial settlement inhabited mainly by people working in the shipyards on the river Nervión and the local iron and steel works, the second on part of the mining district. The results of their respective studies were not heartening, and José Iñigo opened his with the comment that describing the state of religious practice in the Vizcaya mines was like talking about rivers in a desert.[14] Also, just before the civil war, a Catholic youth organization in Catalonia conducted an enquiry into religious practice in the region and concluded that only 5% of young people in the regional capital, and in Catalonia as a whole, could be described as practising Catholics after leaving school.[15] Small-scale and technically unsophisticated though such contemporary surveys are, their general accuracy is unquestionable. As Canon Arboleya put it in his famous analysis of the Church's failure presented to a Church conference in 1933, the dimensions of the problem were those of mass apostasy, especially among the urban working classes.[16]

A generation later, more sophisticated sociological studies began to fill in the detail of the general picture. An early contribution was Duocastella's work on the Catalan coastal town of Mataró, whose population of 35,000 in the late 1950s included fishermen and agricultural workers as well as industrial personnel. When a head count was made at Sunday Mass one week in October 1955, just under 30% of the population was present, including the children, with women outnumbering men. Fishermen were the least observant, closely followed by unskilled industrial workers and rural labourers (3.5%, 3.7%, and 4.6% respectively). The next category was that of skilled workers, almost one in ten of whom attended Mass that day, and then there was

[13] F. Peiró, *El problema religioso-social en España* (Madrid, 1936).
[14] J. Azpiazu, 'La religiosidad del arciprestazgo de Portugalete', and J. Iñigo, 'La situación religiosa en la zona minera vizcaína', *Idearium*, ii (1935), 92–101, 327–36. *Idearium* was published by and for priests of the Vitoria diocese.
[15] *La federació de jovens cristians de catalunya—contribució a la seva historia* (Barcelona, 1972), 12.
[16] M. Arboleya Martínez, *La apostasía de las masas* (Barcelona, 1934).

an enormous gap with, on the other side, the men in liberal professions, white collar workers and the industrial managers, all between 45 and 50%. The equivalent figures for women were higher throughout, but fell just as clearly into two occupational blocks, with unskilled urban and rural workers on one side and clerical workers and professionals on the other. Male and female students—no doubt from, and destined for, the ranks of professional and managerial personnel—exhibited high levels of Catholic practice. When the results were processed to give areas from which immigrants had come to the expanding town, they duly showed that those from the non-practising south were outstanding in their negligence.[17] As in other industrial towns, large and small, religious practice was comparatively low overall mainly because it was extremely low among unskilled manual labourers. In the major urban centres of Madrid, Barcelona, and Bilbao, the overlapping factors of occupation and immigration from beyond the immediate hinterland explain the lower rate of practice within the city than in the surrounding countryside, even in the case of Madrid where the rather miserable, depopulated rural centre of Spain was anyway not noted for its fervour.[18]

One can be confident of asserting, on the basis of the material surveyed above, that conventional Catholic practice in Spain in the last century or so has been a characteristic of the north rather than the south, of property owners rather than manual workers, of the better rather than the poorly educated, of women rather than men. These general patterns recur over and over again in analyses of Catholic life. Areas strong in religious observance also produce very substantial numbers of vocations to the priesthood and the religious life, and proved capable of significant political mobilization in defence of the Church when its interests seemed threatened.[19] They were reasonably well served by parishes with an adequate number of clergy, while the sprawling industrial *barrios* and the neglected south had too few priests struggling to minister to parishes that contained too many people, or covered too huge an area, or both.[20] An apparent exception to this pattern was the concentration of new Catholic institutions—especially schools and welfare establishments—in the cities, where they were staffed by religious personnel largely

[17] R. Duocastella, *Mataró 1955. Estudio de sociología religiosa sobre una ciudad industrial española* (Madrid, 1961).
[18] FOESSA, *Informe sociológico sobre la situación social de España. 1970.* (Madrid, 1970), 450.
[19] See below, pp. 90–2, 65–7, 169.
[20] For ratios of priest to people by area, see below, p. 92.

recruited from the devout rural north. But the exception was more apparent than real, since the most favoured institutions of the Catholic revival, the private primary and secondary schools, were disproportionately concentrated in bourgeois, practising urban sectors, from which the most prestigious of them also attracted recruits. In his study of the Portugalete *barrio*, for example, Fr. Azpiazu noted that although the population had risen from 3,500 in 1887 to about 13,000 in 1934, no new parishes had been created, and almost no foundations made by the religious congregations.

A number of factors accelerated, slowed, or even temporarily halted the trends in Catholic practice over a century, without radically changing them. Political circumstances have been immensely influential. For example, when universal or virtually universal fulfilment of the Easter obligation ceased, and the obligation itself clearly came to be regarded as optional rather than inescapable, as it did some time between 1826 and 1896 in the small Aragonese town studied by Carmelo Lisón-Tolosana, the reasons were probably basically political. There had been no demographic explosion in the town, no determined anti-clerical proselytizing, no overwhelming source of scandal. But the liberal state of the nineteenth century, although usually formally respectful of Catholic doctrines, had between these two dates seized Church property, disbanded most of the religious orders and, in a host of ways, undermined the traditional society in which Catholic practice had—at least in small agrarian towns in Aragón—been axiomatic. Absenteeism then rose particularly steeply in the republican years 1931 to 1936 when the role of the Church in Spain as a whole was a matter of bitter public controversy, and when a local priest cited atheist and 'Marxo-communist' propaganda in the town as part of the local political explanation. Inevitably, the Franco regime stiffened conformist behaviour again, but it never approximated to the norm of the early nineteenth century.[21] This one, local example, could be duplicated many times over. Catholic practice was most buoyant when firmly supported by state policies, most feeble when anti-clerical ideologies were permitted their puncturing or even capsizing attacks on religious orthodoxy. But buoyancy once lost was only ever partially regained, as Catholic apologists, who had expected Franco's victory in the civil war to herald a second Counter Reformation, eventually discovered. The general trend, as elsewhere in western Europe, was deflationary.

Like political and ideological influences, those of demographic and

[21] Lisón-Tolosana, 288–95.

economic change varied in time and place but were not random. Where class conflict was most acute, Catholic practice became unthinkable for the propertyless. This was the case—reinforced by anarchist and socialist militancy—in the *latifundio* regions of the south, classical location of both anti-landlord and anti-clerical violence between the 1870s and 1939. In the towns as well, poverty discouraged religious practice. Peiró, for example, noticed that many proletarian families in Madrid in the 1930s lacked shoes or a clean shirt for Sundays and would not go to church without them. More radically, he saw that the urban poor profoundly mistrusted Catholicism as an essentially bourgeois phenomenon, defending property against the propertyless and hypocritical in the altruistic morality it preached. Earlier in the century, proletarian fury at state policies was expressed in the 'tragic week' in Barcelona of 1909 in an orgy of violence against ecclesiastical personnel and buildings, because the Church was seen as a class enemy.[22] Religious communion did not usually manage to embrace both partners in acute, polarized class conflict.

Small, stable agrarian settlements of small peasant farming were its most congenial setting. In such villages, everyone knew everyone else and was used to co-operating in both work on the land and in social life; the village and the parish were conterminous; communal and parochial life were almost indistinguishable. William Christian noted in one such settlement in Santander that 'virtually every man, woman and child' turned up for Sunday Mass. Another anthropologist, Susan Tax Freeman, studied a Castilian village in the 1960s where everyone attended Mass on feast days but not necessarily Sundays, and she observed that these feast days were the occasion of important communal activities and business, for which the religious ceremony provided an essential element of shared identity. Valdemora was not a particularly devout village, and its inhabitants disliked priests, but because feast days remained the traditional focus for village affairs, 'the imperatives of community action are thus religious imperatives as well'. In this unstratified, fairly homogeneous community, religious observance united the whole village on important occasions.[23] But of course such

[22] J. Connelly Ullman, *The Tragic Week: A Study of Anticlericalism in Spain, 1875–1912* (Harvard, 1968); J. Romero Maura, *La rosa de fuego: El obrerismo barcelonés de 1889 a 1909* (Barcelona, 1975).
[23] W. A. Christian, *Person and God in a Spanish Valley* (New York and London, 1972), 19, describing agricultural villages in Santander province in the 1960s; S. T. Freeman, *Neighbours. The Social Contract in a Castilian Hamlet* (Chicago, 1970), 92–7, also for the 1960s.

settlements gradually dwindled, both absolutely and relative to the population as a whole, as the twentieth century wore on. Perhaps more relentless in its effects than even the relativistic values of liberalism or the erosive opposition of early socialism and anarchism, demography—and the economic forces behind its modern shapes—was not on the side of Catholic practice.

More strongly marked than changes and variations in religious practice over time, therefore, has been the underlying continuity of a sociological and geographical definition of Catholic Spain from before the 1870s for a century. That Catholic identity has usually been virtually synonymous with conservative politics in some form or other, even though the forms have ranged from extreme authoritarianism through gentler oligarchic preferences to democratic reformism. Most Catholics could be relied upon to be anti-socialist for both religious and economic reasons, and to be on the whole more impressed by order and stability than by programmes for radical change. In the 1960s and 1970s the political and moral bankruptcy of Franco's dictatorship on the one hand, and the remarkably fresh and open perspectives on civic, political, and social responsibilities streaming from the Second Vatican Council on the other, together provoked substantial numbers of practising Catholics to prefer repudiation of the status quo to its protection.[24] They had some predecessors in earlier decades, but not many. Usually, Catholicism implied some form of conservatism, just as the politics of the Left—from progressive liberalism to anarchism—had more often than not embraced anti-clericalism. If you knew a person's religion, you were likely to be able to identify their politics, or vice versa. As the British anthropologist Julian Pitt-Rivers pointed out in a preface to his pioneering study of the village of Grazalema in Cádiz province, 'the distinction between politics and religion, as we conceive of it in our own society, has no anthropological validity' in the Spanish context.[25] Catholic practice and conservative politics were inseparable parts of the same cultural reality, facing their mocking reflection in alternative cultural worlds where radical politics and alienation from the Church reinforced one another.

In Grazalema in the early 1950s 'the members of the ruling group share certain common standards of conduct, the most important of which is their adherence to the Church', and the men of this little local élite 'consider more the political implications of religion, and to them

[24] See below, pp. 243–8.
[25] J. Pitt-Rivers, *The People of the Sierra*. 2nd edn. (Chicago, 1971), xiv.

anti-clerical is synonymous with "Red"'. Pitt-Rivers explored the recent history of the area as interpreted by his interlocutors and concluded that 'in Andalusia the civil war might be likened to a religious conflict, in that the most important criterion of political action was allegiance or opposition to the Church'.[26] His observations were valid beyond the Andalusian border. In the utterly contrasting socio-economic world of a small town in the Ebro valley, Lisón-Tolosana arrived at similar conclusions a few years later. Inhabitants remembered that before the civil war the church pews were occupied by well-to-do families who also governed the town, while the poor were uninterested in religion. In the political mobilization of the republic, family traditions of piety or the lack of it were a major factor in the choice of party allegiances. Inevitably, the larger landholders who attended church also identified themselves with the political Right, against the Left's attempts to subvert both religion and property relationships.[27] Catholic practice in modern Spain has very rarely been politically neutral—a fact due both to the Church's fear of political and intellectual pluralism and of social change, and to the peculiarly harsh class conflicts in Spanish society not created by the Church, but within which it had to preach its message of salvation.

An analysis of religious practice and its cultural and political implications cannot end here, however, because piety has never been expressed only through attending church on Sundays and receiving the sacraments. Even brothels in Almería—and no doubt elsewhere—had pictures of the Virgin Mary over the beds, and one brothel mistress explained in 1920 that 'although I don't say we went so far as to go to Mass, we never missed a novena to the *purissima*'.[28] In addition to private and family devotions, Spanish Catholics participated in an enormous number of religious rites quite separate from the minimal obligations of orthodoxy. Among these, the most public have been processions and cults connected with statues and shrines, and their relationship with post-Tridentine, let alone post-Vatican II, Catholic sacramental liturgy has often been quite complex. Ideally these public devotions were ancillary aids to a life of piety centred on the Mass. In practice, priorities have been less clear. Not all those who have visited the statue of the patroness of Spain, the Virgin of Pilar in Zaragoza, were as interested in attending Mass in her cathedral church as in

[26] J. Pitt-Rivers, *The People of the Sierra*. 2nd edn. (Chicago, 1971), 68, 134, 132.
[27] Lisón-Tolosana, 42–50.
[28] G. Brenan, *South from Granada* (London, 1974), 199–201, originally published 1957.

asking of her some special favour or thanking her for favours received. The banks of votive candles left near the Virgin of Montserrat by Catalan devotees were certainly not incompatible with utterly orthodox Catholicism, but none the less suggested a preference for a tangible, informal, perhaps non-institutional approach to sacred power and protection. And the candles and votive offerings at Montserrat—written notes of thanks, surgical appliances no longer needed, a garment belonging to someone prayed for, wedding bouquets—were replicated on different scales not just in the large regional shrines but in thousands of humble local equivalents.[29] Individual, group, and even, in a railway age, mass pilgrimages to centres of devotion associated with Mary or one of the saints were encouraged by bishops and priests as a consoling or uplifting complement to the Church's liturgy, and as an additional encounter with the sacred, mediated through hymns, prayers, and images more accessible to many than the Latin universally used in the celebration of Mass and the sacraments until the 1960s.

One particularly interesting feature of these practices, however—as of other popular devotions like the rosary and novenas—is that although they were often led by priests they did not actually depend upon sacerdotal participation for their very existence, as did the Mass and the sacraments. They were lay rather than sacerdotal forms of worship. Paradoxically, the existence of two discreet but interdependent kinds of worship was nowhere more obvious than in the ordinary low Mass (so called to distinguish it from the more ceremonial, sung high Mass) of pre-Vatican II experience. While the priest, with his back to the people, got on with his duties and esoteric Latin formulae at the altar, many of the congregation 'heard' Mass—and the passive term is entirely accurate—by reciting the rosary silently, or reading devotional prayers or visiting favourite statues in the church. Many lay people treated the priest's liturgy as a kind of efficacious sacred context for their own pious practices, but also recited the same prayers and visited the same statues at other times, quite independently of it. And very many processions and other cults associated with holy places and holy images had no immediate relationship at all to the Church's official, sacerdotal, sacramental liturgy. The ambivalent feelings and views sometimes expressed by bishops and priests about such devotions arose precisely because these were lay traditions, never fully under clerical

---

[29] The most detailed anthropological study of shrines and sacred images anywhere in Spain in this period is W. A. Christian, *Person and God in a Spanish Valley*. See also J. R. Mintz, *The Anarchists of Casas Viejas* (Chicago, 1982), 64–5.

control. In a rich variety of ways they depended upon and expressed the social and value systems of secular rather than ecclesiastical life.

One example of this is the way in which sacred statues belonged to and symbolized specific localities. In sixteenth-century England, Thomas More noticed the territorial significance of local saints and local appellations of the Virgin Mary. '"Of all Our Ladies, I love best Our Lady of Walsingham", "and I", saith the other, "Our Lady of Ipswich".'[30] Similarly in Spain, while Begoña, Pilar, Montserrat, and Rocío are all titles of the Virgin Mary, they nevertheless have a firm geographical base in, respectively, Vizcaya, Aragón, Catalonia, and Andalusia. At a more local level, villages honoured the images of their patron saints and, especially, images of Mary either called by the place's name or by the devotion depicted in the statue itself—the Virgin of Sorrows, or of Mount Carmel, or of the Rosary—or by some detail of a local apparition of Mary—the Virgin of the valley, or the heather, or the snow. This enormous proliferation of Our Ladies, backed by innumerable other patron saints, helped differentiate one region or settlement or parish from its neighbours. Anthropologists have recorded how village identity has often been most clearly expressed to the outside world on a patron's feast day, the favoured time not just for communal celebrations but also for rituals of rivalry with nearby villages.[31] Shrines were often located near village boundaries, marking off one settlement from another. These cults of local Virgins and saints were territorial and communal rather than ecclesiastical, and inevitably proved most popular within an ecclesiastical unit of parish or diocese when these coincided with the cultural world of a village or town or self-defined region.

Priests knew perfectly well that participation in local patronal rites and processions was no guarantee of Catholic orthodoxy. In the dark years of the early Second Republic, for instance, there was a spontaneous protest amounting to a riot when the Council of Almonte, in Huelva province, decided to remove from the town hall a statue of the very famous local Virgin of Rocío (of the dew). The priest was carried shoulder-high by an indignant crowd from the church to the town hall to pray before a photograph of the Virgin, and this was followed by a ten-hour procession from six in the morning until four in the afternoon bearing the original statue from its remote shrine to the parish church. The mayor and some of the councillors fled; there were edifying scenes of devotion and the local people even asked the teachers to put recently

---

[30] Quoted in K. Thomas, *Religion and the Decline of Magic* (London, 1971), 29–30.
[31] See, e.g., Lisón-Tolosana, 11–13, and Pitt-Rivers, 11.

Religious Practice and Piety 25

banned crucifixes back on the school walls. The parish priest was pleased but not deceived. It all happened, he commented, 'in spite of the poor religious spirit of the people of Almonte'. He knew better than to infer from their demonstration of pride and loyalty for the Virgin of Rocío any change in the usual neglect of the Church's sacraments, ceremonies, and general ministrations. Popular religiosity within its own cultural structures was a phenomenon quite distinct from conventional Catholic practice, and especially in the south the relationship between the two was hard to establish. A further example of this in the correspondence between Ilundain and his priests concerned the destruction of a statue of Our Lady in a public shrine in the parish of Valencina and Castilleja de Guzmán. The local authorities were indifferent and inactive, but popular feeling ran high and within twenty-four hours a complaint was presented to the civil governor. To indicate the strength of popular indignation the priest explained that the complaint carried 'seventy signatures of men', obviously a rallying of male support to which he was not at all accustomed. Local councillors had not understood a most important aspect of Spanish religious behaviour and sensibilities. While at one end of the spectrum practising Catholics attended Mass and the sacraments and also held local patron saints in great reverence, and at the other end convinced opponents hated church religion and popular piety equally, in between were many indifferent or anti-clerical Spaniards who felt intensely loyal to their particular community's patron and practices. There were many southern villages where almost no one ever went to Mass, but where feast days were joyfully celebrated as ancient, often pre-Christian festivals.[32]

On the whole, priests seem to have been canny and discriminating in their assessments of popular religiosity, knowing that it might accompany orthodox faith, or exist without reference to it, or even compete with it. Year after year, for instance, archbishops of Seville fruitlessly pleaded with the people of the archdiocese not to abandon the Church's official Holy Week ceremonies in favour of the dramatic street processions of the traditional brotherhoods with their costumes and music and immensely elaborate tableaux of Virgins and Christs and apostles carried through the city by droves of bent and panting, but not necessarily believing or practising, men.

Often similarly fruitless was the injunction to behave with decorum

[32] References from Ilundain correspondence, Archivo diocesano de Sevilla, Parroquial 1932, Legajos 1–4. For the Rocío shrine, see J. Infante-Galán, Rocío, La devoción mariana de Andalucía (Seville, 1971).

during the week of processions, and not to mar it with 'secular' festivities of drinking and dancing.³³ But the drama of the church services on Maundy Thursday and Good Friday had more to compete with than the alternative drama going on for longer periods in the streets. The brotherhoods and their rituals were originally rooted in the old guilds, and some are still united by a common trade or profession. Even new brotherhoods demonstrated the importance of such connections: one founded in 1946, for example, in honour of Saint Martha, was the creation of a group of hoteliers; one founded in the sixteenth century was given new life in the twentieth by its success in gathering together bank employees, while a seventeenth-century brotherhood of coachmen recruited three hundred years later members of the Spanish air force. The brotherhood of Our Father Jesus of Good Health, and Most Holy Mary of Sorrows, based in the Sevillian parish of San Ramón, is better known locally as the brotherhood of the gypsies, and for good reason. Equally accurately, the brotherhood of the Sacred Column and Whipping of Our Lord Jesus Christ, and Most Holy Mary of Victory, which is based on the tobacco factory, has a more colloquial title as the association of cigarette makers.³⁴ Where trade or profession no longer provided common ground, family traditions supplied continuity of group identity and boys were often registered in the brotherhoods at birth by their fathers. The third unifying factor has been locality, with many of the brotherhoods acquiring an identification with a part of the town, and sometimes even taking its name. For instance, the brotherhood of Our Lady of Light bears the popular name of La Carretería not because of any link with road workers but because that is the name of the suburb it is based in.³⁵ Probably most famous of all the statues carried in procession in Seville, and without question the most loudly and joyfully acclaimed as its escort of Roman soldiers noisily clatters through the crowded streets before dawn on Good Friday morning, is Most Holy Mary of Hope, popularly known as the Macarena. She and her devotees are inescapably identified with the densely populated proletarian quarter of Triana.

Many of the diocesan clergy have, of course, supported and encouraged these brotherhoods, but none the less there have been problems, of which the most permanent has been their tendency to cut across

---

[33] E.g., *BEAS*, xxxi (1899), 136–8.
[34] *Semana Santa Sevilla 1980. Horario e itinerario oficial*, 11, 19, 40, 36, 28.
[35] F. García de la Torre, *Estudio histórico-artístico de la Hermandad del gremio de Toneleros de Sevilla* (Seville, 1979), 12.

parochial structures. Some of the sacred images honoured by these associations are housed in parish churches, some in chapels constructed for the purpose, with chaplains funded by the brothers themselves; but in all cases the images draw enthusiasts irrespective of parish boundaries and quite significantly disrupt the normal pattern of church-going, since members are very likely to attend Mass in the church of the brotherhood rather than the local parish church. Furthermore, some priests have always been sceptical of the crowds thronging the churches in the days before the Holy Week processions when the elaborate floats are being prepared, when for the rest of the year they scarcely put in an appearance. In order to sympathize with this one has only to watch a priest attempting to celebrate Mass with some kind of order a week or so before the most popular images, such as the Macarena, are due to be taken out in procession, while large numbers of people mill about admiring the float and lifting children to see it better and paying no attention at all to the priest's efforts at the altar. Since the Second Vatican Council many younger priests have become very critical of these non-liturgical pieties, which they see as the expression of folklore rather than 'true' religion, and in a recent survey brotherhood members complained of a lack of sympathy from priests and bishops in general and from younger priests in particular.[36]

At stake is the definition of 'true religion'. From an ecclesiastical point of view, processions, and the time, money, and fervour lavished upon dozens of decorated floats were all very well if strictly subordinated to and aiding a life of sacramental observance and personal piety. Since the Council, those conditions have been extended to include active concern for social problems, which many of the brotherhoods have indeed tried to promote.[37] Ranged alongside this view—and sometimes utterly opposed to it—is an appreciation of Holy Week street processions in many parts of Spain, and at their most elaborate and numerous in Seville, as a uniquely genuine religious phenomenon precisely because of their popular character, largely independent of the doctrinal and disciplinary structures of the Church, and immersed in a communal rather than individualistic culture of group or neighbourhood tradition.

[36] DIS, *Estudio de las hermandades* (Seville, 1972), 35–40. This is one of a number of studies prepared for the archdiocese in preparation for a synod by the Departmento de Investigación Socio-Religiosa of Madrid.
[37] For example, members of the Santa Marta brotherhood in San Andrés parish ran free courses to prepare young people for examinations to gain jobs in local banks. Information from interview with Santa Marta members and their girl friends, Seville, 23 Sept. 1980.

They belong to the streets not the churches, the people not the priests, the lay singers of *saetas* and noisy bands not the church choirs, just as the brotherhoods themselves are essentially lay in organization, composition, and leadership. From this perspective, young men walking barefoot and carrying penitential crosses do not have to be weekly communicants to validate their painful participation, and the boisterous reception traditionally given to the Macarena is just as authentic a part of the religious ritual as the grave sobriety surrounding the appearance of Jesus the Nazarene and Jesus of Great Power, carried in procession just ahead of her well before dawn on Good Friday.

The popular traditions of these street rituals have not safeguarded them from accusations that they belong to the same class politics of piety as orthodox religious practice. There is no doubt that in modern times the brotherhoods have been largely, though not exclusively, middle or upper class in membership, and that the most substantial proletarian participation in the processions, other than as spectators, have been the hundreds of labourers paid to carry the huge platforms with their heavy statues and drapes and candles. (Only in very recent years have some of the brotherhoods produced the *costaleros* from their own members.) It is very revealing that in the anti-clerical atmosphere of the early Second Republic, only one brotherhood ventured on to the streets of Seville in 1932, and in 1933 none at all of the usual forty or so. Brotherhood chapels and statues were damaged and some destroyed in the violent early days of the civil war; for example, groups from Triana quarter showed their evaluation of this 'popular' religiosity by destroying the church of the Macarena, before General Queipo de Llano showed his evaluation of them by laying waste their streets and homes and later rebuilding the church. In areas of acute class conflict, popular religion shared some of the class alignments of church religion, but never so rigidly.[38]

Meanwhile, for Church authorities the trying aspect was not the class politics of processions and shrines, but the ecclesiastical, institutional issue of control and orthodoxy. This was inevitably more prickly in the south, where conventional observance and popular piety could so easily part company than, for example, in Segovia or Valladolid, but even in areas of robust Catholic practice there were tensions. William Christian, for instance, noted the attempts by priests in the devout Nansa valley in Santander province to restrain some of the pious customs of the rural

---

[38] Information from numerous conversations in Seville.

Religious Practice and Piety 29

populations round local shrines in the 1950s, and the strong disapproval by younger priests after the Vatican Council of the traditional devotional focus on statues and shrines and pilgrimages.[39] Sacerdotal religion was often uneasy when finding itself in the company of potent sacred images, accounts of apparitions that often gave shrines their fame, and alternative, if discreet, holy persons, like the women *sabias* of Grazalema who were healers, counsellors, and purveyors of hidden knowledge.[40] Occasionally such phenomena resulted in open heterodoxy, of which the most notorious example is probably Palmar de Troya, near Utrera, in Seville province. There an alleged apparition of the Virgin Mary to some little girls in the mid-twentieth century began to draw huge crowds, as has often been the case. But matters did not stop there. A large, convinced, disciplined group gathered round a leader, Clemente, in the Order of the Holy Face, which was—and is—a strange cross between a religious order and a secretive, fanatical sect like the Moonies. In Palmar de Troya they have created an alternative church, denouncing the pope in Rome as an anti-pope and proclaiming Clemente as Pope Gregory XVII. On the whole, however, Spain has no more been heterodox than it has been Protestant: but its Catholicism has not always been to the taste of the clergy.

In very many other public religious rituals, the vital question was not the orthodoxy of the people involved, but whether the ritual was primarily religious or political, in so far as those two elements could be separated at all. The Jesuits, for example, campaigned consistently for many years to spread the cult of the Sacred Heart; and many of the practices associated with this cult of the heart of Jesus in Spain—as in France where it had originated—were inextricably linked in the late nineteenth and early twentieth· centuries with the integrist values of the extreme Right of the Catholic political spectrum. Devotion to the Sacred Heart was propagated most forcefully through the Apostleship of Prayer, founded by the French Jesuit Francois Xavier Gautrelet in 1844, and its publication, the *Messenger of the Sacred Heart*, of which an independent Spanish version was firmly established by the Jesuits in 1886 and published monthly thereafter. The *Messenger* was anti-liberal, anti-Semitic, bitterly opposed to the limited religious toleration granted by the 1876 constitution, and enthusiastic to see 'the social reign of Jesus Christ' in Spain.[41] A favourite way of hastening that theocracy at

[39] W. A. Christian, 56, 182.
[40] J. Pitt-Rivers, 189ff.
[41] For further examination of the *Messenger*, see below, p. 126.

the end of the nineteenth century was by 'enthroning' an image of the Sacred Heart in Catholic homes. But when the campaign shifted from private homes to public places, it was evident that the aim was not just to strengthen the piety of the faithful but to claim Catholic conservative influence over civic and political life.

The *Messenger* called for the enthronement of the Sacred Heart in offices, schools, banks, town halls, and city streets, and reported progress to its readers under headings like 'Madrid—the Sacred Heart in the Bank of Spain'.[42] From about the year 1915 statues were erected in hundreds of towns and villages, often by local subscription, and with as much pomp and representation of local authorities as possible. They appeared in provincial government buildings and even on hill tops. Nationally, the movement reached its climax in 1919 when, at the newly erected statue in the Cerro de los Angeles, estimated to be the geographical centre of Spain, King Alfonso XIII, accompanied by the whole government, read a consecration of the entire nation to the Sacred Heart. The preparation of this event and the fund-raising for it had been well publicized, and for some at least of those present the significance was far from being purely religious. Remigio Vilariño, SJ, director of the *Messenger*, for example, attended the ceremony and drew his own lessons in the report he wrote for the magazine. He contrasted the consecration with 'the entire despicable history of mean and miserable politicking which oppresses and enslaves us', and imagined Spain's kings in heaven exclaiming, 'Well done! This is Spain as it is, as it must be. If it cannot be so, it is better not to exist at all.' Meanwhile, below, 'revolutionaries', 'intellectuals', and 'enemies' were horrified and outraged.[43] These statues, in other words, were a protest at religious and political pluralism by many of those who erected and honoured them. That the message of Catholic conservative intolerance was clearly received by foes as well as friends was amply demonstrated by the care with which some anarchists and socialists 'executed' the statues in the early months of the civil war in 1936.

Processions of a rather provocative kind were another speciality of the Apostleship of Prayer. In March 1889, for instance, groups throughout the three Basque provinces processed from one of the city churches in Bilbao to the sanctuary–shrine of the Virgin of Begoña, along with local Catholic students and school children. About 13,000 people were involved in this act of Marian piety, but it could equally well be regarded

---

[42] *Mensajero del Corazón de Jesús y del Apostolado de Oración* (May, 1926), 466.
[43] Ibid. (July, 1919), 520–34.

Religious Practice and Piety 31

as an anti-liberal, anti-progressive political demonstration, since the primary avowed aim was 'solemnly to proclaim the rights of God and the social reign of the Heart of Jesus, in opposition to the diabolical centenary of "the rights of man" '.[44] In another Marian procession in Bilbao some years later, the political provocation proved too much for a rival, socialist gathering, and in the ensuing clash one man was killed and a number injured. Interpretations of these events on 11 October 1903 varied: Church sources criticized the civil governor for not providing adequate protection for a legal religious act, and the archbishop of Burgos complained to the government; but the Left-wing press regarded the procession as an act of deliberate provocation and much later the communist leader Dolores Ibarruri referred to it as a Carlist celebration.[45] Meanwhile the *Messenger* gave its own serialized account in which the October pilgrimage was presented as the beginning of a new reconquest of Spain in the name of Catholic unity. It had opposed Jerusalem to Babylon, Jesus Christ to the devil, and the battle would continue. So great was the symbolic significance of the event for Fr. Luis María Ortiz, SJ, that twenty-five years after his series of articles, he published a commemorative pamphlet.[46] Symbols, however, resist single readings, and the banners and hymns that Ortiz saw as an expression of faith seemed to many others an exploitation of religion for political ends.

Other processions and pilgrimages also ended in violence. Students for the priesthood in the seminary of Oviedo in the last decades of the nineteenth century used to carry sticks while taking part in religious processions in the town, 'to protect the sacred images against liberals and republicans', and both sides suffered broken bones.[47] Mass pilgrimages to national shrines like Compostela or abroad to Lourdes or Rome could be equally bloody. In 1894, for instance, some of the 13,000 pilgrims on their way to Rome were stoned on the quay at Valencia. This aggression was certainly expressed not just out of dislike of religious jamborees, but because the pilgrimage took place under the aegis of the immensely wealthy Catholic shipping magnate, the Marquis of Comillas, and the national association of Catholic workers that he

---

[44] Ibid. (June, 1889), 472.
[45] *BEOV*, xxxix (1903), 405–8, and D. Ibarruri, *They Shall Not Pass* (London, 1966), 29–30.
[46] *Bodas de plata de la jornada sangriente pero gloriosa para el catolicismo en Bilbao* (Pamplona, 1928).
[47] A. Viñayo, *El seminario de Oviedo* (Oviedo, 1955), 109.

dominated—an association widely disparaged among militant workers as a blacklegging traitor.[48]

The interpenetration of religion and politics in Spain has been so complete that the devout have frequently been unaware of political messages in acts of piety. To many people throughout fifty-five years of the restoration monarchy, for instance, it seemed quite unexceptionable that the royal march should be played at the consecration in solemn high Mass, that police and members of the armed services should salute statues being carried by in procession, that prayers for the king should be incorporated into Catholic liturgy. These, or their equivalents, are familiar in any state with an established Church. They inevitably became controversial, however, when the monarchy itself was disputed, and rapidly assumed the character of subversive disloyalty once the republic was proclaimed in 1931. For their part, anti-clerical republicans recognized and strengthened the political function of religious symbols by banning the crucifix from Spanish schools.

During the civil war, Catholic ritual became the unifying ideological sign and expression of one of the opposing sides. While Catholic liturgy was proscribed in most areas under republican control, and secret house Masses in circumstances of great danger—especially where anarchists were dominant—recalled the persecuted life of the catacombs, on the insurgent side Mass was celebrated before enormous crowds in cities and in military camps, bishops blessed guns and exhorted the troops, and the capture of towns from the republicans was celebrated with solemn *Te Deums*. Catholic ritual proclaimed the war a struggle between religion and the forces of revolutionary atheism at least as effectively as did the bishops in their official statements and pastoral letters.[49]

The division was not as clear nor as neatly defined by religion as the symbols suggested, of course. One insurgent general, Vigón, laconically recorded in his diary his amusement at seeing his colleague Cabanellas—a notorious sceptic and Freemason—on his knees in front of his troops leading a prayer of consecration to the Sacred Heart.[50] Several generals on the other side, including the famed defender of republican Madrid, Miaja, were conversely, firmly Catholic. Muslim soldiers and Nazi airmen were flagrantly unsuitable agents of the Catholic crusade, just as devout Basque troops on the other side modified at least in the north the anti-clerical character of the republic's defenders.

[48] For Comillas, see below, p. 148.
[49] For bishops' pastoral letters during the war, see below, pp. 202–4.
[50] H. Raguer, *La espada y la cruz* (Barcelona, 1977), 64.

Religious Practice and Piety   33

Nevertheless, Catholic ritual assumed enormous importance because defence of the Church emerged as a kind of agreed shorthand for the varied and sometimes conflicting currents of conservative, reactionary, and counter-revolutionary values for which the insurgents fought. Suddenly the bellicose language of the *Messenger* in one cultural world and crude anti-clericalism in another had been translated into real war, and the opposed camps set up in words now confronted one another with guns and bombs. Religious images and rites camouflaged as much as they expressed the inspiration and aims of both sides in a conflict rooted in class hostility as much as in religion. Catholicism was the badge of the insurgents—even if worn on the uniform of a Freemason or a Muslim—and Catholic liturgies unified one half of the Spanish population against the other.

Some ecclesiastics recognized at the time the danger for the Church in this situation, especially as it continued after the war ended, making Catholicism the religion of the victors, flaunted before the vanquished. The most eminent critic was the cardinal archbishop of Tarragona, Francesc Vidal i Barraquer. In spite of his escape from almost certain death at the hands of anarchists, and the appalling massacre of many of the priests in his archdiocese, he deplored the political manipulation of religion in nationalist Spain and warned the pope in 1939 of the likely consequences. The religion of the nationalists, he said, seemed to consist mainly of

promoting great Catholic spectacles, pilgrimages to Pilar, huge processions, enthronements of the Sacred Heart, solemn funerals and funeral orations for the war dead. They organize dramatically mass participation at confirmation and first communion ceremonies, and above all they open almost every act of propaganda with outdoor Masses of which they have made a veritable abuse.

All of these lacked religious depth and were rather, ephemeral 'cultic demonstrations' expressing a political reaction against recent persecution and laicism. They could do little good, but threatened to make Catholicism hateful to the indifferent and to all those who remained loyal to the republic.[51]

Particularly in the first years of Franco's Spain, Catholic rites dominated social and civic life. The 'patriotic religion' lamented by Vidal i Barraquer and later dubbed 'national-Catholicism' by its Catholic critics launched again all the campaigns of earlier decades in an attempt to effect the decisive religious transformation of the country. Hilltops and

[51] Quoted ibid., 246–7.

town squares again boasted enormous statues of the Sacred Heart, Marian pilgrimages were organized on a vast scale, street processions in Holy Week were encouraged; inevitably, a military pilgrimage to Cerro de los Angeles took place in 1945 in which fifty generals and fifteen hundred officers participated. Military or political authorities appeared conspicuously in all these events.[52] Religion and victory went hand in hand, which is to say also that religion offered its hand to certain very well-defined social and political groups and not to others. Anyone attending the Corpus Christi celebrations in Toledo until very recent years indeed, for example, would see a glorification of the Church, the military, and the conservative, propertied classes in which it was extremely difficult to see where one ended and another began. The political force of religious ceremonial was indirectly attested by a strange episode in 1967 when Catholic, Catalan nationalists 'kidnapped' a Romanesque statue of the Virgin of Nuria, patroness of Catalonia. They wanted to prevent her imminent ritual coronation by a Francoist bishop, which seemed to them an offensively anti-Catalan gesture.[53]

In the 1970s, Spain remained what the Counter Reformation had made it and what Franco's victory in the civil war had confirmed—a Catholic country. 95% of the population were baptized Catholics; 84% declared themselves believers and only 5% non-believers; other denominations could claim at most 3% of the population as adherents.[54] Sociologists of religion noticed trends towards greater agnosticism and atheism, especially among young people in their twenties, and the better educated.[55] For many Spaniards, however, belief in God and self-definition as Catholics coexisted peacefully with total neglect of the basic Catholic obligations of attending Sunday Mass and receiving the sacraments once a year. And the determining factors here remained what they had been for generations—region, size of settlement, occupation, class, and sex, although age joined the list as younger Spaniards proved generally less interested in religion than their elders.

Preachers continued to be preoccupied not only by those who, according to the conventional criteria, did not practise their religion, but also by the quality of faith and commitment of those who did. The fears of

---

[52] For post-war religious rituals see A. L. Oresanz, *Religiosidad popular española (1940–1965)* (Madrid, 1974), 9–21; F. Urbina, 'Formas de vida de la iglesia en España, 1939–1975', in *Iglesia y sociedad en España 1939–1975* (Madrid, 1977), 12–17.
[53] *El Vaticà i Catalunya* (Geneva, 1967), 257–61.
[54] FOESSA, *Estudios sociológicos sobre la situación social de España. 1975* (Madrid, 1976), 543, 704.
[55] Ibid., 542–57.

bishops and priests that religious observance might be an empty formalism for too many of the laity were sharpened in the 1960s and 1970s as a more immanentist theology became prevalent, bringing with it an expectation that genuine religious commitment would be expressed by action for social justice as well as pious exercises. Sociological statisticians confirmed these fears as they processed endless questionnaires on the exact content of people's beliefs and the correlation between belief and action, theology and life-style. In the most exhaustive compilation of data made in the 1970s, researchers estimated that 36% of believing Catholics rejected the idea that love of neighbour should be a fundamental norm governing daily behaviour, and that 44% thought it impossible to follow Christian principles of justice in business dealings and money matters. There was little comfort, however, for those still more concerned about traditional sexual mores, since a large minority did not consider pre-marital sex sinful, and a convincing majority wanted divorce to be made available in Spain in certain circumstances. Nor did devotional criteria produce more comforting results than those of morals and mores: even among those who attended Sunday Mass regularly, large numbers rarely received communion, and this choice seemed perhaps more revealing of the degree of personal commitment than Mass attendance itself.[56]

The Catholic character usually claimed by the Spanish state between the 1870s and the 1970s, and almost universally claimed by individual Spaniards at the end of the Franco regime, covered an enormous variety of religious practice and conviction. To be Catholic could and did mean quite different things according to place, local culture, education, and class. One of the crazier enquiries of the 1960s concluded that just as city dwellers laughed more than those in the country, the young more than the old, the rich more than the poor, so those who counted themselves 'good Catholics' laughed more than the rest of the population.[57] The enormous, probably insoluble problem for the Church in modern Spain until very recently has been that 'good Catholics' have had cause for joy not just in spiritual certainties and continuity of cultural tradition, but also because, on the whole, they were not numbered among the poorest, the propertyless, the illiterate, and the unemployed.

[56] Ibid., 566–73.
[57] FOESSA, *Informe sociológico sobre la situación social de España. 1970* (Madrid, 1970), 610–11.

2
Cultural Values

SPANISH Catholicism was, as every child learned to repeat, one, holy, Roman, and apostolic. There was one creed, one hierarchy, one central liturgy. Yet the epithet Catholic was so universally appropriated by the devout and the bored, the observant and the negligent, the ascetic and the lax, that its meaning was extremely elastic. Even among the more devout, observant, and ascetic who went to church, received the sacraments, and prayed, the cultural experience and expression of a common faith differed according to region, class, sex, occupation, and innumerable other variants. There was not—nor could there be—a single Catholic culture. Fr. Carles Cardó published in 1946 a very influential study of contrasting spiritual values developed over centuries in Castile and Catalonia respectively, arguing that whereas Castilian tradition encouraged a crusading fervour, the Catalan tended instead towards tolerance and even indifference.[1] No doubt similar distinctions could be elaborated elsewhere, but regional peculiarity was not always the decisive factor. An outsider seeking to understand Spanish Catholicism in the early 1930s, for example, would gain from the fierce Jesuit periodical *Razón y Fe* a quite different impression than from the experimental new journal 'of affirmation and negation' *Cruz y Raya*, produced by laymen, both published in Madrid and both expecting to reach a serious and educated readership. Even the Mass itself acquired an infinity of cultural incarnations once it was celebrated in the vernacular instead of Latin after the Second Vatican Council. There had always been more and less ceremonious and solemn modes, but a stranger attending Mass in one of the stuffy, fashionable baroque churches in the centre of Madrid in about 1970 and then straying into a folksy liturgy in a working-class area like Vallecas or Moratalaz where the celebrant might improvise many of the prayers, and the atmosphere be reminiscent of something between a political meeting and a huge family party, could well imagine that these were different denominations

---

[1] C. Cardó, *Histoire spirituelle des Espagnes* (Paris, 1946).

altogether. Nor was any one of the myriad cultural worlds within Spanish Catholicism immune to modification over time. On the contrary, in addition to earlier oscillations between stability and change, all of them were abruptly exposed to inescapable demands for reappraisal and conscious updating in the 1960s as the Vatican Council produced authoritative new models for Catholic self-understanding.

It is nevertheless possible to identify characteristic values or emphases that permeated most Catholic language and activity for much of the century under discussion, and to trace lines of development. The young polymath Marcelino Menéndez y Pelayo captured the prevailing tone of contemporary Catholicism in the early 1880s when he surveyed Spanish religious history with a discontented eye in his rebarbative *History of Spanish Heterodoxy*. With many a rhetorical flourish perfectly pitched to echo through the decades in irresistible quotation, his analysis of Catholic identity was nostalgic, nationalist, and defensive. In religion as in literature, art, and imperial expansion, the sixteenth and seventeenth centuries had constituted the golden age. The Catholic Church had transformed 'a crowd of assembled people' into a great nation, strong in spiritual unity, called by God to dominate the world.[2] Thenceforth, subsequent history was a sorry tale of 'how the beautiful building of old Spain was demolished, stone by stone, and how its religion and its language, its science and its art, and all that had made it wise, powerful and feared in the world was gradually forgotten'.[3] The introduction of the Bourbon dynasty early in the eighteenth century was followed by other pernicious foreign influences through the Enlightenment and the French revolution: Spain's originality and creativity was sapped, together with its religious unity. In this account, the best hope for Catholicism in Spain lay in restoring what had been destroyed, and eradicating debilitating foreign influences.

It would be difficult to exaggerate Menéndez y Pelayo's influence: a rare intellectual giant of orthodoxy in very undistinguished company, he created a vigorous, memorable, and polemical version of Spanish history that claimed Catholic responsibility for a glorious past, and Protestant, liberal, and foreign responsibility for national decline. To be Catholic was therefore patriotic, whereas religious dissent or indifference undermined Spanish greatness. This argument was repeated *ad nauseam* in textbooks, sermons, and political propaganda for decades. Bishops agreed with Menéndez y Pelayo that even the most circumscribed

[2] M. Ménendez y Pelayo, *Historia de los heterodoxos españoles*, vii, 556–7.
[3] Ibid., v, 483.

toleration of religions other than Catholicism in Spain amounted to a dangerous denial of patriotism as well as being a form of national apostasy. On this basis they went on deploring the loss of 'Catholic unity' decades after the constitution of 1876 guaranteed a modicum of religious toleration; and they welcomed on religious grounds any authoritarian regime that promised to restore it.[4] A history of the Church for school children published in the early 1920s referred confidently to 'the invasion of Freemasonry and impiety, the source of all the evils which our country suffered in the nineteenth century'.[5] A textbook compendium of world history widely used in schools in the same period attributed all the ills of modern Europe to the Protestant reformers.[6] (Its author, the Jesuit polemicist on educational matters, Ramón Ruiz Amado, was a prolific writer of textbooks, many of which—including a history of Spain—were officially approved for use in schools by the Ministry of Education after the civil war.) During Primo de Rivera's dictatorship, political propagandists repeated Menéndez y Pelayo's familiar identification of Catholicism with patriotism to justify a Catholic autocracy, just as they did again during the civil war and in the Catholic dictatorship that followed it.[7] Other ideologies and their adherents became the destructive and hated 'anti-Spain', unworthy of tolerance or respect. Nostalgia for a former golden age became a ferocious weapon in the present. Since the past provided such powerful legitimation of intolerance and repression as a patriotic duty, it is not difficult to see why modernity was regarded with suspicion. It carried connotations of Enlightenment scepticism and mistrust of established authority, free enquiry, and liberal principles, the rights of man rather than duties towards God and God's ecclesiastical and secular representatives. The dominant Catholic culture in Spain was profoundly anti-modern, and hostile to those European influences that had helped identify modernity with pluralism.

One of the clearest examples of Catholic xenophobia and defensive archaism was the long, obsessive campaign against an alternative, Europeanizing and liberal intellectual culture promoted by the Free Educational Institute (*Institución Libre de Enseñanza*). Set beside the vast educational resources of the Catholic Church, the ILE looked puny, but

[4] See below, pp. 120–32.
[5] Hermanos de las Escuelas Cristianas, *Historia de la iglesia católica* (Madrid and Barcelona, c. 1922), 351–2.
[6] R. Ruiz Amado, *Compendio de historia universal (edad moderna)*. 6th edn. (Barcelona, 1926), epilogue.
[7] See below, pp. 173, 220–1.

Catholic apologists were right to fear it as a latter-day David capable of wounding, if not slaying, Goliath. It appeared on the scene in 1876 when a circular from Orovio, the Minister responsible for education, precipitated the exit from university teaching posts of professors and lecturers unwilling to make their teaching conform to Catholic doctrine. Numbers remained so small that in the golden jubilee year of 1926 the ILE could boast only 158 pupils. Moreover, because until the late 1920s it did not prepare pupils for the state examinations it despised, based on textbooks it deplored, many pupils stayed for only part of their education and then went elsewhere to acquire the necessary qualifications for university entrance.[8] But the ILE's influence was out of all proportion to its size. It is best seen, not as a small school, but as the institutional centre of a remarkably high-powered cultural world.

That world was first called into being in 1857, when Julián Sanz del Río, professor of the History of Philosophy at Madrid university, dedicated the inaugural lecture of the academic year to a philosophical enquiry closer to humanism and rationalism than to Catholic dogma. Sanz's philosophical model was an obscure German idealist called Karl Christian Friedrich Krause (1781-1830), but the genealogy of his vague, spiritual, tolerant, humanitarian, individualist thought is less important than the immense attraction it held for Spanish intellectuals who had no desire to repudiate religious or even Christian experience and sensibility, but disliked the doctrinal formulations and narrow ecclesiastical discipline of Roman Catholicism.[9] 'Krausism' meant in Spain a high-minded, idealist search for the rational, harmonious development of the whole individual and of a tolerant society. It was as much concerned with spiritual growth as with learning, and it inevitably produced a pedagogical theory utterly opposed to the traditional Catholic preoccupation with assimilating already defined truths and morals. It was not so much a detailed philosophical system as an alternative cultural style. Sanz del Río gathered round him before his death in 1869 an impressive group of collaborators and disciples especially eminent in academic life. For many of them, Pius IX's onslaught on liberalism in the *Syllabus of Errors* of 1864, then the solemn declaration of papal infallibility in 1870, closed whatever doors to orthodoxy had still

---

[8] L. Luzuriaga, *La Institución Libre de Enseñanza y la educación en españa* (Buenos Aires, 1957), 90–1.
[9] For a classic study on the cultural reasons for the attraction of Krausism in Spain, originally published in Spanish in 1956, see J. López-Morillas, *The Krausist Movement and Ideological Change in Spain 1854–1874* (Cambridge, 1981).

remained open. They would worship God 'in spirit and in truth', but privately, not according to Roman Catholic prescriptions.[10] When a group of Sanz del Río's followers resigned their university posts in 1876 and united round Francisco Giner de los Ríos to found the ILE, they claimed that their institution was profoundly respectful of spiritual values but neutral in religion. To their orthodox critics, those two assertions were mutually contradictory, since only Catholicism embodied true spiritual values. The notion of religious neutrality itself constituted for them, particularly within the interpretation of Spanish history that Menéndez y Pelayo was soon to elaborate, a denial of Catholicism and an affront to patriotic sentiment.

Orovio's imposition of confessional uniformity on Spanish universities lasted only until 1881, after which many of the Krausists returned to university posts. They were later joined by former ILE students. When Catholic writers inveighed against the ILE, their target was not just the school, but the whole intellectual group centred on it, and spreading ever further into the universities and then politics. By the turn of the century many of the luminaries of Spanish intellectual culture and reformist politics were members of that distinctive group, and the same was still true thirty years later. Against the novelists Benito Pérez Galdós and Emilia Pardo Bazán, the poet Antonio Machado, the philosopher José Ortega y Gasset, writers and social reformers Concepción Arenal and Joaquín Costa, politicians ranging from the Liberal leader Segismundo Moret to the Socialist theorist Julián Besteiro, and many other very eminent figures, Catholic orthodoxy boasted few names of comparable intellectual prestige.[11] In 1907 ILE circles created a commission to encourage advanced study and research (the *Junta para ampliación de estudios e investigaciones científicas*) which from 1910 gave grants to about fifty scholars each year to study abroad and won a formidable academic reputation. Krausist influence was diffused also through a small training college established in 1907 and a students' residence opened in Madrid in 1911.

The Catholic assault on Krausism was begun by the scholastic philosopher Juan Manuel Ortí y Lara in his reply in Granada in 1857 to

---

[10] One of the first Spanish Krausists, the priest Fernando de Castro, described his conversion 'from Roman Catholic into a genuinely and truly religious man, according to the spirit of Christianity which is not at all opposed to universal human reason, adoring God privately in spirit and in truth'. See M. D. Gómez Molleda, *Los reformadores de la españa contemporánea* (Madrid, 1966), 38–9.

[11] All cited as professors or collaborators of the ILE in the appendix to L. Luzuriaga, op. cit.

Sanz del Rió's seminal inaugural lecture. He was later joined by his fellow Thomist the Dominican and successively bishop, archbishop then cardinal Ceferino González, and by Menéndez y Pelayo. They accused the Krausists of pantheism, heresy, hypocrisy, and corrupting the young.[12] The ILE also proved a favourite target of the Jesuits who seemed both dazzled and appalled by this brilliantly successful counterpart to their own attempts to shape national culture through educating a dominant élite. In the anti-liberal Jesuit press—ranging from the popular *Messenger of the Sacred Heart* to the serious *Razón y Fe* (*Reason and Faith*), begun in 1901—religious toleration was consistently vituperated as a poisoning of the wells of national culture, contaminating truth with error.[13] The tone of many campaigns was set in the bellicose presentation of *Razón y Fe* to its readers, in which the editors stated that men of learning were abandoning reason, truth, and the supernatural, but Jesuits fought along with others to defend the sacred, indissoluble trinity of truth, Church, and fatherland.[14] That patriotism and Catholicism were inseparable in Spain was reiterated frequently right up to the 1960s.[15] Free-thinking intellectuals were therefore doubly disliked as perpetrators of error and anti-patriotic values. The educational polemicist Ramón Ruiz Amado launched a fierce attack on the ILE and the *Junta para ampliación de studios* in 1924; in 1926 the review reported a speech by the bishop of Jaén designating the ILE as an enemy of Spain as well as of religion; four years later F. Alonso Barcena argued in a series of articles that Giner de los Ríos's exaltation of tolerance was unacceptable; in November 1937, with the civil war still at its height, F. Cereceda unleashed an angry diatribe against the intellectuals of the ILE as corrupters of youth and agents of anti-patriotism, and the theme was taken up again in 1939 and 1941 by S. Cuesta; an editorial in 1943 attacked Pérez Galdós on the centenary of his birth as 'one of the great falsifiers of the national spirit' in a liberal age that was itself a 'national aberration'.[16] In fact a flurry of post-war articles on Ortega y

---

[12] See the accounts in A. Ollero Tassara, *Universidad y política. Tradición y secularización en el siglo XIX* (Madrid, 1972); Gómez Molleda, 20–6; J. J. Gil Cremades, *El reformismo español. Krausismo, escuela histórica, neotomismo* (Barcelona, 1969), section IV.

[13] For the *Messenger* campaign against liberalism, see below p. 126.

[14] *Razon y Fe*, i (1901), 2–5.

[15] The lines of argument were established by Ramón Ruiz Amado in numerous articles, see e.g., 'Los privilegios de la enseñanza religiosa en España', *RyF*, vii (1903); 'La paz religiosa', *RyF*, xvii (1907); 'Psicología del patriotismo', *RyF*, xxiv (1909).

[16] R. Ruiz Amado, 'La junta para ampliación de estudios y sus instituciones', *RyF*, lxviii (1924); bishop of Jaén's speech in D. Domínguez, 'El segundo congreso catequístico nacional', *RyF*, lxxvi (1926); F. Alonso Barcena, 'Cultura y tolerancia', *RyF*, xci (1930);

Gasset, Unamuno, and others clearly presented the ILE as one of the great evils extirpated by the victorious Crusade of Franco.

Because Catholic writers looked back longingly to an earlier ideal age of national and religious grandeur and bemoaned the influences they thought responsible for its disappearance, they very often defined Catholic culture negatively, against what threatened it. Free-thinking intellectuals and politicians associated with the ILE were abhorred because they imported foreign influences, and Spanish Catholicism was seen as an anti-foreign, anti-liberal, anti-Protestant fortress besieged by its enemies. Enlightenment values were dangerous, but so were Jews, socialists, and Freemasons—all of them foreign in origin or inspiration and hostile to Catholicism. It would be otiose to catalogue instances of the paranoid conviction that conspiracies in any one or any combination of these endangered both Church and nation; it was a permanent feature of Catholic siege mentality on the defensive against the alien and the modern. But an obituary for the cardinal primate Isidro Gomá in 1940 by his Jesuit admirer Fr. Bayle is a typical example. Looking back on the great confrontation between true religion and patriotism and their joint foes during the civil war, Bayle described how 'the enemies of the Cross ... were assisted by the international marxist hordes, supported by Jewish gold and masonic intrigues, urged on by liberalism and regarded benevolently by Catholics whose vision had been darkened by a blinding love for democracy'.[17] Such outbursts never explained what groups as diverse as Protestants, Jews, intellectual advocates of tolerance and liberalism, reformist socialists, and revolutionary Marxists had in common. For integrist Catholicism, that rejected any form of secularization, and in which religion and political and cultural values were therefore inextricably bound together, the connection was simply that they were all its enemies and they were all false. It was not just in Spain that socialism—whose classical texts were often overtly atheistic and whose adherents were often loudly anticlerical—appeared entirely antithetical to Catholicism. Neither was Spanish Catholicism unique in its suspicion of Freemasons or its fear of the relativizing effects of liberalism. Anti-Semitic rhetoric was probably inevitable in a country whose national myths of unity and glory gave pride of place to the expulsion of Moors and Jews in the fifteenth

---

F. Cereceda, 'Siempre fueron los mismos. Los "intelectuales"', *RyF*, 478 (1937); S. Cuesta, 'Los "intelectuales" increyentes', *RyF*, 500–1 (1939), continued in no. 516 (1941); on Pérez Galdós, see *RyF*, 545 (1943) 481–2.

[17] *RyF*, 512–13 (1940), 206.

century. But all of these were exacerbated by the paradox that although Catholicism in Spain felt itself desperately threatened and on the defensive, it also retained fervent hopes of restoring ideological hegemony long after these had faded in, for instance, France or Italy. Its enemies were powerful, but perhaps they could still one day be overcome: this uneasy balance kept integrism alive, poised between nostalgia for a lost Spanish Catholic world and determination to shape a new one against the combined trends of modernity and foreign influence.

Integrists, however, never went completely unchallenged in the Church. Just as many devout Catholic politicians favoured the limited toleration of other religions in the 1876 constitution, so other Catholics attempted peaceful coexistence and even co-operation with free-thinkers and non-Catholics, and welcomed international contacts. In intellectual life, the best example of this before the civil war was *Cruz y Raya*, a literary and philosophical periodical published from 1933 to 1936 that set out to emulate the quality and range of Ortega y Gasset's famous *Revista de Occidente*. Its contents were international and ecumenical.[18] Among foreign authors it published Claudel, Victor Hugo, Charles Péguy, Jacques Maritain, Étienne Gilson and André Malraux, Blake, Milton, Newman, Gerard Manley Hopkins and Eliot, Heidegger and Höderlin, and Luigi Sturzo. Progressive Catholicism in France, especially round Mounier's journal *Esprit*, was a particularly strong influence, but *Cruz y Raya*'s editor José Bergamín wanted to incorporate many different literary and philosophical approaches, especially contemporary ones. Even more striking was the list of Spanish contributors, which included a generous selection of nonconformists from Unamuno to Ortega y Gasset, from Pio Baroja to Julián Marias, as well as orthodox Catholics ranging from the fascist Rafael Sánchez Mazas to the young poet Miguel Hernández. In its pages Giner de los Ríos and the ILE could be referred to appreciatively.[19] Abstract and surrealist drawings and works of Picasso heightened the impression of modernity. Bergamín invited an 'open, free, independent collaboration' of all spiritual values, and affirmed the Catholic inspiration of the review while denying that faith implied or required any single cultural embodiment.[20] Similarly anti-integrist was *Cruz y Raya*'s political orientation, since it denounced Right and Left indiscriminately without ever committing itself to any one political

[18] There is a published analytical index (not always accurate): R. Benítez Claros, *Cruz y Raya (Madrid, 1933–1936)* (Madrid, 1947).
[19] *Cruz y Raya*, 30 (Sept. 1935), 89–92.
[20] Ibid., 1 (April 1933), 7–10.

group. It was the opposite end of the Catholic intellectual spectrum from *Razon y Fe* but although it enjoyed a buoyant reputation during the Second Republic, it remained a rather isolated initiative and was drowned by the integrist flood of Crusade Catholicism.

Many integrist characteristics of the Catholic restoration in the late nineteenth century and its recapitulation through the civil war in the 1930s helped keep it combative and assertive. They reduced the infinite possibilities of cultural classification to simple alternatives: everything was either true or false, good or bad, right or wrong. In July 1931, for example, just as preparations for a new, democratic, republican constitution were beginning, the *Messenger of the Sacred Heart* proclaimed that 'the time is approaching when all ideologies and all social systems will be resolved into two—either Communism or Catholicism, either Rome or Moscow'.[21] Whether the obsession was with Russian communism or, as earlier, with liberalism, the method remained one of extreme polarization. It is probably not surprising that a mentality so rigid and unselfcritical proved intellectually sterile. Spanish Catholicism produced few important writers and none of outstanding international calibre. It was virtually untouched by the European modernist anguish at the close of the nineteenth century, and had no equivalent of Loisy or Von Hügel. The best-selling Catholic novel in Spain in the 1890s was Luis Coloma, SJ's integrist and didactic *Pequeñeces*, originally published in serial form in the *Messenger* in 1890–1. Coloma saw himself as a pious equivalent to the impious Zola, using a crude realism to shock his readers into conversion, 'preaching to those who otherwise would not listen to me, telling them necessary home truths clearly in their own language in a way that could never be done under the dome of a church'.[22] Pardo Bazán admired the work, although most contemporary Spanish novelists did not, but it clearly did not constitute nor herald any significant Catholic literary revival like that in France to set beside the marvellous renaissance of heterodox novelists and dramatists. In philosophy, the Thomism encouraged by Leo XIII held sway in Catholic education, but it produced no Maritain.

Up to the civil war, only poetry among the literary arts overcame the odds, but the greatest achievements belonged to Catholic cultures away from the mainstream. The priest Jacint Verdeguer's poetic language was forged in the new fire of the Catalan revival, far removed from integrist rigidities. Miguel Hernández wrote sublime lyric poetry in the

[21] *Mensajero del Corazón de Jesus* (July 1931), 578.
[22] From Coloma's preface in L. Coloma, *Pequeñeces*, ed. R. Benítez (Madrid, 1975), 55.

Cultural Values   45

1930s but died in 1942 with his health ruined at the age of thirty-two in a Francoist gaol in which he had been imprisoned after a commuted death sentence for his commitment to the republican side in the war: he had worked with Federico García Lorca and Pablo Neruda and had written prolifically while fighting against the Crusade; his life and his poetry did not fit into the neat alternatives offered by Catholic apologetics.[23] Probably the most internationally famous Catholic artists of the period were Manuel de Falla whose musical inspiration owed more to his native Granada and Andalusia than to religion, and the Catalan architect Antoni Gaudí whose amazing fantasies in stone certainly sprang from Catholic cultural sources, but those of an interiorized, ecstatic medievalism rather than a sclerotic nineteenth-century version of the Counter Reformation.

The Catholic revival after the painful experiences of earlier decades in the nineteenth century, eliminated ambiguity, discouraged innovation, and fostered intellectual certainty rather than enquiry. Its hermeticism protected the fortress of truth against all the insinuations of error. It promoted moral clarity and sincere devotion. But it could not generate great art or literature, or even noteworthy theology. The dominant intellectual and artistic figures of Spain developed at its margins, often finding its crudity offensive. The tragic civil war of 1936-9 was a struggle over the country's intellectual and cultural values as well as its religion and its social and political systems, and Catholic victory dispatched many of the intellectual élite into exile. Typically, that victory was symbolized in the massive, ostentatious basilica in the Valle de los Caídos (Valley of the Fallen) where those who had fought and died for religion and the true Spain were commemorated.

The stridency of post-war national Catholic culture could no longer be directly challenged by heterodox Spaniards, nor by the handful of Catholic intellectuals who had fought on the battle field or in the propaganda war alongside 'the enemies of God' and paid the price of death or exile. Catholic unity and uniformity—so long desired—were imposed by force during and after the war. While Menéndez y Pelayo's interpretation of Spanish destiny was regurgitated in dozens of books and periodicals, and thousands of speeches and sermons, it could be effectively queried only by those within the gates of the Catholic fortress. After the first decade a few voices were raised, pleading the inclusion rather than exclusion of alternative traditions. Pedro Laín Entralgo

[23] There is a brief biography in M. Hernández, *Obra poética completa*, eds. L. de Luis and J. Urrutia (Madrid, 1982).

pointed out in his book *España como problema* (1949) that liberals and free-thinkers constituted an essential part of Spanish cultural history. José Luis Aranguren in *Catolicismo y protestantismo como formas de existencia* (1952) argued that Catholic perceptions and values could be enriched and complemented by those of Protestants and existentialists.[24] From 1951 to 1955 José María García Escudero contributed a regular column on religious affairs to *Arriba*, in which he consistently chose to replace the usual vindications of Catholic life and values with an independent, discriminating appraisal that appreciated ecclesiastical self-criticism more than complacency.[25] Catholic experience elsewhere in Europe also challenged Spanish exclusivism. One of the earliest examples of this was the insistence by French participants at annual international conferences organized by Spanish laymen in San Sebastián that religious liberty was a basic human right and that individual conscience must be freely and fully respected. Even the pages of *Razón y Fe* disapprovingly recorded this controversy in 1948 and 1949, although only in order to repeat the old, contrary argument that error could not and should not enjoy equal rights with truth.[26] A dynamic awareness of progressive Catholic trends in other European countries in the 1950s was evident in two unpretentious religious periodicals, *El Ciervo* and *Espiritualidad Seglar* published in Barcelona and Salamanca respectively. In spite of the efforts of a few brave liberalizers, however, the patriotic religion of post-war Spain remained predominantly intolerant, and insular.

Ironically, the decisive saboteur of defensive integrism proved to be the Vatican. It was through the encyclical letters of Pope John XXIII and the Vatican Council in the 1960s that the Spanish state was forced to admit religious liberty, and the Spanish Church to learn the new ways of ecumenism and dialogue. Pope John's call for *aggiornamento* (updating), enervated the fighting strength of self-conscious Catholic archaism. With the Vatican addressing itself to all people of good will instead of just the faithful, calling Protestants no longer heretics but 'separated brethren', and extolling the advantages of pluralism and tolerance, many of the distinguishing features of Spanish Catholic tradition were suddenly declared obsolete. So unexpected and severe was this

[24] For national–Catholic propaganda see below, pp. 220–1; for the influential and controversial works by Laín Entralgo and Aranguren, see below, pp. 242–3.
[25] Reprinted in J. M. García Escudero, *Catolicismo de fronteras adentro* (Madrid, 1956).
[26] E. Guerrero, 'El problema de las libertad religiosa. A propósito de las "Conversaciones" de San Sebastián', *RyF*, 610 (1948); and 'Las conversaciones católicas de San Sebastián', ibid., 623 (1949).

reversal that Spanish cartoonists could skilfully exploit a whole new theme of bemused disorientation. One exploited the current tourist advertising slogan 'Spain is different' by showing a worried priest lamenting that 'Even in the Council Spain has to be different'. Another depicted a cleric in traditional soutane and broad-brimmed hat peering into a book called 'Teach yourself the Council in 15 days'. A third caught traditional xenophobia perfectly as it showed laymen—perhaps government ministers—wearily deciding that 'This is what happens when we allow Councils to be held abroad'. But the disorientation was painful, and a fifty-year-old priest talking to the compiler of a book on post-conciliar humour expressed the sentiments of many in his remark, 'Our generation has been really unlucky—first the civil war, and now the Council'.[27]

An enclosed Spanish Catholic culture which had prided itself on its past and its national purity suddenly had to modernize by absorbing the experience of Catholics in democratic, pluralist societies, and the findings of foreign biblical scholarship and theology, even from within the tradition of the long-maligned Protestant Reformation. As more theological students studied in France or Germany, so the religious book market was flooded with translations of works ranging from popular spirituality to learned exegesis. The trend was clearest in serious, academic theology: whereas in 1950 only 25% of such works published in Spain were of foreign origin, in 1965 that had risen to a stunning 90%. From theological autarky, Spain switched abruptly to very heavy dependence on imported goods. A document studied by the Spanish clergy in 1971 used another image drawn from economics to make the same point when it described the Spanish Church as suffering from 'theological and cultural underdevelopment'.[28] In terms of intellectual creativity, even in religious studies, the price of defensive ideological hegemony had been very high.

Before the Council, some Spanish scholars already found the price too high. The scripture scholar José María González Ruiz returned as a young priest to his native Seville from studying in Rome a few years after the civil war ended, and found the contrast between the two ecclesiastical worlds shocking. Nor was this due simply to the presence of the most integrist of all prelates, Cardinal Segura, as archbishop there, for on appointment as lecturer in the seminary in Málaga, he

[27] J. L. Martín Descalzo, *Dios es alegre—antología del humor español posconciliar* (Madrid, 1971), 33. The cartoons mentioned are among those collected in this work.
[28] *Asamblea conjunta obispos-sacerdotes* (Madrid, 1971), 90, 42.

soon discovered that there too, clerical life was lived in an intellectual ghetto. Bishop Angel Herrera—who as a layman had been a leading figure in Catholic social action—disliked the fact that González Ruiz's scripture lectures disturbed and excited the seminarians. Combining seminary teaching with continuing biblical research in Rome throughout the 1950s, he avoided major conflict but discovered in 1960 that a large file of complaints against him had been prepared for submission to Rome, based partly on suspicion of his biblical exegesis, partly on disapproval of his insufficiently deferential attitude to ecclesiastical authority, and partly on fear of his political nonconformity. González Ruiz was certainly not the only theologian to find himself caught in a 'secret, underground war' like something in a spy story. As he himself wrote, 'the years before the Second Vatican Council were full of secret investigations'. His seminary students were warned not to communicate with him outside class and the most promising were removed. If this experience was far from unique, so too was his exhilaration when he first realized that the Council was battering down the walls of the ghetto. He was in Rome by chance during it, worked informally, especially with Dutch theologians, and had the satisfaction of seeing many of the orientations for which he had been criticized only a few years before transformed into Council doctrine. At the same time he discovered the liberating properties of the newly consecrated 'dialogue' as he made friends with Italian communists, undeterred by the accompanying sense of guilt inevitable in anyone brought up in Crusade Catholicism. One of the most respected of Spanish biblical scholars, González Ruiz was typical in his experience of how both the Council and knowledge of other European countries affected Catholic intellectual life in Spain.[29] It was not possible to study in Paris or Rome or Munich and then find the orthodoxies of the Spanish ghetto in the 1950s and early 1960s other than stifling. Nor was it possible to engage in serious discussion with foreign Marxists or even Catholic democrats and then tolerate the stultifying complacency of the Spanish Catholic dictatorship.

Theories about the relationship of Catholic orthodoxy to other ideologies were never politically neutral. In Spain, theological and cultural integrism necessarily belonged to the authoritarian Right. Similarly, the connections between liberal or sceptical thought and reformist or radical politics under the restoration monarchy and the Second Republic, although complex, had been evident to all. The erosion of integrist

---

[29] For his own autobiographical account, see J. M. González Ruiz, *"¡Ay de mí, si no evangelizare!"*. 6th edn. (Bilbao, 1976).

principles within Catholic intellectual culture therefore necessarily threatened to undermine also the values that made dictatorship acceptable. Ecclesiastical conversion to ecumenism, human rights, and dialogue permitted and even propelled Catholics to think that orthodoxy should coexist with non-Catholic ideologies, which in practice in Spain implied political pluralism. The sociological implications were also clear. Just as formal religious practice in Spain coincided generally though by no means perfectly with ownership of property, so mass support for anarchist, socialist, and then communist movements came primarily from wage labourers. For Catholic writers and preachers, distaste for integrist theology and authoritarian politics frequently accompanied dissatisfaction with the class basis of religion. It is not accidental that writers who were progressive—or conciliar—in their theology were nonconformist in politics and committed to social reform. This was true of a whole generation of theologians such as González Ruiz, Olegario González de Cardedal, and the Jesuit Alfonso Álvarez Bolado, for whom the Vatican Council represented an enormous intellectual and ethical liberation. Sometimes it was a changing social or political awareness that revolutionized theology and spirituality, as in the case of the Catholic communist Alfonso Carlos Comín, radicalized in university conflicts in Barcelona in the mid-50s and then in labour disputes in Málaga, or the extraordinarily influential Jesuit José María Llanos who already in 1955 opted to live poorly in a working class district of Madrid—El Pozo del Tío Raimundo—instead of in bourgeois or university surroundings.[30] But in whatever order of personal or chronological priority, theological renewal, social criticism, and political disaffection combined to dissolve integrism. And behind the personal histories of individual, but very important writers, lay the widespread class and regional discontent of large numbers of Catholic lay activists and clergy.[31] By the last years of the Franco regime, the ecclesiastical culture of national nostalgia and exclusivist intolerance had lost its theoretical underpinning and its socio-political basis; integrists found themselves, unbelievably, a heterodox minority.

It often seemed that, however hostile Spanish Catholic tradition was to European rationalism and liberalism, the greatest enemy of all was sex. One aspect of a consistently clerical culture was its idealizing of celibacy. Spanish Catholicism was unremittingly puritanical. Schools,

[30] For autobiographical accounts, see A. C. Comín, *Fe en la tierra*. 3rd edn. (Bilbao, 1977); J. M. Llanos, *Creo* . . . 6th edn. (Bilbao, 1977).

[31] See below, pp. 105–13, 232–8.

youth organizations, publications, and the confessional all concentrated on the preservation of sexual innocence, and warned girls and boys against 'bad companions', unedifying books and papers, and later the cinema. The human body, and particularly the female body, was dangerous. In 1926 the metropolitan archbishops issued an apoplectic pastoral letter to all Spanish Catholics on immodesty, largely provoked by the contemporary female fashion for short skirts. In behaviour as in ideas, the trouble was traced to fascination with imported modernity (*extranjerismo modernista*) at the expense of ancient Spanish customs. The archbishops denounced the 'anti-traditional and anti-Christian' practice of coeducation, which some wished to introduce into Spain from abroad. They protested at 'exaggeratedly brief' sportswear, mixed bathing and sports activities, unsupervised dating, and provocative modern dancing. Women were warned that they might be refused holy communion by their parish priest if they did not dress acceptably, and the head teachers of convent schools were asked to refuse admission to girls who came to school improperly clad.[32] Thirty years later, little had changed except that the bishops were less preoccupied by short skirts—the miniskirt still lay in the future—than by a state of undress (*desnudismo*) on beaches and city streets in the summer, which was certainly not limited to tourists 'who came from beyond the frontiers of our fatherland' and of whom, presumably, nothing better could be expected. The cinema and sexual behaviour that undermined the family joined the list of evils to be countered.[33]

Autobiographical memoirs of childhood in Catholic bourgeois families and schools are pervaded by the ignorance, fear, and guilt induced by omnipresent sexual and physical taboos. Art reproductions of the human form in school textbooks were regularly shaded over or blocked out to protect children from the sight of nudity. To see another human body unclothed, or to undergo the first glimmerings of sexual self-awareness in puberty were experiences inextricably associated with notions of sin.[34] So prudish was Catholic life in Barcelona in the 1940s that even reading Fr. Coloma's fifty-year-old moralist, but also realist,

[32] Text in J. Iribarren, *Documentos colectivos del episcopado español 1870–1974* (Madrid, 1974), 117–23.
[33] Text of 1957 pastoral instruction ibid., 302–16.
[34] As examples of this literature, see C. de la Mora, *Doble esplendor* (Barcelona, 1977), 15–24—originally published in English as *In Place of Splendour* (New York, 1939)—for the experience of a young Catholic girl of upper bourgeois family; F. Umbral, *Memorias de un niño de derechas* (Barcelona, 1976), 57–62, and C. Barral, *Años de penitencia* (Madrid, 1975), 111–95, for sexual aspects of post-war bourgeois boyhood.

novel *Pequeñeces* was prohibited a fourteen-year-old boy by his spiritual director, and when some sixteen and seventeen-year-olds went to see a Rita Hayworth and Glenn Ford film in a local cinema, their priest teachers were outraged and extremely pessimistic about the boys' spiritual welfare.[35] In 1955 Enrique Miret Magdalena wrote an article in the journal *Espiritualidad Seglar* in which he surveyed his male, Catholic, Spanish contemporaries and deplored the sexual deformation inflicted by sustained negative teaching on everything to do with sexuality.[36] A reappraisal of sex and the body was an essential element in hesitant new trends in Catholic theology and spirituality from the early 1950s onwards.

One of the institutional guardians of sexual puritanism among the laity for generations was the lay sodality, or congregation, very often dedicated to the Virgin Mary under such titles as Children of Mary, or the congregation of Mary Immaculate and St Luis. These intensified and continued the sexual segregation of the Catholic schools. Although some were parish based, others were connected to the religious orders and used by them precisely as a way of keeping in close contact with former pupils and other associates. In fact many of the educational orders ran a series of sodalities for children of different ages in their schools, and then for young single men or women over eighteen. In the case of the Jesuits, the network was so large and so closely woven as to constitute an alternative to the Catholic Action parish and diocesan lay groups under the hierarchy's direction. For example, there were about one thousand members of the 'Luises' for single young men in Barcelona alone in the 1920s. All these Marian congregations laid heavy emphasis on personal piety and chastity. One famously flourishing example of a Marian congregation for boys up to eighteen was the group dedicated to Mary Immaculate and St Stanislaus that Fr. Ángel Basterra, SJ, directed in Bilbao from 1910 to 1943. For most of that period there were at least 500 active members, expected to attend daily Mass most days, and participate in devotional and social meetings. Congregants were forbidden to join other groups—even football teams—without special permission, or go to the cinema or theatre, all of which might endanger their purity. Talks or slide shows were organized on Sunday evenings 'when nearly all our contemporaries are at entertainments which encourage a relaxation of standards'. In 1917 it

[35] A. C. Comín, *Fe en la tierra*, 35–7.
[36] E. Miret Magdalena, 'Reflexiones sobre el hombre católico español de nuestros días', *Espiritualidad Seglar* no. 27–8 (1955).

was decided as a hygienic measure (*precaución sanitaria*) that no one attending a mixed school could be a member, and when this gradually proved impracticable with the growing attraction of the coeducational state school (*instituto*) in the city, in 1928 'at the beginning of the school year we distributed to the *institutistas* special norms about the dangers they face in mixed education'.[37] Similar attitudes of defensive piety and suffocating prurience were inculcated in dozens of similar sodalities, even if not always with Fr. Basterra's fanatical energy. Even Ángel Ayala, SJ, the founder of a self-consciously modern, active, socially aware association of laymen, the National Catholic Association of Propagandists (ACNP), had no quarrel at all with this kind of morality. He warned young men against the cinema, declared that 'the Church regards outings of two boys and two girls in a car as simply ugly and intolerable', and instead proposed shooting as a healthy, morally sound, and segregated leisure activity.[38]

Sexual experience was readily dismissed as an intrinsic part of the inferior life led by most of the Catholic laity as opposed to priests and religious, although it could be redeemed within marriage by the dutiful acceptance of numerous children. As the eminent founder of another purportedly modern and forward looking lay association, the Opus Dei, expressed it in 1939, 'marriage is for the foot soldiers, not for the general staff of Christ'.[39] The priest was sacred, Christ's own representative; religious had chosen the 'higher way' of poverty, chastity, and obedience; lay life was a poor second best, and sexual activity one of its inferior characteristics. It is not accidental that most lay associations up to the 1960s existed either as an extension of the pastoral work of bishops and priests, or as ancillaries to the religious orders. When a more substantial and autonomous role of the laity within the Church was then gradually explored in theory, if rarely in actual practice, sexual questions did not keep pace. In 1953 a regular contributor to *Razón y Fe* was outraged at the sight of laymen writing theology, and insisted they 'must accept the paternalism of priests' who received a

---

[37] Membership statistics in annual *Breve memoria y catálogo de la congregación de la Inmaculada y San Estanislao* (Bilbao). Rules for behaviour appeared in the 1914 issue, 7–10. Quotations from *Breve memoria* (1929), 4; (1917), 4; (1929), 8. I am grateful to Fr. Gregorio Lizarralde, SJ, who made the annual reports and other documentation pertaining to the Kostkas available to me in Bilbao in 1974. There is a detailed study of the Bilbao Kostkas in F. Lannon, 'Catholic Bilbao from Restoration to Republic' (unpublished DPhil thesis, Oxford, 1975).

[38] A. Ayala, *Obras completas*. 2 vols. (Madrid, 1947), i, 843–80.

[39] J. M. Escrivá de Balaguer, *Camino* (Madrid, 1939), maxim 28.

Cultural Values 53

divine mission to teach and preach. Eight years later the editors were writing enthusiastically about how the laity actually constituted the Church in wider society. That catches exactly the chronology of an incipient, tentative, theoretical change in status of the various groups within the Church. But a more positive view of sex gained only slow and partial official approval. The more extreme forms of physical reticence, and identification of the nude human form with sin were abandoned, and the long battle against short clothes and bare arms and torsos was given up as hopeless. Mixed bathing and recreation ceased to excite comment, though coeducation remained unusual in Church secondary schools. But sex was still seen less as a normal part of human experience and development than as a necessary function—if no longer a necessary evil—of married couples within Church and society. Long after the end of the Franco regime, the official teaching of the Catholic Church everywhere was still that sex was primarily for procreation, inside monogamous marriage, and certainly had no place whatever outside it. Whereas the political conservatism, ideological intolerance, and reactionary socio-economic theories of Spanish Catholicism were revolutionized in the 1960s, the official sexual orthodoxies changed comparatively little. But its practice—often more affected by women's altered role expectations and improved contraceptive methods than by ecclesiastical strictures—frequently bore little relation to its theory. While new ideas within the Church helped open the way for major political renovation in Spain in the 1970s, the sexual revolution happened without and against it.

If seculars found themselves traditionally ranked below priests and religious in ecclesiastical status, lay women were undoubtedly subordinate to men. Urged at every turn to model themselves on Mary, Virgin and Mother, they would have been extremely surprised if a preacher or confessor had widened the range of New Testament models and held up instead for emulation Mary Magdalen who first preached the good news of the resurrection of Jesus, or Joanna, wife of Herod's steward Chuza, who not only helped fund the preaching tours of Jesus and his disciples but wandered round the country with them.[40] Feminist rediscovery of biblical female models lay in the future.[41] Preaching the

[40] Luke 24: 1-12, and 8: 1-3.
[41] As examples of recent feminist reclamation of a range of female models in the New Testament, and criticism of traditional interpretations of Mary and other women connected with Jesus, see R. Ruether, *Mary The Feminine Face of the Church* (London, 1979); E. Moltmann-Wendel, *The Women around Jesus* (London, 1982), first published in the original German in 1980.

gospel, and demanding, extra-familial responsibilities were anathema. The choice was between motherhood and the convent. As late as 1957 Spanish bishops still fulminated against 'an absurd feminism that takes many women away from their destiny in pursuit of pastimes and liberties that are not compatible with decorousness and their maternal duties'.[42] In 1968 the directors of junior seminaries in Spain recognized the need to have more secular staff involved in the education of priests and then guardedly admitted that 'among these there might be an occasional woman'.[43] The old norm of a religious vocation or a life centred almost entirely on the home died very hard. Fr. Ayala advised young women not to smoke or drink, to have only one boy friend ever, and usually not to pursue higher studies or a career since they were 'destined by God to be the angel of the hearth'.[44] Early in the twentieth century the English Superior General of one of the most prestigious female educational orders in Spain argued that academic specialization was not suitable for women, who benefited more from a general education.[45] In 1936 a Catholic conservative politician wrote—with typically mystifying rhetoric—that 'a woman must be nothing other than the eternal feminine of human life, equal to man in dignity, but unequal in function and in the mission each one is called upon to fulfil'. A colleague of his used a blunter style, insisting in a political youth rally that 'by natural law, the man is head of the family' and denouncing 'an exaggerated feminism' that weakened the family hierarchy.[46] During the democratic republic of 1931–6 many Catholic politicians favoured female suffrage because of its likely benefit to the Right, but simultaneously ridiculed campaigns for women's rights or women in parliament.

Women's experience accurately embodied these attitudes. They constituted the majority of practising Catholics, but in church always listened to men preach and celebrate the sacraments. They played no part in ecclesiastical decision making. They were told by male priests to obey their husbands. They were excluded from dozens of male religious societies and events, from the devotional brotherhoods processing in Seville streets in Holy Week to the élitist Propagandists of Ayala's ACNP. The Opus included a women's section, separate from the men's,

[42] Iribarren, 312.
[43] *Asamblea nacional de rectores. Seminarios menores* (Madrid, 1968), 10.
[44] A. Ayala, *Obras completas*, i, 921–1098; quotation, 1080.
[45] J. E. Stuart, *The Society of the Sacred Heart* (London, 1914), 98–9. See also her *The Education of Catholic Girls* (London, 1912).
[46] J. Monje y Bernal, *Acción Popular* (Madrid, 1936), 201, 263.

responsible to men, and utterly opposed to feminism. In religious communities women often enjoyed a certain degree of autonomy, but always had male chaplains, male ecclesiastical superiors and confessors, and usually male spiritual directors. In the home, Catholic teaching against contraception meant that millions of married women were sure to give many years of their lives completely to the strenuous task of raising a large family. At every turn the message was clear: men were born for authority and social responsibility; women were born for domesticity, motherhood, or sexual renunciation. In its patriarchal structure and values, as in so much else, the Spanish Church exhibited in an intensified form patterns common throughout the Catholic world.

The role models usually proposed for Catholic women were perplexing. Women embodied the 'eternal feminine' and were 'angels', but were also frequently reminded of how sexually dangerous they were to men. Virginity was idealized and sex denigrated, yet married women were instructed by priests that they must be always sexually available to their husbands under pain of serious sin. They were the temptress Eve, and they were Mary, Virgin and Mother. Although they were encouraged to a passive sexual role and discouraged from careers, they were nevertheless supposed to be active, albeit without genuine responsibility, in parish life and charitable ventures. Various harmless options were open to those who did not become nuns. If they were pious, and unmarried, they might tread the narrow path of the devout but unimaginative *beata*, so often pilloried by Spanish writers. If they were married and their husbands enjoyed a certain degree of affluence, they might channel some of his money and their energy into charitable foundations for educating the poor or caring for the sick or homeless. Many convent schools urged pupils to be energetic, 'virile' Christians and fighters for the faith, a tradition taken over by the women's section of the fascist political organization, the *Falange*, during and after the civil war with its mobilization of women to propagate aggressively an authoritarian, anti-feminist and ever more conservative ideology.[47] The style could be strong, assertive, and determined, without in any way challenging the essentially dependent and subordinate role accorded the female in the Church and in Spanish society. There were, of course, exceptional individuals and institutions, for example the Teresian Insti-

[47] The *Sección femenina* of the *Falange* was responsible for civic and political education in girls' schools for decades after the civil war, and published innumerable textbooks for girls of different ages on political, social, and family values, and the role and duties of women.

tute founded in Covadonga in 1911. Its members were—and are—devout lay women interested in education who opened secondary schools but also fostered higher education for Catholic women and have often themselves attained very high academic and professional qualifications. They pioneered in Franco's Spain an unusual combination of specialist training, research, and university teaching with lay, female spirituality and pastoral work.[48] The norm, however, was very different. Piety, duty, and domesticity remained the female cardinal virtues, even when practised 'heroically' or 'virilely'.

Political militancy did not fit easily with these stereotypes, and it was among socialists and anarchists in the 1930s, not the Catholic Right, that some women adopted local and even national positions of leadership. There was no Catholic equivalent of Socialist parliamentary deputy Margarita Nelken, or Anarchist leader Federica Montseny. Exceptions at local level aroused the wrath of the more conventional. When some Catholic Basque nationalist women, for example, turned their attention in the 1930s not only to clerical and welfare work in support of the nationalist cause, but also to organizing meetings and making public speeches, they shocked Catholic contemporaries. After conquering the Basque country during the first year of the civil war, soldiers of the Catholic Crusade expressed their loathing for both Basque nationalism and politically active women by subjecting some of these *Emakumes* to the humiliation of being dosed with castor oil in public and having their heads shaved, a fate usually reserved for wives and girl friends of known 'Leftists'.[49] Idealization of the 'eternal feminine' was swiftly abandoned when Catholic women transgressed the limits ordained for them. In post-war years, the first major claim to independent public responsibility was made by Catholic women in the Church's industrial and agrarian workers' associations of the 1950s and 1960s, who took a very active part in what the Franco regime regarded as subversion in industrial relations and criticism of the dictatorship. Along with their male counterparts they were eventually overwhelmed by the frightened opposition of the bishops in 1966–9. Until then, their repudiation of the usual female stereotypes had been partially disguised and therefore protected by exactly the same cloak that covered the unprecedented

---

[48] For an introduction to the Teresians, their founder Fr. Pedro Póveda, and their pedagogical principles, see A. Galino, 'Pedro Poveda—una pedagogía para nuestro tiempo', in *Textos pedagógicos hispanoamericanos* (Madrid, 1968).

[49] P. de Larrañaga, *Emakume Abertzale Batza. La mujer en el nacionalismo vasco*. 3 vols. (Donostia, 1978), gives a detailed account of their activities and fate 1931–6.

Cultural Values 57

radicalism of both the male and female associations, their identity as religious and pastoral rather than overtly political or syndical organizations.[50]

The first major reference by the Vatican to the rights of women as citizens, in John XXIII's *Pacem in Terris* in 1963, linked the issue to working-class aspirations and decolonization as distinctive characteristics of the modern world. Pope John recognized with obvious approval that women increasingly 'demand rights befitting a human person, both in domestic and in public life'.[51] But there was no further definition of such rights, which remained rather nebulous. The bishops of the Church assembled in the Second Vatican Council were not very preoccupied by the question of women's status, although they did appeal for their 'access to the same educational and cultural benefits as are available to men'.[52] This plea was then taken up by the Spanish hierarchy in an important document on education published in 1969. Moreover it was given some social realism by the inclusion of statistics on women's employment mainly in poorly paid, unqualified work. The bishops proceeded to blame Spanish families and society for the inadequate professional formation of women, without any mention of the Church's own contribution.[53] Their analysis was almost certainly not so much disingenuous as culturally blind. Church leaders in Rome and in Spain, all of them male, always failed to see the irony of advocating the cultural and professional emancipation of women while simultaneously forbidding 'unnatural' birth control (reaffirmed in Paul VI's *Humanae Vitae* in 1968) and divorce, let alone abortion. They offered no advice on how to combine a career with prolific motherhood.

Traditional attitudes to sex and the role of women altered much less decisively than criteria on politics, labour relations, and wealth distribution. In spite of the fact that the Vatican Council theoretically revolutionized the role of the laity, and declared sex within marriage 'noble and honourable', male, celibate clerics continued to dominate

[50] For an account of male and female sections of the Catholic workers' associations HOAC and JOC, see below, pp. 232–8.
[51] Official translation by the Catholic Truth Society, *Peace on Earth* (London, 1963), 19.
[52] The quotation is from *Gaudium et spes* in A. Flannery (ed.), *Vatican Council II. The Conciliar and Post Conciliar Documents* (Leominster, 1981), 929. For a brief but devastating feminist visual impression of the Council, see the autobiographical introduction to the reprint of the 1968 classic feminist critique of the Catholic Church, M. Daly, *The Church and the Second Sex* (New York, 1975), 9–10.
[53] Conferencia Episcopal Española, *La iglesia y la educación en España, hoy* (Madrid, 1969), 80–3.

every aspect of Church life. Seculars who tried to construct a different model rather than accept a slightly enlarged place in the old one often found their relationship with the ecclesiastical hierarchy troubled. A good example of this was the cluster of informal, small, mixed communities on the model of Latin American *comunidades de base* that sprang up after the Council. These were typically composed of young people of both sexes, often including one or more priests, and were self-financing, autonomous groups without any canonical status. They combined prayer, study, and work with immersion in the life and problems of their expressly chosen deprived neighbourhoods. Many bishops, admiring their dedication and fervour, regarded them as one of the most vital manifestations of Catholic renewal. But their tendency to see themselves as a pure, authentic, alternative Church distinct from the compromised institution, to blur distinctions between priestly and lay roles within the group, and to bend ecclesiastical discipline and even teaching to their own circumstances sometimes caused unease in the hierarchy and frustration to their own members.[54] They revealed both the depth of creative commitment tapped by the communal, populist orientation of the Council, and the immense problems of channelling so much enthusiasm through the cultural and institutional structures of traditional Catholicism.

It is noteworthy that the Church was able to be much more radical in politics and questions of social justice, that primarily challenged the state and interest groups in Spanish society, than in matters concerning lay life and sexuality which threatened more nearly its own internal organization and values. Male, celibate, clerical supremacy resisted modification more successfully than nationalist nostalgia and xenophobia. It remains to be seen whether the Church might eventually have to launch an *aggiornamento* of this, too, in a changing culture whose transformations it influences strongly but does not control, and within which it tries to maintain vitality and credibility.

[54] For the emergence and early experience of *comunidades de base* see A. Alonso, *Comunidades eclesiales de base* (Salamanca, 1970); J. J. Tamayo-Acosta, *Un proyecto de iglesia para el futuro en España* (Madrid, 1978). There is an interesting reflection on a few years' experience by one community that began in Valencia in 1968; Comunidad del barrio del Cristo, 'Comunidades de base', *Iglesia Viva*, 35–6 (1971).

3

The Professionals I: Religious Communities

THE religious congregations were to the Catholic revival in late nineteenth-century Spain what the urban bourgeoisie was to industrial growth; they empowered it, led it, symbolized it, and flourished because of it. Indeed, the link with industrial and urban expansion is direct, since the burgeoning religious congregations founded their orphanages, hospitals, and reformatories to assuage the miseries of the new working classes, and their secondary schools and colleges to educate the children of the Catholic bourgeoisie. After the catastrophic history of the congregations earlier in the century, this new growth was startling. Measures to appropriate and sell their property had been established policy for radical governments in 1812, 1820, 1833, 1854, and 1868. After previous smaller scale expropriations and some recuperations, the definitive *desamortización* was initiated by Mendizábal. Between 1836 and 1845 83% of the property belonging to the religious orders was seized and sold, a process completed after Madoz's legislation of 1855.[1] Similarly, restrictive legislation on the very existence of the orders culminated in outright abolition of almost all the male communities on 29 July 1837. Of the estimated 2,051 such communities in being at the end of the eighteenth century, only a few dozen survived in the 1840s, and the nearly 50,000 male religious enumerated in the 1797 census had almost vanished.[2]

It is instructive to note that the womens' orders suffered less harsh treatment. Of 1,075 communities in 1797, over 800 survived even at the nadir of their fortunes in mid-century when women religious, although reduced by more than half, still numbered over 11,000.[3] In addition to being less directly affected by the Napoleonic and Carlist

---

[1] For a good survey of *desamortización* see S. Segura, *La desamortización española del siglo XIX* (Madrid, 1973), which stresses fiscal motives. R. Herr, 'El significado de la desamortización en España'. *Moneda y Crédito*, 131 (1974), examines wider economic implications.
[2] Figures from J. Sáez Marín, *Datos sobre la iglesia española contemporánea 1768–1868* (Madrid, 1975), 168, 78–80.
[3] Ibid., 38–9, 81–2, 264–5.

wars, and less politicized than their male counterparts, they were also less lucrative a prospect for *desamortización* and able often to point to their social utility in works of welfare and education. These considerations were evident in the suppressive legislation of 1835–7, including even the sweeping abolitions of 29 July 1837. The Daughters of Charity of St. Vincent de Paul were exempted from dissolution because of their hospital work, together with nuns involved in education, just as the Escolapios among the men escaped liquidation because of their widely respected unpretentious schools. Popular perceptions seem to have coincided with those of the government, since neither the women religious nor the Escopalios suffered in the anti-clerical violence of 1834–5. However, the legal exceptions were made grudgingly with an explicit statement that they were to endure only until alternative facilities could be provided.[4] It is possible to discern at this worst moment for the religious orders the basis of their eventual but precarious triumph: until such time as adequate state provision for welfare and education made them socially redundant, they would always have open a way to survival and growth.

In the concordat of 1851 this way forward was already signposted.[5] Skilfully ambiguous terminology about permission for the establishment of an unnamed third male congregation as well as the communities of St. Vincent de Paul and of the Oratory led to controversy over whether this meant one other in each diocese or only one for the whole country. More practically and more significantly, it also allowed for a generous interpretation of this article 29 that could transform the male congregations in Spain from a trickle to a flood. But beyond all ambiguity was the motive given for the implicit rejection of the measures of 1837: the religious were needed to help with pastoral work and 'to look after the sick and for other works of charity and public utility'. Article 30 named the Daughters of Charity as falling under government protection, but also generally safeguarded congregations of women engaged in teaching and other charitable works. Less sympathetic governments than the Moderates of 1851 could and did ignore this concordat, but found it hard to suppress effectively religious communities for whose work there was no immediate replacement. On the eve of the 1868

---

[4] See articles 3, 4 and 5, ibid., 77.
[5] Text in R. García Villoslada (ed.), *Historia de la Iglesia en España*, v (Madrid, 1979), 719–30. For a careful study of the legal status of the congregations, see J. Buitrago y Hernandez, *Las órdenes religiosas y los religiosos—estudio jurídico sobre su existencia legal y capacidad civil en España* (Madrid, 1901).

revolution there were under 2,000 male religious in Spain, and about 20,000 female.[6] The latter figure is remarkable on two counts: it approximated to the level of a hundred years before, showing that womens' communities had not experienced any major diminution; and it greatly surpassed the total for men, thus setting a new pattern which continued to characterize the revival of the religious congregations in the late nineteenth and twentieth centuries as primarily and unprecedentedly a female phenomenon.

The revolution of 1868 brought in its wake the inevitable anti-clerical decrees, including once more the standard dissolution of the resilient Society of Jesus and many other orders. Notwithstanding the overthrow of Isabel II, however, and the subsequent legislative insecurity through the turbulent years of revolutionary *juntas*, a further Carlist war, a short-lived experiment with a different dynasty and finally a republic, the religious congregations were much better placed in 1875 than they had been in 1840 or 1850 to take advantage of the auspicious new beginning heralded by the restoration of the monarchy in the person of Isabel's son. Paradoxically, the sector of the Spanish Church that seemed in danger of extinction forty years before was now to become the unrivalled spearhead of Catholic revival as the number of religious soared. The basis of this expansion was not to be the great mortmain estates which had gone for ever, but the capacity of religious communities to meet some of the pressing needs of changing Spanish society, especially in the growing cities, and the willingness of the state to accept and rely upon these services. Once that willingness disappeared, as it abruptly did under another republic in 1931, then the religious congregations and the immense investment of Catholic resources and energy they represented were immediately at risk. Meanwhile, from the restoration until the monarchy's collapse in 1931, Catholic Spain was dominated by the schools, colleges, missions, publications, clinics, and hospitals of the religious orders.

In 1904 a worried anti-clerical drew attention to the 'appalling reversal' of enlightenment and progress represented by the expansion of the religious congregations. They then comprised about 11,000 men and over 40,000 women.[7] In 1930 the totals had reached over 20,000 and over 60,000 respectively.[8] During the restoration monarchy, women religious trebled in number, and men religious increased tenfold

---

[6] Sáez Marín, 229–30, 281.
[7] L. Morote, *Los frailes en España* (Madrid, 1904), 10.
[8] *Anuario Estadístico de España* (Madrid, 1930), 672–3.

from their low and unpromising base. The contrast with the steady decline in number of the diocesan clergy in the same period is remarkable. Moreover, while ordinations to the secular priesthood clambered slowly upwards after the civil war, membership of the congregations again soared. Just before the crisis of the late 1960s hit them hard, they boasted 34,000 male religious—nearly 10,000 of them priests—and 85,000 female.[9] Both the rate of growth and the contrast with the fortunes of the diocesan clergy make the highly visible phenomenon of the religious congregations as inescapable a puzzle to the historian of Catholic Spain as they were a subject of comment, both adulatory and contemptuous, for their contemporaries.

Spectacular expansion was undoubtedly one reason why religious attracted so much anti-clerical attention, but more important still was their influence in Spanish culture and society. When Liberal governments in the early years of the twentieth century, and republican governments between 1931 and 1933 sought to curb their activity, the attacks were directed at their schools and colleges, which they deemed illiberal and anti-pluralist.[10] The most sustained intellectual onslaught against religious was probably the philosopher Miguel Unamuno's criticisms of the Jesuits. In 1908, for instance, he charged them with a disastrously low religious, moral, and intellectual calibre, with narrow illiberalism, and with subservience to an anti-intellectual industrial plutocracy. Twenty years later he called them 'degenerate sons' of Ignatius of Loyola, and described the cult of the Sacred Heart with which they were so closely identified as the very tomb of genuine Christianity. In 1921 he accused them of bad taste in literature and the arts, sensuality in the devotions they inculcated, and materialistic and apologetical aims in all their educational endeavours.[11] Unamuno's bitter complaints against the Jesuits were an extreme case of the liberal intelligentsia's charge against the religious orders in general—that they choked modernity, reform, creativity, and even true spirituality in Spain with their philistinism and intolerance.

No one entering a religious community saw the matter in those terms, however. Nor—in spite of the great popular myth best expressed in Pérez Galdós's sensational and successful play *Electra* performed in 1901—were the convents of Spain filled with unfortunate young

---

[9] *Guía de la Iglesia en España* (Madrid, 1970), 34–5.
[10] See below, pp. 77–82.
[11] For these three texts, see M. Unamuno, *Obras Completas*, ix (Madrid, 1971), 232–45; vii (1969), 305–64; ix, 1101–5.

Religious Communities 63

women held against their will, but with highly motivated and often very determined recruits. Why did an austere, restrictive life-style attract so many Spaniards, male and female, in this period? The great majority of those entering religious communities chose congregations with a clear pastoral commitment rather than the purely contemplative orders. They chose to teach, or preach, or nurse, as well as to pray. The combination of a religious way of life and work that was seen as simultaneously missionary and a welfare service to the wider community was obviously very attractive. Most conspicuously, thousands of Catholic women sought in the educational, medical, and welfare establishments run by the religious communities a more satisfying outlet for their piety, energy, and initiative than was available in the home, much as evangelical women in nineteenth-century England did in social work and reforming societies. In a society that gave women stiflingly few opportunities for professional training or responsibility beyond their own family, the religious orders, despite their discipline and sexual and social restrictions could, paradoxically, offer liberating scope. For women and men, the desire to dedicate the whole of life to God was quickened by the opportunity to take part in a shared, noble enterprise of caring for the sick, or orphans, or the aged, or providing education for children who otherwise would receive none at all or one that was Godless. Moreover, a certain sense of urgency pervaded this activity. Particularly in the cities, social and religious needs were glaringly obvious and pressing, and it was in the cities that many communities concentrated their resources. And there were other foes to be vanquished in addition to ignorance, poverty, and disease. The religious congregations which virtually constituted in themselves the Catholic revival of the late nineteenth century wanted precisely to revive or restore Catholic doctrine, practice, and culture, radically undermined by the liberalism and radicalism of the preceding decades and further threatened by the new emerging secular ideologies of socialists and anarchists. The bodies and minds of individual Spaniards were to be tended and nurtured, but it was the health and soundness of Spain herself that was at stake.

This campaigning enthusiasm and determination required certain kinds of theoretical underpinning. Most important was the conviction that the Roman Catholic Church was indeed, as it proclaimed itself, the one ark of salvation in a world of sin and error and misery. It was for this reason that elementary education, or old people's homes, or reformatories for prostitutes had to be Catholic, so as to provide the most crucial benefit of all—Catholicism itself—along with literacy or geriatric care or an escape from the streets. In the highly combative, strident apologetics of the Catholic revival there was no room for secular welfare and secular social reform; they were seen rather as an integral part of religious reconstruction. What was secular was of the world, worldly and suspect. Schools and clinics and orphanages were therefore consistently viewed as agencies of redemption and conversion. Every religious—whether teacher, nurse, bursar, or cleaner—was an essential part of a great missionary enterprise to save the soul of Spain from apostasy. It would be impossible to understand the unquestioning abnegation and toil of so many thousands of religious in the century after the restoration of the monarchy without some awareness of the seriousness and urgency of their calling in their own eyes and in the eyes of those who supported and encouraged them.

The second essential kind of theoretical justification was closely dependent upon the theological position outlined above. If the Church was defined over against a fallen and dangerous world, holiness lay in as complete a separation as possible from the ways and wiles of secular life. With their distinctive dress, their repudiation of family ties and personal possessions, their strictly segregated, enclosed living quarters, the religious communities were generally and officially regarded as the ideal Catholic life-style. Poverty, chastity, and obedience were the 'higher way' to holiness, intrinsically superior to life 'in the world'. Catholic teachers and preachers, and local priests in the confessional and in private conversation held out to countless boys and girls the ideal of a selfless life in the service of God and of the people of God that was sealed with the prestigious mark of a special election to holiness. To give an extreme example—in 1918 a nun in northern Spain recording in her convent's journal the arrival of two new postulants from the small Basque town of Azpeitia commented laconically that their local priest, Fr. Larrañaga, a man with 'a gift for discerning vocations and directing them well' had guided no fewer than 114 of his protégées into religious communities of one kind or another.[12] The bare statistics of recruitment give some notion of the force of this ideal but cannot convey the enormous human pain, energy, stamina, and certitude that fuelled the Catholic revival. It is not coincidental that recruitment plummeted and professed religious left their convents and monasteries in droves in the 1960s and 1970s. The Second Vatican Council forced even into the hermetic

[12] Archive of the Sociedad del Sagrado Corazón, Bilbao, manuscript 'Diario de la Casa' v, 557.

Catholic culture of Franco's Spain a startlingly more positive evaluation of the secular world and a greatly modified account of the Church's role within it. It also abandoned the interpretation of religious life as a superior way of holiness, and in fact had some difficulty in ascribing any very clear function at all to the religious congregations within the Church.[13] With such profound shifts of theory, the decades of expansion ended.

While urgent need and vigorous promotion go some way towards explaining the success of the religious congregations as both root and fruit of the Catholic revival, other factors were also crucial. The variety of community and work was enormous, in stark contrast with the more circumscribed parochial duties of most of the diocesan clergy. Medieval foundations like the Franciscans and Dominicans competed with earlier Benedictine and later Jesuit traditions, with the sixteenth-century Escolapios and seventeenth-century Brothers of the Christian Schools, and the plethora of nineteenth-century foundations, while various small congregations began life in this period in Spain. There was room for those who sought silence, those who wanted to be part of a disciplined group entirely committed to one enterprise, those who preferred a wider range of rather more freelance activity—though this last option scarcely existed for women and was usually the preserve of religious who were also ordained priests. The scholar, propagandist, administrator, or doctor could practise his or her skills in a context that promised to sanctify and make of them an act of worship, but that same promise extended also to those who cooked and cleaned and gardened. That a life of useful and religious service was offered to many kinds of gift and temperament, and to many levels of education, was a necessary although not sufficient cause of the communities' success.

Variety existed too in terms of social prestige and sophistication, and this was reflected in recruitment patterns. Until well after the civil war, when many vocations came from their own schools, the rapidly expanding orders of teaching brothers drew the bulk of their members from lowly rural settlements rather than from the urban environments where so many of their schools were located. The recruitment director of the northern province of the de La Salle brothers, for instance, depended heavily on the good offices of parish priests and school masters in the *pueblos* of Castile.

These pointed out to him the boys who, in their judgement, could be recommended for their intellectual and moral qualities. In the first meeting ... he

---

[13] For the Second Vatican Council, see below, pp. 246-9.

spoke in a very simple way of the religious life in general and of our Institute and Holy Founder in particular ... After some weeks he returned, and asked the boys questions to ascertain what effect the first session and the literature he had left had had. His last question probed the intentions of the child with regard to the proposition of embracing the religious life, and more especially in a teaching institute like ours.

Some months later he returned to inspect the progress of those boys who had expressed interest. The next step was admission to the junior noviceship 'usually at the age of twelve or thirteen'.[14] The Marist brothers used a similar method. Brother Antonio Agustín, for example, spent the summers of 1921–1928 foot-slogging from village to village in Castile and 'he would return with six, seven, up to twelve boys for the juniorate. Naturally, not all persevered.'[15] For many young boys of poor background in rural areas with a high level of Catholic practice, the prospect of becoming a teaching brother was evidently attractive, and the way to the desired end was open and well signposted. The same held true for teaching congregations that permitted some of their members to be ordained priest, such as the Salesians and the Escolapios, and for many congregations involved in welfare work. Whereas this pattern was very similar to that for recruitment of the diocesan clergy, however, the vital difference was the ability of more prestigious orders to draw the children of the urban bourgeoisie.

Pre-eminently successful in this were the Jesuits, but the phenomenon was not limited to them nor to the handful of mens' orders with relatively high educational requirements and priesthood. Exactly the same sociological hierarchy of recruitment obtained in the womens' congregations. Bankers, industrialists, or generals from Madrid or Burgos or Cádiz or Zaragoza did not expect a son of theirs to become a diocesan priest or to join the Marists, but could scarcely regard it as strange or unbecoming if one entered the Jesuits or Benedictines or Augustinians. Their daughters were highly unlikely to end up in the habit of the Daughters of Charity, but would not find themselves at all out of place in the novitiate of the Ursulines or the Society of the Sacred Heart. More important than any other single factor was the level and range of apostolic activity. Those involved mainly in primary or tech-

---

[14] From a paper prepared for me by the late Brother Josué (Jesús Santamaría), Bilbao, 9 Apr. 1974.
[15] Obituary of Brother Antonio (Hipólito Gutiérrez Pardo, 1893–1957) in *Norte—revista mensual de la provincia Marista de esta nombre*, v (1957–60), 27–38.

nical schools or in social work usually recruited at a lower social level, and younger, than those running the top level of Catholic secondary schools and colleges. These latter usually admitted entrants at eighteen rather than thirteen, after a secondary education that was, inevitably, the preserve of those rich enough to pay fees. When they did admit poorly educated boys and girls of few means, it was to the subordinate position of lay brothers or sisters. What critics might—and did—castigate as the preservation of an unacceptably rigid class hierarchy both between and within the religious orders, the religious themselves defended as their only way of not excluding and disqualifying the poor and ill-educated from the greatest of all privileges—a religious vocation. It was certainly true that the social hierarchy within many religious houses accurately duplicated that of the outside world, but by the late 1950s it was also true that the religious communities were preserving patterns already changing in civil society as the harshest poverty of the post-war years receded and an expanding economy opened up new opportunities.

Two other factors remain to complete this interpretation of the success of the religious orders—the existence of resources and opportunities. It is fascinating to see how often new foundations were made possible by the gift of a house, or land, or money, or all three, by wealthy benefactors. When the Society of the Sacred Heart opened its first house in Madrid in 1859 it was on an estate then outside the city at Chamartín de la Rosa, a gift from the Duke of Pastrana.[16] That same year the Daughters of the Cross opened their first orphanage in Spain in Bilbao: they were invited from France by local priests and a pious society 'composed of thirty of the most distinguished and most influential ladies of the town' who together provided a house, furniture, and running expenses.[17] In 1870 seven men attacked the home some miles southeast of Seville of an Andalusian landowner, Don Diego María Santiago Calvo de la Banda y Aragón, Marquis of Casa Ulloa. Because the Civil Guard had been alerted beforehand, the family had evacuated the house which was temporarily occupied by the Civil Guard. When the attackers resisted arrest they were killed outright. It seems that this experience jolted Casa Ulloa into trying to do something to improve conditions in the area, and at the archbishop of Seville's request he eventually founded

[16] For this and other Sacred Heart foundations see RR. del Sagrado Corazón, *Cien años de educación cristiana* (Zaragoza, 1946).
[17] Archive of Hijas de la Cruz, Bilbao, manuscript document of 15 Apr. 1859 entitled 'Fondation de Bilbao'.

in the village of Utrera in 1881 a school for girls, to be staffed by a local congregation founded by Sor Angela de la Cruz, and one for boys under the direction of the Italian Salesians. In Barcelona, Salesian and other foundations were funded by a wealthy industrialist's widow, Dorotea de Chopitea; in Córdoba their benefactor was the Count of Cortina; in Seville their women's branch was substantially aided by the Infanta María Luisa Fernanda.[18] Such examples could be repeated almost indefinitely. The Spanish landed aristocracy and upper middle classes boosted the Catholic restoration by giving buildings and income to the religious congregations to found schools, hospitals, and orphanages. Probably the single most conspicuous gift was of Tibidabo hill in Barcelona, given to Don Bosco, founder of the Salesians, in 1886 to be a kind of Spanish Montmartre—a purpose duly recognized in their own way fifty years later by anarchists who during the civil war pulled down the statue of the Sacred Heart that had been erected to dominate the city and cut into it the defiant initials of the C.N.T. and the F.A.I. The less flamboyant benefactions that were the bread and butter of the revival were made by individuals or pious associations, sometimes for the foundation of colleges and schools for their own children, often for schools and welfare institutes for the poorer classes.

Foundations came thick and fast especially in cities where demographic growth caused by industrial development rapidly created new needs. Bilbao is a particularly good example because shipbuilding and other heavy industries dependent on local iron deposits began to operate on a grand scale precisely in the last decades of the nineteenth century, and because pious mining, steel, and shipbuilding magnates turned to a number of religious congregations for help as the population soared from 32,734 in 1877 to 153,690 in 1929.[19] They had two quite distinct requirements, a suitable education for their own children, and some religious and general preparation of the children who would one day man the mines and foundries, and staff their offices, and service their homes. Beyond this again were the city's resourceless poor, whose plight some of Bilbao's plutocracy took to heart.

One of the most ambitious and controversial collaborative ventures of a religious order and a local bourgeoisie was the Jesuit university opened in Deusto, Bilbao in 1886 and followed in 1916 by a second

---

[18] A. Martín González, *Los Salesianos de Utrera en España* (Sevilla, 1981), 58–60 and *passim*.

[19] 1877 census in *Censo de Población de España* (Madrid, 1878); 1929 figures in *Anuario Estadístico de España 1929* (Madrid, 1931).

college specializing in commercial and engineering studies.[20] The former was mooted in 1879 by a group of wealthy local notables who petitioned the Jesuit provincial for a college of higher studies. In 1883 the group formed itself into a limited company, *La Enseñanza Católica*, which included powerful industrialists bearing well-known family names like Ibarra, Careaga, Moyua, Vilallonga, Smith, and Urquijo. They bought land in Deusto and always retained legal ownership of the property. The college for commercial studies had a similar genesis. In 1916 Pedro de Icaza set up a trust to finance a centre of higher commercial and industrial studies to be directed by the Jesuits. The board of the trust included the chairmen of many of the mining, engineering, naval, and iron and steel companies of Bilbao, not forgetting the chairman of the brokers' association of the Bilbao stock exchange. The benefactors wanted a high level of studies, chiefly law at one college, engineering and accountancy at the other, and solid Catholic instruction—a combination they thought unobtainable in the established universities. In sharing these aims, the Jesuits explicitly saw themselves as preparing a lay Catholic élite to counter the influence of the prestigious Free Educational Institute which was being remarkably successful in providing from its pupils a large number of often free-thinking university and secondary school teachers who dominated Spanish intellectual life. A prospectus of 1888–1889 explained that 'Christian families, wise men and princes of the Church have been longing for some time for a truly Catholic University, where sciences will be learnt with orthodox criteria and which young men will leave fully armed against all modern errors'. Catholic revival through the formation of an educated élite was the ultimate aim of both foundations at Deusto. In addition to a steady output of engineers, accountants, lawyers, and journalists to re-Christianize Spanish society, Deusto produced its first cabinet minister in the late 1920s when Francisco Moreno Zulueta became Minister of Finance under Primo de Rivera, and in the crucial 1933 election no fewer than twenty Deusto men were elected to the republican Cortes for various parties of the Right and Centre. A few of the Jesuits and their benefactors were proud, the majority appalled, when a Deusto graduate, José Antonio Aguirre y Lecube became president of the short-lived autonomous Basque region of Euzkadi after civil war broke out in 1936.

---

[20] Information on Deusto university, including early prospectuses, from C. Sáenz de Santa María, *Historia de la universidad de Deusto (1886–1961)* (Bilbao, 1962); on the commercial college, from L. Chalbaud, 'La universidad comercial o la formación económica superior', *RyF*, xlvii (1917), 56ff.

Given the preoccupation with Catholic restoration, however, the most influential Deusto man was probably Ángel Herrera, founder member and head of the most potent lay association of the pre-war period, the National Catholic Association of Propagandists (ACNP), director of *El Debate* newspaper, inspirer of the Catholic mass party the CEDA, and then president of Catholic Action in Spain before becoming priest, bishop, and cardinal.[21]

In Deusto, as in various secondary schools opened in the town by religious communities for fee-paying pupils, the interdependence of the religious and the bourgeoisie in the joint purpose of Catholic education was clear. The balance of advantage was more complicated when the two groups combined to educate poorer children, to make of them a competent and Christian work-force in a city where socialist unions were gaining a very secure base.

In 1887 a primary school was opened in the Deusto area of the city. The de La Salle brothers taught there, and the industrialist Gabriel María de Ibarra provided the building. The five grades of instruction included the rudiments of algebra, drawing, bookkeeping and accounts. There is no doubt that this foundation, and a sister establishment opened in 1925 in Baracaldo in premises donated by the Altos Hornos iron and steel company, was meant to give an elementary vocational training for boys who would later find employment in local industry.[22] The de La Salle brothers also staffed a school and working-men's centre which a Catholic lay association, the Society of St Vincent de Paul, opened in Iturribide Street in the heart of old Bilbao, again in 1887. The president of the SVP at the time was Fernando de Ibarra, Gabriel's son, and the family contributed funds on a fairly large scale, as did other wealthy benefactors like Casilda Iturriza who bought outright the land and buildings rented for the venture and donated them to the Society. Rules drawn up in 1891 summarized the aims of the school and centre as 'the free education, welfare, protection and moral care of the working class'.[23] For its sponsors, the enterprise contributed to 'the glorious compaign for a Catholic restoration'.[24] To further the social and religious

[21] On the Propagandists, see below, pp. 163–4.
[22] C. Gabriel, *La obra Lasaliana en España* (Madrid, no date), 226–8.
[23] *Génesis e historia de la fundación católica de escuelas y patronato de San Vicente de Paúl de Bilbao* (Bilbao, 1952), 38. The anonymous author says the archive was destroyed between 1936 and 1939, and that he gathered the data from private records of contemporaries.
[24] *Escuelas y patronato de obreros de San Vicente de Paúl de Bilbao. Memoria 1895–96* (Bilbao, 1897), 14. Printed year books also survive for 1897, 1898, 1901, and 1902. Information in these paragraphs is from the *Memorias* and *Génesis*.

Religious Communities 71

purposes of the centre, various subsidiary institutions came into existence, including a mutual aid scheme, a savings bank, recreational facilities, and *uniones profesionales*, which last represented an unsuccessful attempt to bind working men together in associations resembling guilds rather than trade unions. Every effort was made to create and control a securely Catholic world of entertainment and financial benefits as well as instruction. By 1900 there were 1,200 working men connected with the centre, while the de La Salle brothers taught 300 day school pupils and 900 evening class students. Within the fundamentally religious nature of the foundation, the orientation of the actual studies was technical, and this double emphasis was clearly reflected in the later careers of the pupils. While most of them went into local industry, more than 300 priestly and religious vocations were claimed for Iturribide Street by 1928.[25] Economic and religious interests converged. A specific social and industrial need was met partly by capitalists acting through a paternalistic charitable association within the Catholic Church, and partly by a religious congregation that provided the essential ingredient of dedicated, competent, and cheap teaching personnel. The industrialist benefactors were also prime beneficiaries since they acquired a better educated and—it was hoped—devout and non-revolutionary workforce.

A comparable situation obtained in two foundations made by the brothers in mining villages near Bilbao.[26] They opened a school in La Arboleda in 1907 on land given by the Orconera company which also provided free transport for building materials. Fernando de Ibarra, who owned mines in the area, also contributed, and after his death his widow María de la Revilla paid for the maintenance of three brothers to teach in the day school and give night classes. 1909 saw a similar foundation in Gallarta, with financial help from the Franco-Belga mining company and the Ibarra, Durañona, Zubiría, and Salcedo families.

There was a close female parallel to this collaboration in the work of the Daughters of the Cross, who in addition to the orphanage already mentioned earlier, opened a school in the factory area of Baracaldo at the express request of the Altos Hornos company.[27] Often the girls from the school and orphanage went into domestic service with the *gente acomodada* of Bilbao, just as their brothers went into their mines,

[25] *Los Hermanos de las Escuelas Cristianas en España. Su labor educadora durante medio siglo 1878–1928* (Madrid, 1928), 159–60.
[26] See Gabriel, 478, 481–2, and S. Mantilla, *Un jesuita en las minas. El P. Juan Manuel Obeso en la zona minera de Vizcaya* (Valladolid, no date).
[27] Information on Baracaldo from Sister Angeles Aparnaga, Bilbao, 4 Feb. 1974.

factories, and shipyards. Philanthropy, self-interest, and piety combined neatly and efficiently.

The most fascinating local female venture, however, was the Institute of the Guardian Angels, a congregation founded in the late 1890s by Rafaela Ibarra de Vilallonga, daughter of Gabriel, and wife of José Vilallonga, a dominant figure in the early development of the Altos Hornos foundries.[28] During the 1880s the devout and ascetic Rafaela had been involved in various projects designed to help young women coming into Bilbao from the countryside and finding themselves without home or work and sometimes drifting into prostitution. In 1893 she gathered some friends into a new charitable lay association to visit women in hospital and prison and to run a hostel for young unemployed or homeless women. The hostel had small workshops and gave some schooling, while imposing an austere religious routine. Still unresolved was the issue of stability for the project, since no religious community could be persuaded to assume responsibility. The solution emerged in 1896 when Rafaela decided to found a new religious congregation for the task. It was officially approved by the bishop of the diocese in 1901, just after her death, and prospered modestly with nine Spanish houses and others in Rome, Argentina, and Brazil by the 1930s. Middle-class recruits did the teaching and administration and were called 'mother'; those from peasant or urban working class background were 'sisters' and coped with the domestic chores.[29] The Institute of the Guardian Angels is an excellent example of the way in which religious communities seemed the obvious instruments for welfare and educational work, and of the links between such communities and the Catholic bourgeoisie. One of Rafaela's sons, Gabriel, became a Jesuit; her daughter entered the Handmaids of the Sacred Heart; her niece Luisa Urquijo y Ibarra was Superior General from 1916 to 1952 of the congregation Rafaela had founded. Meanwhile other relatives were financially involved either directly or as members of lay associations like the SVP in many if not all of those charitable foundations designed to meet the formidable new social problems created by the very industrial growth that brought these pious benefactors their great wealth.

It is not possible to understand why religious communities appeared to so many people the obvious and only way of remedying social

---

[28] There is a hagiographical biography, P. M. Abad, *Vida de Doña Rafaela Ybarra de Vilallonga*. 2 vols. (Bilbao, 1919).

[29] Information on the congregation's growth and recruitment from data sent by its archivist in April 1974, and interview with Mother Juana Iprota, Bilbao, 15 Mar. 1974.

needs unless one gives due weight to the last factor explaining their expansion—the opportunities afforded by the lack of state, provincial, or municipal resources in an era of rapid demographic change. Disease, poverty, and illiteracy were urgent problems, but in a country with a ramshackle fiscal system that left most real wealth untaxed, and a large army budget, little public money was directed towards meeting them. A law of 9 September 1857 enacting free, obligatory, primary education for all existed on the statue book but not in the practical reality of buildings and teachers. In 1900 only 1.5% of the state budget was dedicated to education (in Germany it was 12% and in France 8%), and the census reckoned that 60% of the population was illiterate. In 1910 Education Minister Romanones acknowledged that Spain needed another 9,579 primary schools just to implement the 1857 law by providing education for children between the ages of six and nine.[30] Inevitably, the situation at secondary level was correspondingly bad, and the preamble to a law of 17 August 1901 aimed at broadening the secondary syllabus admitted that 'of course the penury of our Treasury, which at least for the present allows of no increase in the state education budget, is an insurmountable obstacle in the way of any project for educational reform'. Whether the politicians liked it or not, and most Liberals did not, the religious communities continued to open schools in Spain because schools were needed and the state lacked the will, or the resources, or both, to set up an adequate educational system of its own.

What was true of education was true *a fortiori* of welfare. Since the mid-nineteenth century, responsibility for different kinds of welfare had been divided between the state, the province, and the municipality, just as different levels of education had been, but those responsibilities were met only patchily. Religious communities filled the spaces between the patches with hospitals, old peoples' homes, soup kitchens, reformatories, and orphanages. To take this time the example of industrial Barcelona, of thirty-nine residential homes of one kind or another in the city at the turn of the century, twenty-three were run by religious congregations, all but four or five being foundations made since 1876.[31]

Even more striking, however, was the extent to which even insti-

---

[30] For education at the turn of the century see Y. Turin, *Education et l'école en Espagne* (Paris, 1959), especially 395 on the budget. The figures for 1910 were presented to the Cortes on 15 May and are quoted in C. Silio y Cortes, *La educación nacional* (Madrid, 1914), 32.

[31] R. Albó y Martí, *La caridad, su acción y organización en Barcelona* (Barcelona, 1901), 309–62.

tutions funded by the state or provincial or municipal authorities were dependent upon religious personnel. In 1909 the Ministry of the Interior published a massive survey of welfare institutions in Spain in which it was apparent that without the nursing, clerical, administrative, and cleaning staff fed in by the religious congregations, most welfare institutions funded by central and local government would collapse.[32] It is noteworthy that nearly all of the sixteen residential homes in Barcelona that were not the direct responsibility of the religious, but grew out of private or municipal or provincial initiative, nevertheless were actually staffed by religious brothers and sisters. For example the Provincial Maternity Home and centre for abandoned babies was run by the Daughters of Charity of St. Vincent de Paul, as was the enormous Provincial House of Charity for the helpless poor, that in 1899 housed 665 boys, 369 girls, 321 men and 333 women. Similarly, Barcelona province maintained 305 men and 370 women—almost half the total number of inmates—in the San Baudilio del Llobregat mental asylum, where forty Brothers of St. John of God looked after the men and fifty Hospital Sisters of the Sacred Heart took care of the women, all under the direction of the provincial superior of the Brothers of St. John of God.[33] These brothers—re-founded in Spain by the Italian Angel Menni in 1867 when he opened in Barcelona the first children's hospital in the country—specialized in childrens' hospitals and mental homes. Arrangements like that at San Baudilio del Llobregat were common. For example, of the almost 1,000 patients in their mental hospital outside Madrid at Ciempozuelos in the Jarama hills in 1914, only 184 were paid for privately; all of the others were maintained by the provincial administrations of Madrid, Cáceres, Cuenca, Ciudad Real, Albacete, Segovia, Burgos, Guadalajara, and Salamanca, and the town council of Linares.[34] Even in the education system the division between Church and publicly funded establishments was not as clear as has often been supposed because at primary level—in the charge of the municipality—local officials sometimes paid grants to assist Church schools.[35] But where welfare—or in the idiom of the time, charity—

[32] Ministerio de la Gobernación, *Apuntes para el estudio y la organización de España de las instituciones de beneficencia y de previsión*. 2 vols. (Madrid, 1909).
[33] Albó y Martí, 323, 548.
[34] J. Álvarez Sierra, *El Padre Menni y su obra* (Barcelona, 1968), 65.
[35] E.g., Barcelona *ayuntamiento* in the 1880s subsidized a few primary schools set up by a Catholic men's association, see R. Alberdi, *La formación profesional en Barcelona* (Barcelona, 1980), 673-6; up to 1931 de La Salle schools in Mallorca and Herrera (San Sebastián) enjoyed some municipal subvention, see S. Gallego, *Sembraron con amor* (San Sebastián, 1978), 503-4.

was concerned, central and local government relied absolutely on the religious congregations to staff as well as supplement their institutions. This was explicitly and regretfully recognized by anti-clerical deputies in the impassioned debates on the religious congregations in the constituent Cortes on 8–14 October 1931, and was a major reason then, as a century earlier, why the congregations were not entirely disbanded.[36] Nor did the situation significantly change until quite late in the Franco regime. The poverty of the Spanish state and its local authorities in the late nineteenth and twentieth centuries was itself one of the reasons why so many young men and women poured into the religious communities in order to perform there all those traditional corporal works of mercy that seemed certain otherwise to be left undone.

During the restoration monarchy—and for that matter in the Franco regime too—tending the sick, instructing the ignorant, feeding the hungry, clothing the naked, and visiting the sick and imprisoned all bristled with controversy. Religious dedicated to these necessary and laudable tasks found themselves revered by some but excoriated by many. Sometimes this was because of the different cultural worlds inhabited on the one hand by religious brothers and sisters who were almost always from devout and traditional *milieux*, and on the other by the urban poor. To the former it seemed obvious that religious practice should play a prominent part in the daily lives of all their various charges, be they children, workmen, or reformed prostitutes. The hostels and workshops of Rafaela Ibarra's nuns, for example, had a routine for the residents that would not have shamed a strict religious novitiate. They attended daily Mass, sang hymns, recited prayers, and observed periods of silence during their hours in the workshops, made a chapel visit at the end of the day's work, and considered points for the next morning's meditation.[37] There is overwhelming evidence to show that this typical imposition of religious observance as a condition of eligibility for aid was widely resented. Working-class areas of the large cities were notorious for the virtual absence of formal religious practice: obligatory piety was irksome and degrading. Commenting on just this point in the 1920s the Socialist politician and feminist Margarita Nelken said that anyone enquiring among the poor residents of the most rundown areas of Madrid about the charity given by womens' lay associations and the

---

[36] See, e.g., the interventions of Fernando de los Ríos, Rodríguez Pinero, Humberto Torres, in *Diario de Sesiones de las Cortes Constituyentes de la República Española* (Madrid, 1931), 1527, 1554–5, 1558–61.
[37] Abad, 189.

nuns would hear 'truly terrible things and not a single word of thanks, ever'.[38]

Those struggling to eke out a living on the umpromising margins of urban society had more against the religious, however, than their custom of wanting everyone else to share their passion for praying. Very frequently religious houses presented them with formidable economic competition. For the thousands of nuns involved in orphanages and reformatories and refuges for the poor, it was simple common sense that their female charges should spend some time sewing, or making fancy goods, or working in the convent laundry. It was part of a general practical training, and the income earned helped solve the ever-present problem of how to keep the good work going.[39] For teaching brothers intent on equipping their pupils with at least the rudiments of a trade in carpentry or joinery or metalwork, the only way to do it without charging fees the pupils could not pay was the sale of goods produced in the practical workshops. The pattern was set by what was probably the first general technical school in Spain, the *escuela profesional* opened in Sarría, Barcelona in 1884 by the Salesians, who went on to develop a chain of technical schools with their own workshops throughout the country. In 1966 these schools had over 22,000 pupils. Already by the 1930s many of the Sarría pupils could be described as of lower middle-class origins, but earlier they were of more humble background and many of them were orphans. The original trades of carpentry and tailoring were joined by others, including printing, all with a theoretical and practical training. It was understandably a source of pride to the brothers that this eminently useful education was free, something that could not have been achieved without the sale of the boys' work.[40] From other perspectives, of course, this was all cheap labour, undercutting the local women who took in washing or sewing and the local men who made items of furniture or did household repairs. The common sense, and sometimes the ingenuity and inventiveness of the religious acquired a damaging double edge in a society where schools and welfare institutions were inadequately funded and forced to find ways of financing themselves.

Perhaps the resentment generated by making charity dependent upon religious tests, and by the sale of goods and services from religious

---

[38] M. Nelken, *La condición social de la mujer en España* (Barcelona, no date), 166.
[39] This system prevailed in the Guardian Angels and Daughters of the Cross convents already described, and in hundreds like them all over Spain.
[40] Alberdi, 653–69; *Don Bosco. Cien años en España* (Madrid, 1980), 112–22.

houses goes some way towards explaining why so many brothers and even some nuns whose laudable work might have saved them from popular hatred were massacred in 1936 in the first months of the war, along with thousands of diocesan priests. Even the Brothers of St. John of God were not spared. On 30 July, for example, fifteen of them from the children's hospital at Calafell, Catalonia were killed. Twelve more, this time from the hospital for epileptics near Carabanchel, Madrid, were killed on 1 September. Fifty-three brothers working in the mental hospital at Ciempozuelos were imprisoned in San Antón, Madrid, where they perished in the appalling massacres at Paracuellos throughout November as Franco's assault on Madrid spread panic among its republican defenders.[41] Perhaps their work was irrelevant to their persecutors and they died simply because they were religious, over-conspicuous representatives of a Church identified as an enemy to be annihilated on both ideological and political grounds. Be that as it may, it is certain that involvement in even the most ungrateful and demanding social or medical work did not expunge, in the eyes of their assailants, the offence of belonging to a religious community. A total of 2,365 male and 283 female religious were killed in deliberate, ferocious attacks during the war.[42]

The bitterest controversies about the congregations in pre-war years, however, had always centred on their schools and colleges to which about one half of all male communities and one third of the female were dedicated. The first major, explosive confrontation was in the early years of the twentieth century with Liberal governments. In 1901 and 1906 attempts were made to apply to the indignant congregations the 1887 law of associations, and in 1910 these efforts at some kind of control culminated in José Canalejas's famous but entirely ineffective 'padlock law', designed to prevent their further expansion.[43] It has often been suggested that these anti-clerical moves served mainly as a much needed rallying call for a Liberal party in imminent danger of fragmentation. But on the contrary, Liberal governments quite clearly, explicitly, and understandably feared the influence of the religious schools.

The politicians principally responsible for anti-clerical measures, like Canalejas and Romanones, were not hostile to the Church and never

---

[41] A. Montero Moreno, *Historia de la persecución religiosa en España 1936–1939* (Madrid, 1961), 224, 324–5, 329–46.
[42] Ibid., 765–7.
[43] See below, pp. 137–8.

bore any resemblance to the ogre-like persecutors of religion depicted in much contemporary Catholic propaganda. But they mistrusted the cultural values and ideological orientation of many Church schools, and were painfully aware of the inadequacy of the state's own resources. In an important speech in the Senate in April 1902 Education Minister Romanones argued that an unrestricted liberty of education,

> may prove fatal for those of us who love and defend true liberal principles. This is the root of my suspicions and of my attitude, the attitude of a man who is fearful that the principle of freedom to teach may be utilized to form the national soul ... in so definitive a way that afterwards, all other freedoms will be rendered quite useless.

On 27 June 1903 he outlined his dilemma:

> I do not oppose the educational work of the religious congregations: what I oppose ... is their monopoly of education. Over against their education and teaching, the Spanish state has no other to offer. For, in order to offer a state education system with equal facilities, it would be necessary to dedicate to this purpose far greater sums than the budget actually does so dedicate.

The issue, then, was partly one of numbers and resources, partly one of the actual content of education.

This was seen much more starkly in the different political context of the Second Republic. One of the most divisive articles in the republican constitution was article 26 that, among other radical provisions, debarred religious from teaching, though not from welfare work. This attempt to close the religious schools altogether and to keep religious out of the state system was unsuccessful, since the necessary legislation was only completed in June 1933, to take effect for secondary education on 1 October 1933 and a little later for primary education: the victory of the Right in elections at the end of 1933 immediately rendered it a dead letter. But the intention could not have been more forthright. Was such incurable nervousness of the religious schools justified?

It is extremely difficult to construct a dependable statistical account of the number of children in Church schools before the civil war. The enthusiastically reforming republican Ministry of Education worked in 1931–3 on the figure—supplied by the municipalities—of 350,000 children in Church primary schools compared with about one and a half million in state schools. Marcelino Domingo, Fernando de los Ríos, and Rodolfo Llopis as successive Ministers of Education urgently sought to create the schools necessary to absorb these children, as well as the mass of over a million without any provision at all. According to the ill-fated law of June 1933, all 350,000 were to be withdrawn from Church schools by the beginning of 1934. Equally widely quoted in studies of the period is the calculation that in 1931 there existed 295 secondary schools run by the religious congregations, with a total of 20,684 pupils.[44] But these figures are seriously misleading. They were estimates concerning education leading to the *bachillerato*, and do not cover thousands of children of post-primary age receiving a non-*bachillerato* education. To take just one example, the province of Vizcaya was reckoned in these statistics to have 633 boys in religious secondary schools and no girls at all. In fact, in Bilbao alone a number of schools took girls up to the age of eighteen, but very rarely submitted any of them for the *bachillerato*. Similarly, the 633 boys could not have included all those studying accounting, bookkeeping, technical drawing, and other vocational subjects with the Marists and Escolapios and brothers of the Christian Schools and Claretians and Menesianos in the provincial capital alone. The figure of 20,684, then, is hopelessly low as a total for all those children in post-primary education with the religious: it is the total of those studying towards the *bachillerato* and is very close to the figure of 26,265 for the same category in the state *institutos*.[45] On the other hand, it is extremely unlikely that these girls and boys were included in the municipal estimates of children receiving primary education with the religious congregations, for whom the state should make basic provision. Therefore, while 20,684 is certainly a grave underestimate of post-primary children attending the religious *colegios*, 350,000 is very probably a figure that does not absorb the remainder. But whether there were 370,000 children in the congregations' schools, or 400,000 or closer to half a million, their opponents were determined that soon there should be none at all. The secularizing of education was treated as just as urgent a priority as the assault on illiteracy. Paradoxically, while Church personnel were often suspected of the reactionary opinion that learning to read and write was no good if it did not foster religious orthodoxy, republican educational reformers were equally persuaded that learning to read and write was no good if nuns and religious brothers were the instructors. Sustaining the accelerating rate of state provision achieved under Primo de Rivera in

[44] e.g. M. de Puelles Benítez, *Educación e ideología en la España contemporánea* (Barcelona, 1980), 340, and M. Samaniego Boneu, *La política educativa de la segunda república* (Madrid, 1977), 334–5, where there is a breakdown of the figures province by province.
[45] Samaniego Boneu, 327–33; J. M. Castells, *Las asociaciones religiosas en la España contemporánea* (Madrid, 1973), 438–9.

the 1920s was not enough: illiteracy and the religious were to be outlawed together at top speed.

There was no dearth of people who thought that Church schools were bad schools. Margarita Nelken wrote indignantly of barely literate nuns teaching in primary schools in the 1920s. Constancia de la Mora, granddaughter of the Catholic Conservative politician Antonio Maura, but herself a Left-wing republican and notorious beneficiary of republican legislation permitting divorce and civil marriage, included in her autobiography a brief but passionate denunciation of stifling years endured at the *colegio* of the Slaves of the Sacred Heart in Madrid. Her less flamboyant uncle Gabriel also committed his memories of school to paper, describing his time at the Escolapio *colegio* in Madrid a generation earlier as more a process of domestication than education, with a heavy stress on conformism and learning by rote.[46] But these well-known criticisms of the religious schools need to be put in context. If primary schools run by the nuns left much to be desired, it was simultaneously true that not even Ministers of Education could find much to admire in the ill-equipped state alternatives staffed by poorly paid and often inadequately trained teachers. The fashionable convent secondary schools concentrated on giving a smattering of general culture rather than a disciplined academic education, but there were few girls studying for the *bachillerato* in the state *institutos* either before the republic. And if the boys' schools were crammers intent on getting pupils through the official examination, this was because of a state examination system based on memorizing textbooks, and as Gabriel Maura and many others recognized, the state *institutos* did not escape it any more than the schools of the Jesuits or Escolapios.

The religious schools had many defenders, of course. In the Cortes debate of 12–14 October 1931, for instance, Gil Robles praised the Salesians whose pupil he had been in Salamanca, and the Catalan deputy Carrasco Formiguera paid a personal tribute to his teachers, the Jesuits.[47] In the debates of May 1933 on the law of religious congregations, Catholic deputies lined up to protest the virtue, innocence, and efficacy of this or that congregation, and in doing so they spoke for many thousands of like-minded constituents. However, noisy championing by deputies like Gil Robles, or Lamamié de Clairac, or Antonio Pildain, or Dimas de Madariaga virtually proved the point

---

[46] Nelken, 167; C de la Mora, *Doble Esplendor*, 21–4; G. Maura Gamazo, *Recuerdos de mi vida* (Madrid, no date), 12–26.

[47] *DSCC* (1931), 1713–14, 1708–10.

that republican anti-clericals were arguing. The charge against the schools was not that their standards were noticeably lower than those in the state sector, nor that the syllabus was suspect—since in the case of boys preparing for official examinations the texts were the same as in the *institutos*—but that they fostered anti-democratic politics. Círilo del Río claimed in parliament on 8 October that 'the most outstanding collaborators of the dictatorship (of Primo de Rivera) were formed ideologically in Deusto and the Escorial', that is, by Jesuits and Augustinians. On 13 October Jiménez de Asúa accused the religious schools of deforming their pupils by teaching them that the advanced politics even perhaps of their own fathers was 'truly a disease of the spirit'. Later that night, in one of the most famous and misquoted and misunderstood parliamentary interventions in Spanish history, Manuel Azaña persuaded the Cortes not to outlaw all the religious congregations, but was adamant that their teaching work was a danger to the republic and must go. 'The continuous action of the religious orders upon young consciences is the very heart of the secret of the political situation Spain finds itself in, and it is our responsibility as republicans—and not as republicans but simply as Spaniards—to prevent it by every means.'[48]

An accumulation of accusations does not prove the charge. The religious themselves would and did argue that their schools were entirely apolitical, a claim that was more or less true if political meant advocating the cause of one particular, named, political party or group. It was demonstrably the case, however, that the ideological ambience and spirit of the congregations was anti-socialist, illiberal, and pervaded with the values of the political Right. This was scarcely surprising, given the sociological and geographical catchment areas for recruitment to religious communities and the completely self-contained, closed nature both of the training of teachers through and beyond the religious novitiates and of the enclosed life-style of most of the nuns and teaching brothers that insulated them from wider political and cultural influences. Many religious communities inevitably displayed and transmitted in extreme form the dogmatic mistrust of pluralism that marked the Catholic revival. As late as 1929 a newly published version of the old Ripalda catechism repeated the integrist conviction that liberalism was a serious sin, that no Catholic could call himself a Liberal and that it was usually a mortal sin to vote Liberal at elections.[49] A religious

[48] Ibid., 1542, 1663, 1671.
[49] G. Márquez, *Explicación literal del catecismo de Ripalda, con una exposición y refutación de los errores modernos* (Madrid, 1929), 407, 428.

textbook widely used in the 1920s described the separation of Church and state as 'the great heresy of our times, worse, perhaps, than all the preceding ones' and insisted that the state must be officially Catholic and that all citizens must conform to this identity. Accordingly, 'allowing everyone to write, propagate and teach whatever they please would have to be considered a crime no whit less grave than peddling toxic substances, poisoning water supplies, setting houses on fire or destroying the dykes of a river'.[50] A Church history compiled by the de La Salle brothers who were educating some 30,000 Spanish boys in the 1920s attributed all the country's ills in the nineteenth century to the influence of Freemasonry and impiety, insisted that the overthrow of Queen Isabel II in 1868 had been motivated by hatred for the Church, and criticized the limited toleration of other religions in the 1876 constitution.[51] A textbook published for use in girls' schools as late as 1934 still included vicious outbursts describing freedom of opinion as 'this disgusting sewer, this ravenous wild beast, this insatiable and bloody liberty for error' which had, among its other crimes, 'engendered the law of majority rule, a savage law of the strongest, the germ of ruin and death in its hankering after liberty'.[52] A similar publication of 1908 pointed to a possible remedy in a passage by J. M. Remesal, SJ, calling for an iron surgeon to purge the body of Spain of the gangrene of liberalism, cutting off without compassion all that was not wholesome and Catholic.[53] These examples could be multiplied indefinitely. The liberal democrats and socialists who formed the majority in the constituent Cortes were not indulging in idle rhetoric when they described the schools that used these books as a danger to the republic.

The religious communities themselves confirmed the view of the anticlericals when they welcomed the dictatorship, feared the republic, lamented the election results in 1931 and 1936 but not, of course, 1933, and settled happily—with the exception of some Basque and Catalan nationalists—into a new and firmer dictatorship in 1939. Pluralism meant heterodoxy, persecution, and a denial of Spanish Catholic identity. It is not possible here to trace the responses of religious communities up and down the country; perhaps a couple of small

---

[50] J. Pons, *Curso de religión (para servir de texto en las clases de religión)*. 6th edn. (Barcelona, 1924), 243, 246, 250–4.
[51] HH. de las Escuelas Cristianas, *Historia de la Iglesia Católica* (Madrid and Barcelona, no date c. 1922), viii, 351–5.
[52] RR. del Sagrado Corazón, *Manual de la clase 4* (Barcelona, 1934).
[53] RR. del Sagrado Corazón, *Manual de la clase 2* (Madrid, 1908), 205–6.

examples will convey the wider reality. In 1932 a de La Salle brother protested in the annual report of his school at a crude attempt by the republican government to secularize the national holidays of 7 and 11 October, feasts respectively of Our Lady of the Rosary and Our Lady of the Pillar. In his view the secularizing or privatizing of such feasts was an insult to Spain's long tradition of Catholic patriotism and patriotic Catholicism.[54] The argument was unremarkable but illustrates, none the less, the characteristic identification of religion with fidelity to the true Spain that made a liberal, aconfessional state virtually impossible to understand.

Much more overt is the political message of a manuscript journal kept by a women's community with a prestigious convent school in Seville, The entry for 12–18 April 1931 gloomily recorded the results of the municipal elections and the departure of the king 'who with his supreme dignity and patriotic abnegation addressed to all Spaniards an admirable manifesto', appended in full. Among various dramatic events recorded for the next couple of years was a police search of the house on 12 August 1932 because of rumours that someone involved in the Sanjurjo rising against the republic was hiding there. On 19 November 1933 the journal writer described how the nuns went to vote for the first time since 'grave circumstances' made it a 'sacred duty'. On 24 November she commented that 'the result here, as almost everywhere, was even better than we could have hoped'. Commenting on the revolutionary rising in Asturias in October 1934 she thankfully observed that 'the conduct of the army was magnificent, and the rebellion crushed step by step'. In February 1936 the nuns again sallied forth to do their sacred duty, but in spite of prayer and penance, 'by a secret judgment of God, neither in Seville nor in other provincial capitals could we record a success for the good cause'. After this victory of the Popular Front no good could be expected, and the journal's tone was anxious and full of foreboding until a long, jubilant entry entitled 'Relation of the heroic patriotic days of Seville, July 1936'. Not only was the account of the rising against the republic fervent and euphoric; a new page was added later, in 1937, with details learned by the community directly from Queipo de Llano himself, leader of the Seville rising. On 14 August a republican postage stamp with the insurgents' 'Sevilla—Viva España' superimposed on it was stuck in, with an explanation that it was the first such stamp received in the convent. Amid delirious accounts of

---

[54] *Colegio Santiago Apostol. Memoria Escolar 1931–32* (Bilbao, 1932), 11.

military parades and speeches by Queipo, Millán Astray, and Franco in August, other postage stamps signalling the victory of the rebels elsewhere were added. The journal became a kind of scrapbook of the war, culminating in the official recognition of the school on 18 April 1939 and a letter from Franco's secretary from Burgos on 16 May thanking the community for its good wishes.[55] This journal is not exceptional: its wariness of the republic antedated any republican move against the Church, although it almost certainly drew on bitter memories of persecution of the Church in the First Republic of 1873. In the cultural world of the religious, Catholicism belonged unquestionably with the political Right and could live happily with an autocratic regime but not with a pluralism that had in the past proved so perilous. The critics of the religious communities could scarcely be blamed if they came to exactly this same conclusion.

The politically reactionary sympathies of the teaching religious were formed and sustained not just by fear of a repetition of nineteenth-century suppressions, but also by the sociological context and limitations of the schools. It seems ungenerous to describe the teaching congregations as belligerents in the class war when, as they rightly pointed out to their armchair critics, they actually worked hard to make free education available in many places where otherwise it would not have existed. To a large extent they were victims, like so many others in Spain, of unsatisfactory social conditions. Their free primary and technical schools certainly offered a different kind of education from that in the fee paying *colegios*, but then the Spanish middle classes literally paid for the difference, and no one has ever explained how schools with facilities and staff to *bachillerato* level could be established and run without state subvention and yet free of charge. It was only with state subventions in the closing years of the Franco regime that many of the religious schools lost or greatly modified their class basis. Until then, they depended on the Catholic bourgeoisie not only for the upkeep of the secondary *colegios* but also for funds to keep the free schools going. As has been seen in the case of Bilbao, that dependence inevitably resulted in schools that were geared to sustaining the established social order with its evident class divisions.

For most of the Franco regime the religious communities and their schools flourished in an atmosphere of Catholic reconquest. In 1901

[55] Archive of Sociedad del Sagrado Corazón, Seville, 'Journal de la Maison—Seville', manuscript, in French, in 2 unpaginated volumes for 1 Jan. 1927–30 Oct. 1934, and 3 Nov. 1934–27 May 1937, and a paginated volume for 28 May 1937–19 Sept. 1940.

Pope Leo XIII had called religious the very apple of the Church's eye; now they were the apple of the state's eye too, with no Canalejas or Azaña to trouble them. Few would contest and many thousands affirm that the schools of the Jesuits or Marists or Ursulines or Sisters of Mercy were much the same in the 1950s as they had been in the 1920s. It was probably clearer in the schools than in any other aspect of Church life how victory in the civil war had frozen and preserved attitudes that already in the 1920s seemed extreme in Catholic Europe. Imperviousness to cultural influences from beyond the frontiers, the subordination of women, a puritanical and obsessively negative view of sexuality, a highly authoritarian interpretation of politics and social relations were all dominant features of Catholic post-war education so well known—because so widely suffered—that they hardly need documenting. Eventually these were challenged by voices within as well as without the Church. It is ironic that the new theology of the 1960s with its emphasis on personal experience and responsibility, its upgrading of sexuality and doubts about celibacy, its criticism of social injustice and coercion, succeeded in emptying the convents and changing many of the schools as resoundingly as anti-clerical politics and the terrifying violence of 1936 had failed.

One spectacular instance of this change was in the social composition of the secondary schools run by the religious congregations. Occasional earlier voices, dissatisfied with the concentration of religious schools in the cities and especially their dedication of resources to the bourgeoisie, became an insistent chorus in the 1960s as Catholic complacency waned. A sociological study in 1968 noted that 35% of all children in courses leading ultimately to the *bachillerato* were studying in Church schools—the vast majority of them run by religious—notwithstanding the enormous recent expansion of the state system. It went on to analyse their structure and distribution. Their average size was much smaller than the state schools and they were located in areas of higher per capita income, greater religiosity, and greater population density. 53% were in the north (though very few in the poor region of Galicia), 32% in the centre, mainly in Madrid itself, and only 15% in the south. Half were situated in provincial capitals, less than a third in rural zones and very few in urban working-class areas. When these rather disturbing facts were set beside other findings, such as the problems of adaptation that rural religious had in the cities, and the fact that a slightly higher proportion of former pupils of religious than of state schools seemed to doubt the existence of God, it was likely that some changes would occur.[56] Similar conclusions were presented more crudely to the enormously important joint assembly of bishops and priests in 1971; if Spain were divided into rich, poor and intermediate zones, then 80% of Church secondary schools would be found in the rich and intermediate areas, and over half in the rich zone alone.[57]

This was the same pattern that unfriendly critics had found unacceptable forty or sixty years before. What was new was that in the early 1970s many religious themselves also found it unacceptable. Not surprisingly, when the 1970 general education law of Villar Palasi was under discussion—with its ambitious range and its determination to extend and improve the state system—the Spanish episcopate published a plea for more state subventions of Church schools even though the state's own schools were Catholic, because of the bishops' fear that the schools run by the religious congregations would be forced to be ever more élitist.[58] The final years of the Franco regime saw an extraordinary effort by many of the orders to democratize their schools, and where this proved impossible because of location, sometimes to move them or even close them altogether rather than see them dependent on rising fees and consequently more and more exclusively the preserve of the *gente acomodada*. In many Spanish cities in the 1960s and 1970s fashionable schools in the centre—usually built between 1875 and 1910— were emptied and the sites sold to chain stores or property developers while the religious constructed new schools in the sprawling suburbs with a much more socially diverse intake. This phenomenon was only possible because state subventions were available to schools that qualified for them through the modest background of a proportion of their pupils. In the immediate post-Franco years, there would be nothing the bishops argued harder for than continuing state subvention of Church schools. While religious instruction and traditional Catholic teaching on marriage, family life, and abortion pitted the schools against many campaigns of the political Left, most of them were no longer in general socio-political terms quite the forcing grounds of reactionary ideology that the Right had formerly relied on.

It was fashionable in religious communities in the 1970s to contrast the 'institutional' Church of pope, bishops, and priests with the 'pro-

---

[56] ISPA, *La formación religiosa en los colegios de la Iglesia* (Madrid, 1968), especially 455–90.
[57] *Asamblea conjunta Obispos–Sacerdotes* (Madrid, 1971), 88.
[58] Confederación Episcopal Española, *La iglesia y la educación en España, hoy* (Madrid, 1969), especially 94–5.

phetic' Church of those outside the clerical hierarchy, notably the religious. According to this analysis the religious—though with the puzzling case of those who were also ordained—belonged firmly in the lay rather than clerical camp and their role was that of pioneers, free-shooters, mystics, critics, and prophets. Throughout the preceding century there had always been some members of the congregations who fitted part of this description. Enclosed contemplatives of both sexes had continued to remove themselves from the world of history and hierarchy to pursue an inner life of prayer. A few brave men early in the century had tried to use religious life as a base for social criticism and the exploration of new ways.[59] They were emulated decades later by many religious who tried to live close to the poor and to oppose the Church's involvement with the dictatorial regime and with wealth. Thousands of religious abandoned their habits and their large conventual houses to live unassumingly in groups of three or four—seven or eight at most—in cramped flats in working-class suburbs. To be of the people (even if by adoption rather than birth in some instances) and for the people in a life of service and prophetic presence emerged as the de-institutionalized ideal of the new religious life. Many an aged and monied parent looked on in uncomprehending amazement as their spirited but devout sons and daughters who had entered a highly respectable congregation twenty or thirty years before were suddenly converted to populism or even socialism.

Between the 1870s and the 1970s, however, most religious were not prophetic critics of the establishment, nor pioneering radicals. On the contrary, they manned and womanned the institutions that made visible and active the great institution, the Roman Catholic Church of Spain. They taught and nursed and administered the Catholic revival. They flourished with it, and declined as its aims and values faltered. In their own terms at the time, the achievement was stupendous. In the eyes of many others—and by the 1960s, sometimes in their own—it was profoundly ambiguous. Nor were all earlier critics anti-clerical. Among Catholic Catalan and Basque nationalists, for example, the teaching congregations in particular were regarded as agents of an imposed Castilian culture and, after 1939, an armed conqueror.[60]

However their achievement is assessed, it was undeniable by the mid-70s that the religious congregations in Spain—as elsewhere—were in

[59] See below, pp. 154–8.
[60] See e.g. I. Moriones, *Euzkadi y el Vaticano 1935–36* (Rome, 1976), 54–7; H. Raguer, M. Estrade, and J. Massot, *La integració de les religioses a Catalunya* (Montserrat, 1977).

crisis. While the old monastic establishments and the orders that included ordained priests with a wide range of pastoral work looked likely to shudder and survive, the congregations whose work had been an institutional one of running schools and hospitals and old peoples' homes could not be sure they had a future. If the analysis offered ealier in this chapter of why so many people entered the non-ordained, active religious life is at all correct, then its reverse is some explanation of why thousands have abandoned it since the mid-60s, why few have entered it, and why its future is uncertain. The theology, the patronage, the social circumstances, and state passivity that fostered its enormous extension have all disappeared. The kind of religious life that was peculiarly characteristic of the century studied here has been a casualty of Pope John XXIII's *aggiornamiento*, of the professionalization of teaching and welfare, of the extending social responsibilities of the state, and—not least important—of increasing career opportunities for women.

4

The Professionals II: Diocesan Priests

BEING a diocesan priest has not proved a very attractive option for Spanish male Catholics over the last century. Numbers declined absolutely between 1867 and 1951 from 40,872 to only 21,298, and although the total rose to reach 26,190 by 1968, that improvement was merely a short-term trend, brought to an abrupt halt by the crisis that devastated the seminaries in the late 1960s and 1970s.[1] The secular decline is even more marked when considered in relation to population growth. In 1859 there was one diocesan priest for every 401 inhabitants: by 1962 the equivalent ratio was one to 1,228.[2] It is interesting to compare this with the situation in other west European countries, and to note that the supply of priests relative to Catholic population has not only been more sparse in Spain than in countries where the Catholic population is a fairly well-defined and clerically serviced minority—as in Great Britain or Scandinavia—but also more sparse than in Ireland, Belgium, or Italy. In Great Britain in 1959 there were 746 Catholics to every priest, in Ireland 917, in Italy 1,109 and in Spain 1,336. Only Austria and Portugal were less well provided.[3]

There are clues to understanding these trends both in Spanish politics and in internal Church developments as well as in the sociology of recruitment to the priesthood. Within the general decline during the first half of the twentieth century, for example, there was a sharp fall in numbers in the seminaries in the politically inauspicious years of the Second Republic. Between 1931 and 1934 they dropped about 40%. A particularly dramatic exodus occurred in Valencia, where the seminary was sacked by anti-clericals on 12 May 1931 and the seminarians were forced to flee, many never to return.[4] Conversely, the heady atmosphere

[1] Figures based on Sáez Marín, 358; *Guía de la Iglesia en España* (Madrid, 1954), 294; *Guía de la Iglesia en España* (Madrid, 1970), 34.
[2] FOESSA, *Informe sociológico sobre la situación social de España. 1970.* (Madrid, 1970), 461.   [3] Ibid., 459.
[4] S. Aznar, *La revolución española y las vocaciones eclesiásticas* (Madrid, 1949), 43–9; V. Cárcel Ortí, *Tercera época del seminario conciliar de Valencia (1896–1936)* (Valencia, 1970), ii, 50.

of Catholic victory and reconstruction after the civil war stimulated a great influx of boys and young men, for whom huge new seminaries were built with a confidence that proved misplaced. Whereas at the low point of 1934, there were only 7,516 seminarians in Spain, by 1951 there were 18,536, and in 1961 a peak of 24,179 before the stream of applicants began to run dry and those already in training began to trickle and then flood away.[5]

If political circumstances were influential, so too were ecclesiastical changes. The crisis of the 1960s and 1970s was not peculiar to Spain, and was obviously generated by the radical rethinking about the Church and the role of the clergy and laity opened up by the Second Vatican Council, although it is also true that the new theology and ecclesiology were themselves partly a response to social, political, and cultural changes beyond and outside the Church. At the peak of 1961/2 there were 8,397 students who had persevered through the earlier stages to reach the courses in theology and philosophy; by 1972/3 only 2,791 were registered for such courses. Indeed in the late 1960s more people were leaving the seminaries than entering them. The effect on numbers admitted to the priesthood was inevitably drastic. In 1965/6, 800 men were ordained priest, but in 1972/3 fewer than 300.[6] Furthermore, this period brought in Spain as elsewhere an unprecedented exodus of men from the ordained ministry. Five priests were secularized in 1962/3, but 85 in 1966 and 125 in 1968; in the years 1975/7 no fewer than 845 left the priesthood.[7] The great majority of these were young or middle-aged. At the end of the Franco regime the Spanish Church found itself with a depleted and ageing clergy.

While political and ecclesiastical circumstances largely explain the sharp decrease in the numbers choosing to become priests in the 1930s and the 1970s, more continuous factors help account for the underlying downward trend over a whole century. Peasant smallholders have provided a very substantial proportion of entrants into Spanish seminaries. As late as the mid-60s over 35% of seminary students came from that social stratum. Up to mid-century, the sons of smallholders and agricultural labourers between them accounted for over half the total.[8] To approach the issue differently, small rural settlements have

[5] *Guía de la Iglesia en España* (1954), 284; FOESSA, *Estudios sociológicos sobre la situación social de España. 1975.* (Madrid, 1976), 617.
[6] FOESSA (1975), 621, 618, 622.
[7] Ibid., 625; *Iglesia Viva*, 91/92 (1981), 150.
[8] FOESSA (1970), 468.

Diocesan Priests

Table 1. *Density of priestly vocations by size of settlement*

Settlement	Population	Seminarians	Seminarians per 10,000 inhabitants
Under 500	964,396	4,851	50.3
From:			
500–1,000	1,334,468	3,344	25.0
1,000–2,000	2,132,502	2,952	13.8
2,000–5,000	4,406,789	3,617	8.2
5,000–10,000	4,371,489	2,162	5.0
10,000–100,000	5,880,742	3,843	6.5
Over 100,000	8,483,048	1,888	2.2

Source: J. M. Díaz-Mózaz, 'Les Vocations en Espagne', *Social Compass*, xii (Dec. 1965), 310.

been nurseries of priestly vocations in stark contrast with the low percentage from big towns. Table 1 demonstrates that more seminarians were produced from centres of population of under 500 than from any other category, even though only a small proportion of the total population lived in such centres. As the author commented, the contrast between the fifty seminarians per 10,000 inhabitants of the small rural settlements and the two seminarians per 10,000 in the large cities is too clear to need further exposition. When both the occupation of the fathers of seminarians and the size of the settlement is taken into account it is evident that recruitment to the priesthood has been adversely affected by the occupational shift away from peasant farming and the concomitant exodus from the countryside.

The discouraging effect of urban life has also been demonstrated in a survey published in 1970 of attitudes towards the parish priest. Those questioned who lived in centres of under 2,000 regarded him as a man with a very prestigious occupation, but as the size of the population centre increased, so regard for the priest diminished.[9] As Spaniards living in villages where the priest was regarded as very important have declined in numbers both absolutely and relatively to the rest of the population, so family encouragement to boys to become priests has necessarily become less and less prevalent. It was one thing to have a son a priest in a village in the north where he might rival in prestige the local doctor or even the mayor; it was quite another in the religious indifference of the big cities or the poor agricultural villages of Extremadura, where priests could expect no such status.

[9] Ibid., 541.

In patterns of recruitment to the priesthood—as in everything else Spanish—regional differences have been acute. Predictably, regional variation in the supply of candidates matched the pattern set by levels of religious practice. Where the latter was low, for instance in the centre and Andalusia, Madrid, and Barcelona, there were relatively few seminarians; where it was high, as in Old Castile and the Basque provinces, there were far more. It is difficult to assemble comparative statistics for the early part of the period, but those available for the 1960s reflect well-established and commonly acknowledged trends. For instance in 1967 Navarre topped the list with twenty-six seminarians for every 10,000 inhabitants, while Barcelona and Madrid formed part of the tail with only two. Such contrasts were, of course, self-reinforcing. If Navarre produced so many seminarians, it was partly because it already had so many priests. Its diocese, Pamplona, boasted one priest for every 371 inhabitants in 1967, the best ratio of any diocese in Spain. The dioceses of Madrid, Barcelona, and Seville, on the other hand, struggled along with one priest for every 2,180, 3,147, and 3,334 inhabitants respectively.[10] It was not pastoral need that produced aspirants to the priesthood, but a high incidence of religious practice in areas where priests were already plentiful. Boys—and their parents with them—considered a clerical career more easily in those circumstances where such an option was not out of the ordinary, and required no esoteric justification.

This was necessarily the case in a Catholic culture where the first steps towards ordination were usually taken by entering a junior seminary at the age of eleven or twelve, and this has only ceased to be the norm quite recently. In the Barcelona diocese between 1940 and 1951, one-third of those embarking on training for the priesthood were over seventeen years old; and in the immediate post-war years a large number of adolescents and young men of urban middle-class background entered seminaries after devout participation in the flourishing Catholic Action lay groups that characterized the years of victory.[11] But this was exceptional, probably reflecting both the hiatus of the war years and the expectation of middle-class families that their sons should receive an ordinary secondary education before making vocational choices. Most entrants, however, until very recent years, were young

[10] *Guía* (1967), 19, 61–124.
[11] R. Prat, 'La crisi vocacions—Seminari a Barcelona (1960–71)', in 'Correspondència de diàleg sacerdotal' any viii, no. 100 (Dec. 1971), 48–53, cyclostyled; *Iglesia y Sociedad en España 1939–1975* (Madrid, 1977), 29.

boys from rural areas, often encouraged and recommended by some local priest. As late as 1968, when priests working in junior seminaries with boys of secondary school age were consulted, a substantial majority regarded junior seminaries as either essential or very useful.[12] In the early twentieth century some variations from the standard pattern were phased out. For example, studying Latin and the humanities at home under the guidance of a priest before going later to the seminary for theology and philosophy was common in the 1890s but not thirty years later, when full-time boarding education had become the established norm. Similarly, abbreviated courses were discouraged.[13] The great majority of diocesan priests spent most of their time between the ages of about twelve and twenty-three in an entirely male and clerical educational environment. When Comillas seminary was founded by its eponymous marquis in Santander province in 1892, its stated purpose was 'to provide a completely free education throughout twelve or fourteen years' preparation for the priesthood for boys who are poor but of special talent'.[14] Jesuit-run Comillas was exceptional in recruiting across diocesan boundaries and in its concentration on gifted students, but not in the poverty of their home backgrounds nor in the length of training from eleven or twelve years old through to ordination in the early or mid-twenties.

Until the 1960s, separation from lay society was required of candidates for the priesthood. In the later stages of training this was imposed by external circumstances as well as by ecclesiastical discipline. Theology faculties were definitively suppressed in Spanish universities in 1868, so ordinands were segregated from their lay contemporaries. Physically, intellectually, and culturally the world of the priest was self-contained and self-sustaining through the long years of formation. It was usual for students to be visited by their families only at set times, while other visitors were discouraged and required special permission. Mail was read on its way in and out by priests in charge of discipline. Even during vacations a kind of isolation had to be constructed: seminarians were warned against going to the cinema, the evening *paseo*, or political meetings, reading novels or the secular press, and dressing or behaving in a 'secular' way.[15] The clerical world was defined as

---

[12] *Primera Asamblea de rectores de Seminarios Menores* (Madrid, 1968).
[13] For this change in one diocese, see F. Lannon, 'Catholic Bilbao from Restoration to Republic' (unpublished DPhil thesis, Oxford, 1975), 323–4.
[14] L. Frías, *La provincia de Castilla de la Compañía de Jesús* (Bilbao, 1915), ii, 162.
[15] See, e.g., *Reglamento general del seminario de Vitoria* (Vitoria, 1933).

different from and opposed to the secular world. When seminaries had non-boarding as well as boarding students, the two groups were kept apart. In Valencia, for instance, they had separate study-halls, chapels, organs, and choirs, and a different priest was in charge of each.[16] Mistrust of outside influence could not be clearer. This mistrust was rooted in a spirituality that regarded the world as dangerous. Eventually a more complex and positive theological assessment of the world beyond the seminary and even beyond the Church completely undermined the basis of this defensively enclosed system. Until this happened, physical segregation remained a powerful symbol and determinant of a separate clerical culture.

The intellectual components of that culture are not hard to identify. A secondary education notably weak in the sciences was followed by seven years of theology and philosophy. Dogmatic theology was the dominant course, edging out scripture studies and pastoral theology. Canon law was studied in detail; Latin was taken so seriously that it was actually the language of instruction for parts of the syllabus, while some Greek and Hebrew were also included. In the seminary, philosophy meant studies in the scholastic tradition, particularly after Leo XIII's encyclical letter *Aeterni Patris* of 1879 stimulated renewed interest in Thomas Aquinas's Aristotelian based system of thought. Priests were educated, therefore, in a medieval intellectual discipline which largely ignored the revolutions in science and philosophy from the seventeenth century onwards, and their theology relied upon the terminology and concepts of the scholastic system. Many of them left the seminary with esoteric skills for advancing religious propositions in carefully structured, syllogistic arguments. Truth could be defended against many kinds of error, but on grounds and with weapons that intellectual contemporaries viewed as bizarre and anachronistic. Seminarians remained ignorant of the radical biblical criticism developed in Protestant circles in Germany through the nineteenth century, and were taught to regard Kant, Hegel, Marx, and most other non-Catholic philosophers merely as sources of pernicious error. Dogmatics and apologetics were the staple fare, but the diet was dangerously low in scripture and in post-medieval thought.[17] In spite of the long and careful preparation, newly ordained priests were intellectually undernourished. It is not surprising, then, that Spanish clerical culture produced no major

[16] Cárcel Ortí, ii, 26–8.
[17] For detailed programmes of seminary life and studies see, e.g., *BEAS* (1884), 122–58; *BEOV* (1880), 164–5; *Reglamento general del seminario de Vitoria* (Vitoria, 1933).

figure to command respect in circles of secular learning, and no theologian or philosopher or scripture scholar of international repute in the Catholic world, and no modernist crisis to echo those in France, Italy, or England. It was self-propagating, narrow and defensive. Even when seminary syllabuses were widened to include new disciplines, the motive was usually defensive and the subject treated accordingly. Anthropology, political economy, Hebrew, and Greek were introduced in Valencia in 1893, but quite explicitly to combat determinism, anarchism and socialism, and rationalist interpretations of scripture, respectively.[18] The sudden interest in sociology after the turn of the century sprang from the desire to counter 'revolutionary' propaganda on the need for social change. And when a lecturer in Vitoria seminary surveyed the work of Kant, Comte, Durkheim, and Lévy-Brühl in one lecture in 1916, he did so only to dismiss it as misguided and unimportant.[19]

The average diocesan priest no doubt got on very well without the aid of a sophisticated and modern philosophical education. In Almería or Ávila, Teruel or Toledo, unfamiliarity with the writings of Hegel would be no more a handicap in the work of a busy curate than in Lyon or Los Angeles or Liverpool. But other omissions were more immediate liabilities. The lack of pastoral theology and practice meant that priests were often ignorant or naïve about social conditions, the economy, and politics. When lecturers in Vitoria seminary in the 1920s and 1930s directed their students to read articles from the liberal and socialist press, to investigate the structures of capitalist industry, to learn about local social conditions, history, and customs, and then to write short papers on these topics for the seminary journal, they knew their project was controversial. Opponents successfully objected to the journal, in particular, as diverting time and attention away from the proper priestly discipline of the seminary.[20] Knowledge of canon law and fluency in Latin were more central to a priest's education than an ability to understand, analyse, and criticize contemporary political issues or the social context of their parishioners' lives and work. For many, an urban parish proved a fearsome contrast to the environment in which they had grown up. Few of the diocesan clergy involved themselves directly in controversial social problems before the civil war, and those who did often paid heavy penalties of incomprehension and

[18] Cárcel Ortí, i, 44.
[19] Antonio Pildain, in *BEOV* (1916), 499–502, 525–32, 534–46, 572–82, 608–16.
[20] See F. Lannon, 'A Basque challenge to the pre-civil war Spanish Church', *European Studies Review*, ix, 1 (1979), 29–48.

mistrust.[21] Priesthood was primarily to do with the realm of the sacred, with sacramental ministry, parish activities, and the defence of the faith.

The immediate post-war years saw no significant change in seminary discipline or studies. On the contrary, the old system flourished in the congenial atmosphere of Catholic victory and reconstruction. For example, when the bishop of Bilbao compiled a long and detailed rule of the grandiose new seminary in his recently established diocese, he produced a document which might equally well have appeared in 1890 or 1930. Newspapers were still forbidden; secular studies of any kind required special permission; mail was still intercepted; seminarians were urged to mix with fellow seminarians rather than lay companions during the vacations; cinemas, theatres, crowded beaches, and other places of recreation were out of bounds; lecturers in philosophy and theology were particularly admonished to 'remain faithful to the scholastic method and the thought of St. Thomas'.[22] Yet, little more than a decade later, this kind of priestly formation lay in ruins in virtually every seminary in Spain. In June 1967 Bishop Gúrpide of Bilbao received a long letter from a group of lecturers and spiritual directors in the huge Derio seminary he was so proud of, arguing for a radical change in the regime he had so carefully decreed in 1956. They reported—and obviously agreed with—complaints of the students at inadequate theological training and especially the lack of pastoral preparation for the needs of their region, with its disaffected industrial working class. They wanted a different kind of formation, directed not to the creation of a sacral, remote figure, but a priest trained in sociology and psychology and immersed in the worldly problems of the mass of the population. So acute was the discontent, that the letter ended with a threat that its signatories would resign if the desired changes were not effected.[23] In December 1968, eight of the seminarians themselves wrote to Gúrpide's successor, Cirarda, a pathetic account of their experience in the seminary, highlighting the insufficiency of their formation in every sphere.[24]

Although political tensions made the Bilbao seminary a special case in the 1960s, the rejection of traditional clerical education was general throughout the country. Quite apart from the incontrovertible evidence of seminarians voting with their feet by the end of the decade, reliable

---

[21] See below, pp. 157, 161–2.
[22] *Reglamento del seminario diocesano de Bilbao* (Bilbao, 1956), 104.
[23] Derio seminary, Manterola archive, legajo 1.1.15, Seminario, carpeta 1, letter of 2 June 1967.
[24] Manterola archive, Seminario, carpeta 2, 20 Dec. 1968.

Diocesan Priests

information was gathered in a questionnaire of older students devised in the spring of 1969 by an episcopal commission. It was followed by a discussion with groups of seminarians at a conference in Avila in November. The students wanted an education that would give them secular professional competence as well as religious, a thorough pastoral preparation including studies in psychology and sociology, a new kind of life-style in small groups in an urban context instead of hidden away in massive seminaries, and a less authoritarian discipline. They raised grave doubts about embarking on education for the priesthood at the traditional early age. Of those questioned, 43% could give no particular reason for entering the seminary, and 50% recognized the strong influence of parents, teachers, and local priests. A high proportion were undecided as to whether they would actually proceed to ordination, and many regarded the usual parish role of the priest as unattractive and wanted experimentation with new pastoral styles.[25] By the mid-70s imposing seminary buildings echoed emptily, since the junior seminaries were in decline and those older boys and young men who remained often lived in small groups in flats, studying at theology institutes that were also open to the laity, and gaining pastoral experience in the cities. Recruitment to the priesthood has not stopped since then, and in the 1980s there are signs of a patchy increase, but the former pattern of child vocations from rural areas trained in a separate clerical world has almost disappeared.

These abrupt changes in education for the priesthood, were, of course, reflections of a more fundamental shift in the self-understanding of the Spanish clergy and the expectations placed on it by the laity. The priest had been a man set apart. His training prepared him for a sacerdotal role marked by differences from those around him. Just as that apartness had been most plainly expressed and symbolized in distinctive clerical dress and the discipline of celibacy, so the abandonment of the first and a loss of conviction about the second very often became the signs of a different role emerging in the 1960s. And a changed understanding of the life and work of the priest was itself a part of the wider reassessment of the whole Church's relation to the modern world eventually incorporated into the ecclesiology of the Second Vatican Council.

The classic apartness of the Spanish cleric could be a social distance of prestige or of disparagement. In small settlements of high religious practice he enjoyed an authoritative status in the network of social

[25] See *Iglesia Viva*, 28/29 (1970), 385–444 for commentaries on this questionnaire and the Ávila meeting.

relationships, whereas elsewhere he sometimes attracted contempt and hatred. At one extreme he was a cultural and political as well as spiritual guide: at the other, a pariah. For many people the celibacy of the clergy was suspect. In the hamlet of Valdemora, north-east of Madrid, villagers were wary of both priests and shepherds as men without family ties, and discouraged their sons from taking up either way of life.[26] In his study of the village of Yegen, south of Granada, Gerald Brenan described how the local inhabitants were quite unconcerned at priests who had housekeeper lovers, and were indignant when a very popular priest left the village after falling in love with the doctor's sister-in-law.[27] In this isolated village that was not anti-clerical, nor anarchist, nor socialist, and where religious practice had very little to do with the sacraments and centred rather on communal celebrations of ancient nature feasts with Christian dates and images superimposed, the niceties of sacerdotal sexual discipline were not perceived as important. It is extremely difficult to gain an accurate idea of what proportion of the diocesan clergy before the 1960s rejected the obligation of celibacy. Brenan noted that very remote villages like Yegen were 'dumping grounds for bad specimens', while the clergy in other settlements in the locality were above reproach. Elsewhere a confident disparaging of priests in general, stereotyped as scandalous libertines, often went hand in hand with respect and affection for the actual local parish priest, known by everyone to be a thoroughly conscientious man, a disparity noted by J. R. Mintz in his study of Casas Viejas in Cádiz province. In Casas Viejas too, however, sexual misdemeanour was not necessarily viewed negatively as long as the priest was a responsible man, and respected on other grounds.[28] In another cultural world, pre-1914 Madrid, a bemused and rebellious teenage Arturo Barea met the priest he most admired in a Madrid park and was introduced to his wife and son.[29] The discipline of celibacy was not universally observed, and those who side-stepped it were not necessarily the least adequate priests. Responsibility towards lover and children, or the impossibility of abandoning the priesthood with no qualification for another career could account for sexually unconventional priestly behaviour as much as cynicism or weakness. The Church's obsession with celibacy was not shared by everyone, and as

---

[26] S. T. Freeman, *Neighbours. The Social Contract in a Castilian Hamlet* (Chicago, 1970), 181.
[27] G. Brenan, *South from Granada*, 68–71.
[28] J. R. Mintz, *The Anarchists of Casas Viejas*, 71–3.
[29] Movingly related in A. Barea, *The Forging of a Rebel* (London, 1972), 215–16.

Barea's moving account of his childhood vividly illustrates, celibates could be more preoccupied with sex than anyone else. But celibacy—for good or ill—marked off the great majority of priests from the people they served.

The sacerdotal role did not inhibit priests from political activity. Carlist and Integrist clergy of the restoration period had few qualms about overt political involvement, as the writings of the most famous Integrist priest polemicist, Sardá y Salvany, amply demonstrated.[30] Navarrese clerics formed a 'sacerdotal *junta*' in 1931 to keep watch during meetings of the Carlist militias, and later actually manufactured hand grenades in the cause of God and the old laws.[31] There were eight diocesan priests among the Cortes deputies who faced in 1931 the daunting task of giving Spain a new constitution. More subtle than such explicit political engagement, however, was the defence of specific and religious values which almost always aligned priests somewhere on the conservative Right. For decades, sermons reiterated the legitimacy of a hierarchically structured society and preached the virtues of obedience, hard work and deference.[32] Anti-socialism seemed to its clerical as to many of its Catholic lay champions not a political option but a religious duty. Similarly, disputes over confessional education inevitably meant that priests and other Catholic spokesmen opposed liberalizing policies in the name of religious truth. A world view in which the defence of Catholic doctrine and Catholic institutions was the overriding priority meant that although many priests did not have a political vocabulary recognized as such, they in fact talked politics when simply defending the faith. The three members of the clergy who participated in the constituent Cortes of 1869 were an excellent example of this, and they had innumerable successors throughout the country in subsequent generations. The three—a cardinal, a bishop, and a priest—shared a distinctive intellectual style and ecclesiastical outlook which resulted in intolerance of views derived from any source other than Catholicism, and they consequently insisted on the Church's right and duty to exercise cultural hegemony and political tutelage in Spain.[33] In that

[30] See below, pp. 126–7.
[31] A. Lizarza Iribarren, *Memorias de la conspiración. Cómo se preparó en Navarra la Cruzada 1931–36* (Pamplona, 1953), 15, 81–2, where the priests are named.
[32] For nineteenth-century sermon material see J. A. Portero, *Púlpito e ideología en la España del siglo XIX* (Zaragoza, 1978), and A. Martínez Albiach, *Religiosidad hispana y sociedad borbónica* (Burgos, 1969). These patterns were little challenged in the first decades of the twentieth century, and greatly intensified under the Franco regime.
[33] For an analysis of their contribution, see S. Petschen, *Iglesia-estado. Un cambio político. Las constituyentes de 1869*, 29–66.

radical assembly, it was not just that they voiced ideas their audience did not want to hear, but that they spoke a different political language.

In so far as priests were regarded as official representatives of a Church that valued the established social hierarchy, they necessarily played a political role, however far such an aim was from their intentions. As men trained to oppose political and cultural pluralism they belonged—primarily for religious reasons—on the political Right. Where class conflict and political discontent were most acute, priests suffered from identification with the forces of property and repression, for instance in Barcelona in the 'tragic week' of 1909, in the 'Bolshevik years' of hunger in Andalusia at the end of the First World War, and in the revolution in Asturias in 1934. Where class relations were less violent, and the distribution of property less provocative, priests fitted more harmoniously into the social hierarchy. It is not surprising, therefore, that the minority of priests who moved away from conservative assumptions were those who had come to dissociate their religion from the established social and political order and even to experience the two as contradictory. That was the case of men whose pastoral work amid rural or urban poverty led them to criticism of social injustice. And it was true too of priests in particular regions, especially Catalonia and the Basque country, where the centralized political system was widely interpreted as repressive and ripe for challenge. Often the two strands were intertwined. Policarpo de Larrañaga is a good example of a Basque nationalist priest who loathed rule from Madrid and poured his organizing and oratorical energies into Catholic trade union work in the 1920s and 1930s. Catalan nationalist sympathy separated many of the Catalan clergy from the politics of the Right in the same period, while a very few of the Gallegan clergy followed a parallel autonomist path. Probably the most radical theoretical work on social relations from any priest was the work of Ángel Carbonell, who boldly argued in 1927 that collectivist solutions to social problems were not incompatible with Catholicism, and indeed harmonized more easily with traditional Catholic teaching on the social function of property than did pernicious economic liberalism, with which the Church had coexisted for so long. Given the contemporary Catholic fear of socialism, this was a brave argument. Carbonell stated in the prologue to his book that it sprang from his pastoral work in Barcelona slums, and that he had originally written it in Catalan.[34]

[34] P. de Larrañaga, *Contribución a la historia obrera de Euskalerría*. 2 vols. (San Sebastián, 1976, 1977); F. Carballo and A. Magariños, *La iglesia en la Galicia contemporánea*

Diocesan Priests 101

An interesting sign of the increasing range of political opinion among the clergy is the odd assortment of priests who were elected deputies to the constituent Cortes of the Second Republic in 1931. Leaving aside Basilio Álvarez whose canonical situation was irregular, there were seven, of whom five belonged to the Agrarian or Basque–Navarrese minorities. Luis López-Doriga Meseguer was, astonishingly, a Radical Socialist representative from Granada who agreed with the notion of a non-confessional state, and divorce legislation, because he recognized ideological pluralism in Spain and argued that the constitution must reflect that reality rather than attempt to change it.[35] More orthodox but still surprising was the position of Jerónimo Garciá Gallego, independent Republican from Segovia, who claimed Catholicism as the 'religion of the rights of man, the religion of democracy, the religion of liberty'. He berated powerful Catholic groups—notably those connected with the influential Catholic daily *El Debate*—for failing to embrace democratic values and for having supported Primo de Rivera's dictatorship. As a convinced republican he pleaded for a lenient treatment of the Church by the republic on the grounds that the groups he criticized were not actually the Church. His was the unrewarding task of proclaiming his republican sentiments unfashionably in the 1920s and his Catholic belief to a sceptical republican Cortes in 1931.[36] The remaining clergy were of a more traditional mould, lining up with the Right because they wanted to embody Catholic values in the constitution and laws of the land. And it was a priest and seminary teacher, Antonio Pildain of Guipúzcoa, who eventually invoked Catholic doctrine in parliament as justification for armed resistance to the anti-clerical articles of the constitution.[37] The political pluralism explored by García Gallego and taken to far greater lengths by López-Doriga might have continued to exist and diversify in clerical circles had not the civil war closed off all possibilities of such nuanced disagreements in its brutal polarizing of options. As it was, the Cortes debates of October 1931 demonstrated both the continuing strength of a clerical tradition that understandably feared the bitterly anti-clerical Left and sought to impose Catholic orthodoxy by political or even military means, and the emergence of tolerant but ill-fated alternatives.

(Madrid, 1978), 30–55; A. Carbonell, *El colectivismo y la ortodoxia católica* (Barcelona, 1927).

[35] *Diario de Sesiones de las Cortes Constituyentes de la República Española* (Madrid, 1931), 1658–9, 1776–7.

[36] *DSCC*, 1569–77, 1659–60.   [37] *DSCC*, 1706–8.

Once the attempted coup of 18 July 1936 divided Spain into two warring segments, it became almost impossible for priests to retain allegiance to a republic that immediately became associated with terrifying anti-clerical violence on an unprecedented scale. Over 4,000 diocesan clergy were hunted down and killed in republican areas of Spain during the civil war, mainly in the first months of administrative chaos, and mainly where anarchism was strongest. It was a cruel price to pay for identification with a system of class and property relations that the Church had not created. Back in 1899, after priests preaching a mission in rural Andalusia had been stoned by villagers, Archbishop Spínola had predicted that some day torrents of blood would flow in a popular persecution of priests there.[38] His successor in the early 1930s knew that some of his clergy went in fear for their lives,[39] while in another region noted for its conflictive class relations, Asturias, priests and seminarians were assassinated during the revolution of 1934. As Canon Maximiliano Arboleya, an Asturian priest wholly immersed in social-Catholic enterprises, including unions, in the local coal mines despairingly commented, it was ridiculous to attribute such violence simply to subversive propaganda.[40] The thousands of priests who died in 1936 were victims of anarchist determination to do away with the Catholic Church in Spain. They were also victims of the Church's failure to analyse and attempt seriously to rectify the grave, urgent, predicament of the urban and rural poor.

Only in the Basque country, where the strength of the Catholic Basque Nationalist Party restrained anti-clerical violence, could significant numbers of the clergy continue to support a regime from which they still hoped to obtain regional autonomy. Elsewhere a tiny handful of priest republicans like Leocadio Lobo in Madrid, José Manuel Gallegos Rocafull in Córdoba and Josep María Llorens i Ventura in Barcelona constituted an embarrassment to Church leaders.[41] But clerical sympathy for the republican cause in the Basque provinces was a major scandal. It jeopardized the propaganda campaign of ecclesiastical and military authorities seeking to convince the world that they represented Christian civilization fighting to the death against atheistic communism. A photograph of a large group of Basque priests held in a Francoist gaol near Seville did no good to that campaign, nor did the execution of

[38] *BEAS*, xxxii (1899), 400–3. [39] See above, p. 15.
[40] Letter of 30 Oct. 1934 from Oviedo, in D. Benavides Gómez, *El fracaso del catolicismo social* (Barcelona, 1973), 553–6.
[41] For these priests, see H. Raguer, *La espada y la cruz* (Barcelona, 1977), 178–87.

fourteen Basque priests, almost all of them in October 1936, by the forces of Catholic Spain as they pushed the northern front into a collapsing Basque republican territory.[42] Statistically the fourteen executions might seem paltry when set beside over 4,000 priests killed on the other side; but the significance of these Basque priests put to death in the name of a Catholic crusade preserved them from the ultimate indignity of being weighed by numbers. There was no danger of Martín Lecuona, Alejandro Mendicute, José de Ariztimuño, Celestino de Onaindía, and their colleagues ever being dismissed by either side as of no particular importance.

It is ironic that those responsible for these deaths claimed that the fourteen priests were executed for political offences, while simultaneously interpreting the massacre of priests in republican territory as ideologically and irreligiously motivated, without any connection with the politics of the victims. But just as the recently ordained Martín Lecuona was regarded as politically suspect to conservative, centralizing anti-republicans because he was immersed in Basque trade union affairs, so even the most other-worldly or radically reforming priest caught in the anti-clerical vengeance on the other side, represented to his persecutors a Church politically identified with the social groups and institutions that supported Franco's rising. Political definition sometimes lies in the eye of the beholder, a truism equally fatal to the few on one side as to the many on the other. Just as sacerdotal credentials failed to exculpate the Basque priests from the political suspicions of their Catholic captors, so the credentials of reforming interest, Catalan loyalty, poverty, political ignorance, or innocence equally failed to redeem the crime of ordination of their colleagues across the battle lines. The tiny group died although they were priests, the great mass because they were priests; in both cases, the preconceptions of what priests were expected to be and to represent were clear.

In the twenty years after the end of the civil war, the image of the diocesan priest was probably simpler, clearer, and more uniform across the length and breadth of Spain than before or since. Victorious Francoist army chaplains, traumatized men coming out of hiding in the last strongholds of republican resistance, the new recruits flooding into the seminaries all saw their task as the reconstruction of Catholic Spain, providentially saved from obliteration. Enemies of the priesthood outside the Church, and enemies of a centralized, conservative Spanish govern-

[42] For details of the executed priests, and the famous photograph, see J. de Iturralde, *La guerra de Franco. Los vascos y la iglesia* (San Sebastián, 1978), ii, 331-80.

ment within it had been silenced. In the new regime priests had a well-defined task whose only ambiguity was the ineradicable one that as far as the vanquished were concerned, reconstruction meant repression. For an institution as convinced of its own righteousness as the postwar Spanish Church, however, and as securely backed by a sympathetic regime, hostile exterior perceptions were less dangerous than confusion or self-doubt among its own leaders, the priests. It is paradoxical that while in the short term the civil war banished any confusion of self-image, in the long term it inevitably embedded it deeply. The hatred that had claimed so many priests' lives was a fact of history susceptible of many explanations, and the notoriety of the republican priests of the 1930s remained an uncomfortable pointer away from the accepted versions of what had gone wrong.

Meanwhile fervid public processions, insistent catechesis and government funding combined to re-create Catholic Spain. In 1939 the government subvention of clergy stipends that the early republic had pledged to stop was re-established, with explicit mention of the clergy's efficacious co-operation during the war. On 10 March 1941 a decree committed the state to funding the rebuilding of parish churches. On 8 December 1946 the government and the Vatican reached an agreement by which the state contributed substantially to the reorganization and maintenance of Spanish seminaries and universities for ecclesiastical studies. When, in December 1972, Franco's prime minister Carrero Blanco estimated that 300,000 million pesetas had been poured into a not always adequately grateful Church, many observers disputed his figures and pointed out that state payments had not kept up with inflation. But there can be no doubt that the sums were enormous and that the diocesan clergy, if not well paid, were none the less paid by the state, as they had been prior to the republic. The extreme nervousness of the Church when Franco's system was dismantled, lest the clergy budget be abolished, was evidence enough of its reliance on state support.[43] Given this financial dependence, and the ideological interpenetration of Church and state, it is not surprising that the unease and dissatisfaction with the Church and with their own role experienced by some priests in the 1960s and 1970s were very often connected with criticism of government policies, particularly on social and regional issues.

[43] For state support of the Church post-1939 in the light of episcopal views towards the end of the Franco regime, see T. G. Barberena, 'Las subvenciones económicas a la iglesia', in *Iglesia y comunidad política* (Salamanca, 1974).

Diocesan Priests 105

One obvious stimulus of a critical social and political consciousness among priests was the network of Catholic lay associations in both industrial and rural milieux. As these workers' associations within Catholic Action became more radical and more threatening both to the regime and to conservative bishops in the late 1950s and 1960s, they took their chaplains with them. When the national lay officers of the male and female branches of HOAC (Worker Brotherhoods of Catholic Action) and JOC (Young Catholic Workers) issued in May 1962 a declaration on labour conflict in Asturias, the national chaplain, Ramón Torrella, was suspended by the bishop of Madrid, while the authors were imprisoned. Special meetings and courses were organized for clergy connected with JOC and HOAC, which further sharpened their group identity. In September 1967 six national chaplains of the various movements were sacked by the hierarchy for political involvement. In December no fewer than 360 chaplains of the Young Catholic Workers' associations met to look at their task in the light of the new theological trends of the Second Vatican Council. They addressed to the hierarchy a plea that the Church should extricate itself from close identification with a political system experienced by so many workers as oppressive. These skirmishes with both the dictatorship and their own bishops left many of the priests involved wounded and bitter. In 1968 Felipe Fernández Alia, national chaplain to the female branch of JOC, wrote to Bishop Morcillo of Madrid of the widespread defeatism among radical laity at the sight of a corrupt Church, and he asked God for the 'miracle' of having faith in the Church. When the inevitable sacking duly followed, his opposite number in the male association protested to the president of the Episcopal Conference. Little hope was placed in the protest, however, for its author, Vicente Amargos, wrote that the pastoral style of the bishops had little to do with the gospel or with the new conciliar Church, and that nothing good could now be expected of them.[44]

While some of the priests caught up in the conflicts of the 1960s survived to enjoy the altered balance of forces within the Episcopal Conference in the early 1970s—Ramón Torrella was himself consecrated bishop in December 1968—many suffered disillusionment to the point of seeking laicization and often abandoning the Church altogether. The enthusiasm for a new pastoral commitment in the factory and the field that had marked some seminaries in the 1950s, especially

[44] This account is based on J. Castaño i Colomer, *La JOC en españa* (Salamanca, 1978), especially 90, 139, 172–80, 185–6, 193–5.

Barcelona, Vitoria, Valencia, and Comillas, ended for many of the then seminarians in sterile confrontations both in their own dioceses and at a national level. One of the peculiarities of the JOC and HOAC network which was eventually modified by the bishops was precisely that it provided an extra-diocesan structure for the laity and their chaplains alike, cutting across the traditional, diocesan based, hierarchical controls. And although conflict with the government and the law might not have proved in itself a deflating experience for priests imbued with a call to denounce injustices like the prophets of the Old Testament, simultaneous opposition from their own ecclesiastical leaders denied them the ground on which they stood. For many, it was a bitter discovery that against the Church there was no salvation, followed by the fundamental question as to what salvation with and within the Church might mean. The answer frequently seemed too insubstantial, too other-worldly, too compromising to invest a life in.

In the Catalan and Basque dioceses, disputes over wages, working conditions, and civil rights necessarily fused with nationalist resistance to a centralizing regime backed by military force. The appointment of a non-Catalan, González Martín, to the see of Barcelona in 1966 aroused the furious indignation of clergy and laity alike. Two years earlier 400 priests and religious in Catalonia wrote a letter to their bishops on the pastoral problems in the area, pointing out that cultural minorities and workers were experiencing a crisis of faith exacerbated by the Catholic character of the state that repressed them. González Martín's appointment, then, was one focus among many of anger at both ecclesiastical policies and the state whose needs and values the Church was seen to serve. Police harassment of Barcelona university students was another sensitive issue, and it was mainly violence against the student Joaquín Boix i Lluch that 130 priests denounced with a silent march on Barcelona police headquarters on 11 May 1966. Four leaders were arrested and eventually tried in February 1969 in Madrid, found guilty of participating in an unauthorized demonstration, and sentenced to a year and a day's detention. The trial provoked a new wave of protests in Catalonia, including a silent solidarity march of 280 priests to the archbishop's palace. The state of exception, declared in January 1969 and accepted by the hierarchy, enabled the police meanwhile to raid parishes like San Pablo del Campo and Nuestra Señora de Montserrat in search of subversive material in a way that was becoming all too familiar in the Catalan and Basque provinces in these years. Other priests were put on trial for attending illegal clandestine meetings of workers, or for allowing their churches to be used for such meetings. At the height of this activity in March 1969 no fewer than 400 Catalan priests met to discuss the situation. The number of priests involved was immensely important: the phenomenon was not that of a few young radicals who could be allowed to tire themselves tilting at armoured windmills, but rather a major shift in the self-understanding and social and political role of hundreds of post-civil war priests. The other notable feature of the turbulence was the seriousness of the new commitment, ending for some in imprisonment and hunger strikes. In the last months of Franco's life, the Escolapian priest Luis María Xirinacs from Barcelona embarked on his fifth hunger strike, this time from Carabanchel gaol and with the unsuccessful aim of gaining an amnesty for political prisoners. The prophet's role was costly.[45]

The cost was highest, however, in the Basque provinces, especially in Vizcaya and Guipúzcoa where Basque nationalism was strongest. It was also here that the overlap between regionalist militancy and the radicalizing effects of the industrial and rural Catholic workers' associations was particularly powerful. Both for its overwhelming political importance—as viewed from Madrid as well as from Bilbao—and for the extreme version it presented of tensions between diocesan clergy and their bishops that existed less acutely elsewhere, the mobilization of a sector of the Basque clergy must be studied in some detail. Bitter memories of the civil war were ineradicable, and the first expressions of clerical discontent from within the Basque dioceses—as opposed to those emanating from numerous groups in exile—were in direct continuity with claims made before the war. Demands in 1950 for Basque-speaking bishops and the use of Basque in seminaries and in preaching already had a long tradition behind them. They were accompanied by newer complaints arising from the war itself and the regime that followed it, such as Bishop Múgica's prolonged exile, the deafening silence of Church authorities about Basque clergy executed, imprisoned and exiled during the war, and the Church's reluctance to speak out for human rights in the dictatorship.[46] Much fiercer was the famous letter of 30 May 1960 signed by 339 Basque priests and addressed to the incumbents of the four Basque sees. It gave a long list

[45] Many of the conflicts are detailed in *El Vaticà i Catalunya*. 2nd edn. (Paris, 1971). By courtesy of Don Ander Manterola, I also had access to a collection of cyclostyled and typescript documents in Derio, Manterola archive, legajo 1.3.1. Iglesia catalana y otras.

[46] See, e.g., the letter from Guipúzcoan priests in 1950 to Font, first bishop of San Sebastián, in A. Onaindía (ed.), *Ayer como hoy. Documentos del clero vasco* (St. Jean de Luz, 1975), 160–72.

of Francoist infractions of human rights normally defended by the Church, ranging from a servile judiciary and censorship to police use of torture, and governmental policies in the area tending towards genocide.[47] The real crisis, however, came in the last decade of Franco's dictatorship, when the new liberal and reforming consciousness inspired by Pope John XXIII combined with a more combative social and political stance by priests and laity on the one side, met ever harsher official measures on the other, notably a brutal use of the 1960 decree on banditry and terrorism which equated many kinds of political action with military rebellion, and the states of exception declared in part or all of the Basque provinces in 1967, twice in 1968, 1969, twice in 1970, and twice in 1975. During states of exception—in which constitutional rights were suspended—large numbers of people were imprisoned without trial, and tortured.

On 1 November 1964 Fr. Albert Gabocacogeascoa, a young chaplain to the agrarian branch of Catholic Action (JARC), preached a sermon in Ajurias y Magunas, Vizcaya, which was firmly based on the writings of Pius XII and John XXIII concerning the basic right to self-expression and access to true information. Having established this theoretical base, however, he went on to a detailed analysis of contraventions of these rights in the Basque area, particularly in the police use of torture.[48] This sermon launched Gabocacogeascoa into sustained criticism of the local and national civil authorities, in which many local priests followed him. There were demonstrations of solidarity by other priests when he was brought to trial, first in Guernica then in Madrid, and for the next ten years new meaning was breathed into the traditional opening address of homilies 'my dear brethren' as priests suffered heavy fines for what they described as denunciations of injustice and what the civil governors described as offences against public order. In the parish of San Fernando, Bilbao, on 7 January 1966 the Jesuit David Armentia, worker-priest and chaplain to HOAC, listed some of the errors and evils perpetrated in the name of God, including the death of Jesus, the Inquisition, and the Spanish civil war.[49] In Menaca on 3 December 1967 Fr. Patxi Bilbao Atxikallende marked the beginning of Advent by distributing a signed protest at the arbitrary arrest and torture of young Basque nationalists. On 28 January 1968 in Baracaldo, an industrial suburb of Bilbao, Fr. José Manuel Olabarría preached on the theme of

[47] *Ayer como hoy. Documentos del clero vasco* (St. Jean de Luz, 1975), 174–243.
[48] Text in Manterola archive, legajo 1.1.4. Escritos del clero.
[49] Ibid.

the liberating work of God as revealed in the Old Testament, going on to draw a parallel between the Jews oppressed in Egypt and the Basques. Both men were brought to trial, but sixty-six local priests signed a letter affirming the truth of the charges of torture made by their two colleagues, and lamenting the failure of the bishops of the Basque dioceses to do the same.[50]

In a very tense atmosphere, relatively small incidents set up chain reactions. For example, in May 1965 a children's *fiesta* in Ibarruri, Gabocacogeascoa's parish, was deemed by the authorities a demonstration of solidarity, and they fined the parish priest and Fr. Ander Manterola, diocesan chaplain of the female branch of JARC. The police auctioned the latter's car to raise the fine, which in turn led to a protest demonstration by about 100 priests and many lay people.[51] A group identity was developing, especially among the younger priests. In March 1966 the chaplains of the Basque-speaking section of the female JARC groups wrote to the nuncio stating that dialogue with their bishop was impossible, and calling attention to the entry of some of their young laity into clandestine political-patriotic nationalist organizations (that is, into ETA), and begging for some hierarchical backing of priests who denounced police violence.[52] Finally, in 1968, battle was joined on a large scale and irrevocably. In June an ETA leader, Xabier Etxebarrieta Ortiz, was killed by the Civil Guard in Guipúzcoa. Requiem masses arranged for him in his home town of Mondragón and elsewhere were banned by the civil governor. A couple of months later, in August, ETA embarked on a new policy of deliberate assassination of political, military, and police leaders when they killed the head of the *Brigada Social* in San Sebastián, Melitón Manzanas, and provoked a state of exception in the area in which hundreds of people were detained.[53] Also in August Bishop Bereciartua of San Sebastián published his unprecedented pastoral letter criticizing the state's recourse to military justice and violence in Guipúzcoa.[54] And in 1968 the extraordinary phenomenon of a prison exclusively for priests was inaugurated in Zamora with the detention there of Alberto Gabocacogeascoa, soon to be followed by many others. (The provision of special centres for priests convicted in

---

[50] Ibid., 1.1.1. Conflictos clero.
[51] Ibid., 1.4.1. Erri-Gaztedi (JARC/F). Documentación general.
[52] Ibid., 1.4.3. Erri-Gaztedi. Informe sobre Vizcaya. For the links between Catholic Action groups and ETA, see below, p. 234.
[53] On Etxebarrieta and Manzanas, see *ETA Documentos* vi (Donostia, no date), 525–39.
[54] See below, p. 251.

civil or military courts was agreed in theory in the 1953 concordat, article 16 clause 5, but the requirement in clause 4 that the local ordinary's permission be sought before proceeding against a priest was often ignored, or his refusal overridden.)

Amid extreme political tension, the public interventions by sectors of the Basque clergy culminated with a sit-in by sixty priests in the Bilbao diocesan seminary at Derio in November, after earlier occupation of the diocesan offices in Bilbao. From there they addressed a letter to Pope Paul VI. It was written in Spanish and Basque, and declared the aim of the clergy to be ecclesiastical reform. After an analysis of the Basque situation and of the Church, it detailed the proposals of the group for a poor, independent, dynamic, and indigenous Church, liberated from the various captivities represented by wealth, affiliation with the Francoist state, Spanish culture and personnel, and the authority of the Spanish Episcopal Conference.[55] The twenty-five-day occupation of the seminary was a dramatic crisis that is both instructive in retrospect and was decisive in many different ways at the time. It is interesting to note that almost all of the sixty priests were from rural parishes with strong connections with JARC associations.[56] Their frustration had reached an intolerable pitch because it combined so many different strands: shame at the Church's support of a dictatorship; anger at the social and economic changes in the Basque area, especially the immigration of a non-Basque proletariat before and after the civil war and the progressive emptying of the rural areas where both Basque language and Catholic practice were most widespread; despair at the evolution of ETA into full-scale terrorist activity and the distancing of its members from—in many cases—their original Catholic allegiances; and fury at an uncomprehending local Church hierarchy. Their occupation of the seminary, guarded without by police and suffering within the indignity of suspension by the bishop from use of their sacerdotal faculties was all too apt a symbol of the total impasse in which they were trapped.

A way out was created by the timely—from their point of view, perhaps providential—death of Bishop Gúrpide on 18 November. With uncharacteristic speed the Vatican named his successor within hours, and Cirarda defused the situation by swiftly creating new diocesan pastoral structures and appointing some of the seminary occupiers to posts of responsibility, lifting Gúrpide's suspension and generally making

[55] Text in P. Iztueta, *Sociología del fenómeno contestatorio del clero vasco 1940–75* (San Sebastián, 1981), 420–33.
[56] A fact noted ibid., 169–70.

clear that dialogue—to use the jargon of the ecclesiastical moment—was possible. Cirarda succeeded in re-integrating into the ordinary life of the diocese many men whose frustration had pushed them almost beyond its limits, and certainly beyond the comprehension of some older and less alienated colleagues. In the bitter years from 1969 to 1975 relations between bishops and clergy in the two crucial dioceses of Bilbao and San Sebastián were on the whole less strident, but the political and nationalist conflict between some priests and the dictatorship became even more intense.

On 30 May 1969 five Basque priests initiated a hunger strike in the diocesan offices in Bilbao. Jesús Naverán, Javier Amuriza, Julen Kalzada, Alberto Gabocacogeascoa, and Nicolás Tellería saw their action as 'a cry of protest and struggle on behalf of the oppressed among our people ... a complement to the still inadequate voice of the Church hierarchy'.[57] In contrast to the seminary occupiers of the previous year, they launched their appeal not just to Church leaders but to the Minister of Justice, the international Red Cross, and the United Nations as well as Bishop Cirarda. They drew attention to torture, the ever intensifying 'hunting of men', and the harsh treatment by police and employers of workers involved in labour disputes in huge heavy industrial firms such as Altos Hornos and Babcock Wilcox. Their way of opposing the terrorism of the state left behind the earlier methods of clerical resistance, and the Catholic state punished their temerity with prison sentences of twelve years in two cases and ten in the other three. In Zamora they were joined by other priests—mainly Basques, but with some Catalans and a few from elsewhere, like Mariano Gamo from the Madrid suburb Moratalaz—usually for short terms imposed for unacceptable preaching and writing. But much fiercer sentences were faced by Zamora's most famous inmates, nineteen years from the infamous trial 1001 for the Jesuit Francisco García Salve, for involvement with the illegal, Communist-led Workers' Commissions, and fifty years and twelve respectively for Jon Etxabe and, again, Julen Kalzada from the equally notorious Burgos trial, for their links with ETA.[58]

The fifteen defendants in the Burgos trial of 1969–1970 were between them charged with a number of terrorist offences, including the murder

[57] Text ibid., 359–60, or in A. Onaindía, *Ayer como hoy*, 308–11.
[58] These facts are well known, but gathered in this instance from accounts written by the Zamora priests themselves in 1972, 73, 74. Manterola archive, legajo 1.2.5. Cárcel concordataria (Zamora). Their 1972 *Informe* to the Spanish bishops is printed in R. Mate and others, *Herria-Eliza. Euskadi. pueblo-iglesia* (San Sebastián, 1978), 427–36.

of the police chief Manzanas.[59] In the course of the trial, Etxabe claimed that fidelity to the gospels led him to side with the oppressed, while Kalzada said priests had a duty to be politically committed and that he had carried arms in order to protect his people against the police and would do so again. Burgos marked the nadir of Church–state relations, not because two priests were on trial for membership of a terrorist organization but because of what that revealed of the sympathies and behaviour of a much bigger network of priests and because of the stance taken by the hierarchy. It was the bishops of Bilbao and San Sebastián, supported by the Spanish Episcopal Conference, who led the successful petition for the trial to be in public and for death sentences (there were nine in all) to be commuted to imprisonment, and the unsuccessful request that the hearing be before a civil not a military court. It was the same bishops who implicitly queried the regime's credentials as arbiter of justice when they condemned institutionalized violence as well as the terrorist variety.[60] The role of sectors of the Basque clergy is harder to define. After ETA's switch to assassination tactics in 1968 very few like Etxabe committed themselves openly to its cause. Others were caught up in the struggle by declining to hand over to the police terrorists who sought their help, as was the case with the five priests who helped ETA militant Mikel Etxebarria evade the police after the killing of taxi-driver Fermín Monasterio in March 1969, and two of whom, Fr. Joseba Atxa and Fr. Martín Orbe, were tortured when being questioned by the police.[61] More were involved indirectly in a way best summed up in the words of one of the men condemned to death at Burgos, Eduardo Uriarte, who later wrote, 'the clergy created many ETA militants, through what was a kind of religious mysticism combined with political mysticism'; or, more succinctly, 'they preached, but we did it'.[62] And beyond these was the much greater number who simply suffered and criticized the effects in the Basque provinces of a centralizing military dictatorship. Perhaps the best index of the relative strength of these different groups is the tiny nucleus of irreconcilables

---

[59] For an account of the Burgos trial see K. Salaberri, *El proceso de Euskadi en Burgos* (Paris, 1971).

[60] See below, pp. 251, 252.

[61] Interview 24 Sept. 1981 in Bilbao with Fr. José Ángel Ubieta, who in 1969 was Vicar General of the Bilbao diocese, named by Atxa and Orbe under torture as approving their act (though retrospectively), imprisoned for 72 hours, but released because Cirarda and other bishops refused permission for any process against him.

[62] Teo Uriarte, 'Un condenado a muerte en Burgos pone a ETA contra la pared', *Muga* no. 17, año ii, 4–18. José Ángel Ubieta kindly drew my attention to this article.

left after the dictatorship was dismantled, who saw their Herria-Eliza organization as the true precipitate of the ferment of 1960–75.[63] But their stridency was no substitute for a wider solidarity: for the great majority of Basque priests who came through these appalling years without total disillusion, changes first in the Church and then in the state defused, if they did not eradicate, the emphasis on confrontation.

The personal and pastoral price of the closing years of Franco's regime was high. A study of the figure of the priest in Bilbao diocese, commissioned by the bishop in 1969 and published in 1971, could scarcely avoid the title *Sociological Analysis of Sacerdotal Conflicts in the Diocese of Bilbao*. It was based on a questionnaire to the clergy and reflected clearly the 'chaotic and desperate' pastoral situation invoked by 516 priests as their reason for writing to the nuncio asking for intervention from Rome during the 1968 seminary occupation. 46% were discontent with the traditional role of the priest and over 25% positively endorsed 'dissident' or 'prophetic' action. While almost half saw no overwhelming pastoral problems in the area's political situation, one third thought it effectively annulled any and every pastoral undertaking, while 13% denied even the possibility of working as priests until political conflict was resolved. More than half wanted the hierarchy to back up more firmly priests in difficulty with civil authorities. At one extreme twenty priests considered it a duty to inculcate loyalty to Spain, and at the other, five priests thought it right even to resort to violence in the Basque cause, while the majority reckoned they should expound the political teaching of the Church and thereby clarify 'the legitimate claims of our Basque people'.[64]

In very many ways, however—for instance in widespread dissatisfaction with their own formation and with the sacerdotal role they had inherited—priests in Vizcaya shared confusions and criticisms common throughout Spain, and aired in the exhaustive questionnaires preparatory to the joint assembly of bishops and priests in September 1971. Of approximately 16,000 priests in sixty dioceses who answered the questionnaire, 41% felt insecure in their theology, and 51% in moral issues; three quarters felt they lacked the doctrinal preparation to help lay people think out economic, social, and political questions. If the old doctrinal and moral certitudes had gone, so had political conformism:

---

[63] For Herria-Eliza priests as seen by themselves, see especially R. Mate and others, *Herria-Eliza. Euskadi. pueblo-iglesia.*

[64] *Diagnóstico sociológico de los conflictos sacerdotales en la diócesis de Bilbao* (Bilbao, 1971), 23, 56, 68–71, 91–92 (published for circulation only to priests of the diocese).

only one in ten approved of the contemporary political regime, whereas the sympathies of more than a third lay with socialism or workers' movements. For more than half, disagreement between different groups of priests in their dioceses seemed a real problem. Some thought it inappropriate for a priest to be also a worker, or teacher, but more disagreed. Only a minority approved of the way Spanish bishops used their authority, and nearly half wanted celibacy to be optional.[65]

Much the most famous happening in the joint assembly was the passage by a majority, but not the requisite two-thirds majority for formal acceptance, of the statement that,

> we humbly recognize and ask pardon that we did not know how, when it was necessary, to be true 'ministers of reconciliation' in the midst of our people torn by a fratricidal war.[66]

Behind that confession lay not just a shift in political perspective but a revolution in ecclesiology, and behind that in theology, that both depended upon and informed a critical socio-economic analysis of contemporary Spain. While right-wing critics decried what seemed to them the new phenomenon of priestly involvement in politics, what was in fact new was the kind of politics, the kind of theology, that accompanied it and the kind of self-understanding many priests had espoused. Just as the range of clerical dress now extended from the traditional soutane to coloured open-necked shirts and jeans, so there was no unanimity about what a priest should be. Preachers of 'prophetic' homilies had little in common with Opus Dei priests, for instance, or with the Spanish Sacerdotal Brotherhood of St. Antonio María Claret and St. John of Ávila that appeared in 1969. Its members confidently repudiated 150 years of biblical criticism and proclaimed the Bible 'the holy book written by the finger of God and, therefore, infallible in every part'. They wanted authority and obedience reinstated in place of new-fangled 'maturity and responsibility' and inveighed against communism, immorality on the beaches, 'prophetic groups', pluriformity, and ecumenism. Less democracy and more discipline, less sociology and more piety was their message. With their campaign for a continuation of the confessional state went a rather forlorn struggle to maintain status, as they lamented the loss of that dignity formerly enjoyed by Spanish priests.[67] For them,

[65] *Asamblea conjunta obispos-sacerdotes* (Madrid, 1971), 651, 688–92.
[66] Ibid., 170.
[67] Manifestos in 'En defensa de la verdad de la Iglesia', *Iglesia Viva*, 35/36 (1971), 401–12.

the status quo just after the war had been ideal and they found the retrospective communal confession of inadequacy during a war glorious for its martyrs quite grotesque.

It would be difficult to catalogue all the books, symposia, lectures, questionnaires, and special issues of ecclesiastical journals dedicated between 1968 and 1975 to the crisis in the Spanish clergy. Analyses of worker priests, married priests, ex-priests, reactionary priests, priests in prison, abounded, testifying to the irreconcilable disagreements within the ordained ministry. In the profusion of images the old stereotype of the pious but narrow peasant's son who entered a seminary at twelve and lived in ignorance thereafter of contemporary culture was lost for ever. Many Spanish priests in every generation had been devout, conscientious men, respected for their personal austerity. Now, however, it was often unclear how to strive towards the ideal of holiness in a modern world in which the old conventions governing priestly behaviour were crumbling. Uncertainty was compounded by the unanswered question as to what the new roles of the clergy, and the committed laity, might become in an age with far fewer priests.

PART II
Catholic Politics

Carlists + Integrists
hostility to article 11 of 1876 constitution which permitted
private non-Catholic religious practice torments Carlists
etc. Jesuits esp. imp. – campaigns + concentration
Basque Country + Catalonia : issue steadily (from 1870,)
marginalised by nationalism/separatism
equation Liberalism + Sin

no large Cath. party, but no Kulturkampf, by contrast
clergy paid, protected, richly privileged
various unsuccessful attempts form Cath. party, Conservative
party more committed to em

Cath revival b. not pop., ↑ c-r properties fear

5

The Politics of Restoration   *liberal Carlism cons.*

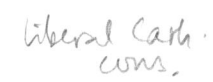

CATHOLIC attitudes to Spanish politics between 1875 and 1975 were determined as much by their basic attitude toward the regime in power as by any current problem or controversy. There never was a single unchallenged Catholic option, nor a comprehensive Catholic political organization. Nevertheless, it is evident that Primo de Rivera's dictatorship of 1923–30 and the first decades of Franco's dictatorship met with a general approval denied the republic of 1931–6 and never fully accorded the constitutional monarchy of 1876–1923. The Spanish Church found it hard to come to terms with parliamentary democracy and pluralism, and for a long time much preferred an authoritarian regime that defended its doctrines and controlled its enemies.

The constitutional monarchy of Alfonso XII caused more controversy among Catholics at its inception than any of the others because it neither threatened anti-clerical disasters nor promised tranquillity. On the one hand it protected the Church mightily, which was extremely welcome after the battering received since the September revolution of 1868 deprived Isabel II of her throne. It acknowledged the Catholic, Apostolic, Roman religion as the religion of state in article 11 of the 1876 constitution; it paid stipends to the diocesan clergy; it prohibited any public expression of other religions; it stipulated that all education in Spain must be Catholic; it made archbishops ex officio senators and rapidly filled more than thirty vacant episcopal sees; it restored the validity in civil law of canonical marriage; it facilitated the expansion of the religious congregations. There might seem little left for Catholics to desire in this confessional state. On the other hand, however, article 11 of the constitution explicitly granted toleration to the private practice of cults other than Catholicism, in contravention of the first article of the supposedly still binding concordat of 1851. Article 11 of the new constitution read:

The Apostolic, Roman, Catholic religion is the religion of the state. The nation binds itself to the maintenance of this cult and its ministers. In Spanish territory, no one shall be molested on account of his religious convictions or participation in religious rites, as long as Christian morals are duly respected. However, no public ceremonies or demonstrations other than those of the religion of the state shall be permitted.

Hopes for total religious uniformity were dashed. Spain would not be entirely and exclusively Catholic.

Cánovas del Castillo had carefully constructed the new constitutional system to accommodate as wide a spectrum of the political nation as possible. But just as some Republicans remained irreconcilable at one extreme, so did many Catholics on the other, especially among the Carlists who had just fought their second civil war in forty years to try to secure not only an acceptable branch of the Bourbon dynasty on the throne, but also an uncompromisingly Catholic monarchy. For these Traditionalist Catholics, article 11 was unclean meat that could not be digested without incurring impurity and falling into apostasy. Their abhorrence of the new diet would have disrupted the Church as little as it did the recently pacified state, however, had it not been in perfect harmony with wider ecclesiastical distaste for Cánovas's religious compromise.

Toleration of 'untruth' was liberal, and no adjective was more charged with disdain and opprobrium in Catholic nineteenth-century vocabulary in Spain and in the Vatican. Rather than accept this most moderate of concessions to liberalism, then, as the best that could be hoped for in a country that had recently experimented with a constitution granting full religious liberty,[1] the Vatican pressed for the restoration of complete Catholic uniformity. Pius IX's Secretary of State, Antonelli, protested against the draft article 11 in the autumn of 1875 to the Spanish government, and a month before the debate on religious toleration opened in parliament in April 1876 the pope himself wrote an intransigent repudiation to Cardinal Moreno of Toledo with explicit orders to publish it.[2]

In letters from each ecclesiastical province to the king or Cortes, speeches in the Senate, and pastoral letters to priests and people, the Spanish bishops adopted a hostile stance and called on all Catholics to do the same. Catalan bishops, among others, argued that Catholics

[1] For a detailed study of the constituent Cortes of 1869, see S. Petschen, *Iglesia-estado. Un cambio político. Las constituyentes de 1869.*

[2] This account of Vatican and episcopal initiatives and their repercussions in Spain is based on D. Benavides Gómez, *Democracia y cristianismo en la España de la restauración 1875-1931* (Madrid, 1978), 21-5, and M. F. Núñez Muñoz, *La iglesia y la restauración 1875-1881* (Tenerife, 1976), 211-32.

could not vote in the 1876 elections for any candidate who should approve article 11. The archbishop of Seville ordered public prayers to safeguard Catholic unity and asked dolefully whether Jesus Christ would be permitted exclusive dominion in Spanish institutions, laws, and customs as heretofore, or whether he would have to compete with 'error and heresy'.[3] Since from the point of view of the government this stream of protests represented unwarranted intervention in political matters, it attempted to censor episcopal documents before publication. The bishop of Orihuela seems to have been the only bishop to see things the government's way and actually forbade his clergy to get involved.

It is impossible to understand episcopal opposition to the 1876 liberal constitution and the consequent sympathy for Carlist and then Integrist alternatives if one does not recognize that the roots of disagreement lay in theories and convictions not primarily political but ecclesiological. For pope and bishops, the identification of other religious traditions with error was axiomatic. Because they regarded the Catholic Church—as their entire ecclesiastical, apologetic education had trained them to do—as the unique source of pure truth in a world contaminated by error, they lacked a conceptual framework which could comprehend religious pluralism of even the most limited kind. The ideal remained Catholic hegemony as promised in the 1851 concordat: any dilution of this hegemony was interpreted less as political accommodation to changing circumstances than as religious infidelity and apostasy. The sanctioning of limited pluriformity seemed, therefore, a national perversity to avert which the bishops campaigned against the private practice of non-Catholic cults with all the moral fervour expended a little later in England against the supposed undermining of a different national morality by the private practice of homosexuality.

Profound regret for an apparently irrecoverable Catholic uniformity had a more pervasive influence on the Spanish hierarchy than the more direct political option of Carlist loyalty. Moreover, during the first five years of the restoration, thirty-one new bishops were consecrated for Spain and its remaining colonies—an enormous number which accounted for half the total. It was fortunate for Alfonso XII that the political chaos of the previous years had prevented a more gradual filling of vacant sees, and with the Carlist war hardly over, the major preoccupation of the government was inevitably the dynastic loyalty of candidates for episcopal consecration. In accordance with well-established regalist tradition, the governments of Alfonso XII and Alfonso

[3] *BEAS* (1876), 73-4.

XIII intervened directly in the selection and translation of bishops. The new restoration appointments were chosen sometimes from lists prepared by the Vatican and the nuncio, but sometimes the initiative came from the Minister of Grace and Justice, to whom members of parliament for the relevant area were not shy in proposing candidates.[4] Cánovas himself prevailed on a rather reluctant Vatican to appoint the insignificant Pedro Sánchez Carrasco to the vacant Ávila see because of his alacrity in announcing from the pulpit Alfonso XII's succession.[5] As late as 1899 the then Minister of Grace and Justice, Durán i Bas, sought firm reassurances that Torras i Bages was not a man of Carlist sympathies before proceeding with his nomination to the see of Vich, which had been a noted centre of clerical Carlism and Integrism.[6]

Within a decade of Alfonso's accession, the great majority of the hierarchy were not directly associated with Carlism. Moreover, only two years after the bitter confrontation over article 11, Pius IX died and his successor, Leo XIII, soon urged that Spanish Catholics should accept a constitution so recently rejected as ungodly. But Vatican and hierarchy were largely responsible for what both soon came to deplore, namely that a small but articulate minority of Catholics within Traditionalist circles continued to equate article 11 with national apostasy and therefore to oppose the liberal constitution—and the majority of Catholics who accepted it—with a ferocity drawn from a conviction of righteousness.

To substantiate their claim against the liberal monarchy, Traditionalist Catholics could point not only to the papal and episcopal views expressed so vehemently in 1875–6 but also to the immensely influential *Syllabus of Errors* attached to Pius IX's encyclical letter *Quanta Cura* of 1864. That exhaustive denunciation of all that was liberal and secularizing in the modern state, and the notorious final item of the long list that rejected the 'error' that the pope in Rome should accommodate himself to 'progress, liberalism and modern civilization' was quoted constantly in Traditionalist literature as proof that Catholics could not be assimilated within the Canovite system.

Leo XIII set out to rally Spanish Catholics to the constitutional monarchy as he rallied French Catholics to the Third Republic with, in both cases, rather indifferent results. In an encyclical letter addressed

[4] For details of these appointments, see Núñez Muñoz, 98–119.
[5] Ibid., 107–8.
[6] J. Bonet i Baltà, 'Eclesiàstics de Barcelona enaltits en el consistori papal de 1899: Vives i Tutó—Morgades—Torras i Bages', *Analecta Sacra Tarraconensia*, xxxvii (1964), 231–72.

specifically to Spanish Catholics in 1882, *Cum Multa*, Leo appealed for unity and pointed out the error 'of those who confuse and virtually identify their religion with one political party, even to the extent of regarding as little less than alienated from Catholicism those who belong to another party'. Priests were asked not to give themselves up to party passion, and newspapers conducting campaigns ostensibly in the name of the Church were reminded of the need for charity. Three years later, *Immortale Dei* developed a doctrine of reconciliation applicable to the recalcitrant Catholic Right in Spain and France when it insisted that no form of government was condemned by the Church unless it was directly repugnant to Catholic teaching. The form of government was 'accidental' from an ecclesiastical viewpoint, rather than in itself of fundamental importance—an argument that was to be given another stormy passage in the troubled constitutional waters of 1931–6.[7] In *Libertas* of 1888 the pope invoked the principle of the lesser evil in order to combine a denunciation of modern liberties, including freedom of the press, freedom of conscience, and religious toleration, with an acknowledgement that public authorities sometimes have to permit these things 'for the sake of avoiding a greater evil, or of obtaining or preserving some greater good'.[8] In other words, Leo did not disagree with his predecessor that total interpenetration of Church and state in complete Catholic harmony was the ideal: but as Bishop Dupanloup of Orleans had done when the *Syllabus* was issued, he urged that where the ideal could not be achieved, compromise to avert further harm was acceptable. The Catholic Church did not recognize freedom of religion as a human right until the 1960s.[9] Pope and bishops alike, therefore, were reluctant to consider Catholic religious monopoly a lost cause. Article 11 was a necessary and tolerable, but perhaps reversible evil. A negative, or at best a provisional air, continued to emanate from Church statements with a bearing on the regime.

Catholic Traditionalists, to whom these pleas for compromise were mainly addressed, were not impressed. Liberalism was evil, and must be opposed in the name of Catholic truth. Not only did article 11 permit the existence of heterodoxy on Spanish soil, but article 12 allowed any

[7] See below, pp. 189–90.
[8] The quotation from *Cum Multa* is my own translation. Authorized English translations of *Immortale Dei* and *Libertas* were published, viz., *On the Christian Constitution of States* (London, 1886), and *On Human Liberty* (London, 1888).
[9] For a useful account of this fundamental controversy on the eve of the Second Vatican Council, see A. F. Carrillo de Albornoz, *Roman Catholicism and Religious Liberty* (Geneva, 1959).

Spaniard to found an educational institute 'in accordance with the laws'. The suspicion that this would open the way to institutions unsympathetic to Catholic principles was not fully allayed by the earlier ministerial circular of 1875, reaffirming the Catholic character of all university education and thereby provoking an exodus of university lecturers unwilling to conform. When Orovio's circular was abrogated in 1881, confessional control of university education lay in ruins, and the concordat had been contravened. Ideological pluriformity secured a base; bishops and many other Catholics were dismayed, and the unreconciled Right was, in its own eyes, again vindicated.

The religious force behind the Traditionalist position can best be seen in the appearance as late as 1888, and survival for some years thereafter, of a dissident integrist wing that abandoned the eponymous dynastic leader in favour of an extreme religious programme for 'integral' unsullied Catholicism separate from Carlism. From the time of the 1875–6 controversies, however, the Integrist trend within Carlism under Candido and then Ramón Nocedal with their newspaper *El Siglo Futuro* had constituted the irreducible core of Catholic opposition to the Alfonsine monarchy. The manifesto they issued in 1888 as they left Don Carlos and his—to them—unduly compromising and conciliatory tendencies reveals the extreme though imprecise theocratic aspirations that fired Integrist zeal.

God is first and most important, and Catholic unity is the first fundamental law of Spanish society ... It is the social reign of Jesus Christ; it is Jesus Christ ruling in the laws and customs, in public and private institutions, in all teaching, in all spoken and written propaganda, in the king as in his subjects; it is, in one word, the government of Christ the King, absolute Lord and Master of all things.[10]

Given the tiny number of Traditionalist deputies in parliament (for example two Carlists after the 1881 elections, and two Integrists and four Carlists in the 1890 elections after the Integrist excision), the disruptive vigour of the Traditionalists within the Church requires some explanation.[11] The first immediately obvious feature of the Carlist and then Integrist movement was its concentration in well defined areas, especially Navarre, the Basque provinces and Catalonia, within which

[10] In M. Tirado y Rojas, *León XIII y España* (Madrid, no date but *c.* 1903), 91.
[11] For a brief study of Integrism, see J.N. Schumacher, SJ, 'Integrism: a study in nineteenth century Spanish politico-religious thought', *The Catholic Historical Review*, xlviii (1962), 343–64. The interpretation I offer gained in detail and depth from a conversation in Barcelona, 12 July 1982, with Fr. Joan Bonet i Baltà, who probably knows more than anyone else about the Catholic Traditionalist controversies of the period.

it had overwhelming clerical support.[12] In these areas wounded religious sensibilities were sharpened by regional disaffection from the untrustworthy centralized state. It is not accidental that the notorious and sustained Traditionalist commitment of the Basque and Catalan clergy declined in the 1890s at the same time as the Basque Nationalist Party and a programme for Catalan autonomy began to offer an alternative Catholic, Basque, or Catalan, but not Carlist political option. Just as there is a continuity from the Navarrese guerilla priests who took up arms in the 1820s against the liberal constitution, through the Navarrese Carlist clergy of the later nineteenth century to the clerical enthusiasts for the armed uprising planned against the republic in the 1930s, so is there continuity from the Vizcayan or Guipuzcoan anti-constitutional priests of the 1820s whose successors were Carlists in the 1870s and Basque Nationalists fifty years later.[13] Only the Navarrese maintained *en masse* their Carlist allegiance well into the twentieth century, but in the Basque provinces and Catalonia, the formidable fusion of religious and regional, anti-centralist convictions in Carlism and Integrism also found different, nationalist expressions later, both in the early twentieth century and in the second half of the Franco regime.

One other clerical group must be mentioned if the force of Integrist Traditionalism within the Church is to be understood. The Integrist political views of many Jesuits provoked a scarcely veiled rebuke by Leo XIII in 1890. In a forthright letter to the bishop of Urgel he complained of the role of some ecclesiastics in causing division among Catholics on political matters and then went on to lament as even worse that 'some religious, distinguished of old by their fidelity to and love for the Apostolic See should secretly or publicly help in the ever wider propagation and total penetration of this evil, to the most grave danger of the highest interests of Church and country'.[14] As the pope's criticism recognized, Jesuit influence was most marked in propaganda, and the extension

---

[12] Joan Bonet i Baltà estimated that in the early 1880s, about 90% of Catalan priests were Carlist.

[13] For militant Basque and Catalan clergy in the first half of the 19th century see, P. de Montoya, *La intervención del clero vasco en las contiendas civiles (1820–1823)* (San Sebastián, 1971); J. F. Coverdale, *The Basque Phase of Spain's First Carlist War* (Princeton, 1984), e.g., 76, 79, 90, 115, 141, 145–6, 151, 273. For the transition from Carlism to Basque nationalism in provinces other than Navarre, see M. Blinkhorn, 'Ideology and Schism in Spanish Traditionalism 1876–1931', *Iberian Studies*, i (1972). For Navarrese priests preparing the uprising of 1936, see A. Lizarza Iribarren, *Memorias de la conspiración. Cómo se preparó en Navarra la Cruzada 1931–36* (Pamplona, 1953), 15, 81–2.

[14] Letter of 20 March 1890 published as an appendix to *Exhortación pastoral del obispo de Urgel sobre las actuales divisiones entre los católicos* (Madrid, 1890), 61–2.

and force of Integrist written propaganda was another cause of the movement's disproportionate influence. A constant Integrist campaign was waged in the *Messenger of the Sacred Heart* from 1883—when the Jesuits took it over—until well after Integrism as a separate political movement had disappeared. In August 1889 José García Romero, SJ, rued the day when 'Catholics forgot their faith' and passed the liberal constitution with its eleventh article on religious toleration; in 1895 José María Remesal, SJ, was still feeling scandalized at Catholic acceptance of the now twenty-year-old constitution; in 1896 Julio Alarcón, SJ, railed against 'false Catholics' and declared that one could be a sinner and a Catholic but not a liberal and a Catholic. In 1905 another Jesuit writer—almost certainly the editor Remigio Vilariño—assured his readers that liberalism 'is sinful in all its forms. And it is mortal sin. And it is not only probable but certain that it is mortal sin.' As late as 1916 Vilariño glanced back over the preceding years and noted with pleasure the *Messenger*'s untiring struggle against 'the error of liberalism in whatever shape or form', which still continued.[15] Jesuits also contributed frequently to the *Revista Popular* of the Catalan priest Sardá i Salvany, the most famous of all clerical Integrist propagandists, and a close collaborator of the Nocedals. They encouraged and advised him, and greeted triumphantly the approval of his extremely controversial work *Liberalism is Sin* by the Sacred Congregation of the Index in Rome in 1887. Luis Coloma, SJ, exalted him as the 'popular Balmes of our time' and F. Echevarría, SJ, thought his book should be 'the banner of all Catholics'.[16] Without the busy application of many Jesuit pens to the cause in popular religious publications, especially the *Messenger* and Sardá i Salvany's *Revista Popular* (distributed mainly in Catalonia), the political tenets of Integrist Traditionalism would not have been so widely and confidently proclaimed as tenets also of the Catholic faith. The Jesuits enjoyed an authority to assert that connection which no lay Integrist newspaper, however fervent, could possibly rival.

Priest journalists exploited two major attractions of Integrist Traditionalism. They identified a political option with religious doctrine and piety, thereby imbuing it with all the force of a sacred loyalty, while at the same time presenting a beguilingly simple choice between good and bad, fidelity and betrayal, truth and error. Both elements were likely to appeal to Carlist Catholics who in the 1870s had been prepared

[15] *Mensajero* (Aug. 1889), 97; (Apr. 1895), 304; (June 1896), 489–90; (Sept. 1905), 234; (June 1916), 522.
[16] Ibid. (Feb. 1887), 120–1; (June 1888), 482.

to face death in battle for the cause they held to be just. These characteristics were exemplified in Sardá i Salvany's *Liberalism is Sin*, whose incomparable fame and centrality among Integrist writings was demonstrated in bizarre fashion in 1891 when a polyglot version in eight languages appeared in Barcelona with a format similar to that of a huge illustrated family Bible. The argument was simply that all liberalism was sinful and that the 1876 constitution was liberal. The conclusion demanded by elementary syllogistic logic was not in doubt, and was applied ruthlessly to Catholics who combined orthodox religious practice with any kind of liberal, pluralist opinion in politics. In fact liberalism occupied, according to this book, a unique category of sinfulness, worse than—for example—blasphemy, adultery, or homicide. After the furore aroused by the Sacred Congregation of the Index's approval of the work, it was re-submitted and the Congregation then explained, not particularly helpfully, that it had merely judged the book's doctrinal orthodoxy and not the correctness of its application of doctrine to the actual political circumstances in Spain.[17]

Finally, newspapers remarkable for their stridency, headed by *El Siglo Futuro*, enabled 'Integral Catholicism' to make its presence felt in a way that was difficult to ignore. The Nocedals' paper engaged in polemics that set it against not only its liberal enemies but also the hierarchy and eventually Don Carlos himself. As early as 1881 he was repenting his decision two years earlier to have Candido Nocedal as his unique representative in Spain since *El Siglo Futuro*'s total rejection of the Canovite system seemed less and less realistic. On Candido Nocedal's death in 1885 Don Carlos declined to name his son Ramón as his representative, and in 1888 he withdrew authorization of *El Siglo Futuro*, precipitating the excision from Carlism of the Integrists and no fewer than twenty-five newspapers.[18] The parting of the ways in 1888 gravely weakened an already numerically small political movement, but Carlism before 1888 and its Integrist offshoot after, demonstrated the peculiar pugnacity of traditional Catholicism when allied with regional passion and confronted by a centralized state it found offensive on both political and religious grounds.

It took the Vatican and the restoration hierarchy thirty years to silence the clamour of Traditionalist opposition to the constitutional

---

[17] F. Sardá i Salvany, *El liberalismo es pecado* (Barcelona, 1884). For the controversy with the Sacred Congregation of the Index see Tirado y Rojas, 29–65.

[18] For the content and influence of *El Siglo Futuro*, see Benavides Gómez, *Democracia y cristianismo*, 13–207.

monarchy. Even among the bishops a few die-hards continued to regard party politics and religious toleration as aberrant. In the early 1880s Bishop Serra, titular of Daulia, quoted St. Paul's injunction 'to obey the higher powers' to demand obedience for the Carlist pretender, and disputed the need for any Catholic political organization other than the Traditionalist communion. Catholics content to operate within the liberal constitution should be repudiated as decisively as fourth-century Arians had been; if necessary the contest should go on for eight centuries, as had Catholic Spain's crusade against Islam. Even after Leo XIII's repeated calls for reconciliation in the 1880s, such die-hards could not bring themselves to believe that the pope meant what he said. As late as 1890 Bishop Casas Souto of Plasencia advised his clergy that none among the three republican and two Alfonsist monarchist parties could be supported by Catholics, since they were all liberal. This left, of course, only Carlist and Integrist options. Equally, it was only in 1890 that Cardinal Casañas, bishop of Urgel, eventually conceded defeat and—to the pope's immense satisfaction—wrote a famous pastoral letter urging sincere compliance with papal directives to recognize a legitimate plurality of political options.[19]

In Catalonia the dispute continued until almost the turn of the century. An Escolapio priest, Fr. E. Llanas, directed *El Criterio Católico* from 1884–1887 against Carlist Integrism and in 1888 published a commentary on the encyclical *Libertas* which, as its title *Is Liberalism Sin?* reveals, was also a refutation of Sardá i Salvany's work. Also in 1888 Josep Torras i Bages, then still a diocesan priest, published in Barcelona his brief but measured and influential study of the role of the clergy in modern social life in which he criticized the destructive character of much Catholic journalism and the political use of sermons by anti-liberal priests.[20] Such arguments, allied with papal pressure, the evident stability of the Canovite system, and disillusionment at the 1888 split, gradually deprived the intransigents of crucial support. In 1896 Sardá i Salvany himself published his dramatic article 'Cease fire' in the *Revista Popular* recognizing Carlists and even Alfonsists as 'Catholics like us', no doubt to the chagrin or scandal of many of his regular readers, long accustomed to quite different sentiments from his pen.[21]

[19] Serra's letter is in *La Ciencia Cristiana*, xvii (1881), 474–8; for Casas Souto, see Benavides Gómez, op. cit., 155; for Casañas's letter and the pope's response, see *Exhortación pastoral del obispo de Urgel sobre las actuales divisiones entre los católicos* (Madrid, 1890).
[20] J. Torras i Bages, *El clero en la vida social moderna* (Barcelona, 1888), especially 14–18, 64–6, 77ff.
[21] '¡Alta el fuego!', *Revista Popular*, 11 June 1896.

Last to lay down their arms were the Jesuits. Their journal *Razón y Fe* carried in 1905 an article by Venancio María Minteguiaga, SJ, expressing the view that Catholics could and should vote for Liberal candidates in the forthcoming municipal elections, especially if such candidates were Catholic themselves, in order to avoid the greater evil of Socialists and Republicans.[22] *Messenger* contributors remained unconvinced,[23] but the defection represented by Minteguiaga's article in the recently founded and much more weighty *Razón y Fe* was decisive. Moreover, Pius X continued his predecessor's policy of accommodating the lesser evil when—three years after becoming pope—he ratified Minteguiaga's views in his letter *Inter Catholicos Hispaniae* of 20 February 1906.[24] This Vatican line was reaffirmed in 1908 by Pius X's widely publicized series of norms for Spanish Catholics worked out with the help of a Catalan Capuchin resident in Rome, Cardinal Vives i Tutó. While maintaining, as always, the ideal of a state conforming in every way to Catholic teaching, these norms urged co-operation with the actual best available and discouraged abstention from elections or a priori opposition to the liberal system.

There the long and fruitless controversy might have rested, but for one further campaign, this time in the Basque country. The parliamentary debates on Canalejas's 'padlock bill' of 1910, designed to limit the religious congregations, provoked particular dismay in the Basque provinces. Since the beginning of the century José María Urquijo y Ibarra had been campaigning, both in the Cortes where in 1903 he took his seat for Bilbao as an anti-dynastic, independent Catholic, and in the Bilbao newspaper *La Gaceta del Norte* of which he was a founder, for a so-called Vaticanist policy of intransigence against the liberal monarchy. He now berated not just the 'padlock bill' but the liberal regime in its entirety, urging Catholic hostility, while contrary appeals for Catholic involvement to defend the Church were made in *El Pueblo Vasco*, notably by members of the Ibarra family. A deputation of Basque catholics associated with José María Urquijo went to Rome in the spring of 1911 to seek guidance. (Interestingly, the deputation included the young Angel Herrera whose views on the legitimacy of the 1931 republican regime were to be so crucially important for Catholic politics.) The

---

[22] V. M. Minteguiaga, 'Algo sobre elecciones', *Razón y Fe*, xiii (1905), 141–56. See also the article by P. Villada, SJ, on the same lines after the elections, 'De elecciones', *RyF*, xiv (1906), 450–63.
[23] *Mensajero* (Sept. 1905), 222–8, 234.
[24] Published as a supplement to *RyF*, xiv (1906), no. 55.

response to this and other requests for a papal ruling was, inevitably, a revised version of the 1908 norms, this time repudiating with particular energy the catastrophist tactics dear to the Catholic extreme Right of weakening or opposing the political system in the hope of subverting it altogether. Even in this final statement, however, in a letter from Secretary of State Merry del Val to Cardinal Aguirre, acceptance of the constitutional monarchy was finely balanced with encouragement of a Catholic reconquest aimed at the re-establishment of Catholic unity in Spain, and at the overthrow of all the errors listed in the *Syllabus* of 1864.[25]

Although Integrism was dead as a political force, and political participation within the terms of the 1876 constitution was actively encouraged, that constitution was still just the *mal menor*. Catholics were to participate in its elections and parliaments in the hope of transforming society and the state into the ecclesiastical ideal. And what was this ideal? Ultimately, it was the Counter-Reformation ideal of a confessional state in which the laws, and for that matter all the institutions of social and political life, would embody religious values and further religious aims. This remained the hope, if not the realistic expectation, of popes and bishops. While the hope persisted, the Church was bound to look to the state for defence and support. It could not irrevocably accept the process of secularization already discernible in article 11, that would gradually leave the Church to fight more of its own battles with ecclesiastical and religious, rather than political, weapons.

The 1876 constitution established the rules of the political game, but Church leaders never lost the hope of taking their places within a more congenial structure. Political implications were therefore rarely far beneath the surface of pastoral statements, while constitutional implications lay just one level further down. When the bishops of the Burgos ecclesiastical province in 1884 penned a forty-page tirade to be read in churches throughout the north of Spain protesting at the corruption of youth in contemporary society, they were fulfilling what they saw as an urgent pastoral obligation. But their ferocious onslaught on socialism, as well as naturalism and rationalism, as forces of corruption was also propaganda against political pluralism. Equally, their appeal to young people to avoid bad teachers, bad company, and bad books constituted

---

[25] Letter from Secretary of State Merry del Val to Cardinal Aguirre, 20 Apr. 1911, published in *RyF*, xxx (1911), 273-4.

at one level an unexceptionable defensive pastoral strategy while at another, it was, because of the ample definition of 'bad', a forthright denunciation of the liberal state that corrupted truth and right.[26] In 1883 the highly respected Archbishop Ceferino González argued in a pastoral letter that the only explanation for the lamentable loss of Catholic uniformity was ignorance and passion, and that rationalist or Protestant propaganda was anti-patriotic as well as anti-Christian.[27] The scope of the desired state defence of Catholicism was sketched in a later pastoral by González when he enumerated some dangerous influences to his no doubt bemused flock, most of whom until that moment would never have heard of eclecticism, Hegelianism, biblical criticism, materialist positivism, physiological psychology, ethnography, or geology.[28]

When, in 1916, Cardinal Guisasola Menéndez, archbishop of Toledo, wrote a courageous pastoral letter on the social injustices perpetrated against Spanish workers in the liberal capitalist economy, he criticized specific political abuses such as the manipulation of parliament. But since he also dismissed socialism as a bearer of hatred and war, and condemned liberal democracy in general, and its disrespect for the 'Catholic spirit of the country' in particular, for the evils he diagnosed, it is hard not to see again the usual longing for a Catholic, autocratic political system.[29] Competition from other ideologies was never tolerable, and could not be when they were automatically categorized as both erroneous and evil. The Church was a beleaguered fortress stoutly resisting the ungodly attacks of intellectual and moral modernity. Such an interpretation had budged little if at all from the utterly assured categories of the 1864 *Syllabus*, and was inherently anti-pluralist and anti-democratic. Moreover, these political preferences were all the firmer for being derived not from a political or economic analysis that could be modified, nor even from scriptural images and texts that could be argued over, but from a static ecclesiology which repelled complexity and ambiguity. Conversion or re-conversion to Catholic truth and rectitude remained the episcopal solution to the nation's problems. Inevitably, therefore, Spanish bishops greeted Primo de Rivera's coup in September 1923 with immense relief. National, Catholic regeneration

[26] *BEOV*, xx (1884).
[27] *BEAS* (1883-4), 3-43.
[28] *BEAS* (1886), 379-405.
[29] V. Guisasola Menéndez, *Justicia y caridad en la organización cristiana del trabajo* (Madrid, 1916).

was now, at last, on the agenda.[30] The rules of the game were, eventually, being decisively changed, and in the new dictatorship Church leaders expected to breathe a purer air while benefiting from partnership with a sympathetic, autocratic state partner.

Meanwhile, since such a solution could not be predicted, it was important to further Catholic interests by working within the structure of a regime which—if not ideal by the exacting standards of Catholic political theory—at least offered some enormous advantages. Ecclesiastical representation in the Cortes was already assured. Although the 1876 constitution stipulated that priests could not be parliamentary deputies in the lower house, all archbishops and the patriarch of the Indies were ex officio senators. Moreover, each of the nine archdioceses also elected a senator-representative, almost certain to be a bishop, and bishops formed one of the categories from which senators could be nominated by the crown. The senate regularly included, therefore, a contingent of at least nineteen bishops.

As to the political mobilization of the laity, a large confessional party on the model of the German Centre was unlikely to emerge for the very good reason that there was no Spanish equivalent of the *Kulturkampf*. On the contrary, in the Alfonsine state, the Church was paid, protected, and richly privileged. An early attempt to rally and organize Catholics failed. Inspired by the initiative of the French bishop, Freppel, in inviting his Catholic compatriots to unite on confessional matters notwithstanding political differences, Alejandro Pidal i Mon issued a similar call in the Spanish parliament on 16 June 1880. The oddity of the enterprise was betrayed by both the meticulous avoidance of the word 'party' in favour of the vague 'union', and by the variety of political views among the founders, who could only have been held together by discriminatory policies against Catholics. But the defence of family, property, and religion scarcely provided an adequate programme for action in a Spain in which none of the three was in danger. When a group of eminent laymen of strikingly diverse political convictions wrote in January 1881 to the hierarchy to launch the Catholic Union, the direction to be taken remained indistinct.[31] A concern for confessional control of education—already widespread and secure in practice except

---

[30] See, for example, the circulars by the archbishops of Seville and Toledo respectively, in *BEAS*, lxvi (1923), 277–80.

[31] Letter of 14 Jan. 1881 from Orgaz, Guaqui, Pidal i Mon, Mirabel, Canga Argüelles, Galindo y de Vera, and Carbonero y Sol, is in *La Ciencia Cristiana*, xvii (1881), 180–2.

at university level—and pious aims such as Sunday observance and the prevention of blasphemy were not powerful enough to galvanize Spanish Catholics into active association.

The Catholic Union was warmly encouraged by many bishops, including Cardinal Moreno, archbishop of the primatial see of Toledo, who presided over the enterprise and drew up a statement of its aims.[32] Others were not convinced. The archbishop of Valladolid responded very cautiously, unable to see what could come of the initiative except a 'monstrous and heterogeneous amalgam'. Archbishop Bienvenido of Granada was indignant that anything bearing the name Catholic had been launched by laymen, without prior ratification by the whole episcopate. He was also sceptical of an association of 'all good Catholics' that might give cover to those who approved liberal measures such as the seizure of papal lands, the *desamortización* of Church property, religious toleration, and freedom of the press. The bishop of Daulia was even more scathing of this attempt to unite true Traditionalist Catholics and liberal catholics, and wept to see the signatories of the latter along with Carlists like the Count of Orgaz.[33] Its episcopal critics suspected the Catholic Union of being a device to fudge crucial issues and neutralize the Carlists by diluting them within an amorphous Catholic association; its episcopal backers hoped it might shift Catholic attention from constitutional to religious matters while, precisely, neutralizing the troublesome Carlists.

Lay responses were similarly varied. Admirers of Cánovas argued that the natural organization for politically-minded Catholics was now Cánovas's Conservative party which had Church interests at heart but also embraced a proper range of other political concerns. From this perspective, the Catholic Union could never be more than an association of Catholic defence without any wider political scope.[34] Most Traditionalists inevitably loathed it as an attempt to stifle them in a sinful embrace.[35] The influential Traditionalist intellectual Juan Manuel Ortí y Lara had in 1875-6 bitterly opposed eminent lay Catholics like Vicente de la Fuente who accepted as inevitable the beginnings of a secularization of the state. In 1881, however, he welcomed the Catholic Union as a useful Trojan horse carrying dedicated Catholics into the enemy camp where they might be more effective, but soon withdrew

[32] His reply, and those of some other episcopal supporters, ibid., 182-7.
[33] Ibid., xviii, 94-6; xvii, 279-87, 474-8.
[34] See, for example, J. Sánchez de Toca, *Católicos y conservadores* (Madrid, 1885).
[35] For Carlist responses see Benavides Gómez, *Democracia y cristianismo*, 41-78.

his support on recognizing that this was not at all Pidal i Mon's intention.[36]

It is not surprising that the new association provoked such different reactions and a great measure of confusion. Indeed it is very difficult to see what Catholic mobilization for confessional purposes that did not challenge existing political commitments could have meant in practice. In the 1884 elections (from which Traditionalists abstained) twenty members of the Catholic Union gained Conservative seats, a development that had always been the natural Catholic alternative to the Traditionalist position. Pidal's appointment as a Minister in the Conservative government earned him unbridled scorn from the unreconciled Right, especially as he held responsibility for education where he necessarily failed to achieve the Catholic ideal of total ideological hegemony.[37] Carlist contempt notwithstanding, his political course from 1881 to 1884 was as realistic as it was predictable.

The Catholic Union gradually disappeared from the political scene but it left behind some unresolved questions and unfulfilled aspirations. Religious uniformity had been lost in 1876, but might not Catholic unity be made visible in some great national movement that influenced public and social life without creating a political party? In the desire for a permanent and comprehensive Catholic organization that would be neither overtly political nor merely devotional but, in Cardinal Moreno's words in 1881 'religious and social', there lay the seeds of future mobilization campaigns by a rather amorphous Catholic Action movement, controlled by the hierarchy and destined to greater longevity than its political expression—the Catholic Union—but equal sterility.

The choice of words is very revealing. A Catholic union or Catholic action was acceptable, while the notion of a Catholic party was suspect. 'Politics' was taken to mean party politics, and was often a pejorative term in Catholic vocabulary. This distaste lasted for decades beyond the initial controversies of the restoration. As late as 1931 Gil Robles's first mobilization of the Catholic Right called itself Popular Action and denied that it was a party, even though it issued manifestos and programmes and intended to fight elections. Similarly, Catholic associations with quite evidently conservative political values, like Angel Herrera's Propagandists, and the Opus Dei, consistently claimed they were apolitical

---

[36] For Ortí y Lara, see A. Ollero Tassara, *Universidad y política. Tradición y secularización en el siglo XIX* (Madrid, 1972), especially 147–71. He eventually rallied to the papal line in 1893 and left Nocedalian Traditionalism.

[37] Benavides Gómez, *Democracia y cristianismo*, 85–113.

because they did not constitute a party. The terminological idiosyncrasy is very significant. It has regarded permissible political differences as being of relatively minor importance, and assumed an underlying Catholic consensus or national religious identity that no political group could legitimately challenge. The limits of valid political disagreement were quite narrow. Accepting radical political pluriformity within Catholicism, and respecting the legitimacy of non-Catholic or anti-Catholic political options remained until almost the end of the Franco regime a difficult task for the Spanish Church.[38]

Paradoxically, this was again demonstrated in the last nineteenth-century plan for the political mobilization of Catholics, which actually did use the word 'party' although in a way that virtually emptied it of meaning. Between 1891 and 1896 Bishop Antonio María de Cascajares was distressed by not only the disunity of Catholics but also the crisis of the Canovite system as disagreements began to rend the Conservative party. Perhaps because of his noble lineage, so unusual among Spanish bishops, he was able to communicate his dissatisfaction to various eminent politicians and even the Queen Regent as well as within ecclesiastical circles. His solution to colonial problems, economic difficulties, and party fragmentation was a Catholic political party capable of offering the country timely, effective government. But, like General de Gaulle's *Rassemblement de Peuple Français* after the Second World War, Cascajares's projected organization was really to be an anti-party, an alternative to the ordinary political parties distrusted alike by the nineteenth-century cardinal—as he was from 1895—and the twentieth-century general, and for broadly similar reasons. Just as de Gaulle wanted a national movement of French patriots to counteract the sectional confrontations of the parties, so Cascajares wanted 'a truly national party, comprehending all honourable and truly patriotic men'. Since those left out would therefore be the dishonourable and the unpatriotic, the Catholic party would presumably not be one of two or more in a pluralist regime so much as the necessary instrument of a government for national unity with no viable alternative or competitor. This initiative from the archbishop of Valladolid was an early example of attempts to 'regenerate' a political system that in 1898 was powerless to prevent the loss of Cuba and the Philippines, and that was progressively weakened by the fragmentation of the two major parties, Conservative and Liberal. Like many other proposals for regeneration,

[38] For Catholic Action, the Propagandists, Acción Popular, and Opus Dei, see below, pp. 147-8, 163, 189, 227-8, 229-30.

it was ineffective, but not before it revealed again Catholic willingness to dispense with pluralism.[39]

Many lay Catholics with no stomach for the catastrophist extremisms of Nocedal or Urquijo, or for the pessimism of Cascajares, found a congenial political base in the Conservative party. Cánovas had restored the Church along with the monarchy, and after his assassination in 1897 his party continued to be associated with the defence of the Church, especially under the pious leadership of Silvela and then Antonio Maura. Up to the turn of the century its Liberal opponent seemed relatively uninterested in religious issues, as it concentrated on establishing universal male suffrage (a more impressive achievement on paper than in its very patchy reality), trial by jury, and legal rights of association—all enacted in the 1880s. There was scant enthusiasm for campaigns to widen religious toleration or even bring in complete freedom of religion, and the party included many devout Catholics, among them José Canalejas, who was soon to be ruthlessly and wrongly represented in ecclesiastical polemics as a monstrous enemy of the Church.

Partly because earlier Liberal causes had been achieved, and partly because of the profound disquiet about Spanish society and politics triggered by the obliteration of the Spanish navy in 1898 by the United States and the consequent loss of Cuba, Puerto Rico, and the Philippines, religion reappeared on the political agenda at the turn of the century. While many bishops predictably attributed loss of empire to national apostasy and interpreted the naval disasters as divine retribution for infidelity,[40] others sought explanations in the backwardness and cultural and technical inadequacy of a Spain facing American power. National regeneration became the urgent aim, talked and written of wherever political and social questions were discussed; and competing projects for reforming the country dominated politics from then on.[41]

This was the context of Liberal attempts to modernize Spanish society, not by attacking Catholicism but by loosening its dogmatic monopoly. A Liberal ministry had de-confessionalized university education in 1881. Now in 1901 a Liberal ministry made religion an optional instead of obligatory subject in the secondary school *bachillerato*, and another

[39] For Cascajares's project, see Andrés Gallego, *La política religiosa en España 1889–1913* (Madrid, 1975), 55–91.
[40] For a typical example, see Bishop Fernández Pierola's pastoral letter of 11 Feb. 1899, *BEOV*, xxxv (1899).
[41] There is a survey of regenerationist politics in R. Carr, *Spain 1808–1975*. 2nd edn. (Oxford, 1982), 473–563.

would in 1913 permit the children of parents who did not consider themselves Catholic to be exempted from religion classes in state secondary schools. Later still, in 1923, the bishops were seriously alarmed by the intention of García Prieto's Liberal government to reform article 11 of the 1876 constitution in the direction of much wider religious liberty, a danger providentially averted for them by Primo de Rivera's coup later in the year.[42] Much the bitterest controversy, however, played out in noisy street demonstrations and the press as well as in parliament and pastoral letters, revolved round the religious congregations, particularly those involved in education.[43]

During a discussion of education and the religious congregations in the Cortes between 27 June and 4 July 1903, the Liberal politician Romanones asserted, on the basis of information from the *Dirección General del Instituto Geográfico*, that in 1900 there were approximately 44,000 nuns and 13,000 male religious in Spain, one quarter of the former and one half of the latter dedicated to education. Since the corresponding figures he quoted for 1886 were approximately 17,000 female and 2,000 male religious, the total had trebled in fifteen years. Clearly the congregations had flourished under the restoration monarchy, even though the legal status of most of them was uncertain.[44] As the radical press and anti-clerical demonstrations made even more apparent, this expansion of religious organizations often identified with reactionary values and intolerance was resented by Liberals. The attacks on the orders in France by Waldeck-Rousseau and Combes highlighted the problem. The Liberals tried in 1901, again in 1906, and finally in 1910 to impose controls, on the first two occasions by bringing the orders within the regulations of the 1887 law of associations, and in 1910 by Canalejas's ill-fated 'padlock law'. Episcopal protests and Catholic rallies in towns all over Spain denounced these measures as an affront to the Church and an unforgivable assault on the country's religious identity and traditions. State relations with the Vatican were strained, and the international Eucharistic Congress being held in Madrid in the last week of June 1911 could scarcely avoid taking on the character of an anti-governmental demonstration, especially with its vast procession through the centre of the capital on 28 June.

Out of this polemical ferment and popular mobilization by both sides,

[42] Text in Iribarren, 116–17.
[43] On Liberal attempts to control the congregations, the essential works are, Andrés Gallego, *La política religiosa en España 1889–1913*; J. M. Castells, *Las asociaciones religiosas en la España contemporánea* (Madrid, 1973), 271–373.
[44] See above, p. 60.

the Liberals achieved very little. The 'padlock law' had imposed restraints on the further expansion of the congregations while a new law of associations was being prepared, but had stipulated that this must be produced within two years. When no legislation materialized, Canalejas's law lapsed. Many commentators then and since have argued that if little was achieved, little had ever been intended, except to galvanize a fragmenting Liberal party whose political programme had been exhausted. Sardá i Salvany spoke for many on both sides of the divide when he called early twentieth-century anti-clericalism 'a comedy pure and simple', a disingenuous party manoeuvre to rally support.[45] A Liberalism unable to move on from its nineteenth-century achievements to radical social reform fell back instead on old-fashioned anti-clericalism, providing its Conservative rivals simultaneously and unnecessarily with the role of champion of an endangered Church—or so a very common theory goes.

It is misleading, however, to dismiss the anti-clerical campaigns of the early 1900s and the Catholic protests they provoked as merely the results of political manipulation. The conflict was not a phantom battle between opportunism on the one side and a groundless persecution complex on the other. The fact that Liberal politicians tried to use anti-clerical passion for their own purposes did not mean that they created it, any more than Canalejas's care not to alienate the Vatican completely, disproved the genuineness of his worries about the strength and ideological orientation of the religious congregations. It was possible to be anti-clerical and shy away from the separation of Church and state; it was possible to be a devout Catholic and yet feel uneasy about convent workshops undercutting the labour of the urban poor. It was certainly possible to be Catholic and a Liberal and strongly out of sympathy with the illiberal, authoritarian culture of the Catholic revival, often most glaringly apparent in the religious schools. Liberal fears of missing the road to modernity and greater pluralism because of an ecclesiastical control over secondary education that the state lacked the resources to counter, were neither wild nor disingenuous, but very often sincere.[46]

Traditionalists organized protests in demonstrations, in parliament, and by post against the 'padlock law', the latest abomination in a country that had reneged on its Catholic past.[47] It was as much a part

[45] Andrés Gallego, *La política religiosa*, 298.
[46] For convent workshops and schools and their critics, see above, pp. 76, 80–2.
[47] For their parliamentary speeches and campaigns, see R. Rotllan (ed.), *La ley llamada del 'candado' y la oposición católica en las Cortes* (Madrid, 1911). Rotllan did not deign to include protests from Catholic Alfonsist deputies.

of a longer and deeper process for them as it was for Liberals, and the more to be feared for that. Limited religious toleration had been anathema; now followed restraints on the religious, whom Pope Leo XIII had called in 1901 the very apple of the Church's eye.[48] Spain was unsafe for integral Catholicism, and Integrists felt justified in describing Liberal policies as persecution. Julio Alarcón, SJ, argued in the newly-founded Jesuit periodical *Razon y Fe* during the earlier confrontation over the orders in 1901 that while the public slogan was 'war on clericalism', the secret and real one was 'war on the Church, war on Jesus Christ'.[49] Many bishops, priests, and laity agreed with this, on the customary grounds that the Church had divine authority to teach and that therefore governmental restrictions on the teaching orders were restrictions on the Church as a whole and ultimately on the saving mission of Christ himself, with whom the contemporary Church so confidently identified itself.

The Conservative party could not afford to take such a metaphysical line, however much some of its notables disliked Liberal initiatives. After extensive abstention during the progress of the 'padlock bill' through the Cortes, for example, Maura himself led Conservatives in voting for the bill eventually, on 24 December 1910, having first exacted as their price the inclusion of the time-limit clause that in practice made the law obsolete before it could have much effect. Conservative politicians might not be religious purists and maximalists in their policies, but they nevertheless provided again in these years an effective bulwark for a threatened Church.

From the early 1890s, however, many Catholics in the productive areas based on Catalan textile and Vizcayan iron-mining industries chose a political allegiance outside the two Alfonsist parties and outside Carlism. They placed their hopes of social and political regeneration in local regionalist and nationalist alternatives to the centralized state based on Madrid. Catalan nationalism first took clear political shape round the politician Prat de la Riba and his demand for home rule in a document known as the Bases of Manresa, drawn up in 1892. In 1901 the autonomist movement was streamlined in the Lliga Regionalista which until the republic of 1931 dominated Catalanist politics. The Lliga was rich, restive at Madrid centralism, hostile to popular radicalism, and

---

[48] In a letter to the Superior General of the congregations, text in J. Buitrago y Hernández, *Las órdenes religiosas y los religiosos—estudio jurídico sobre su existencia legal y capacidad civil en España* (Madrid, 1901), appendix 2.

[49] *RyF*, ii (1902), 16.

kept to the political Right by its industrialist leaders, most notably the millionaire Cambó. The party had no specific religious character or platform, and did not need one. Demographic weight, industrial strength, its own language, and a rich literary and artistic culture combined to make Catalan nationalism formidable in its tests of strength with Madrid.

If the campaign for Catalan autonomy did not need Catholic inspiration or propaganda, however, there were Catholics who thought that the Church needed Catalanism and that Catalonia could only benefit from an acknowledgement of its Catholic traditions. Probably most influential was the learned Josep Torras i Bages, bishop of Vich from 1899 to 1916. His very appointment by the Conservative regenerationist ministry of 1899 was an acknowledgement of Catalanist sensibilities, and in line with a demand for Catalan incumbents of Catalan sees made in the Bases of Manresa, in whose elaboration Torres i Bages had participated. His elevation to Vich, however, and the translation from Vich to Barcelona of Bishop Morgades were secured by the Catalan Durán i Bas during his brief occupancy of the Ministry of Grace and Justice.[50] To most politicians of the dynastic *turno* in Madrid at this time, such appointments seemed dangerous, and from the turn of the century onwards Valencians and Castilians were often promoted to Catalan sees while Catalan clergy were consecrated for dioceses elsewhere, to the chagrin of politicians like Prat de la Riba as well as ecclesiastical personnel.[51]

In a careful investigation of Catalan cultural traditions that centrist politicians like Romero Robledo chose to regard as a separatist tract, Torras i Bages had argued in a famous book published in 1892 that the *gens* or nation was a God-given unit, a kind of natural constitution under the changing formal constitution of states. Catalonia was such a *gens*, and since governmental systems change while the nation abides, 'the Church is regionalist because it is eternal'. Accordingly the Church must respect the culture and values of the local *gens*: in Catalonia preaching and catechesis should be in Catalan.[52] He put these con-

---

[50] See J. Bonet i Baltà, 'Eclesiastics de Barcelona enaltits en el consistori papal de 1899: Vives i Tutó—Morgades—Torras i Bages', *Analecta Sacra Tarraconensia*, xxxvii (1964), 231–72.

[51] For the controversy over episcopal appointments in Catalonia, see J. Massot i Muntaner, 'El Vaticà i Catalunya', *Questions de vida cristiana*, cix (Montserrat, 1981), 43–63.

[52] J. Torras i Bages, *Las Tradició Català* (Barcelona, 1982), especially Book I, Chapters 3, 5, and 6.

victions into practice by breaking with custom and writing his first pastoral letter as bishop of Vich in Catalan. But even more alarming to those who considered all this just one step away from a separatism that would dismember Spain was Morgades's first pastoral letter in Barcelona in 1900, stressing the need for preaching to be in Catalan in Barcelona itself as well as in rural areas because it was the language best understood by the people.[53]

The chief preoccupation of the bishops was pastoral; they wanted to work with and not against the language, customs, and ever more insistent regionalist revival of their dioceses. Notwithstanding government efforts to de-Catalanize the episcopacy in Catalonia, the need for a Catalan pastoral programme remained. In 1914 Torras i Bages refused translation out of the area to the archbishopric of Valencia, just as Francesc Vidal i Barraquer later resisted all attempts to move him after his appointment to the Catalan archiepiscopal see of Tarragona in 1919. Particularly under Vidal i Barraquer as metropolitan archbishop, joint initiatives by all the bishops of Catalonia on pastoral matters became common. Youth movements, clergy meetings, liturgical and devotional organizations were all co-ordinated at an inter-diocesan level, and plans for a Catalan ecclesiastical council were in preparation when the advent of the dictatorship interrupted them. In the spring of 1923 one of the now customary meetings of the Catalan bishops presided over by Vidal i Barraquer issued various joint statements, including a confirmation of the norm that preaching in Catalonia should, except in special circumstances, be in Catalan.[54]

Strong local church leadership from 1900 onwards tended, then, to favour and participate in the nationalist revival, even though it eschewed formal party political commitment. Its aims were pastoral, even when politicians defending the crumbling Canovite system were understandably unable, in their fear of the Catalan resurgence, to distinguish the pastoral from the political. Many lay Catholics, however, were less interested than the bishops in establishing the Catholic credentials of Catalanism, and more interested in Catalanism in its own right. This was true, for example, of Josep Carner in literature and of innumerable Catholics committed to the home rule alliance that swept the Liberal and Conservative parties out of Catalonia in 1907. As the

[53] For both letters, see J. Massot i Muntaner, *Aproximació a la història religiosa de la Catalunya contemporània* (Montserrat, 1973), 18–19.

[54] See R. Muntanyola, *Vidal i Barraquer, Cardenal de la Pau* (Montserrat, 1976), 136–9.

Catalan historian Vicente Cacho Viu has pointed out, this collaboration without religious preconditions necessarily diluted integrist traditions within Catalan Catholicism.[55] Religion might encourage a sense of regional cultural identity, but it did not determine any one political option for religious reasons. Catholic lay participation in the promotion of Catalan culture or nationalist politics because they were Catalanist, and not primarily because they were Catholic, helped both diversify and secularize Catholic politics to a degree that was unusual elsewhere. By the time of the major crisis of the restoration system in 1916–23, local Catholic sympathy for Catalan nationalism of one kind or another was firmly established. Because of it, Catalan Catholics came to view the authoritarian centralism of Primo de Rivera with a distaste uncommon among their co-religionaries. Its vigour by 1931 would prevent the Catholic Catalan vote in the Second Republic from being marshalled as easily as the Catholic vote in many other areas of the country in a confessional campaign to turn defence of the Church into an overriding political obligation.[56]

In sharp contrast to the Catalan movement, contemporary Basque nationalist politics were explicitly Catholic. The first manifesto of the Basque Nationalist Party, the PNV, founded by Sabino Arana y Goiri in 1893 called for the creation of a new trans-Pyrennean Basque state, Euzkadi, that would be officially Catholic and in which the state would be subordinate to the Church, and politics to religion.[57] The ideal of a Catholic state underpinned by a society with social and cultural values derived from traditional Catholic morality was a powerful source of inspiration for pious nationalists. Early enthusiasts resembled the Integrist right wing of Spanish Catholicism, to which, in fact, many of them had belonged. This Catholic character of nationalism was not surprising in provinces with extremely high incidences of religious practice and spectacularly large numbers of recruits to the priesthood and the religious life; although an aconfessional nationalist party, the ANV, later came into being, mainstream Basque nationalism right up to the civil war remained Catholic in its leadership, its membership, its policies, and its voting strength. Priests featured prominently in the study of Basque language and society, including the pioneer lexicographer Resurrección María Azcue and later the famous ethnographist José

---

[55] V. Cacho Viu, 'Catalanismo y catolicismo en el ambiente intelectual finisecular' in *Aproximación a la historia social de la iglesia española* (Madrid, 1978).
[56] See below, pp. 176–7, 193–4.
[57] Text in M. García Venero, *Historia del nacionalismo vasco* (Madrid, 1968), 281–3.

María Barandiarán. Others were active in the Basque trade unions, Basque Workers' Solidarity, affiliated to the PNV, and a very few plunged themselves directly into nationalist political propaganda. Not all Basque Catholics were sympathetic, however, to a cultural revival some saw as artificial and anachronistic; and not all who were sympathetic agreed with the expression of that revival in political nationalism. It was stronger in Vizcaya and Guipúzcoa than in Álava or Navarre. Its adherents—often middle-class and white-collar workers—found themselves sandwiched between the local heavy industrialists and bankers who, unlike their opposite numbers in Catalan industries, remained centralist in their politics, and the Socialist working classes in Bilbao and other smaller industrial centres, who were often immigrants from other parts of Spain.[58] Before the appointment of Mateo Múgica as bishop of Vitoria in 1928, there had been no Basque incumbent of the Basque see, established in 1861, even though Basque bishops headed other dioceses elsewhere in Spain. Indeed, his predecessors opposed the nationalist revival. Early in the century one of them prohibited the use of Basque names in baptism, while another wrote a pastoral letter denouncing the nationalist programme as 'darkening the minds and perverting the hearts' of the young.[59] Catholic sympathies divided over the nationalist issue, but here, as in Catalonia, it stimulated Catholic disapproval of Primo de Rivera's campaigns to enforce Castilian, and it made many extremely wary of the centralizing Catholic Right under the republic. It would eventually set the PNV in complete and armed opposition to Franco's Catholic crusade and imposition of centrist dictatorship.[60]

One further alternative to what was left of the two dynastic parties appeared just before Primo de Rivera opened his 'parenthesis' in the political life of the country. In an attempt to surmount the country's problems, the People's Social Party (PSP) was founded in the closing months of 1922 to gather together Catholic politicians of various traditions. The aim was moderate reform, including regional devolution, genuine elections, social reform, and a new look at Spanish embroilment in Morocco.[61] Since the Liberal and Conservative parties had failed to

---

[58] For nationalism's sociological composition and voting strength in Bilbao, see J. P. Fusi, *Política obrera en el país vasco 1880–1923* (Madrid, 1975), 193–203.
[59] For documentation, see I. Moriones, *Euzkadi y el Vaticano 1935–1936* (Rome, 1976), 45–6.
[60] See below, pp. 213–14.
[61] The standard work is O. Alzaga, *La primera democracia cristiana en España* (Madrid, 1973).

produce the oft-promised regeneration, and since social conflict since 1916 had been bitter and sterile, perhaps a new party might try its hand. The venture bristled with problems and paradoxes. Like Sturzo's People's Party in Italy, on which it was based, it was evidently Catholic in inspiration and composition, and the founders had in common a commitment to implement papal social teaching since Leo XIII's *Rerum Novarum* of 1891. This interest in social problems was dominant in the Zaragoza nucleus formed by members of the earlier Christian Democrat circle there headed by law professor Inocencio Jiménez, and among Herrera's Propagandists. Other founders, however, like the Traditionalists Salvador Minguijón and Ricardo Oreja, or the Maurists Ángel Ossorio Gallardo and Count Vallellano, already belonged to established political groups. The relationship between the new entity and the older organizations was unclear. Minguijón expected many recruits, including future parliamentary representatives, to retain their position within their original party. Yet the PSP itself was to be a party, not just an association for the defence of confessional interests. The confusion over composition—a further instance of Catholic unease with the vocabulary and reality of political pluriformity—was mirrored in the PSP's self-description. No one doubted that it was 'a new political party of the Right', but Francisco Barrachina, the one worker representative on its executive committee, insisted that in this case the Right was defined by ideals and not by interests. This interpretation was repeated in the party's programme and formed part of the rhetoric of inter-class solidarity with which the PSP repudiated any identification with the interest groups that exploited the established socio-economic order for their own sectional advantage.

It is not difficult to specify the ideals in question: although non-confessional, the PSP would necessarily be Catholic, anti-socialist and anti-revolutionary. Because of Primo's coup, it did not survive long enough to demonstrate whether such an orientation could in practice avoid coinciding neatly with the class policies of the 'Right of interests'. There was not even time for this initiative to expand by mobilizing substantial popular support. The alacrity with which the great majority of its leaders accepted Primo's coup suggests at least that the new party lacked democratic conviction—as indeed its interest in corporatist ideas and structures had already indicated. Moreover, little was heard of social reform from those members of the PSP who later became involved in Primo's Patriotic Union and National Assembly.[62] The urgency pro-

[62] See below, pp. 174–5, 177.

voked by the political chaos of 1922 disappeared under the more congenial stability of the dictatorship. Nevertheless, the PSP had briefly sketched a Catholic political style that could accommodate genuine democrats like Ossorio y Gallardo, and advocates of social change like Inocencio Jiménez, and had at least recognized the need for reforming policies including a progressive income tax. Under the republic, the identification of the 'Right of ideals' with the scepticism of parliamentary democracy and the social immobilism often demonstrated by the 'Right of interests' was to be markedly more crude and forthright.

In the closing months of the constitutional monarchy, Catholic politicians were active in a variety of political movements, of which only the regionally restricted PNV, Carlism, and an enfeebled Integrism were concerned with confessional issues as a first priority. With the possible, partial exception of the PSP they all belonged on the socially conservative Right, lined up against the socialist and anarchist mass movements whose emergence and vigour heralded the collapse of the Canovite system. Catholic politics under the restoration monarchy were not monolithic: disagreements between Traditionalists and liberals, Alfonsists and Catalan and Basque nationalists were real and passionate. What considerable common ground they had lay not in confessional issues but in their socio-economic conservatism. Notwithstanding the range of parties, there was little mourning in Church circles when parties and parliament were superseded in 1923 by Primo de Rivera's dictatorship. And there was only a little, localized joy when in 1931 parliament and parties reappeared—this time as the instruments of mass politics with no king and no Cánovas to safeguard the Church and silence its critics.

6
Catholic Action and Social Catholicism

MANY of the major disputes of the sixteenth-century Reformation turned on the rival validities of justification by faith and justification by good works; the Spanish Church of the late nineteenth and twentieth centuries, however, often seemed committed to justification by politics. Many devout Catholics, lay and clerical, hoped that some day politicians would complete the unfinished business of the restoration monarchy by restoring full Catholic unity and abolishing the ignominious toleration of other denominations. Faith in national justification by political change remained fervent. Perhaps because of the long tradition of regalism in the Spanish Church, continued under the Alfonsist monarchy by active state intervention in the choice of bishops and in the political role of bishop-senators, Church leaders thought the state should fight its battles and be its very sword and buckler.

When the Church fought its own battles in the Catholic revival, its efforts were often puny and the style noisy but defensive, looking over its shoulder for reinforcements. In spite of enormous state support, it was unable to produce an intellectual élite of any sophistication or power, and much of its art and literary culture were crudely propagandist. Most damaging of all was the failure to penetrate the worlds of the urban and rural proletariats. The Catholic revival was dominated by nostalgia for past glories in supposedly easier and more congenial times when the philosophical synthesis of St. Thomas Aquinas satisfied the learned, and the simple faithful were untroubled by class conflict and revolutionary ideas. As Pierre Jobit pointed out many years ago, its besetting sin was the sin of archaism.[1] It was a revival for some other society in some other time, not for a post-Reformation, post-Enlightenment, post-imperial Spain undergoing partial and patchy industrialization. Attempts to mobilize the faithful in Catholic Action rarely if ever addressed the fundamental problems of poverty and class conflict. Social Catholic initiatives remained hesitant and were under-

---

[1] P. Jobit, *L'Église d'Espagne à l'heure du Concile* (Paris, 1965), 49–50.

Catholic Action 147

mined at every stage by reactionary Catholic capitalists, notably by the ubiquitous, pious, and baneful Marquis of Comillas.

A bewildering array of meetings, groups, councils, and confederations noted more for their impressive titles than for any achievements comprised Catholic Action in Spain, a movement to rouse the Catholic laity officially launched by Cardinal Moreno with his *Constitutive bases for the Union of Spanish Catholics* of 1881. The political expression of this movement was Pidal i Mon's abortive Catholic Union, but the aims of Catholic Action itself were broader than his parliamentary concerns. It hoped to organize Catholics in order to transform Spanish society.[2] After the failure of Pidal's efforts to draw Catholics into a single political party, the next major campaign to unite Catholics was undertaken by Cardinal Sancha, in a series of six Catholic Congresses between 1889 and 1902.[3] They were dominated by bishops and lay intellectuals and politicians, and pastoral plans became hopelessly entangled in political controversies. The Congresses were designed to overcome Carlist and Integrist intractability to the hierarchy's guidance, as well as the apathy of other Catholics, yet repeatedly deplored precisely those liberal tendencies in the constitution, education, the press, and public life in general to which Traditionalists so strongly objected. This paradox was clear in all the Congresses. In Burgos in 1899, for example, the programme for action promulgated by the bishops required the government to keep religious toleration as narrow as possible, to ban heterodox books, to free Church schools and colleges from state supervision, to enforce Catholic orthodoxy in all education in Spain and place it under the hierarchy's inspection, to extirpate blasphemy, pornography, and drunkenness. The declaration accompanying this programme once again sought the restoration of Catholic unity, and added for good measure a repudiation of 'all those liberties of perdition, offspring of the so-called new rights, or liberalism, the application of which to the government of our fatherland is the source of so many sins, and which leads us to the brink of the abyss'. That no substantial Catholic mobilization ever resulted from these Congresses, which were eventually abandoned as useless, was due only partly to the consistent wrecking tactics from the extreme, irreconcilable Right. The other major impediment was the intrinsic

[2] For a brief survey, see A. Bonet, 'Acción Católica', in Q. Aldea, T. Marín, and J. Vives (eds.), *Diccionario de Historia Eclesiástica de España* (Madrid, 1972), i, 2–5.

[3] A full *Crónica* of each of the six congresses was published in, respectively, Madrid 1889, Zaragoza 1891, Sevilla 1893, Tarragona 1894, Burgos 1899, Santiago 1903. For a brief account, see C. Martí, 'Congresos Católicos Nacionales', in *DHEE*, i, 604–5.

impossibility of stimulating enough interest to create effective Catholic associations or electoral leagues whose task would be that of persuading Spanish governments not just to protect the Church and be its paymaster but to serve its purposes entirely and count them as their own.

After the Tarragona Congress of 1894, the organizing *junta* of the Congresses became also the central *junta* of Catholic Action as a whole, under the presidency of Claudio López Bru, Marquis of Comillas, a position he was to hold until his death in 1925. Comillas was a devout, immensely rich shipping magnate and landowner, determined to serve the Church in his own, rather devious ways, and to keep his employees pious and out of radical unions. For thirty years he dominated Catholic policy-making on labour relations. A workers' section of Catholic Action was set up under his influence in 1894, to be followed in 1919 by a women's and in 1924 by a youth section. None of these, however, had the popular vitality of the special sections of Catholic Action in the 1950s and 1960s; on the contrary, they were firmly under hierarchical and magnate control, associations of leaders with few followers. After being fruitlessly reorganized in 1926 with diocesan and parochial units, Catholic Action eventually held its first National Congress in Toledo in 1929. The following extract from its conclusions gives a clear notion of the style that had too often dominated Catholic Action through the preceding years:

The diocesan committees shall procure:-
1. The extirpation of the social evils of ignorance of Christian doctrine, indifference and irreligiosity; blasphemy, both spoken and written; the profanation of feast days; evil publications; insubordination; indecency in dress, cinemas and other entertainments; pauperism and emigration.
2. The promotion of social well-being by the careful nurturing of religion, morality, obedience to the Church; respect for authority; charity towards the poor; religious instruction of the populace.

The local committee shall stimulate the zeal of priests, religious and lay people to
1. The extirpation of social evils everywhere.
2. The defence of the sacred interests of religion, the family, authority, private property and the poor ....[4]

Right up to the civil war, Spanish Catholic Action often amounted to little more than a ritual lament that things were as they were, and an institutionalized aspiration that they should be different. Bishops loudly

[4] *BEOV*, lxv (1929), 734.

castigated lay complacency and inactivity, but offered no programme for action.[5]

The most characteristic products of Catholic Action were words or gestures rather than purposeful organizations—congresses and processions, rather than flourishing workers' or students' associations. When the Church was not placing all its hope in political aids to salvation, it trusted in flamboyant piety. Comillas financed spectacular pilgrimages for working men to shrines in Spain and abroad, including Rome. The Catholic Congresses of 1889–1902 were followed by congresses of all descriptions, Eucharistic, Catechetical, of the 'Good Press'. Catholic Action rarely addressed itself to limited and clearly identified problems with a coherent plan of campaign; rather, it performed pious incantations in the hope that some particular assembly or demonstration would achieve the correct form of words and gestures to effect the desired transformation of Spanish society. If the politicians would not lead the way to salvation, then perhaps some spontaneous combustion of mass fervour might establish again in Spain the kingdom of Christ.

The Catholic Action initiatives sponsored by the hierarchy had much in common with the style of the Jesuit Apostleship of Prayer with its public consecrations to the Sacred Heart and its determination to erect statues of the Sacred Heart in town halls and village squares. Both wanted to change Spanish society—and if possible even the state—by means of pious practices. And the reliance on piety rather than social analysis and reforming policies was a major reason for the greatest failure of the Catholic revival, its inability to prevent or counteract the alienation of the industrial working class and the southern peasantry from the Church.

The Catholic revival of the second half of the nineteenth century was a mainly bourgeois phenomenon, not a popular one. It became an increasingly counter-revolutionary movement as propertied Catholics faced the threat of collectivist organizations. In particular, the emergence of Socialist and Anarchist unions and the Socialist party in the late nineteenth century sharpened Catholic awareness of social conflict, especially in industrial areas. Leo XIII's *Rerum Novarum* published in 1891 further encouraged a spate of writing and organizing in Spain to confront what contemporaries called 'the social question'. The analyses,

---

[5] See, e.g., the hierarchy's collective pastoral letter published in the social and political crisis of 1917 in Iribarren, 105–11, especially paragraph 6.

however, postulated moral regeneration rather than economic reform. An excellent example of this tendency is a prelate particularly esteemed for his intellectual ability and formation, Bishop Maura y Gelabert of Orihuela, cousin of the Conservative politician Antonio Maura, with whom he had been brought up. Between 1893 and 1901 Maura wrote nine pastoral letters on the social question, later published in book form for wider distribution.[6] His description of the plight of the poor showed that he had few illusions about their living conditions. Their experience of class inequality was, he judged, like a kind of 'blood-drenched sarcasm thrown in the face of the miserable worker by society'. He was realistic, too, in ascribing the violence of the underpaid and downtrodden to their economic misery. But his second letter, especially, was devoted to the primacy of ideas and values and argued that all socio-economic problems were in origin moral and religious problems. Solutions lay not in structural change but in a change of heart and understanding. Positivism and unbelief, for example, must be counteracted. Since, according to Maura y Gelabert, inequality was irremovable and natural, the practical question was how to prevent *abusive* inequality by encouraging justice and charity in employers and demanding that they respect the teaching on wage levels and work conditions in *Rerum Novarum*. While acknowledging that private property rights could not be unlimited and unconditional, he had no proposals for property redistribution and saw no good in socialism. Indeed, in the sixth letter he was anxious to prove that the Church was a better defender of workers' rights than socialism: in exchange for that defence, the worker was to accept his social condition. In Maura's largely theoretical account, the Church was the source of truth on issues of property, work, and social organization. Its teachings supported the status quo while criticizing 'abuses' that were created by egoism and error and consequently capable of reform through moral conversion and doctrinal instruction.

A cruder version of this interpretation of modern social ills was given by one of the pioneers of Catholic workers' associations in Spain, the Valencian Jesuit Antonio Vicent. He was convinced that the principal cause of the social question was 'the denial or total forgetfulness of the ultimate end of the human race'. This was why, since the advent of the French revolution and socialism, people could no longer find happiness within poverty, and why the clergy should preach abnegation and remind their hearers of man's true end. Both liberalism and collectivism

---

[6] J. Maura y Gelabert, *La cuestión social* (Madrid, 1902).

disregarded original sin; the only way forward lay through abnegation, duty, and love, and a reversal of national apostasy.[7] Vicent's *Socialism and Anarchism* (1893) is a curious work, remarkable for its exceptionally clear division of the world—even by the Manichean standards of contemporary Spanish Catholicism—between good and bad, truth and error. No radical social analysis or social action could be expected of a man who urged monied women to prevent their maidservants from leaving the house wearing 'clothes that were indecent, or above their station', and encouraged working men in his Catholic associations to greet one another with the words '*Ave Maria purissima*'. None the less, Vicent's 'Catholic circles' represented a major and characteristic attempt to win Spanish workers to the Church and keep them out of the socialist unions.

Another sign of growing preoccupation with the social problems thrown up by modern industry was the foundation in most Spanish seminaries in the early years of the twentieth century of chairs of 'sociology', demanded by the Catholic Congress of Burgos in 1899. Equally indicative of the interest in both clerical and lay circles was the series of six conferences called Social Weeks held with episcopal backing and participation between 1906 and 1912. Both discussions and the Catholic workers' associations themselves, however, became battle grounds. Those who, like Comillas, sought to improve industrial relations through religious regeneration defended their ground against opponents who wanted to see genuine unions as firmly ranged against liberal capitalist exploitation as against the socialists and anarchists. The confrontation was lengthy and complicated, the strategies of defence often ruthless and unsavoury, but as the forces of innovation were themselves quick to recognize, the conservatives won most of the battles and the whole war, leaving most Catholic efforts at working-class organization looking timorous and puny.[8]

Although Catholic workers' circles existed in Spain before Vicent began his work in the 1880s, they were little more than mutual help associations. The network that he established and inspired in the manufacturing towns of Valencia in the 1880s and 1890s broke new ground with their scope, the numbers involved and uniform structure. His circles became the model for initiatives elsewhere, and by the end of the century Catholic workers' circles or groups very like them were to be

[7] A. Vicent, *Socialismo y anarquismo* (Valencia, 1893).
[8] The fullest account of the period up to 1914 is J. Andrés Gallego, *Pensamiento y acción social de la iglesia en España* (Madrid, 1984).

found in some density in parts of Old Castile, Aragón, and Córdoba as well as right down the Levant coast, with scattered examples elsewhere, especially along the north coast. In all there were probably upwards of 200. Total membership for the same date has been estimated variously from about 70,000 to about 180,000, and many new groups were founded in the following years.[9] The impression of numerical strength given by these figures is misleading, however, because they are so unreliable as to be almost meaningless. Not only were many of the circles ephemeral—a fact well documented, for example, for the Córdoba area[10]—but a substantial proportion of members were 'honorary' or 'patronal', that is, people of means, not workers at all. Furthermore, since many of the activities were devotional and recreational, a total of worker-members, even were that possible to compute, would tell us little about Catholic organization of workers on the shop floor, as opposed to their organization under Catholic auspices for relaxation, social insurance, and religious rituals. Vicent and those round him saw the 'social problem' as a crisis of faith and morals, in which atheism and ignorance of the Church's teachings were greater problems than the widely unbalanced distribution of property and opportunity under liberal capitalism.

In 1893 Archbishop Sancha of Valencia held, with Vicent's help, a General Assembly of Workers' Circles and *Patronatos*, from which developed in 1896 the National Council of Catholic Worker Corporations, the CNCCO. Vicent became chaplain of this national association, and the Marquis of Comillas with his right-hand man, Carlos Martín Álvarez, the dominating influence among a whole host of marquisses, admirals, and generals, while the Duke of Sotomayor was appointed president. Over the years, the CNCCO gradually took on the role of a kind of industrial branch of Catholic Action, and it acquired a reputation for action in a pious rather than an industrial sense. As early as 1901 one of the most articulate and knowledgeable of Comillas's Catholic critics, the Asturian priest Maximiliano Arboleya Martínez, commented that:

The workers in our Circles are talked to about religion, about morality, about resignation, about their obligations—which are sometimes exaggerated; but it is almost never that anyone talks to them about their legitimate rights in a

---

[9] Data on numbers and distribution ibid., 199–217, where the author acknowledges the immense difficulties of quantification.

[10] J. Díaz del Moral, *Historia de las agitaciones campesinas andaluzas* (Madrid, 1977), 143–5 (originally published 1929) for the disappearance by the late 1880s of circles that had flourished a decade earlier.

concrete way, about the injustices of which they are victims, about the obligations of the capitalists....[11]

For the first twenty years of this century, disagreements within what was called 'social Catholicism' frequently hinged on what Catholic workers' associations should be called. 'Circle' gradually gave way to 'syndicate', a title that seemed less anodyne. While many insisted that the word 'Catholic' should be blazoned on all groups, others disliked, not their Catholic composition, but the strong whiff of incense and suborned harmless respectability exuded by a confessional label. And if syndicates might perhaps be free in this sense of not being overtly confessional, a whole host of social Catholics argued that they must certainly be free of patronal domination, with membership limited to workers. Vicent himself was convinced by 1906 that mixed unions of workers and bosses must give way to horizontal associations. 'Pure' syndicates eventually became official policy in 1919, with the foundation of the National Confederation of Catholic Workers' Syndicates (CNSOC), that also recognized the legitimacy of strike action when negotiations had failed, but still insisted on confessionalism.[12]

These resolutions of 1919 were insubstantial, however, because by that date Catholic syndicates had acquired in most parts of the country a reputation for strike-breaking, and it was well known that patronal influence was not blocked merely by exclusion from formal syndical membership. In the wake of the important railway strike of 1912, for instance, a Catholic railwaymen's syndicate was set up with its centre in Valladolid, its orientation largely in the hands of the Jesuit Sisinio Nevares, its enterprises discreetly backed by the two big railway companies, its heart set on breaking the hold of the 'revolutionary' and 'anti-patriotic' Socialists and Anarchists. Inevitably its leader Agustín Ruiz gloried in opposing the railway strike of July 1916 and the general strike of August 1917. Since his organization was numerically small in comparison with the militant unions, it is very unlikely that Catholic blacklegging was particularly influential in the suppression of both strikes, which relied rather on military intervention. But in these desperate years of working-class hardship in an economy dislocated by the impact of the First World War with prices soaring out of reach of wages, Ruiz's syndicates won applause from the government, employers, and

[11] Quoted in Andrés Gallego, *Pensamiento y acción social*, 208.
[12] Structure and programme of the CNSOC in J. N. García Nieto, *El sindicalismo cristiano en España* (Bilbao, 1960), 247–59.

the Catholic press, and vituperation from the defeated strikers. Greatly impressed by this performance, the Marquis of Comillas tried hard to create an accompanying web of Catholic miners' syndicates, especially in the militant Asturian pits.[13] In such circumstances, the 1919 commitment to 'pure' syndicates and to strike action when necessary could not but provoke cynicism.

Such cynicism about the past record and future intentions of the kind of social Catholicism associated with the inescapable Comillas and various Jesuit priests, including Nevares, Villada, Noguer, and many others, was not limited to hostile outside observers. Notable figures within the Church and within social Catholic circles shared it. Among them were eminent laymen, university professors like Severino Aznar of Madrid university and Inocencio Jiménez of Zaragoza, diocesan clergy like Arboleya, and religious like the Augustinian Bruno Ibeas and the Dominican José Gafo. In some cases it is possible to trace in detail both the intellectual influences and practical experience that led individuals to more radical convictions, and the obstacles they encountered in trying to implement them.

Pedro Gerard was elected Prior of the Dominican house in Jerez in 1907, at the age of thirty-six. He was fat and must have looked the stereotypical self-indulgent friar of anti-clerical caricatures. Because of a steep decline in wine exports, the area round Jerez suffered in these years the same kind of economic crisis and consequent social unrest that a glut of wine production was causing simultaneously in parts of southern France. The seriousness of the situation, and the popular identification of the Church with it, were brought home to him when a statue of Our Lady carried in a procession he was responsible for was stoned amid blasphemies and insults in 1910, and a local general strike broke out the following year. A brilliant preacher, he was asked by a group of local magnates in 1912 to organize Catholic workers in reaction to an Anarchist foundation made to their alarm in Jerez. His decision for a workers-only syndicate was not what they expected, but by this time he had rejected the traditional means of welfare and charity as a solution to the dire need he saw round him, and was convinced that workers must receive adequate wages, as of right. This was the immediate background to a talk he gave at the conference on social problems in Pamplona in 1912 which caused havoc among the leading

---

[13] For the Valladolid Catholic railway syndicates see J. J. Castillo, *El sindicalismo amarillo en España* (Madrid, 1977), 34–41, 103–217, on which this account is based.

lights of the Catholic workers' circles and Catholic syndicates, and was one of the reasons why this series of social week conferences was abandoned for twenty years. Gerard's style of public speaking relied on clarity and dramatic intensity, not subtlety: he pulled no punches in denouncing the social Catholic record, repudiating confessional tests and demanding that all syndicates of Catholic workers be *sociedades de resistencia*, militant. This was not at all what the CNCCO leaders who planned the conference wanted to hear, and denunciations of Gerard poured in to the papal nuncio and Rome. Although Gerard's *Sindicatos Libres*—free in the double sense of non-confessional though Catholic, and not open to magnate or entrepreneurial membership—spread to Madrid, Pamplona, Zaragoza, and other centres, and formed a national federation in 1916, he had made powerful enemies. In 1913 the archbishop of Zaragoza forbade him to lecture again in the city, and for a while in 1912–13 he found himself under a prohibition from Rome. A recent analysis of the documentation has identified his major opponents. These were not his Dominican Master-General, nor the Vatican Prefect for Religious, but groups and individuals in Spain. His own provincial superior, Fr. Casas, and other Dominican priors, the nuncio Ragonesi who was close to Comillas, the Jesuits and their lay associates in the Jerez area and elsewhere, all sought to stop his work and in 1916 succeeded. He was ordered by his superiors to withdraw from all activity related to workers' syndicates. Three years later he died.[14]

Gerard's treatment affords a marvellous insight into the mental world of the Spanish Catholic establishment, for although his style was fiery and acerbic, there was nothing new or particularly radical about his proposals. Associations for workers only had been sanctioned back in 1891 by Leo XIII in *Rerum Novarum*, in which he had also spelled out the need for a just wage, not merely a subsistence wage. Gerard's inspirations were the Belgian Catholic unions, and he sought and took advice from a well-known Belgian Dominican, Fr. Rutten, whose orthodoxy was not impugned and whose expertise in union affairs was widely respected. (Gerard's father was Belgian.) He also kept himself informed about Italian Catholic initiatives, and had the works of the social Catholic pioneer, Toniolo, in his library. Even Pius X's traditionally minded Secretary of State, Merry del Val, in an interview with Gerard in March 1913, found nothing to censure. This purportedly

[14] The essential source is S. Carrasco, OP, 'El padre Gerard, fundador y propagandista del sindicalismo católico-libre 1911–1919: ocho años de lucha con la incomprensión de los suyos', *Communio*, viii (1975), fasc. 2–3, which uses Dominican archives.

dangerous Dominican defended private property, was anti-socialist, and certainly regarded Catholic workers' associations as part of a religious aspostolate, one in which effective action on wages and working conditions would be more powerful than acts of piety. In 1917 his Free Syndicates opposed the general strike along with their confessional counterparts. It is evident that the bitter denunciations and the determination to remove him from the scene owed more to offended sensibilities and extreme conservatism than to any putative heterodoxy. For his Provincial the problem seems to have been that he did not conform to the conventional image of the observant religious, absenting himself from singing the Office and from other prayers, negligent about hearing confessions, lax in administrative and financial accountability, stirring up trouble instead of 'sacrificing' himself. For the CNCCO dignitaries he was an unwelcome rival, and one whose ideas if put into practice would cost capitalists like Comillas much more in higher wages than they paid into syndicate subventions and mass pilgrimages. Gerard's views were not exceptionally radical, even by the standards of contemporary Catholic thought in western Europe. The storm they raised was a sign of the culpable unreality—or skilful cynicism—of his scandalized critics.

Others shared and continued Gerard's efforts to foster syndicates that were Catholic in inspiration, but neither chiefly preoccupied by questions of piety nor under the control of the CNSOC. Dominican colleagues, including Tomás Perancho and José Gafo, remained committed to the *Libres* in action and word, ensuring for example that the Dominican periodical *La Ciencia Tomista* often carried articles which contrasted strongly with the confessionalism and conservatism of the Jesuit *Razón y Fe*. By 1921 Gafo was having to defend himself against complaints from the nuncio, and Dominican sources show that employers for their part put pressure on the bishops to block him and the *Libres*. As a sympathetic colleague of Gafo's explained sadly to their superiors, 'these tactics were usually successful, since very few prelates were properly informed on social questions, and few had the courage to refuse the demands of powerful men'. Both the primate, Cardinal Reig, and the bishop of Madrid were hostile.[15] Gafo was not silenced as ruthlessly as Gerard had been, but the *Libres* were always held in suspicion by the hierarchy, while the CNSOC always tried to mar-

---

[15] S. Carrasco, 'Los superiores domínicos ante el "catolicismo social" y la incapacidad de los sindicalistas católicos para lograr fórmulas de inteligencia', *Escritos de Vedat*, iv (1974), 667–86.

ginalize or undermine them. Many Catholic employers undoubtedly found too threatening the analysis of working-class disdain for the Church that Perancho expressed very simply in his diary and that the *Libres* always recognized as their starting point: 'People hate the Church, not because they are immoral, as many priests foolishly preach, but because the Church is at the service of the rich ... undertaking as a primary task the defence of the property of the rich.'[16]

Among the diocesan clergy, Maximiliano Arboleya of Asturias was the greatest stumbling-block for the circle round Comillas, both because of his direct experience with miners working in Asturian pits owned by Comillas and because of his skill as a writer and lecturer. In 1914 he founded the Independent Workers' Syndicates of Oviedo. Like the *Libres*, which they closely resembled, the *Independientes* swiftly ran into difficulties with Catholic employers and some of the bishops.[17] Arboleya recognized that Socialist and Anarchist unions had won enormously important real benefits for their members in the coalfields and had therefore deservedly gained their confidence. There was no point in introducing Catholic unions geared towards enhancing the spiritual life of men who had many more pressing needs. Unions were about industrial relations, not spiritual progress. Arboleya was furious that a policy based in common sense and in what elsewhere in Europe would seem ordinary and orthodox, should in Spain provoke such an angry conservative campaign, supposedly in the name of Catholic social teaching.[18] His fury is understandable, since the *Independientes* were pledged to respect private property, the family, and Catholic doctrines and ethics, and were so far distant from a mentality of class warfare that they hoped to attract funds from wealthy sympathizers.[19] Real willingness to strike, the exclusion of capitalist members, and the subordination of piety to industrial action were apparently sufficient to bring down the wrath of the cautious Catholics who dominated alike the CNCCO, then the CNSOC, and Catholic Action.

Barcelona, the major industrial city of Spain, also produced some social Catholic initiatives of its own. In 1907 Popular Social Action (ASP) was founded by a Jesuit priest, Gabriel Palau. It has been

---

[16] Quoted in Castillo, *El sindicalismo amarillo*, 281.
[17] Arboleya's experience is presented with massive documentation in D. Benavides Gómez, *El fracaso social del catolicismo español* (Barcelona, 1973).
[18] See, e.g., his letter of 16 Jan. 1922 to his friend Juan B. Luis Pérez, bishop designate of Oviedo, ibid., 529–31.
[19] Statutes ibid., 46–7.

estimated that the ASP had over 27,352 members by 1915 in a Catalonia where the Socialist unions of the UGT had never made much headway but where a host of independent unions flourished and where the Anarchist CNT was only just beginning to dominate. Palau was especially interested in the propagation of ideas, and wanted to re-educate Catalan Catholics to an awareness of social problems and then make Barcelona the centre of a national network of social Catholic initiatives. The press activity of the ASP, both at a popular and at a more learned level was prodigious, and its *Revista Social* became one of the most respected publications in the extraordinarily busy world of social Catholic reviews, pamphlets, and newspapers. Its success in asserting its intellectual authority can be gauged from the fact that by 1910 about 40% of ASP membership was outside Catalonia. Palau's institution provided ideas, information, and contacts for Catholics concerned about social tensions and their possible solutions, and social tensions were nowhere more evident than in Barcelona, site of the terrifying 'tragic week' of violence in 1909. This orientation of the ASP as a kind of resource centre necessarily attracted well-meaning bourgeois Catholics, while its financial needs were largely met by the inevitable Catalan industrialist, Claudio López Bru, Marquis of Comillas. It was committed to notions of class harmony. The syndicates that became associated with it were called Professional Unions, and these modernized guilds never comprised more than about 7,000 workers, many of them clerical rather than blue-collar. A recent study has emphasized their paternalism, and estimated that at the most generous calculation they never accounted for more than 2% of the Barcelona manual work-force.[20] They soon established a reputation as strike breakers.

In 1916, the same year that Gerard was ordered to withdraw from activity related to industrial relations, Gabriel Palau was sent by his superiors out of harm's way to a chair of sociology in Argentina. Jesuit documentation reveals the same kind of criticisms within the order as those made within the Dominicans about Gerard—he neglected his religious obligations and created conflict.[21] Since he was also suspected by bishops and other influential Catholics—Comillas included—of trying to take over the co-ordination of all social Catholic ventures country-

[20] C.M. Winston, *Workers and the Right in Spain, 1900–1936* (Princeton, 1985), 38–64, which is the best recent survey of the ASP.

[21] J. Alemany Briz and A. Álvarez Bolado, 'Gabriel Palau SJ y la Acción Social Popular: correspondencia inédita (1913–1916)' in *Miscelánea Comillas*, 72 (1980), 123–78.

wide, making Barcelona rather than Madrid their centre, it is not surprising that he was removed. Some of the propagandist functions of ASP survived, but the collapse of the Professional Unions with Palau's departure indicates clearly enough their lack of substance. They were middle-class missions among the working population, rather than workers' organizations.

Even earlier than Palau's enterprises in Barcelona, Professional Unions had appeared in Bilbao in 1905, already concerned to oppose Socialist unions affiliated to the UGT by offering a Catholic alternative prepared to take strike action and supposedly to be 'pure' in composition. They petered out in 1916 because of their lack of real militancy, and because of competition from Catholic unions within Basque nationalism. Bilbao and the area round it also boasted tougher but small associations affiliated to Gerard's 1916 National Confederation of Catholic Free Syndicates. But easily the most successful unions of Catholic inspiration in the Basque provinces were those of the nationalist Basque Workers' Solidarity (SOV), founded in 1911.[22] Like all Catholic industrial unions of the period, SOV arose from Catholic determination to counter socialism, in this case as a reaction to the miners' strike of 1910. Antisocialism had an additional attraction in the area, moreover, because of the immigration from elsewhere in Spain of manual workers who not only swelled the ranks of socialism but also were not Basque. Socialists, non-Basques working in local heavy industry, and unjust capitalists were all in their different ways targets of the SOV. A generous internal estimate reckoned about 10,000 members by 1920, with heavy concentrations in Bilbao, and most notably among metal and woodworkers and shipyard hands. Solidarity was explicitly Basque and explicitly Catholic, yet while the latter characteristic virtually ensured that it would hope for class harmony and be better at social insurance than class conflict, its nationalist sympathies and consequent rejection of the non-nationalist stance of most local heavy industrial barons suggested from the beginning a possible evolution into a more vigorous later confrontation, as eventually occurred in the 1930s. Its cultural and political roots were quite different from those of Catholic unions elsewhere, capable ultimately of giving quite substantial fruit, but in

[22] See P. Larrañaga, *Contribución a la historia obrera de Euskalerría*. 2 vols. (San Sebastián, 1976, 1977), for an important account of the SOV by a priest immersed in its activities, especially in the 1920s and 1930s. The best scholarly account is I. Olabarri Gortezar, *Relaciones laborales en Vizcaya 1890–1936* (Durango, 1978), 131–66.

the crucial first twenty years of this century its contribution to the cause of a militant Catholic unionism was slight.

Anyone surveying social Catholic perspectives in 1919, the year when the National Confederation of Catholic Workers' Syndicates was formed, might be pardoned for finding it confusing. In addition to the new association of confessional syndicates there also existed the national federation of those syndicates in the tradition of Gerard, Catholic but not primarily confessional, whose representatives had left the 1919 meeting after angry scenes. The Basque SOV would clearly never fit very comfortably within any Spanish confederation of any kind. Gafo's groups were 'free' of non-workers, but relied nevertheless on assistance from other social classes, while the self-proclaimed Catholic unions were dominated by titled dignitaries and yet claimed now to be 'pure' and 'horizontal'. Furthermore, relationships within social Catholicism were extremely strained, with accusations of secrecy, manipulation, and betrayal, coursing through private correspondence and personal interviews, and sometimes erupting in public. More important than all of this, actual achievements in winning industrial workers to the Church, or effectively mobilizing those for whom it had always remained significant were extremely slight. Impressive statistics notwithstanding, there was no solid, purposeful Catholic presence on the shop floor or in the mines, but rather a gathering of Catholic workers for mutual aid, for social exchange, for devotion, even sometimes for negotiation with employers, but rarely for sustained, effective pressure for a better deal in the world of capitalist industry. There were many meetings, speeches, associations, and federations, but not much action. However much Catholic leaders disliked political, moral, and religious liberalism, economic liberalism seemed perfectly tolerable—given a reform here and an adjustment there—when set beside the inflated terrors of collectivism.

It is perhaps, therefore, not as paradoxical as first appears that in 1919 a new and much more aggressive initiative of Catholic inspiration should come precisely from Traditionalists who hated any and every kind of liberalism. The Free Syndicates of Barcelona (a phenomenon totally distinct from the Gerard–Gafo Free Catholic Syndicates except for the unfortunate similarity of title) emerged from working-class groups of Carlists, the majority of them recent migrants to the city from poor rural Carlist strongholds.[23] They were not confessional, though they

[23] The essential work is Winston, *Workers and the Right in Spain, 1900–1936*, on which this brief account is based.

Catholic Action 161

found common ground with clergy close to Gafo, especially Blas Goñí and Bruno Ibeas, while they loathed and disdained the world of Comillas and Palau's ASP. They bore no political label, but pitted themselves against the revolutionary aims of the Anarchist unions while sharing not just their toughness in industrial disputes, but also their willingness to resort to street fighting and assassinations. Carlism had never been squeamish about taking to arms. Between November 1920 and October 1922 the *Libres* acted as enthusiastic accomplices of military governor Martínez Anido in his determination to shoot revolutionary Anarchists off the streets of Barcelona. Yet, if they sided with tough military rule in these years of uncontrolled urban violence, and co-operated happily later with Primo de Rivera's dictatorship, they did not display any of the usual Catholic deference to employers. On the contrary they won various benefits for their members in industrial confrontations. In 1924 they brought into existence yet another National Confederation of Free Syndicates (CNSL) and in 1929 approached the 200,000 mark in membership, although at a time when the CNT was proscribed. The re-emergence of the Anarchists at the end of the dictatorship, together with the *Libres*' anti-Catalanism and dislike of parliamentary democracy, left them hopelessly vulnerable to the new political climate of 1931 and they never recovered their strength. But by that time their claim to form any part of the Catholic world was not one that most Catalan Catholics found at all convincing, any more than Carlist leaders recognized them by then as part of the true communion. They—or their leaders—were free-shooters metaphorically as well as literally, forming an odd and unassimilable growth within Catholic culture, though demonstrating that it was not simply a Catholic background that made the confessional unions incapable of effective union activity, but rather the debilitating effects of employer dominance and an obsessive concern with piety.

The other new venture of 1919 could not have been more different. Severino Aznar, university professor and the doyen of social Catholicism, gathered together lke-minded intellectuals and clergy in a Christian Democrat Group. The title was not felicitous, since although they chose the word 'democratic' to emphasize their allegiance to a modern, reforming, populist Catholicism, alert to the needs of workers in industry and on the land, their integrist critics chose to consider them suspect because 'democratic' seemed—in integrist vocabulary—redolent of liberalism, socialism, and anti-hierarchical attitudes. This very high-powered group, intent simply on discussing and popularizing analyses of social problems and their possible remedies, found itself embroiled in the usual nonsensical attacks from the extreme Catholic Right and the Jesuits, and was ultimately denounced to Rome.[24] In these years of violent agitation in town and country, especially in Barcelona and the south, it was lamentable that active clergy like Bruno Ibeas, Francisco Morán, and Arboleya, academics like Salvador Minguijón and Inocencio Jiménez, and experienced writers on social issues like Ramón Albó y Martí should have to defend themselves against charges of heterodoxy because they dared to insist on the social function of property and the limits to private property rights. The outlook for those wanting energetic new approaches, both theoretical and practical, was bleak, and it became more bleak the following year when Cardinal Guisasola of Toledo died.

Guisasola was born and educated in Oviedo and remained throughout his life extremely sceptical of liberal values. He did not care for parliaments and parties, but unlike many of his episcopal colleagues he was consistent in his anti-liberalism and criticized economic liberalism as forthrightly as its political counterpart. His 1916 pastoral letter, *Justice and Charity in the Christian Organization of Work*, abominated Spanish liberal democracy and socialism, and then went on to castigate in particular the state's failure to protect workers against exploitation. He argued that workers had a right not only to a just wage but also to property, and that in present conditions the traditional virtue of charity had to transcend private acts of generosity and be implemented with justice at a social level. It was Guisasola who urged the union of Catholic syndicates in 1919 and saw the need for them to be genuine associations of workers. He was consistently sympathetic to the convictions born of experience of men like Arboleya and Gerard, and he encouraged the Christian Democrat Group and eventually went to Rome to defend it. When necessary he could assert his authority over against entrenched opposition, even when it came from the nuncio Ragonesi, whose criteria in social matters diverged sharply from his and relied rather on the views of Comillas and Jesuit advisers like Villada. His death in 1920 further weakened the possibility that Spanish social Catholicism would ever develop fighting strength, and his three successors at Toledo in the 1920s, Almaraz, Reig, and Segura showed little interest in the ideas of an Aznar or the practice of a Gafo.

[24] For these attacks, and the history of the Christian Democrat Group, see D. Benavides Gómez, *El fracaso social*, 161–276.

The Christian Democrat Group was not the only one aiming to educate and jolt Catholics into greater social awareness. Ten years earlier the Jesuit priest Ángel Ayala had founded in Madrid the National Catholic Association of Propagandists (ACNP) from young men who were usually former students at Jesuit schools and colleges and members of the Luises, the Jesuits' own version of Catholic Action for their own male élite.[25] It is impossible to exaggerate the importance of the Propagandists in twentieth-century Spanish history, because they managed to give permanent and effective institutional expression to their endeavours in the press, educational initiatives, enduring lay associations and eventually politics. In 1911 they took over *El Debate*—with money from the publishers of the Bilbao *Gaceta del Norte*—and made it a Catholic daily of national circulation and immeasurable influence; they became deeply involved in Catholic agrarian organizations; they provided the nucleus for Catholic political mobilization in the 1930s round *Acción Popular* and then the CEDA (Spanish Confederation of Autonomous Right-Wing Groups). Their lay leader, Ángel Herrera, student of the Jesuit school in Valladolid and the Jesuit university in Deusto, and for many years editor of *El Debate*, created for himself a position of eminence among lay Catholics while retaining the trust of the hierarchy, a trust eventually expressed in his appointment as president of Catholic Action in 1933. The Propagandists were modern in their methods but traditional in their aims. To re-Christianize the élite they used journalistic, public speaking, and public relations skills shining with modernity, and they approached the disadvantaged with a barrage of carefully designed devices to keep them out of socialist temptation. Their newspapers (regional ones like the *Gaceta Regional* of Salamanca as well as *El Debate*), their summer schools, lecture tours, peasant credit associations, and ultimately their political creations achieved an unchallengeable dominance over Catholic life in Spain during the Second Republic.[26] They were less involved in the world of industrial unions. They always remained close to their Jesuit founders and

---

[25] There is a biography of Ayala: F. Cervera, *Ángel Ayala* (Madrid, 1975). The official ACNP history is I. Martín and N. González Ruiz, *Seglares en la historia del catolicismo español* (Madrid, 1968); F. Martín-Sánchez Juliá, *Ideas claras* (Madrid, 1960), is another view from the inside; M. Fernández-Areal, *La política católica en España* (Madrid, 1970), gives an Opus Dei perspective; for a highly critical assessment see A. Sáez Alba, *La ACNdeP. La otra 'cosa nostra'* (Paris, 1974). There is a brief account by Herrera of the foundation and early development of the ACNP, stressing the connection with Deusto, 'La Asociación Católica Nacional de Propagandistas en Loyola', *Estudios de Deusto*, xi (1919), 284–92.

[26] See below, pp. 195–7.

mentors, and shared the traditional Jesuit style of working hard to capture the social élite. Herrera, an energetic, devout, articulate man of rigid, secretive, and authoritarian temperament won the justified suspicion of the Christian Democrat Group when he chose not to join its initiative nor even give its members the space they sought in *El Debate*, the nearest thing Spanish Catholicism had to a national daily interested in social Catholic themes.[27] A lack of co-operation between two groups committed to the propagation of social Catholic ideas—though differing versions of those ideas—added yet another discordant note in 1919 to the cacophony already rising from the competing syndicates.

An excellent example of Herrera's methods and of Propagandist mentality in the last years of the constitutional monarchy was the Great Social Campaign planned at their initiative and with full episcopal backing in 1922. It was first announced in *El Debate* on 18 February, and formally presented to the nation in a pastoral letter of the whole episcopate published on 1 March. The bishops briefly outlined contemporary problems as they saw them—dangerous ideas, working-class hardship and discontent, civil disorder. They then proposed to do 'something important and definitive', and with melodramatic calls for patriotism and decisive action, proceeded to enumerate a plan of reforms astonishing in their abstraction and triviality. There was to be a 'social university' to train Catholic journalists, propagandists, and politicians; new Catholic primary and vocational schools were to be planned, to give a modern and anti-Protestant education; revolutionary ideas were to be countered with an effective campaign; old-age pensions for the diocesan clergy should be negotiated from the state; money should be raised to sustain diocesan social works, and Catholic industrial and agrarian syndicates. In other words, Catholic truth and right were to be more effectively proclaimed and organized in an attempt to mitigate class conflict and prevent anything more radical occurring. It was, in essence, an ideologically motivated counter-revolutionary initiative. As the bishops stated, they hoped that many people had, like themselves, learnt the lessons of the disturbing events of the previous troubled years.[28] Herrera had planned the next stages of the Great Campaign as a cross between revivalist meetings—complete with foreign evangelists imported from Latin America—and a modern advertising exercise. The

---

[27] Benavides Gómez, *El fracaso social*, 167–74.
[28] Text in Iribarren, 112–15.

message was the same as usual, but it would be presented with exemplary fervour: the product was the same, but it would be irresistibly packaged. Even the campaigners were the same—Comillas vice-president of its central committee, surrounded by titled Catholic dignitaries. Arboleya was right to regard the whole thing as ridiculous, and entirely suitable for the time of year, which was carnival.[29] Politicians on the Left found it distasteful and, in its appropriation of the king himself as patron, and its self-designation as a national patriotic movement, intolerable. They secured its cancellation, though it is hard to imagine that such an artificial concoction could actually have had much real impact. There could be no better indication than the aborted Great Social Campaign of the incorrigible faith in words, gestures, and committee resolutions that was so deeply embedded in the culture of the Catholic revival.

The Church's efforts to win over and mobilize industrial workers had not got very far when the hated liberal constitution was suspended in 1923. Failure was dangerous for the Church's credibility and ultimately for its safety, as was apparent in sporadic outbursts of proletarian violence against ecclesiastical personnel, processions, shrines, and buildings. After much the worst of these, the 'tragic week' in Barcelona in 1909, one Catalan Catholic writer, Joan Maragall, had pondered the lessons in a burnt-out church in Barcelona. He concluded that while the Church was identified with peace and order and the status quo, the poor in their impotence and frustration wanted disorder, and war, and something new, because the peace was not their peace, and the established order held nothing for them. Maragall pleaded that Catholics should not simply rebuild the destroyed churches, with stronger doors and more efficient state protection, but that they should instead meet the need for change and movement away from a social order defended at such ferocious cost.[30] The hopeless dilemma of social Catholicism in this period was its domination by people who regarded the complete preservation of the social order as axiomatic. There might have been some scope for the moderate reformism of the *Libres-Católicos* and the *Independientes*, anti-socialist but committed to winning industrial benefits through Catholic unions with some muscle, but even that modest programme was not given the encouragement, or even the operating space, that is so badly needed.

---

[29] Benavides Gómez, *El fracaso social*, 306.
[30] J. Maragall, 'L'esglesia cremada', in *La Veu de Catalunya* (18 Dec. 1909).

The agrarian efforts of social Catholicism in Spain in the same period were more successful for two reasons: firstly, Catholic practice and Catholic popular culture were much more buoyant in rural settlements of the north and parts of the centre than in pit villages and the industrial suburbs of the big cities; secondly, something practical could be done for poor peasant smallholders without causing more than a slight ripple through the extensive wheatfields of big Catholic proprietors. In parts of rural Spain it was not too late, in the first years of the twentieth century, to counter the socialist threat, and indeed neither Anarchism nor the Socialism of the PSOE and the UGT had anything practical to offer the smallholding peasant who wanted his property to be made more secure and productive, not collectivized.

Although Catholic agrarian groups were already evident in Old Castile from the beginning of the century, the firm legal and economic basis of Catholic defence of northern peasants was the 1906 Law of Agrarian Syndicates that gave legal status to farmers' associations and agrarian credit institutes, and promised them tax and import concessions on machinery, seed, breeding animals, and fertilizers.[31] One of the early activists was the indefatigable Fr. Vicent, and it was Vicent who first involved the wealthy landowner, Antonio Monedero, who was to be a central and controversial figure in the enterprise for some years. Vicent wrote to Mondero, then stayed with him for a few days in 1910 on his estate in Dueñas, Palencia province, in Old Castile. Monedero founded there the revealingly named Catholic Patronal Workers' Association, partly because of Vicent's prodding, but partly too because, as he himself explained, he and his fellow proprietors were driven to it 'by violent social circumstances stirred up by the preaching of subversive doctrines among the people'.[32] As early as 1908 clusters of groups were forming into local federations for more effective action; in 1912 a national federation under the auspices of the National Council of Catholic Worker Corporations was mooted; in 1915 a flourishing regional confederation appeared in the heartland of agrarian Catholicism, Old Castile and León; and in 1917 the National Catholic Agrarian Confederation (CNCA), was established as an agrarian parallel to the Catholic industrial syndicates and, like them, part of official Catholic Action under the hierarchy's supervision.

---

[31] For a summary of the law and its implementation see J. J. Castillo, *Propietarios muy pobres: sobre la subordinación política del pequeño campesino* (Madrid, 1979), 75–9.

[32] A. Monedero Martín, *La Confederación Nacional Católica-Agraria en 1920. Su espíritu, su organización, su porvenir* (Madrid, 1921), 14.

Simple though that progression seems in retrospect, it was fraught with all the internal politicking endemic in the social Catholic world. An agrarian secretariat centred on Madrid and expected by Aznar, Morán, Arboleya, and Cardinal Guisasola himself, to be the crux of the various local and regional federations was displaced by the leaders of the Old Castile and León associations, with Monedero and the Jesuit Sisinio Nevares firmly in charge. In spite of Guisasola's reservations about both men, Monedero became president of the new CNCA in 1917 and held the position until 1921.[33] The rise of Monedero had begun in 1912 at a meeting of agrarian propagandists in Palencia organized by Ángel Herrera. It was typical of Herrera and of what eventually became the CNCA that Monedero, one of the great landowners of the province, should be made the president of that meeting and then of the Palencian federation. Herrera completed the work Vicent had begun in binding Monedero into Jesuit circles by introducing him to Nevares, with whom henceforth he worked very closely, relying also on the resources of Herrera's Propagandists for speakers and organizers. For seven years from 1912 Monedero wrote a column on Catholic agrarian questions in El Debate under the name Juan Hidalgo,[34] enjoying just the platform for his views that the Christian Democracy Group was later denied. Monedero had his difficulties with large-scale proprietors who wanted nothing to do with peasant farmers' problems, as he himself related with relish. He even declared that if the CNCA did not remain free of landlord dominance it would become 'an instrument of tyranny over the poor', and he castigated the selfishness of the rich—a moral stance that seemed a bit quixotic in a man forced to resign in 1921 largely because of his extravagance with CNCA funds.[35] But in fact the CNCA was utterly committed to an inter-class programme and was always headed by big landlords and bourgeois propagandists. It was also confessional (rallies often began with religious songs and the rosary), often worked closely with bishops and local priests, always defended religion, the family, and private property, and saw itself as inoculating the peasantry against the dreaded socialist virus.

In its peak year of 1919, the CNCA mustered, according to

---

[33] For the internal wrangles, see Castillo, *Propietarios muy pobres*, 81–103, and Benavides Gómez, *El fracaso social*, 89–93.

[34] Reprinted in A. Monedero Martín, *Siete años de propaganda para organizar la Federación Nacional Católica Agraria* (Madrid, 1921).

[35] See, e.g., *Siete años de propaganda*, 292; *La Confederación Nacional Católica-Agraria en 1920*, 85–92.

Monedero, some 500,000 members, a total that must be drastically reduced to take account of ephemeral foundations, non-existent members, and the president's exaggerated optimism.[36] Even if the real total is more like a half or even a third of that figure, however, there is no doubt that in some areas, notably Old Castile, Navarre-Logroño, and the Levant, these agrarian syndicates functioned successfully. One reason was their diversity, allowing responsiveness to local conditions. Recent study has shown that, for instance, in the near subsistence peasant farming region round Valladolid syndicates concentrated on buying fertilizers and machinery communally, while Burgos syndicates, with the resources of the savings bank of the Catholic Workers' Circles there behind them, lent money to individual smallholders. Clerical backing was often effective. The bishop of Astorga and León promoted agrarian syndicates to help restock small vineyards devastated by phylloxera; Bishop Ramón Barbera of Ciudad Rodrigo and later Palencia urged the exploitation of untilled land on the great estates of these two dioceses, more secure lease terms and even, if necessary, some expropriation. Many diocesan priests participated in a very practical way in local syndicates.[37] Perhaps bishops and priests, often themselves from precisely the social strata within which the syndicates operated best, understood the problems of poor peasant farmers struggling to keep going, and felt more confident about how to help them, than they could ever do when faced with the alien world of irreligious industrial suburbs. Other factors also helped: the CNCA did best in provinces of smallholders and tenant farmers with relatively high literacy rates,[38] so although some of its members were economically very insecure, they were not the utterly resourceless and alienated poor whose plight was described in so many official reports on Extremadura and Andalusia. Credit facilities, bulk buying of fertilizers at reduced prices, shared ownership of expensive machinery, all gave immediate, practical help, without disturbing established property relations on the land.

All these favourable circumstances were thrown into relief by the failure of the CNCA to establish itself in any strength in areas where they did not obtain, like Galicia and the southern provinces. Enormous efforts were made in these regions from 1917 to 1919 when strikes and agrarian unrest frightened the propertied classes with nightmares of

---

[36] See Castillo's observations in *Propietarios muy pobres*, 107–27.
[37] There is very useful information on the activities of different syndicates and clerics in J. Cuesta, *Sindicalismo católico agrario en España (1917–1919)* (Madrid, 1978), 70–181.
[38] Ibid., 30–1.

revolution. In over-populated Galicia with its miniscule, inadequate plots of leased land, the federation recently launched by Nevares and Monedero broke up in confusion in 1919 because it could find no solution to controversies about property rights. In Andalusia and Extremadura, the expensive campaigns of 1918 and 1919 seemed to give immediate results and achieved a little land redistribution of territory given up by owners, but once the greatest scares of revolutionary violence abated, landlord sympathy declined and the campaign ended in failure.[39] In their contrasting ways, the *minifundio* agriculture of Galicia and the *latifundio* agriculture of much of the south and centre were impervious to the kind of palliatives the CNCA could offer. Landless labourers and tenant farmers with too little land even for subsistence could only be effectively helped by being given land: the CNCA could and did appeal to the great proprietors to surrender some of their land voluntarily, but was absolutely unwilling to think of the compulsory reform of property distribution: between the two, Catholic agrarian plans came to grief.

Rural social Catholicism helped keep the small peasantry both from proletarianization and from socialism, while it achieved little where the word 'peasant' was usually synonymous with landless labourer or pitifully poor *minifundio* tenant farmer, both categories frequently already influenced by collectivist or redistributist ideas. This patchy achievement further stabilized the patterns already created by Catholic practice and the density of Catholic institutions in rural areas. Catholic Spain claimed the peasantry of Valladolid and Palencia but not of Almería or Albacete. Eventually, when that electoral mobilization of Catholics that Catholic Action had talked about for decades became a reality in the Second Republic, the interlocking social Catholic achievements of the CNCA, Herrera, and *El Debate* ensured that the CEDA had a popular mass following for practical as well as religious reasons among the northern peasantry. The rural Catholic syndicates undoubtedly did better than their industrial counterparts, but they reflected and exacerbated the established weaknesses as well as the strengths of Spanish Catholicism.

[39] For Galicia, see ibid., 242–7; for Andalusia and Extremadura, 248–74.

7
Dictatorship and Republic

THE dictatorship years of 1923 to 1930 were the decisive lost opportunity for the Spanish Church. So, at least, thought a few frustrated, democratic, and socially aware Catholics. With a handful of exceptions Catholic lay spokesmen had shared the relief expressed by the hierarchy in 1923 as the iron surgeon began his lengthy operation on the country's failing, but not necessarily moribund, constitution. Bishops who had recently pleaded that projects to liberalize article 11 of the 1876 constitution be abandoned could relax. Under Primo de Rivera there seemed no threat of policies hostile to the Church while its usual enemies—anti-clerical Liberals, Anarchists, and Socialists—would be displaced, repressed, curbed or otherwise prevented from doing harm. The new protective calm proved soporific, however, with the result that no enduring benefit was gained from the advantages of a sympathetic regime and its corporatist experiments. So ran the anguished argument of Canon Arboleya's *Sermón Perdido* as he mourned in 1930 the hopes he had placed in the dictatorship in 1923. Far from utilizing the new opportunities to implement Catholic social teaching, Church leaders and organizations had contrived to identify themselves with reactionary social policies and anti-democratic politics.[1] In 1928 the former Maurist conservative Ángel Ossorio y Gallardo made a similar point in a commentary on Sturzo's study of Italian fascism, when he argued that Primo's dictatorship was illegitimate, and that Fascist and other Right-wing dictatorships were too like Bolshevik dictatorial systems to be relied on by Catholics as a bulwark against them.[2] But reliance on political solutions was deeply embedded in Catholic mentality, and in 1923—as in 1939—a military dictatorship seemed in itself a reassuring guarantee of security and success.

Cardinal Reig of Toledo welcomed the task of national 'regeneration' undertaken by the dictatorship, and to judge from their pastoral letters,

[1] M. Arboleya Martínez, *Sermón perdido* (Madrid, 1930.)
[2] A. Ossorio y Gallardo, *Un libro del abate Sturzo* (Madrid, 1928).

bishops were chiefly preoccupied in these crucial years by the continuing fall in real terms of state financial aid to the Church and the rapid rise in womens' hemlines as European fashions invaded the country.[3] The sense of crisis so evident in their recent writings disappeared, as narrowly institutional and pious concerns again took priority over fears of social disturbance and revolution. It was time for consolidation not experimentation. Reig himself did not bring to his short occupancy of the primatial see (1922–7) any reputation for innovative vigour. He insisted that all Catholic social action must be strictly confessional and he treated as a priority a cautious reorganization of Catholic Action in 1926 that strengthened episcopal control over it but achieved little else. He resisted suggestions from the Christian Democrat Group that a new series of conferences on social issues would be useful, often seeming afraid of discussion of economic reform while notoriously sympathetic to the social conservatism of the Integrist newspaper *El Siglo Futuro*. According to Fr. Francisco Morán, who was a member of the Group but also an ecclesiastical administrator well placed to know the views of the Spanish bishops, all but two or three of them shared Reig's reluctance to address the kind of issues that Aznar, Jiménez, Albó, and the other self-designated Christian Democrats kept trying to raise.[4] Claudio López Bru, Marquis of Comillas and the dominant figure in Catholic Action for thirty years died in 1925, but there was no sign that his death might open the way to a more realistic approach to contemporary social problems.

Reig was succeeded as archbishop of Toledo and director of Catholic Action by a man who carried the common Spanish Catholic aspiration to live in an enclosed and protected religious world, free of doubt, ambiguity, and competition, to quite extraordinary lengths. Pedro Segura y Saenz was not just illiberal and a stranger to compromise, lacking—as Cardinal Vidal i Barraquer was later to lament—'the balsam of gentleness and smoothness';[5] he was positively anti-modern with all the passion and ferocity of someone who believed that centuries of intellectual and cultural change could be successfully denied. Even Franco's dictatorship was to prove insufficiently respectful of ecclesiastical claims for his taste. His struggle was not so much for orthodoxy as for total ecclesiastical control of civil and cultural life. He was an

[3] Texts in Iribarren, 117–23, 125–30.
[4] Benavides Gómez, *El fracaso social*, 380–92.
[5] M. Batllori and V. M. Arbeloa (eds.), *Arxiu Vidal i Barraquer: Església i estat durant la segona república espanyola 1931–1936*, i (Montserrat, 1971), 131.

integrist ranged not just against nineteenth-century liberalism but against any inhibition on the Church's sway over human life. Born into a modest family in Burgos province, he later became the star pupil of his Jesuit teachers at the newly founded Comillas seminary.[6] Ordained in 1906 and consecrated auxiliary bishop of Valladolid ten years later, he became bishop of the backwoods diocese of Coria in Extremadura in 1920. From there he was rescued by Alfonso XIII who admired his blunt forthrightness and translated him to the archiepiscopal see of Burgos in 1926 and then, almost immediately, to Toledo. At the precocious age of forty-seven, he was head of the Spanish Church and known to be loyal to his royal patron, devout, utterly devoid of political flexibility or social nuance, unfamiliar equally with intellectual doubt, moral complexity, and analytical sophistication as he embarked on his primatial duties.

Segura appointed as president of Catholic Action Count Rodríguez Sampedro, and with this pious nobleman he planned for 1929 the first National Congress of Catholic Action, similar in many ways to the Catholic Congresses of the turn of the century and equally ineffective. The sessions in Madrid were pompous, fervent rituals without serious content. Comillas's Jesuit ally, Sisinio Nevares, was a speaker in the session on industrial issues, in which the confessional character of Catholic workers' unions was predictably emphasized. Unions were blandly described as instruments of peace and harmony between the classes, dedicated to 'studying, promoting, and defending common interests in determining conditions of work and the work contract'.[7] Perhaps more clearly than ever before, and with a higher authority, came the affirmation that workers' syndicates formed part of Catholic Action, which, given Segura's control of Catholic Action, meant that after more than thirty years of social Catholicism, syndicates were still seen as pious associations rather than unions to represent labour's interests in industrial negotiations and disputes. At the end of the Congress, conclusions of an anodyne generality were solemnly agreed, committing participants to 'the extirpation of social evils everywhere',[8] and Segura equally solemnly demanded the restoration of full Catholic unity to Spain.

While Reig and Segura led the hierarchy in pursuing the Church's

---

[6] There is a biography, R. Garriga, *El Cardenal Segura y el nacional-catolicismo* (Barcelona, 1977).
[7] Benavides Gómez, *El fracaso social*, 403.
[8] See above, p. 148.

institutional and pastoral concerns as they saw fit in a period of political calm, many lay Catholics participated enthusiastically in the structures and ideological validation of the dictatorship. The writer José María Pemán considered Primo's coup of September 1923 as fundamentally in harmony with Spain's 'inner constitution', which was centralist and Catholic. Religion was the necessary basis for order, and Pemán argued their connection more directly when he wrote that 'the wave of critical scepticism in ideas' had to be halted in order to stop 'the wave of revolutionary demolition' sweeping over the country. Pemán's apologia for the regime and its characteristic political institution, the Patriotic Union, claimed that religion was consubstantial with Spanish tradition and identity—a claim that echoed Menéndez y Pelayo and heralded the national-Catholic justifications for another dictatorship ten years later. Religious dissent or disaffection was, therefore, a failure of patriotism. Anti-centralists, anti-clericals and liberal pluralists alike lost at a stroke of the pen any respectable political ground on which to stand: their ideas were unSpanish, and unnatural.[9] Similar arguments appeared in articles by José Pemartín and others on the Spanish dictatorship, and soon became common currency on the anti-democratic Catholic right.[10]

More directly involved in the regime's political experiments was Eduardo Aunós, Minister of Labour from 1924 and the man chiefly responsible for the corporatist labour law of 1926. Aunós thought that the political Right had failed through selfishness, the Left through illusory hopes, while Primo offered a new corporatist alternative that would transcend the horrors of liberalism and combine the Left's desire for social justice with the Right's sense of tradition. He stated that his inspiration for the 1926 law had been drawn not only from Mussolini's Italy, and Spanish experience, but from earlier social Catholic thought in France—especially La Tour du Pin—and Germany.[11] It is curious, however, that Catholic labour institutions did not derive much benefit from corporatist organization rooted in Catholic aversion both to liberal individualism and to assumptions about the inevitability of class conflict. Aunós's law set up joint committees of employers and workers to settle wages and work conditions (*comités paritarios*), but with the Anarchists outlawed it was the Socialist UGT not the Catholic unions that seized the opportunity. Until the end of 1930, when it was too late, the confessional Catholic unions and the non-confessional but none the less

[9] J. M. Pemán, *El hecho y la idea de la Unión Patriótica* (Madrid, 1929).
[10] For a brief survey, see S. Ben-Ami, *Fascism from Above* (Oxford, 1983), 174–89.
[11] E. Aunós, *La reforma corporativa del estado* (Madrid, 1935).

Catholic *Libres* were usually unable to put up a common slate for *comité paritario* elections. Since victory went to the majority union while the minorities went unrepresented, fragmentation of the Catholic vote as well as the small numbers mobilized in much of the country ensured that the Catholic unions rarely gained representation.

Much more successful was Catholic representation in the Patriotic Union, a political association through which Primo hoped to transfer administrative and political responsibilities into civilian hands after the initial military phase of his regime. The Patriotic Union began in Valladolid in circles connected with Herrera's Propagandists, *El Debate*, and the short-lived Popular Social Party. Its extension through Castile and beyond depended largely on the personnel of these interlocking Catholic groups, and it flourished in areas where it could draw on Catholic agrarian organizations and syndicates. Like its successors under the Second Republic—Popular Action and the CEDA—the Patriotic Union was the political expression and political prize of careful social Catholic toil to pre-empt socialist influence, especially among small peasant farmers. Involvement was almost automatic for leaders of the National Catholic Agrarian Confederation, and the CNCA's president, José Manuel de Aristizábal, helped launch it in Madrid together with José María Gil Robles, Propagandist, future secretary-general of the CNCA and future head of the CEDA. The Patriotic Union defended property, religion, the family, and the unity of Spain. It became an essential part of Primo's projected new state, which was to replace corrupt parliamentary wranglings with order and hierarchy while transcending class antagonisms and combining conservatism with social reform.[12]

The balance between conservatism and reform was not easily struck, however. The dictatorship increased social benefits and educational provision, and state representatives on the *comités paritarios* very often gave a casting vote for wage rises. Employers' associations protested, and were joined by Catholic landlords when the government tried to tighten tax controls and reduce rural unemployment. But the regime's reforms decisively outran erstwhile Catholic supporters when a decree of 1928 established in agriculture those joint committees on wages that had operated effectively in industry. The CNCA led the way in opposing this measure and blocking its implementation.[13] It would be the repub-

---

[12] For the origins and activities of the Unión Patriótica, see Ben-Ami, *Fascism from Above*, 126-60.
[13] Ibid., 298–303.

lic, not the Catholic dictatorship, that challenged property relationships in *latifundio* areas.

For most of Primo's regime, however, Catholics found little to criticize and much to applaud. Religion and patriotism held joint sway, not just in political rhetoric but also in education policy and censorship. The religious congregations were officially revered and encouraged; religious instruction was reinstated to the position it had lost in 1913 as compulsory for all children in state schools; conformism was demanded of pupils and teachers since, as Primo himself explained, 'no culture at school will be permitted that is not religious and patriotic'.[14] Catholic sexual mores were preached by Church and state alike. Here at last was a truly Spanish regime acting as Church leaders had always thought it should, as protector and promoter of Catholic values. As an army chaplain enthusiastically proclaimed, Primo was an Atlas holding the family, the monarchy, and the Church on his shoulders.[15]

For a while it even seemed that university education might be redeemed from the non-confessional and often free-thinking ethos that had exasperated traditional Catholics ever since the Church lost control in 1881. Re-Catholicizing the universities was too large an ambition for immediate realization in the 1920s, but the lesser and still fiercely controversial aim of incorporating confessional establishments within the university world had many influential advocates. In 1928 the government proposed to allow students from private colleges 'that had enjoyed a widely recognized and solid scientific and pedagogic reputation for more than twenty years' to be examined and awarded degrees alongside students in the state universities. The prime beneficiaries would obviously be the Jesuit colleges in Deusto and the Augustinian college at El Escorial. No other single domestic issue under the dictatorship provoked such noisy, articulate, and sustained opposition. Student demonstrators clashed with police; the universities of Madrid, Oviedo, Santiago, Valladolid, Salamanca, and Seville were temporarily closed, and protests were often anti-monarchist as well as anticlerical. Moreover, student irritation was shared by many of their most famous teachers. Ramón Menéndez Pidal wrote a letter of protest from Madrid, Fernando de los Ríos from Granada, while Unamuno—the already exiled Rector of the university of Salamanca—wrote not to Primo but to Spanish students, urging militancy, and criticizing the

[14] Quoted ibid., 104.
[15] M. Jover Mira, *La España Inmortal* (Madrid, 1930), 61.

dictatorship and a 'decrepit dynasty' along with Deusto and El Escorial. A few months before Primo lost power in January 1930, the proposed reform was suspended.[16] The whole episode was a warning to the dictator, and through him to the Church, of the enormous resistance among the best educated social groups in Spain to contemporary Catholic intellectual culture. Something stronger than Primo's dictatorship would be needed to impose its acceptance in circles where it was held in profound distaste as reactionary, narrow, bombastic, and impoverished.

The only serious confrontation between Church and government in these years of patriotism and religion arose precisely from conflicting notions of patriotism. In the Basque provinces Primo's extreme centralism infuriated Basque nationalists but won enthusiastic support from Zacarías Martínez, bishop of Vitoria from 1923 to 1928. No episcopal protest was raised when the dictator banned the use of Basque in catechesis, even in villages where young children would have difficulty with Spanish. Moreover, Martínez took the opportunity afforded by the opening of a new railway line in the presence of King Alfonso and General Primo de Rivera to pray that the new lines he blessed would 'communicate good ideas of peace, work, and *españolismo*, and that the criminal notions of separatism would never pass along them'.[17] The bishops of the Catalan ecclesiastical province of Tarragona, however, were not so subservient though they were far from being separatists.

In the spring of 1923 the Catalan bishops had confirmed an already established norm that preaching in Catalonia should normally be in Catalan. After the September coup, the new dictatorship chose to regard the use of Catalan in the pulpit as an attack on Spanish national unity, and kept Vidal i Barraquer and his colleagues under a constant barrage of criticism. The government tried unsuccessfully to move Vidal i Barraquer out of harm's way to the see of Zaragoza or Granada, and non-Catalan speaking bishops were appointed to Lérida and Tortosa. Even more alarming, however, was the bizarre series of documents from the Roman curia that began in December 1928 and took up the government's accusations.[18] The Catalan clergy was charged with political exploitation of the confessional and preaching separatist cam-

[16] For an account of this confrontation by one of the students active in the anti-government campaign, see J. López Rey, *Los estudiantes frente a la dictadura* (Madrid, 1930).

[17] For the PNV's complaint to the Vatican about bishops prior to Múgica, see I. Moriones, *Euzkadi y el Vaticano 1935–36* (Rome, 1976), 44–54, from which these examples are taken.

[18] The best account of this strange incident is R. Muntanyola, *Vidal i Barraquer, Cardenal de la pau* (Montserrat, 1976) 213–29.

paigns from the pulpit; the seminaries were described as centres of exaggerated and pernicious regionalism in need of severe disciplining. These serious accusations from Rome, made without any evidence being adduced, represented a notable victory for the government. The status of the documents was unclear, however, and eventually the affair fizzled out without any result other than to demonstrate that the Church could be divided against itself when pastoral and political matters overlapped. As a much more formidable dictatorship was to learn in the 1960s, such division was not always beneficial to the government in power.

However much Primo disliked regionalist movements, his most fundamental problem remained what it had been all along—the exact shape to be given that rectification of Spanish politics that his coup in 1923 had begun. In October 1927 a new phase began with the opening of the National Assembly, a consultative body charged with making proposals for a new constitution. The National Assembly's composition reflected the corporatist convictions of its creator, with representatives of 'activities, classes, and values' as well as of the state, provinces, and municipalities, along with a block of Patriotic Union members. That Catholic enthusiasm for the Assembly embraced men as different as Gafo and Pemán was not surprising, considering the common ground provided by their loathing of liberalism. To eager Patriotic Union deputies assembled not just in their own right but also among the representatives of other categories, this was the awaited opportunity to construct a new, Catholic, truly Spanish state, more congenial than any known for generations. When the draft of the constitution was published in July 1929, however, Primo's dictatorship was already in crisis. Attempted rebellion, army disaffection, growing dislike among industrial and agrarian élites of state interventionism, economic and currency fluctuations, the irreconcilable opposition of most dynastic politicians and virtually all major Spanish intellectuals, and the growing irritation of King Alfonso were all combining to force his fall which eventually came in January 1930.

Not least because of the poor reception afforded the corporatist constitutional draft of 1929, Primo's successor General Berenguer hastened to abandon newfangled methods and set about returning to the dishonoured 1876 constitution. But the effects of the previous six and a half years were not so easily undone. A Catalanist movement immeasurably radicalized and alienated by Primo's obsessive centralism could no more tolerate a restoration of pre-1923 political structures than would the Socialists. Some of the old dynastic politicians contemplated with increasing confidence doing without the Bourbon dynasty altogether, and not even the army found the prospect of a non-monarchical Spain worse than the likely alternative of a civil war to maintain a hopelessly compromised king. In February 1931 eminent intellectuals like Gregorio Marañón and José Ortega y Gaset, who had been in conspicuous dispute with the dictatorship for some years, founded a Group at the Service of the Republic, thereby signalling a widespread conviction that no hope for the cultural and social modernization of the country could reasonably be placed in a morally and politically exhausted monarchy. By the time Admiral Aznar replaced the defeated Berenguer in February 1931, republicanism had become for many not so much a passionate, crusading commitment as simply the necessary starting-point for political, social, and cultural reconstruction.[19] In April municipal elections were held as a preliminary to national ones. They were manipulated less than any before, and while rural Spain provided an overall monarchical majority vote, the towns and cities repudiated the monarchy. Alfonso XIII left Spain to its republican but otherwise uncertain future.

For decades the Church had relied on the crown for support. More recently, it had shown little of that exasperation and despair experienced both by settled republicans and, more importantly, by the numerous and varied groups converted to republicanism by the dictatorship. On the contrary, Catholic associations had given life to the Patriotic Union, Catholic schools had flourished unhindered, and Jesuits and Augustinians had seen no danger in seeking degree status for their colleges from a dictator despised by the leaders of the intellectual establishment. The Free Unions had expanded enormously in Catalonia and other areas where they profited without embarrassment or thought for the future from the regime's proscription of the Anarchists, and in their new strength they dangerously combined admiration for dictatorship with contempt for Catalanism and a growing taste for Fascist solutions.[20] When, on the last day of 1930, Cardinal Segura eventually brought himself to sanction the alliance of the confessional with the Free unions, this belated move to Catholic solidarity also served to make the Catholic unions even more suspect in the new political climate than they were already. Segura himself watched the events of 1930 with alarm, recognizing in a pastoral letter of 27 February that 'the moral, religious,

---

[19] The essential work on the origins of the republic is S. Ben-Ami, *The Origins of the Second Republic in Spain* (Oxford, 1978).

[20] Winston, *Workers and the Right in Spain, 1900–1936*, Chs. 5 and 6.

and social order' was in question as well as the political.²¹ A man who had recently closed the national congress of Catholic Action with a call for the restoration of Catholic unity could not but lament republican tendencies that were about to sweep away the Church's staunchest ally. His alarm was shared by other bishops who were unable suddenly to rethink their settled conviction that monarchy, patriotism, and religion formed an indissoluble whole.²² Catholic students, religious, bishops, Catholic industrial and rural syndicates, Catholic newspapers and periodicals had backed Primo de Rivera's version of Spanish regeneration, mourning only inadequate clergy stipends and over zealous plans for a new deal for rural labourers. There was reason for Canon Arboleya's pessimism as he wondered in 1930 what would become of the Church after the elections that everyone could see were unavoidable. 'Not only did we neglect the opportunity to prepare to act properly within a democratic regime, now unquestionably close, but we took every means—often perhaps only too effectively—to ensure that we now figure as the enemies of what the whole people considers a great advance and a priceless victory.'²³

While thousands ecstatically greeted the proclamation of the Second Spanish Republic on 14 April 1931 as the dawn of social and cultural modernity, foreboding was justifiably a more usual spontaneous response among Catholics. On 15 April Bishop Gomá of Tarazona wrote to Vidal i Barraquer that 'we have now entered into the vortex of the storm ... I am absolutely pessimistic'. On 16 April, Vidal i Barraquer reported to the papal nuncio Tedeschini that he intended to seek an interview with the Catalan leader Maciá swiftly, 'in order to see if I can manage to avert radical measures, contrary to the interests of religion'. On 17 April, Cardinal Segura addressed a grim circular to all bishops: 'Undoubtedly our country has suffered a severe blow with the events of these days; please God that they do not prove, sooner or later, the cause of its death.' Vidal i Barraquer's reply was less catastrophist, but extremely apprehensive as he prayed 'may God help us, for difficult times await us and we have to be ready for everything'.²⁴ Segura's notorious pastoral letter of 1 May reminded Catholics of their duty to obey the civil authorities but also included a warm appreciation of the monarchy and of Alfonso XIII, 'who throughout his reign knew how

---

[21] Quoted in Garriga, *El Cardenal Segura*, 134.
[22] Ben-Ami, *The Origins*, 175–6.
[23] Arboleya, *Sermón perdido*, 128–9.
[24] Arxiu Vidal i Barraquer: *Església i estat*, i, 19, 20, 21–2, 30–1.

to preserve the ancient tradition of faith and piety of his ancestors'. This inopportune and provocative act of royalist homage which earned Segura rapid government orders to leave the country was not at all characteristic of episcopal statements as a whole, which followed the line set by the nuncio in both promising themselves and demanding of their people a proper respect for the new republican authorities.[25] But it is evident from their correspondence that even the most politically sophisticated and flexible of the bishops faced the republican order with fear from the very beginning, and certainly before any anti-clerical measure was enacted—unless the proclamation of liberty of conscience on 15 April be gratuitously accounted such—or any anti-clerical offence neglected.

Other Catholic responses told the same story. Count Rodríguez Sampedro, president of Catholic Action, left the country the day after the republic was inaugurated. The Jesuit *Razón y Fe* listed the republic's advent 'humbly' and without comment among other April events, like an earthquake in Managua and the opening of a new ecclesiastical college in Rome by the pope. It noted the 'great reception of Don Alfonso in Paris' but not the exuberant reception of the republic in Madrid.[26] *El Debate* had run a monarchist campaign before the municipal elections, balanced its acceptance of the republic on 15 April with a tribute to the king, and began almost immediately to rally the supporters of order, the family, religion, the fatherland, and property against 'the revolution'.[27] Catholics as different in temperament and mentality as Segura and Arboleya, or Vidal and Gomá, knew that the republic was much more than just a change of political or constitutional regime, and that the Church's position was vulnerable. Differences of opinion lay, therefore, not in the expectation of trouble ahead, but in the allocation of blame for the Church's vulnerability and in the assessment of what should be done.

The expected trouble soon materialized. On 10 May in Madrid a group of young monarchists meeting in a building on Alcalá played a record of the royal march through an amplifier as people were returning home to Sunday lunch from the Retiro park. The angry crowd tried to enter the building, and then headed for the offices of the monarchist paper

---

[25] For a brief but balanced survey, see V. M. Arbeloa, *La semana trágica de la iglesia en España (octubre 1931)* (Barcelona, 1976) pp. 11–45.

[26] *RyF*, xcv (1931), 285–6.

[27] For *El Debate*'s coverage of these crucial weeks, see P. Preston, *The Coming of the Spanish Civil War* (London, 1978), 27–30.

ABC whose owner, Juan Ignacio Luca de Tena, was considered largely responsible for the monarchist provocation on Alcalá. Two people were killed and others injured in a confrontation there with the Civil Guard. The following day, in a counter-demonstration of hostility to the republic's assumed enemies, churches, religious schools, and convents in Madrid were burnt, to be followed by others elsewhere. On the grounds that 'all the convents in Madrid are not worth the life of one republican', the provisional government refused to allow the Minister of the Interior to use force to disperse the arsonists.[28] Equally intimidating to Catholics were government orders appearing in the official *Gaceta* on 23 May, that crucifixes and other religious symbols be removed immediately from all state schools. Ecclesiastical nervousness intensified when elections to a constituent Cortes in June 1931 returned a large majority of Republicans and Socialists. The first constitutional draft prepared by Ossorio y Gallardo and others was replaced by a much more daring text, creating a 'democratic republic of workers of every class'. It allowed for regional autonomy and for the forcible expropriation of property for reasons of social utility, and created a unicameral legislature—three measures which seemed to the Right respectively to dissipate national unity, open the way to the socialization of property, and promote hasty, ill-considered legislation. Most unpalatable to the Church, however, were the eventual articles 3, 26, 43, and 48, which between them deconfessionalized the state, introduced civil marriage and divorce, instituted a secular education system inspired by the ideal of human solidarity, and committed the Cortes to end state subvention of the clergy, dissolve the Jesuits, and ban all religious from industry, commerce, and education.

In the sweeping reversal of traditions and values that the republic represented, the Church was a prime casualty. The separation of Church and state and the introduction of civil marriage and divorce rudely terminated those dreams of total Catholic unity harboured by Cardinal Segura. But secular schooling, together with the withdrawal of state support for the diocesan clergy and church buildings, threatened the entire infrastructure of national Catholic culture. The Church was to be a voluntary association for those willing to subscribe instead of guardian of Spain's identity and conscience. It was a poor exchange, but made much worse by the intention to write into the very constitution

---

[28] See the account by the Catholic Minister of the Interior, M. Maura, *Así cayó Alfonso XIII* (Mexico, 1962), Ch. 5.

the dissolution of the Society of Jesus—periphrastically indicated as an order with a special vow of obedience which was not to the state—and the prohibition on the teaching work of the religious congregations. While the other measures, unpalatable as they were, could be interpreted as the sad, but perhaps inevitable, consequence of the secularizing propensities of Republicans and Socialists, these last were an assault on the basic rights of Catholic citizens and through them an intolerable attack on the Church, incompatible, as critics soon pointed out, with the constitution's own liberal principles.

The simplest explanation of this constitutional aggression for Catholics at the time was that it was an act of ideologically motivated hatred. The simplest explanation for historians ever since has been that it was the foolish and gratuitous expression of obsessive anti-clericalism, an elementary mistake that wiser counsel might have avoided. Some Catholics were painfully aware in 1931, however, that the offending articles of the republican constitution had to be seen in the context of Catholic identification with the monarchy and dictatorship, Catholic dislike of pluralism and democratic parliaments, Catholic inertia in the face of social injustice, and Catholic defence of private property rights regardless of social need. Canon Arboleya had recognized in 1930 that Catholics had earned their reputation as enemies of democracy and social reform. Fr. Ángel Carbonnel had written in 1927 of the danger inherent in the conservative classes' defending their property and fervently supporting dictatorship instead of introducing 'just and necessary' reforms.[29] Another Catalan priest, Carles Cardó, who was extremely influential in Catholic Catalan intellectual circles, published in July 1931 a reminder of the Church's teaching on the social function of property, so perilously ignored by Spanish Catholics.[30] Canon José Manuel Gallegos Rocafull of Córdoba had published in 1929 a plea for the hopelessly poor agricultural labourers of Andalusia, and in 1935 argued in his doctoral thesis that Catholic social teaching derived from St. Thomas Aquinas had always emphasized the instrumental nature of wealth, and the social function of property as well as individual property rights. Defending an unjust property distribution in Spain in the 1930s bore no relation whatever to this orthodox tradition.[31] In his charac-

---

[29] A. Carbonell, *El colectivismo y la ortodoxia católica* (Barcelona, 1927), 34–5.

[30] C. Cardó, 'Les funcions de la propietat privada segons la *Rerum Novarum*', reprinted in *La moral de la derrota i altres assaigs* (Barcelona, 1959), 333–48.

[31] J. M. Gallegos Rocafull, *Una causa justa. Los obreros de los campos andaluces* (Córdoba, 1929), and *El orden social* (Madrid, 1935), especially 19, 150–3.

teristically rhetorical and rebarbative style, the Catholic intellectual José Bergamín in 1935 berated contemporary Spanish Catholicism as often not only hypocritical and indifferent but also a mask for political and commercial interests that corrupted what it touched.[32] In the debates on religion in the constituent Cortes itself, the Catholic Catalan deputy Manuel Carrasco i Formiguera acknowledged the 'most grave error' of recent reliance of the Church on both monarchy and dictatorship.[33]

These self-criticisms of a small sector of the Spanish Church rehearsed issues that many anti-clerical deputies to the constituent Cortes gave as their reasons for approving the articles on religion. Some, of course, went much further, and used this unique opportunity to express a lifetime's hatred for the Church and the religious orders. When reminded of the forty-five-minute limit to interventions as he elaborated on the iniquitous behaviour of popes and the nonsense of miracles, Barriobero interrupted his crude diatribe to expostulate 'but this is the great theme of my entire life' before going on to claim that in a modern age, religion without state help would just wither away.[34] The Catalan anti-clerical, Samblancat, similarly explained that he had prepared his speech with his whole life, then went on to demand the 'humanizing' of priests by the provision of marriage, legitimate children, and work, and the complete abolition of the religious orders. Since women religious took money for laundry work and confectionery, and monks for making liqueurs and running guest-houses, they should at least come under the mercantile code. And he renamed the Jesuits the Mercantile Society of Jesus and refrained from calling them the Band of Thieves of Jesus only out of respect for thieves.[35]

Had such outbursts of common anti-clerical insults been the only content of these debates, the Church would have had little to fear. But hostility was more widespread and weighty. Cirilo del Río complained that 'the most outstanding collaborators of the dictatorship were formed ideologically in Deusto and El Escorial'. Humberto Torres argued that the religious congregations must be removed from the classroom because they were anti-liberal and a sect of the political Right. Hurtado said everyone knew of widespread popular hostility against, and even hatred for, the religious orders engaged in welfare work, though he wanted some gentler solution than expulsion. Alberca Montoya

[32] J. Bergamín, 'La callada de Dios', *Cruz y Raya* (August, 1935), 77–84.
[33] *DSCC*, 1652–3.
[34] *DSCC*, 1586–92.
[35] *DSCC*, 1612–15.

reckoned that religious schools deformed their pupils, for instance in matters of sexual values, while Jiménez de Asua—chief drafter of the constitution—detailed the deformation represented by religious teachers telling children that their fathers' advanced political views were 'a veritable spiritual infirmity'. He accused the Church also of defending the dictatorship, and religious communities of forcing the consciences of patients in their hospitals.[36]

Of all the contributions to the crucial debate on religious affairs in the Spanish parliament in October 1931, the most influential was that of Manuel Azaña, an intellectual who came to be more closely identified with the republic by both its adherents and its opponents than any other single figure. In an argument strangely reminiscent of those adduced by Liberal ministers in the first years of the century when trying to restrict the growth of the religious congregations,[37] he insisted that the good of the state took priority over individual liberties, and that the education institutions run by religious were a danger to the state. Claiming to speak from experience—he was educated by Augustinian monks—he told his listeners that the defence of the republic required the closure of the religious schools, committed to propagating 'everything that is contrary to the principles on which the modern state is founded'. He also despised the use of welfare work 'as a vehicle for proselytism that we cannot tolerate'; but on the grounds that there was no immediate substitute available for the hospitals, clinics, and orphanages of the religious, Azaña pleaded successfully that they—together with harmless contemplative nuns—be spared, and that Jiménez Asua's original draft abolishing all religious communities be changed to deal only with the Jesuits and the other teaching congregations. Azaña earned scant appreciation from Catholic commentators for this act of salvage, entering Catholic demonology instead as the evil spirit who dared point out, in the same speech, that in terms of intellectual culture and creativity, 'Spain has ceased to be Catholic'.[38]

Against the anti-clericalism and often the anti-Catholicism of the majority, Catholic deputies asserted their contrary and positive experience of the religious schools and their different view of Spanish culture.[39] While some continued to press the lost cause of a confessional state, a disconsolate Alcalá Zamora, Catholic head of the republican govern-

---

[36] *DSCC*, 1542, 1558–61, 1600, 1628–9, 1663–5.
[37] See above, pp. 77–8.
[38] *DSCC*, 1666–72.
[39] e.g. Gil Robles and Carrasco i Formiguera, *DSCC*, 1713–14, 1708–10.

ment, accepted the separation of Church and state, and the end of state stipends for diocesan priests, but fruitlessly urged a much slower transition, and a later limiting law on the religious congregations rather than any outright constitutional ban. Ossorio y Gallardo rightly but uselessly pointed out the danger of Azaña's elevation of state defence over individual rights, and appealed to the chamber not to alienate from the republic conservative masses who might otherwise be won for it. Alcalá Zamora in a further intervention correctly predicted that the prohibition on the teaching orders would be impossible to implement and would bring the law into disrepute.[40] Their efforts were in vain.

It is impossible to know how republican politics would have developed if the debate had gone differently. It was certainly the case that the dissolution of the Jesuits and the attempted closure of the religious schools provided the Right with a perfect moral justification for opposition sometimes to the republic itself and consistently to the social, economic, and regionalist reforms as well as the religious measures of its constituent Cortes. It was also true that although the Jesuit order was disbanded, many individual members—now technically no longer Jesuit—remained active in Spain, and that the supposed closure of the religious schools was a fiasco as Alcalá Zamora had warned. Changes of dress, nomenclature, and official, though not necessarily actual, head teachers easily created an illusion of compliance at total variance with reality, especially as the law enacting the constitutional ban was passed only in June 1933, just a few months before elections returned a conservative majority utterly out of sympathy with it.[41] That the articles on religion were approved overwhelmingly in October 1931 cannot be simply attributed, however, either to the political naïvety of the majority coalition or to the evident distaste of intellectuals like Azaña or Fernando de los Ríos for Catholic dogma. As a few Catholics saw at the time, many Spaniards thought the Church anti-republican in spirit if not in words because of its entrenched and obvious reluctance to admit that

---

[40] *DSCC*, 1602-11, 1714-17, 1717-18.
[41] A company called SADEL (*Sociedad Anónima de Enseñanza Libre*) was formed to take some schools formally into Catholic lay responsibility; Salesians set up in each of their schools an *Asociación Escolar* which assumed legal ownership while the religious teachers went on as before, but under lay names and with lay dress; the Augustinians opened two schools in place of the two they had to close in Madrid, with the religious adopting lay style; the de La Salle brothers exchanged the entire staffs of their schools, who were then introduced in their new place with lay names. There are many more examples. With the exception of the Jesuit schools, the suppression of the religious schools was a law observed more in the breach than in the observance.

parliamentary democracy, pluralism, and urgently needed reform of industrial wages and the rural economy which together constituted the very essence of the republican regime for the masses who voted in June 1931 for a change of direction. The Church schools were particularly disliked for their class basis and their undoubtedly anti-democratic ethos.[42] The constitutional attack on the Church in fact did the republic more harm than the Church itself; it was counter-effective in its mobilization of a mass Catholic opposition; it was inept in its method and timing. But the fear and determination that inspired it were neither misplaced nor exaggerated. The Church was a danger to the democratic and modernizing republic well before the republic tried, futilely, to disarm it.[43]

The responses to the republic of Catholic leaders fell into three main categories. Most uncomplicated were the catastrophists who saw it simply as a disaster to be endured or even overthrown. At the other extreme were a few positive sympathizers and supporters, though their loyalty was severely strained by the anti-clerical initiatives of the two-year constituent phase. Between them lay a variety of people who accepted the republic with differing degrees of reluctance and resignation while attempting to operate within it and draw it to more conservative positions. But all Catholics, however they differed in their attitudes towards the republic and their interpretations of the reasons for its anti-clericalism, inevitably disliked the attack on the religious orders, worried about how the Church was to be financed, especially in areas with a low level of religious practice, and saw the sharp drop in numbers among those training for the priesthood as another sign of the Church's institutional precariousness when the privileges and state protection of decades were abruptly withdrawn.

Cardinal Segura expected nothing good from the republic. In the supposedly collective pastoral letter he wrote on behalf of the hierarchy in July 1931—and which Vidal declined to sign—he described the notion that authority derives from the people as 'atheism', embodied in the 'Godless democracies of our days'. He depicted his contemporaries as repeating the Jews' repudiation of Jesus, and argued that there would be no true happiness and prosperity if the state had no official religion. Using carefully selected papal texts to back his argument, he denounced the separation of Church and state as false and pernicious, and referred

[42] See above, pp. 81–2.
[43] For a fuller discussion of this theme, see F. Lannon, 'The Church's crusade against the Republic', in P. Preston (ed.), *Revolution and War in Spain 1931–1939* (London, 1984).

to the Church as a 'perfect sovereign society' which the state had no right to subordinate to itself. Liberal democracies were 'enemies of the Church', and freedom of religion an error. He advised Catholics 'to avoid contact with the enemies of the Church as far as possible'.[44] The same total mistrust was evident in instructions Segura sent all bishops about the safeguarding of Church property, including advice that ecclesiastical capital might be well invested in French or English government bonds. When a copy of this invitation to export capital was intercepted by frontier police on its way to Bishop Múgica of Vitoria, the government insisted on the continuing exile of the author and the expulsion of Múgica, as well as petitioning the Vatican to dissolve itself from the whole affair by removing the Cardinal Primate from his see, which in September it duly did.

The regime could hardly exile the whole bench of bishops, but Segura was certainly not alone in his contempt for the republic. Bishops for whom an officially Catholic state upholding the Church's cultural and ideological hegemony remained the ideal could not but regard the republic as an evil to be tolerated only while no alternative existed. Gomá, for example, never moved from his total pessimism. Bishop Irurita, who in 1929 had appealed for the restoration of Catholic unity to Spain and argued that the Church's authority was as omnipresent as God himself, inevitably brought that same mentality to his catastrophist pastoral letters in Barcelona in the summer of 1931.[45]

Some Catholic deputies in the constituent Cortes expressed their impatience with the republic in the clearest of terms during the debates on religion. One of the Basque–Navarrese minority, Beunza, ended his intervention with a threatening quotation and challenged his hearers not to force him to act on it. 'If persecution dawns we shall take refuge in our mountains, and there we shall seek counsel of our despair and of our dignity as free men against tyranny.' Lamamié de Clairac, Traditionalist owner of vast estates in Salamanca province, warned that if anti-clerical measures were passed, 'we shall have no alternative but to go against this constitution ... which we shall be absolutely unable to accept'. The priest Antonio Pildain was even more explicit, explaining that according to Catholic doctrine, resistance to unjust laws might be expressed by passive resistance, by active means within the law, or by armed force.[46]

[44] Text in Iribarren, 135–50.
[45] M. Irurita, *Pastorales 1927–32* (Barcelona, 1932).
[46] DSCC, 1639, 1685–6, 1707.

This was not an idle threat. It was widely known that already in 1931 Carlist groups were undergoing military training in Navarre. By 1935 there were nearly 6,000 of them.[47] In 1934 a canon of Salamanca cathedral, Aniceto Castro Albarrán, wrote a long and detailed book demonstrating the theological propriety of an appeal to force. He called for a great religious and patriotic armed crusade, scorned those Catholic groups working within the constitution for change, and praised Segura.[48] Although Vidal i Barraquer succeeded in having the ecclesiastical licences for this provocative book withdrawn, Gomá—by then archbishop of Toledo—reckoned it was theologically sound.[49] In March 1934 Catholic monarchists and Traditionalists met Mussolini to secure Italian arms and money for the eventual rising against the republic. There were many in the interlocking groups of Traditionalists and Acción Española who held that acceptance of the constitution meant Catholics shamefully accepting second-class status as citizens when they would be more honourably employed planning the constitution's overthrow.[50]

How far were these convictions the result of the offending articles on religion in the constitution? For two important reasons it is more accurate to see them as justified and confirmed by anti-clerical measures rather than created by them. Firstly, scepticism of the republic certainly antedated the religious debates of October and even the June elections which returned the Republican–Socialist majority whose views on the contemporary Church were no secret to anyone. Rooted aversion to liberalism, pluriformity, democratic procedures, and parliaments had been long embedded in the Catholic Right and had recently borne conspicuous fruit in Catholic sympathy and active support for the dictatorship. Segura himself had been no great admirer of Primo, but as his letter of July 1931 showed, he regarded democracies as 'Godless' and abhorred the theory of popular sovereignty. Primo's Catholic apologists found the republic intolerable because it was democratic, not just because it was anti-clerical. The periodical *Acción Española*, for example, that gathered together many of the authoritarian Catholic Right into a political movement of the same name declared in its foundation

---

[47] A. Lizarza Iribarren, *Memorias de la conspiración. Cómo se preparó en Navarra la Cruzada 1931–6* (Pamplona, 1953).
[48] A. Castro Albarrán, *El derecho a la rebeldía* (Madrid, 1934).
[49] R. Comás, *Isidro Gomá. Francesc Vidal i Barraquer* (Salamanca, 1977), 89.
[50] Pedro Sáinz Rodríguez, *Testimonio y recuerdos* (Barcelona, 1978), 183–4 for his information to the Vatican on the futility of the political line taken by the nuncio and Herrera.

programme in December 1931 that Spanish liberalism was both derivative and unnecessary, even a kind of anti-patriotism. In 1934 Ramiro de Maeztu's *Defensa de la hispanidad* developed this programme, rejoicing that at last the liberal democracies were looking degenerate as France, England, and the United States struggled with mass unemployment: since liberalism, socialism, and the Enlightenment were bankrupt, Spain's alternative tradition of Catholicism, patriotism, and hierarchy could begin to come into its own at last.[51] In these circles there was again much talk of Spain's 'inner constitution' and 'national essence', mystical substances apparently incompatible with universal suffrage and party structures.[52]

The second reason to doubt that Catholic hostility to the republic was generated solely by its anti-clericalism is that Catholics who opposed the republic on the religious orders, or clergy stipends, or divorce, often opposed it also on wages, agrarian reform, and regional devolution. This was clearest among those groups who claimed not to oppose the republic as such, but rather to accept its existence while campaigning against particular policies. Much the largest and most important was National Action, later called Popular Action, that formed the core of mass Catholic political mobilization in the CEDA (Spanish Confederation of Autonomous Right-wing Groups). This emanation of Herrera's Propagandists and *El Debate* put out its first manifesto on 7 May 1931, defending religion against atheism and communism, the unity of the fatherland against 'insane' local nationalisms, the family against free love, order against a 'class dictatorship', a free labour market against state intervention, private property against collectivism. With the usual Catholic suspicion of democratic political vocabulary it termed itself not a party but an anti-revolutionary movement of social defence.[53] Seeing the way the political wind was blowing, Herrera had as early as June 1930 worked out on the basis of Leo XIII's encyclicals a clear distinction between constitution and law, that enabled him to argue that Catholics could always work to change the law even within the framework of an uncongenial constitution.[54] In December 1931 he urged Catholics to give their attention not to the secondary or

---

[51] R. de Maeztu, *Defensa de la hispanidad* (Madrid, 1934). The *Acción Española* programme forms a kind of prologue to the work.
[52] See, e.g. Sáinz Rodríguez's prologue to Canon Castro Albarrán's book.
[53] Text in J.R. Montero, *La CEDA. El catolicismo social y político en la II República* (Madrid, 1977), ii, 593–4.
[54] 'Los principios de la política cristiana según León XIII', reprinted in A. Herrera Oria, *Obras selectas* (Madrid, 1963), 11–24.

'accidental' question of monarchy or republic, but to the essential task of saving Spain from 'a socialism at the service of Freemasonry'. But this vaunted 'accidentalism' did not imply loyalty to the republican constitution: it merely meant Catholic aims could be achieved without a king, through the means currently available. Herrera regarded the 1931 constitution as out of date and moribund, and looked to constitutional reform to bring it closer to the new European models, with a stronger executive, a 'modified' democracy, and corporatist representation. In 1928 Herrera had talked to a Propagandist study circle in Madrid about Spain's 'internal, unwritten constitution' that included monarchy and religion and that no plebiscite could overthrow. He had now adapted his theme to changed conditions, but only to the extent of seeking order, hierarchy, and religion in terms quite obviously incompatible with the democratic, secular constitution of 1931.[55]

Loud championing of the Church was linked always by Popular Action and CEDA with, at best, a sceptical indifference to democracy, an indifference shared by those on the Left of the Republican spectrum whose sympathies were more Jacobin than liberal. In election speeches in 1933 Gil Robles stated quite categorically that if CEDA ideals could not be attained through democratic elections and parliament, then parliament and democracy could be abandoned—they were secondary. No attempt was made to curb the increasingly Fascist style and rhetoric of CEDA's youth movement, JAP (*Juventud de Acción Popular*). A mass rally of JAP at the Escorial in April 1934 hailed Gil Robles as Spain's *Jefe*, a translation of the Italian *Duce*. The CEDA parliamentary deputy for Zaragoza, Ramón Serrano Suñer, called for a new state to replace parliamentary degeneracy. The CEDA deputy for Valladolid, Luciano de la Calzada, claimed it was not possible to speak of Right and Left, but only of Spain and an anti-Spain that had to be vanquished and dominated. Accordingly, 'the first step towards a national politics must be the abolition of all political parties'.[56] It is not surprising that when three CEDA ministers were appointed to the government in October 1934, many considered that the republic had been delivered into the hands of its enemies. CEDA's reputation for authoritarian proclivities hardened when its leaders demanded the most severe repression and punishment of those, especially workers in Asturias, who attempted in

[55] 'El acatamiento al poder constituido', ibid., 25–40; 'Patriotismo y nacionalismo', ibid., 69–83.
[56] For a gloating account of these speeches by another CEDA deputy, see J. Monje y Bernal, *Acción Popular* (Madrid, 1936), 260–84.

October 1934 to rise against a republic they thought now dangerously reactionary. When Gil Robles himself became Minister of War in May 1935, he rapidly promoted known anti-republicans to key positions, including Franco as Chief of the General Staff. In CEDA circles, Catholic loyalty often accompanied a disparaging of democracy by word, deed, and omission.

Defence of the Church was also tightly linked with the defence of property, especially landed property. There was no comfort and an enormous threat to the small peasant farmer of Valladolid or Burgos province in both the religious and agrarian legislation of the early republic. His religious sensibilities were grossly offended, while agrarian reform projects which attempted to ameliorate the appalling misery of landless labourers by setting minimum wages and experimenting with exiguous land redistribution, did nothing to help him to keep on, or just above, subsistence level. CEDA deputies claimed a vital interest in social reform, and could have devised policies to secure their smallholding constituents while also aiding the weak efforts to help the landless. But Popular Action deputies opposed the 1932 agrarian bill—mainly on the grounds that it violated property rights—and demanded its repeal after the victory of the Right in the 1933 elections. Worse, they blocked the limited but genuine reforming schemes of CEDA's own social Catholic agriculture minister Giménez Fernández in 1934–5, even though he justified them with reference to the encyclicals of Leo XIII. The record of the overlapping group of CNCA deputies was the same: they repudiated the cautious and limited expropriation measures of 1932, and CNCA Traditionalist vice-president Lamamié de Clairac torpedoed Giménez Fernández's bill on agrarian leases while shamelessly declaring that if the choice lay between schism and his estates, he would choose his estates.[57] Obstruction of minimal reform of cruelly unjust property relations accompanied fervent campaigning for religion and a profound scepticism of democracy. Propertied, conservative Catholics had more to quarrel with in the republic than its expulsion of the Jesuits or its plans to secularize education.

Also in this middle category of Catholics who neither liked the republic nor overtly condemned it were two exceptionally important Church leaders, the papal nuncio Tedeschini and Cardinal Vidal i Barraquer who, from Segura's forced resignation in September 1931 until Gomá's

[57] See especially Preston, *The Coming of the Spanish Civil War*, Chs. 2, 4, and 6, and Montero, *La CEDA*, ii, 172–207.

appointment as his successor in the summer of 1933, was acting head of the Spanish Church. Unlike the 'accidentalist' politicians, they were solely concerned with religious and ecclesiastical issues, and their distinction between respect for the republic and strong opposition to some of its constitutional and legal enactments was simpler and more consistent than CEDA's. Both of them found Segura a thorn in the flesh and warned Vatican Secretary of State Pacelli against 'the defeatism initiated and propagated with blind tenacity by extremist elements in certain Catholic and religious circles'.[58] Their task was an unenviable one, caught between a largely unsympathetic government and a bellicose Catholic Right that also kept the Vatican informed of its version of events in Spain and held the nuncio, Vidal, and Herrera in derisive contempt.

Vidal was well aware that alternatives existed to the careful negotiation he espoused. In a June 1931 report to Pacelli he mentioned rumours of armed training in the Catholic north, and of 'sympathy and promises from some neighbouring country', but concluded that all this was very risky and likely to provoke immense hostility to the Church, although 'it could be a hope for the future'. In a further report in August, he referred to rumours of a rising against the republic by the Right, but judged it would be premature and, in any case, quite wrong for the Church.[59] He chose instead the path of steady, reasoned criticism of government initiatives, and as late as 14 September he and Tedeschini met the President of the republic and the Minister of Justice to secure an agreement—soon proved worthless—to avoid the dissolution of the Jesuits and the attack on Catholic education while accepting as inevitable the separation of Church and state, withdrawal of state funding of the clergy, civil marriage, and divorce.[60] After the collapse of this tentative middle way in the Cortes debates of October, Vidal was left to frame a collective pastoral letter of the Spanish bishops, published in December, that deplored the new lay character of the state and education, and the restrictions placed on the Church. It was followed by a letter of the metropolitan archbishops on marriage in July 1932 and a second in May 1933 on the projected law to enact the constitutional restraints on the religious congregations. All three documents soberly emphasized the Church's discontent with republican religious legis-

---

[58] *Arxiu Vidal i Barraquer. Església i estat*, i, 307. This publishing archive is the essential source for the activities of Vidal, the nuncio, Herrera, and the Vatican.

[59] Ibid., 79–92, 202–9.

[60] Ibid., 313–23.

lation, argued that it exceeded the competence of the state since the Church's authority was divinely ordained, and called for its rapid reform, while avoiding strident or provocative language.[61] The victory of the Radicals and the Catholic Right in the elections at the end of 1933 seemed to augur well either for the eventual reform of anti-clerical legislation or at least for non-implementation of its most offensive elements, particlarly the closure of religious schools. But already Gomá's arrival in Toledo in July brought to that crucial see a man much closer to Segura than to Vidal in his assessment of the Church's proper role in contemporary politics.

It would be very difficult and probably impossible to find any republican enthusiast among the Spanish bishops. Their well-founded fears for the Church's safety would in themselves have provided more than ample reason for caution. Vidal was not alone in recognizing that the rhetoric of 'Catholic Spain' and social reality were two quite different things.[62] Where indifference towards the Church shaded off into hatred, as it did in much of the south and in areas of strong Anarchist loyalty, for example in Catalonia, the removal of state protection was especially threatening. In the first few years of the republic the number of boys training for the priesthood dropped by 40%. Cardinal Ilundain of Seville encountered daunting problems of apathy and hostility when he tried to make the parishes of rural Andalusia financially self-sufficient. Moreover, priests were complaining to him of popular violence against themselves, their churches, statues, and shrines, and of legal harrassment from the new Socialist and Anarchist local authorities.[63] Everyone knew that in crowded working class areas of the big cities there was little love for the Church and few would be concerned for its welfare.[64] In this situation a secularizing republic was too dangerous for dalliance.

Among Catholic political groups, however, some had quite specific reasons for positive republican loyalty. Foremost among these were the regional parties, for which the devolutionary intentions of the republic marked an enormous and welcome contrast with decades of centralist politics and particularly Primo's determined anti-regionalism. Even the one significant regional group linked with CEDA, the Valencian

---

[61] Texts in Iribarren, 160–212. For the text of the December 1931 letter after Vatican amendments had been incorporated, see *Arxiu Vidal i Baraquer. Església i estat*, ii, 672–705.
[62] *Arxiu Vidal i Barraquer. Església i estat*, i, 317.
[63] See above, pp. 14–15.
[64] See above, pp. 16–18.

Regional Right, maintained its commitment to autonomy, and its leader, Luis Lucia, eventually opted for defence of the republic when civil war broke out in 1936. The new Catalan Democratic Union similarly welcomed the move away from centralist politics, but also adopted quite radical Christian Democrat rather than conservative positions on other issues, including industrial relations, which gave it other points of contact with republican policies.[65] Incomparably more important than this miniscule new party, however, was the well-established Basque Nationalist Party with its large popular following and trade unions.

Many local factors led Catholic Basque nationalism, under the youthful leadership of José Antonio Aguirre, towards a moderate, reforming, Christian Democratic stance in the early 1930s. The strength of the Basque Solidarity unions—accounting for about 30% of the area's industrial workers by 1933—and the monarchist, centralizing sympathies of all but a handful of the region's big industrialists and bankers together nudged the PNV away from the Catholic Right. PNV representatives in the constituent Cortes deplored the anti-clerical articles of the constitution, but yearned for a Basque equivalent of the Catalan autonomy statute granted in 1932. In the elections of 1933 the party did extremely well, winning twelve out of seventeen seats. It remained as keen to defend Catholic schools and the family as were its co-religionaries in the Cortes, but the CEDA's centralism and ever more marked conservatism on industrial and agrarian matters held no attraction. Even when the projected Basque autonomy statute had been shorn of the religious powers originally claimed, the PNV still regarded it as the essential basis for all other political plans.[66] The PNV was reliably republican because of its hopes of autonomy; it could find little in common with the non-democratic Catholic Right; it was also unsympathetic to the Socialist left, both on ecclesiastical issues and in labour relations, and most notably in the abortive revolutionary movement of October 1934. In the Popular Front elections of February 1936 the PNV allied with neither Right nor Left, and saw its parliamentary representation cut from twelve to nine, while remaining the chief political party of Vizcaya and Guipúzcoa. Whatever its disagreements with Socialists and Left Republicans, however, it had little choice but to go

---

[65] For the Catalan Christian Democrats see H. Raguer, *La Unió Democràtica de Catalunya i el seu temps (1931–1939)* (Montserrat, 1976).

[66] See J. A. Aguirre y Lecube, *Entre la libertad y la revolución 1930–1935*. 2nd edn. (Bilbao, 1976); J. P. Fusi, 'The Basque question 1931–7', in Preston (ed.), *Revolution and War*.

on supporting the republic even when in July 1936 it was assailed by army generals ecstatically greeted by the Church hierarchy as saviours of Catholic civilization in Spain. For Catholic Basque nationalists, loyalty to the republic was instrumental rather than primary, but none the less firm for that.

With the exception of the Catholic regional parties—and of those only the PNV was big enough really to matter—there was no Catholic political party committed to the republic. Individual Catholic republicans rather than groups spring to mind, and that is of quite crucial importance for an understanding of both republican politics and Spanish Catholicism. It was perfectly possible for convinced, practising Catholics to be equally convinced republicans. One of the two men executed for a premature republican rising against the monarchy in 1930, García Hernández, was Catholic. There were three devout Catholics in the group that formed the San Sebastián pact to prepare a republican takeover, Alcalá Zamora, Maura, and Carrasco i Formiguera. The first head of government and then the first President of the republic was Alcalá Zamora; Miguel Maura was the republican Minister of the Interior who expelled Cardinal Segura and Bishop Múgica. The man chiefly responsible for the doomed first draft of the republican constitution was another notable Catholic, Ossorio y Gallardo, monarchist by preference, but republican by political logic from 1931. If a sizeable Catholic, conservative, republican party had grown round Alcalá Zamora, Maura, and Ossorio y Gallardo, republican politics might have looked very different. But the conservative Catholic vote was mobilized by Ángel Herrera's network of people and institutions which were already active long before any one of the three reluctantly and tardily abandoned monarchism and cast around to measure their support. They were preempted, and a difficult task was then made impossible by the republic's onslaught on the Church. In their attempt to find a middle way between reactionary Catholic politics and aggressively anti-clerical republicanism they were supported by a few priests and a few Catholic intellectuals, but not by any mass Catholic organization or newspaper.

The hostility to the CEDA evidenced by these Catholic republicans always bore the bitterness of betrayal. When the CEDA refused to support any longer a Radical government without CEDA members in October 1934 and successfully demanded three ministries, it was not just the revolutionary Left that judged this the end of democratic and reforming hopes. The fears of Socialists, Anarchists, and Catalan autonomists that CEDA participation in government would mean an authoritarian regime with no commitment to democracy were fully shared by Ossorio y Gallardo. When Gil Robles eventually became Minister of War in 1935, Ossorio reckoned that the republic was virtually finished.[67] At the end of 1935 President Alcalá Zamora dissolved the Cortes and called general elections rather than tolerate a CEDA government, even though CEDA had been since the end of 1933 the political party with the largest number of seats. Alfredo Mendizábal, Catholic professor in Oviedo, lamented that many Catholic conservatives were quicker to rely on police action than to implement Christian social doctrines. More especially he mourned the pitiless brutality with which the right-wing government, including CEDA ministers, put down the attempted revolution in Asturias in 1934, sparked off precisely by the CEDA appointments. Even though he lost about eight years' work with the destruction of his books, was held prisoner himself, and was well aware of murders committed by the miners, he argued that the use of countervailing violence was useless when what was needed was social reform and justice.[68] Similarly, José Bergamín held the parties of reaction—including CEDA—as much responsible as the parties of revolt for the events of October 1934.[69] Carles Cardó wrote despairingly in 1936 of the Catholic Right's 'suicidal, anti-patriotic, anti-Christian' resistance to justice, and particularly blamed the CEDA for siding with the rich against the masses when in power. He was appalled that the restoration of religious schools and street processions in 1934 and 1935 had been accompanied by repressive social and political policies.[70]

These remained, however, individual voices, with no institutional strength. CEDA, by contrast, spoke through *El Debate*, relied upon Catholic agrarian organizations, enjoyed governmental power, and retained close links with the hierarchy and the Vatican. Indeed, these were tightened when in the spring of 1933 Ángel Herrera was appointed director of Catholic Action in Spain; henceforth it was even easier than before to give the impression that CEDA was the natural political emanation of Spanish Catholicism. While those who challenged this assumption from the Left could draw on no reserves other than the puny force of their own arguments, those who did so from the Right

[67] A. Ossario y Gallardo, *La España de mi vida* (Buenos Aires, 1941), 134; *Mis memorias* (Madrid, 1975), 185.
[68] A. Mendizábel, *Aux origines d'une tragédie* (Paris, 1937), 149, 204–12.
[69] J. Bergamín, 'El "tris" de todo y¿ Qué es España?', *Cruz y Raya* (October 1934), 109–19.
[70] C. Cardó, 'La moral de la derrota', republished in *La moral de la derrota i altres assaigs*, 11–37.

increasingly co-ordinated their own anti-democratic alternatives. As the Traditionalists and Acción Española formed a National Block under Calvo Sotelo in 1934 to serve notice on Gil Robles's accidentalism and work for a corporatist, hierarchical, 'spiritual' Spain that would replace the existing constitution, they called confidently on long traditions of Catholic authoritarianism, dislike of liberal democracy, and expectations of salvation through military intervention.[71] The manifesto was signed by Pemán and Maeztu and Sáinz Rodríguez, its drafter, by Aunós, by many Traditionalists, but also by Fr. Gafo. In comparison with this array of Catholic leaders and political groups openly opposed to the democratic republic, and the CEDA forces determined to change it beyond recognition, Catholic republicans were few, isolated, lacking in established tradition and in institutional solidity.

[71] The manifesto, composed by Sáinz Rodríguez, is in J. Arrarás, *Historia de la Segunda República Española* (Madrid, 1968), iii, 58–60.

8
War and Victory

THE armed rising against the republic on 18 July 1936 had been insistently threatened since the victory of the Popular Front in the February elections. It was planned and led by Right-wing generals of various political persuasions, who were alarmed at the escalating disorder and violence in the country as groups on both the Left and Right of the political spectrum took to the streets. Catholics and Socialists helped prepare the way for military intervention by abandoning parliamentary methods of achieving their respective aims. The Socialist leader Francisco Largo Caballero continued to use inflammatory, revolutionary language, as the Socialist youth movement edged further and further away from democratic convictions. For their part, Carlists and Alfonsists had procured Italian arms and money as far back as March 1934, in a meeting with Mussolini, and representatives of both busily plotted in the spring and early summer of 1936. Particularly in Navarre, Carlists provided massed, enthusiastic, Catholic support for the rising, setting out to fight for God and Spain with chaplains at their side and Sacred Heart badges on their breasts.[1] Nor were these declared enemies of the republic alone in their energetic efforts. Gil Robles discussed the possibility of armed intervention with military leaders on various occasions, and as Minister of War between May 1935 and the end of the year did not fortify the army's will to defend the republic. He did not hesitate to place CEDA electoral funds at the disposition of one of the plotters, General Mola, and in June and July gave instructions that CEDA members should join the military action immediately, when it came.[2]

Once the Popular Front won the February elections, the legalist path of CEDA deputies gradually petered out as faith in parliamentary solutions diminished both on the Socialist Left and the Catholic Right,

---

[1] For the Carlists, see Lizarza Iribarren, *Memorias de la conspiración*; M. Blinkhorn, *Carlism and Crisis in Spain 1931–1939* (Cambridge, 1975), especially Chs. 9, 10, and 11. For the monarchists, see Sáinz Rodríguez, *Testimonio y recuerdos*, 194–252.

[2] Preston, *The Coming of the Spanish Civil War*, 153, 168, 179, 157–9, 193–4.

giving way to the proponents of direct action. Anarchists had never placed much trust in the state, even in its democratic, devolutionary form. At the other end of the political spectrum, Fascists increasingly outflanked not only the accidentalists but also the National Block politicians who had always been sceptical of the republic. The reforming governments of Azaña and then Casares Quiroga lacked Socialist—let alone Communist or Anarchist—participation, and were weak. Their ability to govern at all was compromised by terrorist tactics on the streets by both their opponents, notably the Fascist *Falange*, and their supposed supporters.

However, the question of Catholic contributions to the July rising is a much more complicated one than can be elucidated simply by tracing the actions of Carlists, Alfonsists, and accidentalists. There were no formal ecclesiastical involvement, no bishop-conspirators, no prior deal with the insurgent generals, and the primary motivation of the rising's military leaders was not religious. The first rebel statements stressed the insurgents' disgust at decentralizing policies that seemed to them tantamount to a dismembering of Spain, their fear of a disintegrating public order, and disapproval of 'communist' social reforms. With the exception of General Mola they did not mention religion.[3] Cardinal Gomá was quite right to point out to the Vatican the ideological diversity of the generals, and the fact that some of them 'would not be displeased with a laicizing republic, but with strong public order'.[4]

But Gomá was also correct when he argued that all the insurgent generals wished to defend 'Christian civilization' since in Spain that included the defence of national unity against separatist aspirations, of 'material interests threatened by a possible communist regime' and of a 'profoundly disturbed material order'.[5] It was precisely the widespread identification of Spanish Catholicism with social and political conservatism that made it the perfect ideological justification for a military rising against an anti-clerical, but also democratic, devolutionary, and socially reforming republic. Catholicism was a convenient shorthand for a whole series of conservative aims pursued with varying emphases and priorities by constitutional monarchists, Carlists, and law and order republicans. It had a useful and irreplaceable unifying function in the

---

[3] For the early military statements, see H. Raguer, *La espada y la cruz* (Barcelona, 1977), Ch. 2.
[4] A. Marquina Barrio, *La diplomacia vaticana y la España de Franco (1936–1945)* (Madrid, 1983), 44.
[5] Ibid., 44.

absence of any agreed common objective other than the seizure of power from the Popular Front government. Similarly, it united sociological groups of varying religious positions who felt themselves threatened by early republican legislation or by the Popular Front: many a petty bourgeois in Spain's provincial towns feared socialism and his own proletarianization as acutely as did the small farmer of Old Castile, and felt just as disturbed by the reversal of moral values and conventions experienced since 1931. Catholicism served as a positive, respectable, ideological focus for those protecting their sectional interests and social position, as well as those following their consciences, doing their professional military duty, or defending their faith.

Altogether less mutually beneficial was the relationship between Catholicism and the Spanish Fascists, led by José Antonio Primo de Rivera, son of the fallen dictator. The *Falange* saw itself as a revolutionary, nationalist movement destined to lead a united and regenerated Spain away from class conflict and materialism to the fulfilment of its spiritual mission. For some Falangists, like the writer Rafael Sánchez Mazas, that spiritual mission was undoubtedly Catholic. In 1933 he had stressed to a Catholic readership the tradition in Catholic thought that sanctioned armed resistance to civil authorities.[6] At the other extreme, the idiosyncratic Ernesto Giménez Caballero also sought the true identity of Spain in Catholicism, and argued in 1932 that when it abandoned Catholicism in ridiculous experiments with imported liberal values and democratic structures, it was bastardized. Traditionalists and revolutionary syndicalists might yet change this— Sales's *Sindicatos Libres* doubtless gave him some hope—for it was essential to find a Spanish solution that was not democratic nor Communist, nor even Fascist according to an Italian or German model. 'The Fascism for Spain is not Fascism, but Catholicism.'[7] In another work a year later Giménez Caballero traced Spain's spiritual links with Rome— as opposed to Europe—and in words reminiscent of the Italian futurists exulted that 'the essence of life is war, struggle, strife'. Europeanizing intellectuals from Jovellanos to Azaña had perverted Spain's proper character, but it was now to be redeemed. This would come not from Catholicism, which since the reformation had been in crisis, but from catholicity (*catolicidad*) of which Fascism was the new version. The first step needed was a Fascist state in Spain, followed by the subordination

---

[6] R. Sánchez Mazas, 'Siete escolios a la pastoral', *Cruz y Raya* (Aug., 1933), 143–60.
[7] E. Giménez Caballero, *Genio de España* (Madrid, 1932), 317.

to it of the Church.⁸ These odd theories did not so much use the Church for Fascist purposes as displace it altogether to realms of iconographic fantasy, leaving the real world of power to the heroic constructors of the new state. Many Fascists were far less interested in the Catholic question than either Sánchez Mazas or Giménez Caballero, and thought the latter's ideas and neologisms more than a little crazy, but the subordination of Catholicism to Fascism, and Church to state, that he advocated was a common feature of more ordinary *Falange* views on the new Spain.

The *Falange*'s previously small numbers had been enormously swollen in early summer 1936 as groups on the political Right abandoned legalist tactics and joined the rush to Fascism already well in evidence among members of the JAP.⁹ With its heady if vague revolutionary radicalism, and its emphasis on energy and national glory, it had a propagandist potential that could rival Catholicism's appeal where old-fashioned conservatism, regionally concentrated Carlism, and discredited Alfonsist monarchism could not. Its songs, salutes, and blue shirts endowed the rising with a modernity of style belied by the intentions of most of the insurgents. Many on the traditional Right disliked this rowdy upstart, and both Gomá and the Vatican regarded its displacement and deformation of Catholic vocabulary and symbolism and its glorification of the state with justified suspicion.¹⁰

Although some Catholic political parties and movements contributed directly or indirectly to the revolt against the republic, many of the insurgents were not particularly concerned about religion, seeing it rather as a necessary element of a threatened Spanish tradition and social structure than as the central issue for which they took up arms. Nevertheless, the immediate reaction to the attempted coup in July in many parts of the country was a murderous onslaught on ecclesiastical personnel utterly terrifying in its barbarity and extent. Thirteen bishops, 4,184 diocesan priests, 2,365 male religious and 283 religious sisters were hunted down and killed, mainly in the opening weeks of the war, and mainly where Anarchism was dominant. Sometimes they died in general reprisals against presumed local Rightist elements, as did five priests shot in Fuenteovejuna on the Andalusia–Badajoz border together with thirty-eight lay people on 20 September 1936. Sometimes they

---

⁸ E. Giménez Caballero, *La nueva catolicidad. Teoría general sobre el fascismo en Europa; en España* (Madrid, 1933).
⁹ S. Ellwood, *Prietas las filas. Historia de Falange Española 1933–1983* (Barcelona, 1984).
¹⁰ Discussed below, p. 208.

perished in quite separate attacks, like the fourteen Claretian novices shot on a railway platform on their way from Ciudad Real to Madrid, or the twenty-three Adoratrices nuns shot at dawn on 10 November in a cemetery in Madrid.[11] Fr. Gafo's sustained interest in labour reform did not save him; nor did Vidal i Barraquer's caution and moderation with republican leaders shield his auxiliary bishop, Borrás. Pro-Catalanist and pro-republican priests suffered the same fate in Barcelona as centralist and reactionary ones. Identification with the Church was a sufficient death warrant. Almost half of the priests of Gomá's Toledan diocese were killed, and over 60% of two Catalan dioceses in Anarchist areas, Barbastro and Lérida. At the same time, thousands of churches, monasteries, convents, and Catholic schools were destroyed. It was evident that for many on the Left the Church itself figured as an enemy, and that some Anarchists aimed to destroy it for ever, in spite of the appalled opposition of Anarchist leaders like Joan Peiró.[12] Catholic spokesmen had often complained of sectarian legislation as persecution, but here was persecution indeed, in Catholic Spain, on a scale probably never surpassed anywhere in the modern world.

In circumstances of such horror, it was unthinkable that Spanish bishops could be sympathetic to the republican cause in the war. However spontaneous and unauthorized the vast majority of anti-clerical assaults, they were perpetrated by the republic's supporters. For the very survival of the Church the violence against it had to be controlled, and the surest way of achieving that was victory for the insurgents or national forces, as they came to call themselves. Many bishops featured prominently in the war effort as they publicly blessed insurgent guns, said field Masses for the troops, and intoned the *Te Deum* in official celebrations of insurgent victories. Bishop Pla y Deniel in Salamanca lost little time in making his palace and his pen available to Franco and his colleagues. While his palace became a national headquarters, his pastoral letter, *The Two Cities*, of September 1936 provided an early justification of the rising against the republican government. It was eventually followed by a victorious sequel, *The Triumph of the City of God*, in 1939.[13] In November 1936 Gomá argued that the war was

---

[11] A. Montero Moreno, *Historia de la persecución religiosa en España 1936–9* (Madrid, 1961). The examples here are from pages 290–3, 298, 495, of this definitive study.

[12] For Peiró, see Raguer, *La espada*, 171: his efforts to restrain religious persecution did not save him from execution in 1942.

[13] First published in, respectively, *Boletín Eclesiástico del Obispado de Salamanca* (30 Sept. 1936), 265–314, and (28 May 1939), 167–253.

War and Victory 203

neither a class war nor a conflict over politics, but a confrontation between two civilizations, Catholic Spain on the one hand and foreign, Marxist, anti-Spain on the other. Gomá was sure the insurgents were fully justified, and he had nothing but praise for the mass support for the rising in Navarre, where the war caught him and where he was writing. In January 1937 he wrote that the roots of the war lay in national apostasy as demonstrated by civil marriage and a secular education system. He poured scorn on 'the farce of parliamentary government and the lie of elections'—foreign to Spanish culture and tradition—that had brought about such aberrations.[14]

When at the end of the war, on 20 May 1939, Franco presented his victory sword to Cardinal Gomá in a ceremony in the church of Santa Bárbara in Madrid, the gesture symbolized the close interdependence of the victorious army and the Church, but in reverse. It was not so much that generals had fought for the Church, but rather that the Church had offered its ideological and propagandist services to the insurgent army. Franco, Mola, and their fellow-conspirators fathered the coup that developed into a civil war: but the Spanish bishops were the godfathers of the Crusade, of the theory that the generals—even if they were non-believers or Masons—and their troops, even if they were African Muslims, fought for Catholic Spain against anti-patriotic error and corruption, for Christ against anti-Christ.

This interpretation of the war was most authoritatively expressed in the collective pastoral letter prepared by Gomá at Franco's suggestion and addressed to the bishops of the whole world in July 1937.[15] Unable to comprehend the religious legislation of the republic, and the democratic system that had produced it, the hierarchy took upon itself the responsibility for identifying the true spirit and interests of the nation—an institutional prerogative also traditionally claimed by the army. Not only did the bishops argue that this spirit had been betrayed, but they accepted and retailed, without any substantial evidence, a fantastic story according to which the Comintern decided on 27 February 1936 to plan and finance a Communist revolution in Spain.[16] The July rising, therefore, was a defensive, pre-emptive strike against foreign Communism and its Spanish adherents. On this basis, the usual ecclesiastical

---

[14] Gomá's wartime pastorals are collected in I. Gomá, *Por Dios y por España* (Barcelona, 1940), together with some of his other writings and speeches of the time.
[15] Text in Iribarren, 219–42.
[16] For a devastating critique of these 'documents' see H. Southworth, *El mito de la cruzada de franco* (Paris, 1963), 247–58.

polarized version of Spanish ideological conflict was constructed. True Spain fought apostate Spain; spiritual aims combated materialism; Christian civilization challenged Bolshevism. Consequently, the Church 'could not be indifferent'. It was not. In this letter Gomá and his brother bishops formally committed it to the defence and justification of one side in the war.

If episcopal rejection of the republican cause in the war was inevitable after the anti-clerical violence of the first days and months, it is also true that the grounds for rejection were firmly established much earlier. Gomá's letters are quite explicit: the parliamentary republic was already morally indefensible long before the rising; Catholicism's ideological opponents already deserved to be silenced long before they had the blood of martyrs on their hands. Gomá described Basque desires for autonomy as 'a great error', denied that economic injustice was a cause of the war, reckoned that not even a dozen men on the insurgent side had taken up arms to defend their estates, and asserted that Franco was not on the side of the rich.[17] But in fact there was no doubt that those who fought for religion usually fought also for a centralist, authoritarian regime and for the preservation of an unreformed socio-economic structure, especially on the land, and that they fought against the urban and rural propertyless masses. It is not surprising, therefore, that the Catholics who disagreed with the sentiments of the 1937 collective pastoral tended to be those who already disapproved of Catholic identification with centralist and socially reactionary politics.

Three bishops declined to sign the pastoral letter: Vidal i Barraquer of Tarragona, Múgica of Vitoria, and Francisco Javier Irastorza Loinaz of Orihuela. Only about the third is there any mystery, since he was living in England with papal dispensation from his diocese—probably in disgrace because of financial irregularities—and only the keepers of the Gomá archive know whether he ever replied to the letter from Gomá seeking his signature.[18] Múgica explained his refusal to Gomá by saying he was away from his diocese and therefore unable to exercise pastoral responsibility.[19] This disclaimer arose from Múgica's enormously complicated and painful situation. The Basque Nationalist Party had opted to defend the republic against the insurgents, even though this aligned

---

[17] 'Respuesta obligada. Carta abierta al Sr. D. Antonio Aguirre', in Gomá, *Por Dios y por España*, 54–69.
[18] There is no information on Irastorza in M. L. Rodríguez Aisa, *El Cardenal Gomá y la guerra de España* (Madrid, 1981), written with access to the Gomá archive.
[19] Letter from Múgica to Gomá, 28 July 1937, ibid., 248–9.

it with the 'enemies of God', a decision described in the collective pastoral as lamentable obfuscation. In August 1936 Gomá had drafted a pastoral letter which appeared over the signature of the two bishops whose dioceses covered the whole Basque–Navarrese region, Múgica of Vitoria and Olaechea of Pamplona. In it the two prelates called on the faithful not to make common cause with the enemies of religion, arguing that it was quite illicit to do so. In September Múgica sent a circular round his diocese asking for financial help for the 'saviour army'. But then his position became untenable. He had been suspect under the republic as a disloyal monarchist. By temperament and conviction he was indeed a conservative monarchist, and wary of the political claims of Basque nationalism while respectful of nationalist sentiment in his diocese. He was suspect to the insurgents because during the republic he had defended the right of Catholics to support the PNV and work for an autonomy statute. Gomá himself told Múgica of General Cabanellas's order that he should again—as under the republic—leave the country, an order obeyed on 14 October 1936. He returned to Spain only as an ageing man, without pastoral responsibility, many years after the war ended. In 1945, when still in exile, Múgica explained both his initial outrage at the decision of Basque leaders to oppose the rising and then his gradual disillusion with the Crusade. He described his horror at the execution of Basque priests by the insurgents in October 1936, his protest to the Holy See, and the pressure put on him to keep those and later complaints, and his vindication of clergy executed purportedly as political activists, confidential to the Holy See rather than public.[20] The Vatican and the Spanish Church had condemned him to an anguished and unheroic silence that made his long life—he was nearly one hundred years old at his death in 1968—probably the most searing and burdensome of any Spanish bishop this century. Rather more than absence from his diocese inhibited Múgica's pen when asked to sign the July 1937 letter.

Vidal i Barraquer was afraid not only that a public statement by the hierarchy might provoke dreadful reprisals in republican held Catalonia, but also that the actual content of the text he was asked to approve would compromise the Church politically when the war was over.[21] Anti-clerical purges had been nowhere more ruthless than in Catalonia, where he himself had had a narrow escape, yet he remained unwilling

---

[20] Text of Múgica's open letter to José Miguel Barandiarán in A. de Onaindía (ed.), *Ayer como hoy. Documentos del clero vasco* (St Jean de Luz, 1975), 76–117.
[21] For Vidal's opinions, see Muntanyola, *Vidal i Barraquer*, 427–46.

to conclude that the insurgent cause should therefore be embraced as the cause of religion, preferring instead that the hierarchy should distance itself from political debate about the war. Unlike most of his episcopal colleagues, he was wary of political and military solutions to religious problems, and in Catalan conflicts with Primo de Rivera in the 1920s and the crises of the republican years had recognized the harm done to the Church's pastoral mission by any alliance with centralism and repression. Later, in written and oral communications with Pacelli in 1939, first as Vatican Secretary of State and then as Pope Pius XII, he criticized the openly political behaviour of bishops and clergy in Spain and pointed out the immense pastoral problems created by identification with one side in civil war that hopelessly compromised the Church and 'changed the spirit of evangelical charity, gentleness and meekness in many ecclesiastics into violence, reprisals and punishments'. Nor was he blind to the dangers of a state Catholicism emerging at the end of the war which concentrated on the propaganda exercises of massive, politicized, religious rituals. He deplored the readiness of bishops to construct a 'patriotic religion' characterized more by Spanish nationalism than by piety.[22] Múgica and Vidal belonged to the same generation, the same clerical calling, and the same hierarchy; apart from that, there are more contrasts than similarities between the simple Basque prelate and the sophisticated and intellectually subtle Catalan cardinal. Their common refusal to sign the 1937 letter owed much to their pastoral experience in peripheral areas where the local nationalist aspirations of many Catholics challenged assumptions about the desirability of a centralizing, authoritarian Catholic state. Vidal had been smuggled out of Spain through the good offices of the Minister of Culture in the Catalan regional government early in the war: the Franco regime never allowed him to return.

The insurgents did not always receive from the Church hierarchy the uncritical backing they sought. In November 1936 Bishop Olaechea of Pamplona, whose Navarrese diocese comprised the area of Spain where popular support for the nationalist cause was most fervent and most profoundly religious, courageously pointed out the unacceptable face of the Crusade. In a public address to Catholic women he appealed for an end to revenge killings in the rearguard that constituted a white terror of fearful dimensions. He also expressed scepticism of the new devotion suddenly shown by formerly non-practising Catholics, which

---

[22] Muntanyola, *Vidal i Barraquer*, 561–2.

he recognized as springing from fear of reprisals.²³ It was as dangerous for a known sympathizer of the Left to be trapped on the wrong side of the front in Catholic Navarre, as for a priest to be trapped on the wrong side in Alicante or Lérida. On both sides, religion served as a marker of political affiliation.

Most problematic for Franco, however, was the Vatican itself. Throughout the republic, Pope Pius XI and his Secretary of State, Pacelli, had maintained a discreet distance from constitutional matters. The encyclical *Dilectissima nobis* of 3 June 1933 catalogued the Vatican's understandable complaints against republican legislation, particularly the law removing the religious congregations from education, but Cardinal Pacelli had seconded in every way open to him the commitment to careful negotiation pursued by the nuncio Tedeschini and Vidal. He much preferred Herrera's accidentalism to the forthright rejection of the republic urged by Sáinz Rodríguez on behalf of the irreconcilable Right. That alone provoked Franco's hostility, which increased with the Vatican's failure openly to condemn the PNV's opposition to the Crusade. Worst of all, however, was the fact that Rome showed no inclination to rush to recognize the nationalist government as the government of Spain. On the contrary, the nunciature stayed discreetly open and functioning in republican Madrid under a secretary, and a chargé d'affaires was not appointed for the Burgos regime until September 1937, more than a year into the war. Even then, the appointment of Antoniutti was irritating for Franco because he had just been acting as Vatican observer of Basque affairs, and he spent a lot of energy pleading in Burgos for better treatment of the Basques. Monsignor Gaetano Cicognani was eventually named papal nuncio in the spring of 1938, although even then he was accredited to the government at Burgos, not the government of Spain. Furthermore, the Vatican resisted consistent pressure from the insurgents for the restoration of the 1851 concordat unilaterally ignored by the republic, and in particular for the right of presentation to bishoprics, a privilege the Vatican found anachronistic and erastian. It also acceded only with the greatest reluctance to the exile of Múgica and Vidal. To Franco's indignation it persisted in exploring possibilities of mediating between the two warring sides while he was adamant that the war would end with total victory.

---

[23] Raguer, *La espada*, 163–5. On reprisals in Navarre see two works by Basque priests, J. de Iturralde, *La guerra de Franco, los vascos y la iglesia*. 2nd edn. (San Sebastián, 1978), i, 433–40; M. Ayerra Redín, *No me avergoncé del evangelio*. 3rd edn. (Bilbao, 1978). Iturralde is the *nom de plume* of Juan José Usabiaga Irazustabarrena.

Franco had many admirers in Rome, not least the Father General of the Jesuits, Ledechowski, but he found Pius XI and Pacelli insufficiently grateful for the service he was rendering the Spanish Church.

From the pope's point of view, the emerging regime looked too much like Fascism. In March 1937 Pius launched *Mit brennender Sorge* against the Nazi regime in Germany as well as a simultaneous encyclical against Communism. Both were published by the beleaguered church in Catalonia, but *Mit brennender Sorge* received no publicity in insurgent areas except through *Razón y Fe*. As the pope became increasingly anxious about events in both Germany and Italy, so too he disliked German and Italian involvement in Spain. The Vatican was appalled by the Hispano-German cultural agreement of January 1939, and extremely suspicious of Fascist designs for a national Church in Spain, and of the glorification of the state. In these circumstances, reactions in Burgos to Pacelli's election as Pius XI's successor in March 1939 were glacial. None of these frictions could ultimately outweigh the profound gratitude the Vatican owed Franco for saving the Spanish Church from its formidable enemies—a gratitude sincerely and emotionally expressed by the new Pius XII in his famous radio message of congratulations on victory on 16 April 1939—but they account for the complex future relations between the two which were never entirely free of doubts and reservations.[24]

Inside Spain, things seemed simpler than they did in Rome. For Gomá, notwithstanding his fears of Fascist leanings towards the subordination of the Church, the war presented absolutely clear alternatives. One side was religious and good, the other irreligious and bad. Even his position as official representative of the Holy See to Franco from December 1936 to September 1937 seems to have caused him little soul-searching. On his own initiative, after consulting Bishop Pla y Deniel of Salamanca, he decided against publishing *Mit brennender Sorge* in the ecclesiastical press lest it embarrass Franco. Even more revealing of his complete identification with the insurgents was his anger in May 1937 during conversations with a Vatican representative in Lourdes who was trying to open mediation channels between the two sides in the civil war. He rejected any idea of an armistice, advising the Holy See not to collaborate in attempts to bring one about. Mediation, he reckoned, would merely postpone the 'fundamental question' being decided on the battlefields

[24] The essential source—on which these paragraphs is based—is Marquina Barrio, *La diplomacia vaticana y la España de Franco*, which publishes a wealth of primary documentation.

of Spain.²⁵ At a Eucharistic Congress in Budapest in May 1938 he told a Spanish audience of his agreement with Franco's judgment that 'no pacification is possible except that of arms'.²⁶ The republic's destroyers could not have wished for a more whole-hearted ecclesiastical ally. Moreover, a religious renaissance seemed to be taking place in insurgent Spain, where the Crusade's effects were better than 'a series of missions',²⁷ while on the other side churches were closed, priests and lay Catholics martyred, and Catholicism vilified: Franco's cause was the cause of the Church.

Few Spanish Catholics disagreed with Gomá's interpretation of events. There were instances of priests spontaneously leading local insurgent groups with a cross held aloft in the early days of war. There were priests who preached not only the blessedness of the Crusade but also the necessity of destroying its enemies in the rearguard, although others were sickened by the assassinations and worked hard to prevent them and to help those in danger to escape. Reprisals seemed not to trouble in the slightest the consciences of those devout Catholic laymen who carried them out, and who publicly humiliated the female relatives of Left-wing militants by shaving their heads, dosing them with castor oil, and sometimes half undressing them before forcing them to walk round town streets and squares. For many Catholics there was no embarrassment in the fact that particularly brutal repression amounting to mass executions in Badajoz and elsewhere greeted the feast of the Assumption of the Virgin in August 1936, one of the great Catholic feasts.²⁸

For other Catholics in the insurgent zones, barbarism under the sign of the cross brought anguish, disgust, and foreboding. But those scandalized by the means employed usually agreed in general terms with the bishops' interpretation of the conflict. As far as they were

---

²⁵ Rodríguez Aisa, *El Cardenal Gomá y la guerra de España*, 160-7.
²⁶ R. Comás, *Isidro Gomá. Francesc Vidal i Barraquer* (Salamanca, 1977). 119-20.
²⁷ Marquina Barrio, 46.
²⁸ There is valuable information on individual Catholic actions and attitudes in the oral history of the civil war: R. Fraser, *Blood of Spain* (London, 1979). See, e.g., a Jesuit leading forces in the Guadarrama hills, 116; priests for and against reprisals, 163-4, 166, 172, 305, 417; lay Catholics involved in reprisals in Córdoba, 162; humiliation of women in Seville, 272; 15 August 1936 in Badajoz, Pamplona, Seville, 164-5. The best-known contemporary Catholic criticism of ecclesiastical involvement in reprisals is the study on Mallorca, G. Bernanos, *Les Grands Cimetières sous la lune* (Paris, 1938). For a detailed appraisal of Bernanos's accusations and the controversy they provoked, see the notes by J. Massot i Muntaner and P. Copiz to the Catalan translation, *Els grans cementiris sota la lluna* (Barcelona, 1981).

concerned, the republic had damned itself in the first month of its existence by allowing the convent burnings of May 1931; it had compounded its damnation by its legislative attack on the Church, and sealed it by banning the crucifix—the most treasured sign of the nation's religious culture—from schools and public offices.[29] They accepted and in some cases welcomed war on the republic because the republic had declared war on religion.

Some of those who had been pro-republican in 1931, and even through the succeeding couple of years, were convinced by the assassinations of priests and religious that they had been wrong. Fr. Albert Bonet had been immersed in Catalan youth work and looked to the republic for Catalan autonomy, but after escaping the orgy of anticlerical violence in Barcelona he wrote a letter of loyalty to Franco and then spent most of 1937 on a pro-insurgent propaganda tour of Europe to counter the criticisms of the Crusade especially by French liberal Catholics. For all his social radicalism, Fr. Ángel Carbonnel was similarly traumatized by the experience of religious persecution, as was another Catalan priest, Lluis Carreras, close collaborator of Cardinal Vidal i Barraquer. In a book written in 1938 he eulogized Franco and referred sarcastically to the 'mental deviation and loss of any sense of justice or humanity' of Catholics who remained republican after the summer and autumn of 1936.[30] In the polarizing of options that civil war always brings, it was indeed extremely difficult for Catholics to do other than align themselves with the Crusade against the Church's destroyers.

A few saw matters differently. Alfredo Mendizábal, close witness of the Asturias rising of October 1934, opposed the war altogether and busied himself in Paris with efforts at mediation. His account of the origins of the war—which blamed both Right and Left—appeared with a preface by Jacques Maritain in which the scholastic philosopher deplored the notion of a 'holy' war, and argued that if it was sacrilege to massacre priests and destroy churches, it was no less sacriligious to massacre the poor and to use Moorish troops to kill Christians. The priest-intellectual, Carles Cardó, was appalled by the hunting of priests and religious he witnessed in Catalonia before escaping with Bonet, but

[29] The decisive negative impact of the convent burnings and the banning of the crucifix becomes apparent to anyone talking to Spanish Catholics about their memories of the republic, and was frequently mentioned by those interviewed by Fraser, see, e.g., 124, 526–7.
[30] L. Carreras, *Grandeza cristiana de España* (Toulouse, 1938), 9. For a survey of the writings of Catalan clergy on the war, see J. Massot i Muntaner, *L'església catalana entre la guerra i la postguerra* (Barcelona, 1978), 31–53.

he published in 1946 a powerful attack on the ideal of the holy war so deeply embedded in Castilian tradition, and on the co-option of Catholicism by the political Right in Spain. He followed these themes through to their logical conclusion, arguing that the rising of July 1936 had its roots in Castilian tradition and recent history but not in Catholic doctrine.[31]

The republic did not lack Catholic propagandists throughout the war, though they were but a tiny band. Their conviction that the Church had itself provoked the popular hatred which culminated in anti-clerical violence in 1934 and then, overwhelmingly, in 1936, by its insensitivity to poverty and repression, enabled them to stand firm in their republican allegiance. Moreover, as they argued, violence against the Church was not the policy nor the responsibility of the republic, but rather of uncontrolled groups acting on their own initiative before the republican government could re-establish its authority after the rising. Canon Gallegos Rocafull wrote a pamphlet to claim that there was no Crusade in Spain, but a class war in which the propertied classes legitimized their self-interest by appropriating religion.[32] Ossorio y Gallardo bitterly cited old and new texts detailing Catholic hostility to oppression and totalitarianism, and asked why Gomá and Pius XII did not act in accordance with them, and why so many Catholics found it possible to make their peace with Fascism.[33] The writer José Bergamín had never inclined to understatement, or cultivated sobriety of tone: in Paris in March 1939 he poured out his contempt for the Crusade in a torrent of denunciations. The Church had 'placed a priestly mask over the bloody terror of the hangman'. Spanish clericalism sowed discord and was 'possessed by the devil'. Referring to the use of the crucifix by the insurgents, and perhaps also by chaplains ministering to those condemned to die, he declared it was better to die in front of the cross than to kill behind it. The Church now had blood on its hands, and the Vatican was wrong to greet Franco's victory as something to celebrate.[34]

Much more sober and scholarly was the paragraph by paragraph refutation of the bishops' 1937 letter composed by the Catalan ex-Jesuit, Vilar i Costa, during the civil war. He pointed out the question-begging

---

[31] A. Mendizábal, *Aux origines d'une tragédie* (Paris, 1937); C. Cardó, *Histoire spirituelle des Espagnes* (Paris, 1946), especially 273–8 for the July rising.

[32] J. M. Gallegos Rocafull, *Crusade or Class War? The Spanish Military Revolt* (London, 1937).

[33] A. Ossorio y Gallardo, *La guerra de España y los católicos* (Buenos Aires, 1942), Ch. 1; after this the book concentrates mainly on the period before 1931.

[34] J. Bergamín, *Detrás de la cruz* (Mexico, 1941), especially 12–13, 41, 47, 141–57.

in the bishops' use of 'Spain', 'anti-Spain' and related adjectives to designate antithetically those they approved and those they disapproved. He called attention to the letter's silence on the Right's record in power in 1934 and 1935, especially on its reactionary and provocative agrarian policies. He also noted the absence of any mention of massacres committed by the insurgents, and the inconsistency of justifying the rising by reference to a supposed plot of the Communist International, for which there was no evidence, while saying nothing of the notorious and prolonged preparations for armed intervention by those whose attempted coup and ferocious treatment of 'anti-Spaniards' behind the lines was elevated to the status of a religious Crusade.[35]

It is evident not only from the values expressed in Vilar's commentary on the 1937 letter, but even from the vocabulary and structure in which he presented them, that his mental world was poles apart from that of most of the Spanish bishops. He, Ossorio, Cardó, Gallegos Rocafull, and even Bergamín, for all his rhetoric, offered a socio-political analysis of Spanish Catholicism. Like Joan Maragall after the 'tragic week' in Barcelona in 1909, like Alfredo Mendizábal after the Oviedo rising in 1934, they traced anti-clericalism to the hatreds and fears aroused by the Church's collusion with those who enjoyed power and resources in the hearts of people struggling to survive. Vilar quoted in his work one of the most forceful statements of this case ever made, Canon Arboleya's address to the ecclesiastical conference on social issues in 1933. The alienation or, as Arboleya put it, 'the apostasy of the masses' was due largely to the class interest that had consistently guided Catholic property owners and politicians and pitted them against working people and the poor. 'The working man saw the Church itself in those who behaved in this way, hence his apostasy ... the masses fled from the Church because they believed it their greatest adversary.'[36] It was not simply that the bishops in 1937 came to different conclusions: they asked different questions, and they employed the language of truth and error, of religious fidelity and religious betrayal, as though these had no socio-economic and political context. There could be no understanding between people who addressed one another from separate cultural worlds, and in different languages. It was easier for Vilar to understand popular antagonism to priests and religious in 1936, deeply though he mourned and regretted its dreadful consequences,

[35] J. Vilar i Costa, *Glosas a la carta colectiva de los obispos españoles* (Barcelona, 1938).
[36] Arboleya, quoted ibid., 113–15.

than to make sense of the public statements of the leaders of his Church.

For many others, too, the way of faith and devotion starkly outlined by Gomá could not be reconciled with their interpretation of the nature of the conflict that divided Spain ineluctably in July 1936. Just as there were Masonic and free-thinking generals fighting with the insurgents, so there were convinced Catholic generals fighting for the republic, including Batet, Aranguren, Rojo, and the famous defender of Madrid, Miaja. The devout Manuel Carrasco i Formiguera, who had bravely but uselessly spoken up for the Jesuits to a totally unreceptive Cortes in 1931, stayed loyal to the republic he had helped usher in with his participation in the San Sebastián pact. After being seized by anti-republican forces while acting as an emissary of the republican government, he was executed on 9 April 1938 at Franco's orders.[37]

Much the most important and embarrassing Catholic deviants, however, were the Basque Nationalists. Their Catholic credentials were unassailable: as PNV leaders explained to the Vatican in January 1936, levels of Catholic practice in much of the Basque country were very high, vocations to the priesthood and religious life abounded, fourteen bishops and nearly 5,000 priests and religious worked as missionaries overseas, and fourteen episcopal sees within Spain had Basque incumbents.[38] They wanted from the Vatican—but did not get—some recognition of the specific traditions and needs of the area, some protection from centralist bishops and anti-nationalist religious orders active in the Basque provinces. When war broke out these devout, orthodox, but nationalist Catholics remained loyal to a republic that eventually, in October 1936, granted them the long-delayed statute of autonomy.

The PNV alliance with Socialists, Communists, and other republicans in the war effort and in local government prevented any outbreak of violence against Church personnel or property, and José Antonio Aguirre y Lecube and his colleagues absolutely refused to treat the war as a confrontation between Catholicism and its enemies. In a radio broadcast on 22 December 1936 Aguirre—now president of the autonomous area of Euzkadi—argued that the war, far from being about religion, was about archaic economic and social structures: the struggle

[37] For Carrasco's execution, see the biography, H. Raguer, *Divendres de passió* (Montserrat, 1984), 334–90.
[38] For the texts prepared for presentation to the Vatican see I. Moriones, *Euzkadi y el Vaticano 1935–1936* (Rome, 1976), 29–65, 82–102.

was for social justice against capitalist abuse and privilege.[39] While the Navarrese, then, joined the Crusade with alacrity, fought for God and religion, and ruthlessly killed republican sympathizers behind the lines and publicly humiliated their relatives, their equally Catholic fellow Basques, especially in Guipúzcoa and Vizcaya, fought on the other side in what was from the beginning a Basque as well as a Spanish civil war. To Aguirre's horror and chagrin, Catholic right-wing captives were assassinated in popular violence in prisons and prison ships in reprisals immediately after insurgent and German bombing of Basque targets, but there was nothing on the scale of the massacres in the Crusade's rearguard.[40] It was tragically ironic that the single most vindictive act of destruction in the whole war was the bombing by German planes at the service of the Catholic Crusade of the market town of Guernica, long the symbolic centre of Basque culture, and utterly Catholic.[41] General Dávila's forces executed fourteen Basque priests and took many more prisoner as the northern front was pushed into Guipúzcoa and eventually Vizcaya. The fall of Bilbao in June 1937, and the loss of Basque industrial output, were among the most decisive blows to republican chances of winning the war. But Basque nationalist resistance until then had not only made the insurgents' task much more difficult, it had irrevocably damaged their ideological image. Aguirre never won from the Vatican that statement of the legitimacy of his cause that he so earnestly sought. Nor did Franco obtain from Pius XI the condemnation of the PNV that he demanded. The Crusade had to endure armed and orthodox Catholic opposition. It was to counteract the effects of both the pens and the guns of Catholic republicans that the bishops took the extraordinary step of addressing their propagandist letter in July 1937 to the Catholic bishops of the whole world.

For most of the war, however, in most of Spain, Catholicism and insurgency were virtually indistinguishable. Huge field Masses were celebrated for soldiers, chaplains urged republican prisoners to make their peace with the Church, solemn religious ceremonies marked the capture of city after city. In much of republican Spain, on the contrary, churches were closed, priests in hiding, and religious services

[39] Text in J. A. Aguirre y Lecube, *Obras completas* (Donostia, no date), i, 609–23.
[40] For an account of these reprisals by an anti-republican and anti-Basque nationalist priest who was held on a prison ship and then in prison in Vizcaya, see J. Echeandía, *La persecución roja en el país vasco* (Barcelona, 1945).
[41] The definitive account of the Guernica bombings is H. R. Southworth, *Guernica! Guernica! A Study of Journalism, Diplomacy, Propaganda and History* (Berkeley, 1977). See also the on-the-spot account, G. L. Steer, *Tree of Gernika* (London, 1938).

clandestine, in spite of the efforts of the Catholic Basque Minister of Justice in the republican government, Manuel Irujo.[42] As early as April 1937 Franco ordered the fusion of all political groups in 'national' Spain into a single movement that necessarily violated some of the aims of 'Carlists, Alfonsines, and Falangists alike, while leaving Catholicism by contrast even more obviously than before the crucial element of ideological unity. Those republican measures that the Right considered anti-clerical, and liberals and the Left regarded as a loosening of Catholic hegemony, were abrogated bit by bit—civil marriage on 12 March 1938, the dissolution of the Jesuits on 3 May, the exclusion of religious from education on 2 February 1939, divorce on 23 September, and, eventually, state funding for the clergy was restored on 9 November. Since the Vatican would not permit the continuation of the 1851 concordat, other matters remained unresolved until the agreement between Spain and the Holy See on June 1941 on the appointment of bishops, and further agreements in 1946 and 1950 on other ecclesiastical appointments, state funding for seminaries and theology faculties, and army chaplaincies.[43] In 1953—fourteen years after the end of the war—a new concordat was eventually negotiated, formally enshrining in its first article that Catholic unity long yearned for by Spanish bishops. From very early in the war it had been apparent that insurgent victory would bring a Catholic restoration greater even than that afforded by the restoration of the monarchy in 1875. The Franco regime protected the Church, showered it with privileges, and silenced its opponents by repression and censorship when they were not eliminated by execution or exile. Few at the time heeded Cardinal Vidal's warnings about the insuperable pastoral problems created by such overt reliance on military and political force. It was time for reconstruction on a grand scale, with the terrain providentially cleared of the usual encumbrances and the atmosphere—so the contemporary image euphemistically put it—cleansed of harmful elements.

Church–state harmony in victory was not quite perfect, however, as Cardinal Gomá himself suddenly learnt only months after the war ended. The lesson was delivered bluntly. On 9 August 1939 the primate released the text of his pastoral letter, *Lessons of the War and the Duties*

---

[42] On the situation in Catalonia, see A. Manent i Segimón and J. Raventos i Giralt, *L'església clandestina a Catalunya durant la guerra civil (1936–1939)* (Montserrat, 1984).

[43] Texts in V. Cárcel Ortí (ed.), *Historia de la Iglesia en España*, v (Madrid, 1979), 740–54.

of Peace.[44] Its circulation was banned by the government. There was nothing to vex the authorities in the first part of the letter, with its familiar theological absurdities about the war's demonstration of God's special favour for the winning side, its tirade against 'Protestant' imported democracy undermining Spain's national greatness in the nineteenth and twentieth centuries, and its conspiracy theory of 'secret forces' dominating the world, especially Jews and Masons combining against Spanish interests. In the second part, Gomá stated proudly that the Church had 'lent the whole weight of its prestige, placed at the service of truth and justice, for the triumph of the national cause'. But he also claimed for the Church a determining role in post-war reconstruction. His strictures on the need to respect the rights of the individual, to allow some form of political participation, to avoid any return to harsh, pre-war, conservative attitudes, and to recognize the limits of state power were not at all what the new military dictatorship wanted to hear. Still less congenial were Gomá's vision of the clergy as the real saviours of society, called to influence every aspect of national life, and his exposition of the right of all Catholics to keep a critical eye on possible governmental deviations from Catholic truth in the future. Furthermore he referred openly to the preference of many among the victors for a political system different from the one that had emerged. The letter faithfully reflected the traditional, natural law-based, Catholic wariness of unlimited state power that had made both Gomá himself and the Vatican suspicious of Fascist influences during the war. Gomá did not have long to meditate on the implications of the censorship of his letter—he died in 1940—but the mistrust of unbridled state power he expressed with such political naivety in 1939 continued to cause intermittent friction between the Church and the Franco regime.

Most vehement in his mistrust was Segura, back from exile in May 1937 and archbishop of Seville in succession to Ilundain. Segura's taste for confrontation had ample scope in Seville, where victorious local Falangists were impatient to limit ecclesiastical authority. As early as January 1938 he protested against Falangist attempts to dissolve Catholic lay associations. In October he refused to allow the Seville Falangists to celebrate the anniversary of their foundation with a military Mass. A month later, when the young civil governor and Falange leader Pedro Gamero prepared to place a commemorative list of the war dead on the cathedral walls, in accordance with the Burgos decree of 16 November,

---

[44] Text in Gomá, *Por Dios y por España*, 224–302.

and common practice throughout the 'liberated' zones, Segura threatened to excommunicate him. The most dramatic encounter in this running battle took place in 1940 and can be followed blow by blow in the diocesan bulletin. While the question of whether it was canonically proper to have lists of the victorious dead on the walls of the cathedral and other churches remained sore and sensitive, a group of Falangists probed the wound by painting Falangist symbols on the walls of the archiepiscopal palace on 24 March. On 26 March a highly combative pastoral letter defended the rights of the Church against civil authorities. When Segura ordered the removal of the offending 'party symbols', an armed guard prevented it. When the civil governor ordered that the name of José Antonio Primo de Rivera, founder of the Falange executed during the war, be inscribed on the outside of the cathedral and the adjoining church—as it was on churches up and down the country—the cardinal archbishop threatened canonical sanctions and eventually won. He followed this up with a thirty-four-page pastoral in April, written in heroic tone and arguing that bishops and priests were not state functionaries, and that even a Catholic state had no right to impinge upon ecclesiastical autonomy.[45]

But Fascistic practices and tendencies were not the only bone of contention. Segura touched an exposed nerve of the Franco regime when in 1939 he complained to the Minister of Justice about the plight of republican Basque priests languishing in Carmona jail in his archdiocese. On Good Friday 1940 he was conspicuously absent from the customary processions when Franco participated in them. In 1952 he contradicted a statement by Franco on Spanish spiritual links with the Arab world, and in 1953 refused to provide a priest to celebrate Mass privately for the head of state while he was visiting Seville. Segura-watching became an irritating necessity for the regime, a delicate task for the Vatican,[46] and a specialized kind of spectator sport for the faithful. The cardinal's Saturday addresses, *sabatinas*, became particularly notorious, and it was in these unofficial talks that he shared his choicest observations with the congregation, pointing out on one occasion, for example, that 'Caudillo'—Franco's usual title—was a term often used to describe the head of a band of thieves, and used by St Ignatius of Loyola of the devil.

---

[45] The two letters in *BEAS*, lxxxiii (1940), 233–43, 261–95, together with communications to the civil governor.
[46] For Vatican handling of the Segura–Falange conflict, see Marquina Barrio, 243–62.

Segura, as always, was exceptional. While he indulged for twenty years in maverick sniping from behind his anti-erastian barricades, other Church leaders were extremely grateful to a congenial, authoritarian regime that had restored the Church to what they regarded as its rightful place in Spanish society and the state. The taming of the Falange that Franco had begun in April 1937 continued after the war: 'old shirts' lamented its subordination to the state and its loss of revolutionary capacity as it gave way to an old-fashioned conservatism much more to the Church's liking. It failed to infuse the new state with Fascist ideology, and it failed to gain control of education. The only major blow to the Church was the dissolution of the confessional unions when vertical state syndicates on a Fascist model were created on 21 April 1938.[47] But the confessional unions had never been very effective, and Church authorities had usually preferred them to approximate to pious organizations of workers rather than to unions seriously involved in industrial and agrarian disputes. And the vertical syndicates seemed to promise the class harmony and co-operation tirelessly preached in Catholic rhetoric.

Not all Catholic politicians were content with the new regime. Liberalism and socialism were defeated, property, order, national unity, and the family preserved, but Alfonsine monarchists and Carlists often felt as cheated of the spoils of victory as did the Falange. There was no restoration of the monarchy, no real concession to Carlism's dislike of centralism, the overbearing state, industry, and urbanization. The Church itself, by contrast, showed every sign of winning the peace as well as the war. In this safe new world, ecclesiastical institutions enjoyed exemption from taxation, Catholic feasts were public holidays, all education at all levels embodied 'the principles of the dogma and morals of the Catholic Church', guarded by Church surveillance and censorship, while the state guaranteed that Catholic values would be conveyed also on radio and television, and that Catholic Action would be dependent on the Church hierarchy, free of state intervention.[48] There was no need for a campaign of rectification like that waged for so long over the toleration of non-Catholic cults in the 1876 constitution. Nor did the Church need a political champion to secure its interests as it had during

---

[47] See G. Hermet, *Les catholiques dans l'Espagne franquiste* (Paris, 1981), ii, 117–19. On the absorption of the rural Catholic syndicates, finalized in January 1940, see Castillo, *Propietarios muy pobres*, 391–444.

[48] All these gains were explicitly guaranteed by the concordat of 1953; text in *Historia de la Iglesia en España*, v. 755–65.

the republic. The Church's contribution to the glorious Crusade was rewarded; the martyrs had not died in vain.

During these years of Catholic victory culminating in the concordat of 1953, the Church worked hard to capitalize on its unique opportunity to make Spain, at last, truly and thoroughly Catholic. Fervent recruits flooded into seminaries and novitiates to replace those killed in the war; less fervent and non-practising Catholics were saturated with religious propaganda. The appeal was to individual conversion, preached in thousands of missions in parishes and schools. Street processions, illuminated crosses, posters and pamphlets, bells and music ensured that a local mission could not be ignored. Employers backed the efforts of the priests, who often preached part of the mission in factories. In the harsh austerity of the 1940s and 1950s, religious conformism was advisable for those wanting a job, promotion, or any other advancement, and security. Had not the war been fought against errors that began with Protestantism and indifference and ended with Communism? The message was accentuated by massive processions and pilgrimages—like those to the national shrines at Zaragoza in 1940 and Santiago in 1948—and public consecrations to the Sacred Heart, as all the devotional phenomena of the early century reappeared, symbolizing this time not defiant Catholic militancy but determined Catholic supremacy.[49]

As soon as the war ended Catholic Action was reorganized. Its task was to create a Catholic 'presence' in every corner of Spanish society through the agency of a committed laity. Its official organ, *Ecclesia*, spelt out in the editorial of the first issue in January 1941 the strictly religious and ecclesiastical nature of Catholic Action, which would abstain from all political activity. It continued the tradition of pre-war Catholic Action in its total subordination to the hierarchy and its emphasis on piety, although post-war euphoria and swollen membership gave it for a while an illusion of strength. Its real vitality began with the gradual emergence of specialized branches in industry and agriculture in the mid-1940s, which would later apply Catholic social doctrine to the situation of workers in Franco's Spain with dramatic results.[50]

In its ideas as well as in its institutions and devotions, the Catholic reconquest offered little new. Innovation would have been inappropriate,

---

[49] For post-war piety, see A. L. Orensanz, *Religiosidad popular española (1940–1965)* (Madrid, 1974), 9–22; F. Urbina, 'Formas de vida de la Iglesia en España: 1939–1975', in *Iglesia y sociedad en España 1939–1975* (Madrid, 1977), 12–26.

[50] See below, pp. 231–7.

since the modern and the novel were suspect. It was a time to fulfil old dreams, not to dream new ones. Post-war Catholic culture, like the culture of the nineteenth-century restoration, was anti-modern and xenophobic. Its affirmation of what later commentators called 'national-Catholicism' was an exercise in recapitulation. Most central was an insistent equation of Spanish identity with Catholicism that left no honourable space either for Spaniards who disbelieved Catholic dogma or were not interested in it, or for Catholics who disliked enforced absorption into a military, centralist, Spanish state. This equation of Spanish national tradition and identity with Catholicism had changed not at all since the time of Menéndez y Pelayo, its most energetic exponent. In the 1880s he had looked back to the glorious achievements of the Counter Reformation and imperial expansion, attributing Spain's later decline to its infidelity; it had wantonly run after strange gods, in the form of foreign Protestantism, foreign liberalism, and foreign philosophy, leaving the paths of Spanish orthodoxy and paying the dreadful price. His ideas had been echoed in school textbooks and devotional publications, sermons and pastoral letters without number, forming the core of an integrism that permeated Catholic thinking and was never seriously challenged by any major alternative tradition.

Primo de Rivera's Catholic apologists spoke from this integrist world when they ridiculed political and ideological pluralism. Pemán, Maeztu, Pemartín, and their colleagues all discerned in Primo's authoritarian regime a fidelity to Spain's 'inner constitution'. The precise features of this mystic substance sometimes altered–Ángel Herrera described it in 1928 as Catholic and monarchist but later decided the monarchist element was not essential—yet it remained recognizable. Spain's inner reality was Catholic, nationalist, centralist, anti-liberal, and anti-socialist. Hierarchy, order, and orthodoxy were its basic requirements.

The civil war took the nostalgia in Menéndez y Pelayo's retrospective analysis of Spain's golden age, and the ephemeral hopes of Primo's adherents, and fashioned them into a theory of the victorious, reliable present. Gomá thought Catholicism and the fatherland had been 'consubsantial' in golden age Spain and were so again now. José María Pemán was convinced that 'the Spanish nation, if it exists at all, is Catholic'. A rare convert to Catholicism in intellectual circles, Manuel García Morente, fitted effortlessly into his inheritance: 'Spain is constituted of Christian faith and Iberian blood. Therefore, between the

Spanish nation and Catholicism there exists a profound and essential identity'. The Crusade against Liberals, Socialists, Communists, and Anarchists had emulated the achievement of the earlier crusade against Moors and Jews, and 'Spain is again the chosen people of God'. Spain had rediscovered its 'ideal substance', its divine mission in the world, which was 'the defence of the Christian faith'.[51] Church and state were conterminous, faith and politics interdependent, in this new christendom, providentially resurrected from its death centuries before.

The reconstruction of a national Catholic culture was an urgent priority. Franco's wartime Minister of Education, the monarchist Sáinz Rodríguez, had worked to prevent the establishment of a single, state education system favoured by the Falangists. A parallel system of Church schools was ensured, as well as the ideological dominance of Catholicism rather than Fascism in all Spanish education. Other former members of Acción Española in the republic, Romualdo de Toledo and José María Pemán, worked with Sáinz Rodríguez in the education ministry to achieve these ends, enshrined in the 1938 law of secondary education. In 1943 the law on higher education made religious studies obligatory for all university students, and after the exodus to South America of many pro-republican university teachers during and after the war, Spanish university education was in the hands of the orthodox for the first time for decades. Catholic control was strengthened with the introduction by the 1943 law of *colegios mayores*, halls of residence with some ancillary teaching functions, and firm moral and spiritual formation and surveillance, many of which were run by the religious congregations, the Propagandists, and the Opus Dei.[52] The Falange won the right to dominate the official presentation of civic and political studies in the education system, but the Church did better still.

The Catholic conquest of the universities continued under the direction of José Ibáñez Martín as Minister of Education from 1939 to 1951.[53] He was linked to both the Propagandists and Acción Española, and had been a CEDA parliamentary deputy for Murcia. He appointed the panels that selected university teachers, and many were selected from the ranks of Catholic Action, the Propagandists (particularly strong in law),

---

[51] All these quotations from a survey of the literature by F. Urbina in *Iglesia y sociedad en España*, 85–120. For a theological critique of national-Catholicism from a later liberal Catholic perspective see A. Álvarez Bolado, *El experimento del nacional-catolicismo 1939–1975* (Madrid, 1976).

[52] For the Opus Dei, see below.

[53] On the universities and the CSIC see D. Artigues, *El Opus Dei en España* (Paris, 1971), 43–63; A. Fontán, *Los católicos en la universidad española actual* (Madrid, 1961).

and the Opus Dei. In November 1939 Ibáñez Martín also set up an enormous state research institute, the *Consejo Superior de Investigaciones Científicas*, and put at its head—where he remained until 1966—the chemist José María Albareda, member of Opus Dei. The CSIC was lavishly funded, involved in a wide range of scientific and arts research, and gave scholarships for study abroad. The schools, the universities, and the CSIC, together constituted the institutional underpinning of a national Catholic culture spanning the whole range from primary education to advanced research and teaching. Manuel Azaña had argued in 1931 that in terms of its intellectual culture and creativity, Spain was no longer Catholic: the Crusade gave the Church an unprecedented opportunity to ensure that such an assertion could not again be made with any validity, since there was to be no Spain other than Catholic Spain, and no Spanish culture that was not orthodox.

This did not mean that Catholicism in the first decade of the Franco regime was politically monolithic. Alfonsine monarchists like Sáinz Rodríguez did not take kindly to a military dictatorship without a king, and longed for the restoration of Alfonso XIII's son, Juan de Borbón. Carlists chafed under a regime that bore little resemblance to the ideal for which they had plotted and fought so ardently. Catholic Falangists like Dionsisio Ridruejo watched Franco's domestication of the Falange and failure to implement a social revolution on even the tiniest scale with revulsion. These differences of opinion were real, and from the perspective of those involved in them, profound and principled. But the range of disagreement was limited, and vitally important common ground was established in the dictatorship's Catholicism. Just as Catholicism had enabled the heterogeneous groups on the insurgent side in the civil war to forge a necessary ideological unity, so now it fulfilled a similar function. Not everyone liked the conservative military dictatorship, but it was extremely difficult in the 1940s to dissociate oneself from the conqueror of the traditional common enemies—communism, liberalism, socialism, impiety. On those fundamentals there was consensus. Since the 1870s bishops had wanted just such a combination of limited political diversity with orthodox uniformity. There was no identification of Catholicism with any one 'party'—the great Traditionalist and Integrist error of the late nineteenth century—but pluralism did not extend beyond the limits of Catholic orthodoxy. It was possible to be Catholic and Falangist, Catholic and monarchist, Catholic and simply conservative, but it was not possible in the aftermath of the Crusade to be a Christian Democrat, since that implied a liberal range of legitimate political allegiances, and it was certainly not possible to be Catholic and socialist. There was no political uniformity, but the Manichean divide between right and wrong, truth and error, was absolute, and it matched precisely the military divide between victors and vanquished.

9
Towards Modernity

WHEN Franco died in 1975, the Catholic Church in Spain seemed barely recognizable as the same institution that in 1950 was still peacefully enjoying the victory fruits of the great Crusade. The enormous change of theological style tried out by a few influential German, French, and Dutch scholars and then adopted officially for the universal Church in the authoritative documents of the Second Vatican Council in the 1960s undermined many old certainties about unchanging, absolute truths and radically debased the currency of the traditional language in which those certainties had been confidently expressed. Political opinion among Catholics was more varied than ever before: some of them were Christian Democrats, some were known to be sympathetic to socialism, and the epithet 'liberal' when used in Catholic circles was now as likely to be laudatory as pejorative. Hierarchical relationships between bishops and priests, clergy and laity, were widely challenged as anachronistic and unsatisfactory, while the Church's professionals—the priests and religious—experienced an acute crisis of confidence that resulted in their withdrawal from priesthood and religious community on an unprecedented scale.

These fundamental and irreversible changes are relatively easy to chart, but extremely difficult to assess. Their causes lay partly in Spanish social and political circumstances and partly beyond Spain's borders altogether; partly in ecclesiastical processes and partly in much more widespread cultural and intellectual trends. While neither exclusively Spanish nor exclusively ecclesiastical phenomena, the changes that some hailed enthusiastically as an almost miraculous renovation of Catholicism and that others lamented as its loss of nerve, assumed in the Spanish Church a peculiarly dramatic speed and suddenness. In the ecclesiastical jargon of the time, they were the great *aggiornamento* or bringing up to date urged by Pope John XXIII. But what did this untoward embracing of modernity mean? Before the startled eyes of observers, in the last decade of the military dictatorship the Spanish Church became as much its critic and opponent as its faithful supporter.

The terminology of human rights and civil liberties was appropriated by bishops and priests brought up to hold both in deep suspicion. Fraternal interest in other Christian traditions and even non-Christian ideologies officially replaced outright condemnation. Within the Church, dialogue and discussion became the accepted orthodoxies in theory, and sometimes in practice as authoritarian modes lost favour. However, it was naïve to conclude from these astonishing shifts of value, as many both within and without the Church hopefully did, that it could now be counted an unconditional ally of democracy, tolerance, and progressive causes. It would be truer to say that the Spanish Church had learnt that the benefits of identification with one political system were limited and increasingly double-edged. Gradual accommodation of irreversible social and cultural trends was sometimes more productive than excoriating them, and essential ecclesiastical interests—particularly in its own institutional security, in Catholic education and in moral influence—could be better secured in a pluralistic regime than in a widely hated dictatorship. This is not to suggest that Church leaders or the thousands of Catholics enthusiastically committed to *aggiornamento* were cynically calculating: it is rather to remember that in dramatically changed circumstances and with radically altered perceptions, they nevertheless did not lose their faith in the overwhelming importance of Catholicism itself as a primary value and loyalty.

In the first twenty years after the civil war, various Catholic movements laid claim to a certain modernity of style. Most influential was the Opus Dei, which was founded by a young Spanish priest, José María Escrivá de Balaguer, in 1928, but expanded enormously in Spain and abroad in post-war years. The Opus Dei was an organization for which at first no category existed in the Church, since it was neither a religious congregation with vows, religious habits, and community life, nor simply a devotional association. It was innovative in emphasizing the pastoral role of the laity, and insisting that this role was properly fulfilled in ordinary working environments by individual lay men and women doing their usual jobs to the glory of God. It saw no reason to think that a desire for holiness could be assuaged only in convents and monasteries, or that the only pastoral duty of the laity was to act as an extension of the clergy. Most of its members lived with their families and saw their task as the sanctification of secular life and work. In this positive assessment of the lay and the secular, the Opus Dei undoubtedly anticipated one of the major orientations of the Second Vatican Council. Much earlier, in 1947, it acquired canonical status when the Vatican created a category of religious organization called secular institutes of which the Opus Dei was both the inspiration and the first beneficiary.[1]

The impression of innovation and modernity vanishes, however, on reading *Camino*, the handbook of 999 maxims to which Escrivá gave definitive form in 1939, and which forty years later had reached a distribution of about three million copies in over thirty languages.[2] *Camino* is a bizarre amalgam of traditional piety, penitential discipline, and crude popular moralizing; it aims at a fusion of devotion with efficiency, inward humility with the exercise of leadership and power. Its readers are exhorted to childlike simplicity, to silence and discretion, and to orderliness; they are encouraged to pray to guardian angels and to the souls in purgatory, and to bless themselves every day with holy water.[3] But they are also urged to acquire professional competence, to stand out from the crowd, to lead and to dominate.[4] Although the book is directed primarily to lay people, it disparagingly describes marriage as something 'for the foot soldiers, not for the General Staff of Christ' and reckons that the prayer most pleasing to God is that of priests and consecrated virgins.[5] Lay people must be disciples, not masters, while priests must be venerated, respected, and treated always with formality and reverence.[6] While celibacy is glorified, the body is an enemy.[7] There is no sign here of a new spirituality: *Camino* is élitist, male, individualist, hostile to sexuality, and silent on economic and social problems. It belongs not to the new currents of *aggiornamento* but to the Crusade Catholicism in which it was developed.

Although its leaders always stressed the primary importance of the individual apostolate of each member,[8] the Opus also undertook corporate ventures very like those of the religious congregations in numerous schools, student halls of residence, and retreat centres. In 1952 it emulated the Augustinians in El Escorial and the Jesuits in Deusto by setting up its own university in Pamplona. Meanwhile, individual members vied with Herrera's Propagandists for academic and research posts in state universities and in the CSIC. An Opus member and

---

[1] On the genesis of the Vatican decree *Provida Mater Ecclesia* see Arigues, *El Opus Dei en España*, Ch. 3.
[2] Figures from 36th Spanish edition, Madrid, 1981.
[3] *Camino*, sections 852–74, 639–56, 78–80, 562–72.
[4] Ibid., 332–47, 19, 24, 32, 365.
[5] Ibid., 28, 98.
[6] Ibid., 61, 66–75.
[7] Ibid., 195–6, 124, 226–7.
[8] See, e.g., *Conversaciones con Monseñor Escrivá de Balaguer*, 13th edn. (Madrid, 1980), sections 10, 18, 70, among others.

friend of Escrivá, the chemist José María Albareda, held the key post of secretary general of the CSIC state research institute from 1939 until 1966, when he was replaced by Ángel González Álvarez, also of Opus Dei. The CSIC publication *Arbor* was dominated by Opus writers led by Rafael Calvo Serer. Many members gained posts in the state universities—it has been estimated that they represented about 25% of all appointments between 1939 and 1951[9]—and often collaborated in and benefited from CSIC enterprises.

It is hardly surprising, therefore, that the Opus Dei attracted just the kind of criticism long familiar to religious congregations on the one hand and the Propagandists on the other, while being frequently regarded with great suspicion by both. And the arguments it adduced 'n its own defence were no less familiar and no less incomplete. To ɔharges that its institutions serviced a moneyed and powerful élite it replied, as religious orders had done for generations, that it also provided education for the poor. It is true that it offered training in vocational skills to those with few resources, but it also became notorious for expensive, exclusive halls of residence and secondary schools, even absorbing into the latter in the 1970s upper middle-class children whose parents were disgruntled with the new social mix in the previously select schools of the religious congregations. To accusations that its own members were drawn from the wealthy and influential it responded, as Jesuits had always done, that many members from humble social backgrounds made an essential and prized contribution to its life and work. In both institutes, of course, different social classes fitted into distinct levels of the membership hierarchy. To those who found the involvement of its members in publishing, higher education, big business, and eventually politics unacceptable, it explained, as Propagandists had been explaining for a few decades, that it was entirely appropriate for lay people to concern themselves, as citizens and as Christians, with all aspects of secular life. Just as Fr. Ayala argued that the political involvement of individual Propagandists—that eventually included ten or so ministries in Franco's cabinets—did not alter the apolitical nature of the institute he had founded, so Monsignor Escrivá maintained that the Opus Dei had no more to do with the political or economic activities of its members than did other voluntary associations, like benevolent societies and sports clubs.[10] In both cases, these

[9] Artigues, 60.
[10] A. Ayala, *Obras completas*. 2 vols. (Madrid, 1947), i, 52-4; *Conversaciones con Monseñor Escrivá de Balaguer*, section 49.

claims were not so much disingenuous as examples of the very idiosyncratic use of the term 'political' in traditional Catholic circles to refer merely to adherence to a particular party or programme.

It was predictable that Opus Dei would arouse some unease among Jesuits and Propagandists since it was an obvious competitor with them for influence among the Catholic social and intellectual élite. But from the beginning certain characteristics made it more widely suspect, in particular its secrecy about its own constitutions and inner organization, and the identity of members. The inclusion from the beginning of diocesan priests—who formed a tiny minority of its total membership—and the relative independence of the Opus from hierarchical control and wider pastoral planning made most Spanish bishops very wary. As early as 1941 Segura reported to the nuncio the 'alarming' information he had received about it from Jesuits in Barcelona where it was already well established, and added his own misgivings about his secrecy, its uncertain relationship to the Spanish hierarchy and his queries about whether it was a pastoral, social, or political entity.[11] Spanish bishops continued to fear what Pont i Gol of Tarragona called in a pastoral letter of May 1973 a 'parallel church', and few of them could ever be accounted staunch advocates of the Opus.

For all its appropriation of modernity, the Opus remained highly conservative theologically, socially, and politically. It made no important theological contribution to the Second Vatican Council and was never at ease with the shift from traditional, individualist piety to the more communal and more populist liturgy, ecclesiology, and ethics of the Council documents. The man most clearly identified with conciliar Catholicism in Spain was undoubtedly Archbishop Vicente Enrique y Tarancón. He was translated by Paul VI to the primatial see of Toledo in 1969, then, on the very day it became vacant, to the more crucial see of Madrid in 1971, leaving Toledo conveniently free for the respectable but harmless promotion of González Martín from his disputed position in Barcelona. Tarancón also became president of the Spanish Episcopal Conference in 1971, and that position held in conjunction with the Madrid see made him the real power in the Spanish Church. He mistrusted the Opus, and was outraged when in 1972 a deliberate attempt to discredit his reformist policies by sensational news releases suggesting that the Vatican disapproved of them was traced to conservative circles around Opus personnel and press in Rome and

[11] R. Garriga, *El Cardenal Segura y el nacional-catolicismo* (Barcelona, 1977), 278–9.

Madrid.[12] So evident was the distance between Opus style and conciliar orientations that through the 1960s and 1970s rumours persisted about a possible Vatican offensive against it. Only later, with the election of the theologically very conservative Cardinal Wojtila as Pope John Paul II, and his promotion of it—against the advice of the majority of Spanish bishops—did the Opus find a protected niche of its own in the hierarchical structure of the Church.

In February 1957 it became hard to believe that there was no Opus Dei political tendency, when three known members were appointed simultaneously by Franco to ministerial posts which between them controlled economic policy. Alberto Ullastres in the Ministry of Commerce, Mariano Navarro Rubio in Finance, and Laureano López Rodó at the head of a governmental economic planning unit, worked together to modernize the Spanish economy by moving from post-war autarky to a capitalism that might eventually permit association with the newly founded European Economic Community. Analysts have never agreed about either the originality of their mixture of free market economics and state planning on the French model, or its success. While some attribute to them the spectacular leap in Spanish industrialization and general prosperity in the 1960s, others interpret these as largely the result—through tourism, emigration, and payments sent by emigrants to their families—of the economic expansion of industrialized western Europe.[13] But some aspects of their contribution are beyond controversy. Firstly, it was made within the political system of a military dictatorship, and there is no sign that Opus economists and politicians ever sought in the 1960s or early 1970s to modify this system beyond establishing a monarchy which they hoped would be its continuation, not its nemesis. Secondly, it would be foolish to claim that Opus politicians were not helped and informed by the substantial numbers of Opus members eminent in banking and industrial circles.[14] Thirdly, several effects of the Stabilization Plan of 1959 and the First Economic Plan of 1964 exacerbated social divisions. Inflation and unemployment severely affected a labour force with only the flimsiest of social security protection; while gross national productivity rose, the traditional regional imbalance of Spain worsened as rural areas decayed, unas-

---

[12] J. L. Martín Descalzo, *Tarancón, el cardenal del cambio* (Barcelona, 1982), 179–85.

[13] See, e.g., J. Esteban, 'The Economic Policy of Francoism; an Interpretation', in P. Preston (ed.), *Spain in Crisis* (London, 1976), 96–8.

[14] For the occupation of alleged members and sympathizers of Opus Dei, see J. Ynfante, *La prodigiosa aventura del Opus Dei. Génesis y desarrollo de la Sante Mafia* (Paris, 1970), anexo.

sisted; a fiscal system that had always been scandalously reliant on indirect taxation remained that way, so that profits went more or less untaxed while prices rose and the poor bore an even more unequal burden than was customary. These characteristics of the economic policies of Opus ministers went hand in hand with a flaunted modernity of techniques—not for nothing were Ullastres and his colleagues referred to as the 'technocrats'. In politics as in pastoral activity, the modernity of the Opus style did not conceal the fundamental conservatism of its values.

In 1969 Opus economics ministers were involved in the worst financial scandal of modern Spanish history—the corrupt use of enormous sums of government money by the textile firm Matesa—and were dismissed. Its political credentials never seemed as promising after that, in spite of later cabinet posts and powerful backing by Franco's most trusted assistant and eventual head of government, Admiral Carrero Blanco. When the dictatorship disintegrated in the months after Franco's death, Opus Dei was conspicuous by its absence—except for maverick deserters like Calvo Serer—from the massed ranks of democratizing reformers. Although it would remain economically, socially, and institutionally formidable in the new Spain, its modernity did not extend to an instinct for democracy, a wider distribution of wealth, or open discussion, any more than it had embraced the Church's equivalent of these in its conciliar emphasis on social justice, dialogue, and *aggiornamento*.

Another new lay movement, far removed from the 'jobs for the boys' networks of Opus Dei and the Propagandists, also laid claim to a rather spurious modernity. This time the target was not the young intellectual élite in the universities, but youth in general. Courses in Christian Life (*Cursillos de Cristiandad*) began in Mallorca in 1949, to continue the sessions instituted by Catholic Action youth sections for pilgrims to Santiago in the great national pilgrimage of 1948. Their attempt to keep the Crusade effective in the personal lives of a new generation thus gained strength from two overlapping conservatisms, traditional Mallorquín Catholicism and triumphalist post-war fervour. They were energetically promoted by Joan Hervás i Benet, bishop of Mallorca from 1947 to 1955, moving outside the island in 1953, proving successful in Vich and Lérida, and then reaching Madrid in 1954.

Enthusiasts later claimed that their stress on inner conversion rather than routine religious practice anticipated the renewal of lay spirituality fostered by the Second Vatican Council. Their style was certainly novel in Spain, relying on a total immersion in intensive prayer, lecture, and discussion sessions in residential three-day courses. The *cursillos* bore many resemblances to the evangelistic techniques of Protestant fundamentalism: they were informal, emotional, proselytizing, and utterly preoccupied with personal salvation attained through a born-again conversion experience.[15] They were disliked both by those who found their neglect of wider moral and theological issues reactionary, and those of more sober traditional tastes who could not stomach their forced jollity and intrusive muscularity, and the banality of the movement's hymn, 'Colours'. To the horror of *cursillo* adepts, Hervás's successor in the Mallorquín see in 1955, Jesús Enciso i Viana, attacked them in a pastoral letter in September 1957 as illuminist, strident, and divisive. But they remained popular and spread to the United States and to Latin America, where *cursillo* links with dictatorial politics were sometimes apparent.[16]

While the *cursillos* took their controversial place, especially in Catalonia, among longer established devotional lay movements like the Children of Mary and groups for eucharistic worship, the decisive break with the past in lay spirituality was occurring elsewhere. Already in the early 1930s a new Catholic youth organization in Catalonia, the Federation of Young Christians (*Federació de Jovens Cristians*), had essayed a less pietistic orientation than those usual in Catholic Action. Its founder, Albert Bonet, had been deeply influenced by the vigour and realism of the Young Christian Workers, founded in Belgium in the 1920s by the priest Joseph Cardijn. Following this model, the FJC eschewed the confessional title of 'Catholic' in favour of the more open 'Christian', and it imposed no qualifying religious test or practice on its members, insisting rather on group meetings and discussions. It resisted assimilation by the Catalan political Right, showed a serious interest in social justice, and sketched the first outlines of what would later be called 'specialized' lay groupings according to trade or profession.[17]

Although the civil war killed off the FJC, its influence was evident in the Young Christian Workers that emerged in Catalonia in the 1940s.

[15] For a good analysis, see P. Llabres i Martorell, 'Cursets de Christiandat: un moviment apostòlic mallorquí pels quatre vents del mon', *Questions de vida cristiana*, 75/76 (1975), 59–75. There is a chilling version of a *cursillo* course in J. Marsé, *La oscura historia de la prima Montse* (Barcelona, 1970), Chs. 15–19.
[16] Llabres i Martorell, note on p. 75.
[17] There are studies by various contributors in *La federació de jovens cristians de Catalunya. Contribució a la seva historia* (Barcelona, 1972). See also the sympathetic but critical view of a close observer in M. Serrahima, *Memòries de la guerra i de l'exili*. 2 vols. (Barcelona, 1978, 1981), i, 22–64.

This association found the contemporary fashion for ostentatious processions entirely unappealing, managed not to get swept into involvement with the International Eucharistic Congress held in Barcelona in 1952, and related uneasily to Catholic Action in the area.[18] Similar initiatives in Bilbao, San Sebastián, and Valencia began to demonstrate the capacity of the JOC (*Juventud Obrera Católica*) to attract working-class support. Catholic Action tried its own version for a while in the shape of JOAC (Young Workers of Catholic Action), but in 1956 JOAC merged into JOC. It had a female branch and an agrarian equivalent. It outstripped its rivals, like the Jesuit VOJ (Young Workers Vanguard) based in Madrid. Alongside it, developed HOAC (*Hermandades Obreras de Acción Católica*), workers' group not specifically aimed at youth, and sharing JOC's style, emerging from separate associations of railway workers and a host of other trades in the 1940s, and receiving early recognition by the hierarchy in 1946 as an official part of Catholic Action. In 1959 important new Catholic Action statutes were approved by the bishops, giving constitutional expression to the fact that it then comprised both the old diocesan and parochial networks, and the new specialized branches, including JOC and HOAC. The contrast with the Catholic workers' associations of one and two generations earlier was stark indeed: where they had been pious, under firm hierarchical control, and organized from the top down, the JOC and HOAC of the late fifties and sixties were a genuinely grass roots phenomenon, profoundly involved in working-class concerns like wages and working conditions, and utterly convinced that these matters were as central to Christianity as saying prayers and going to Church.

Both HOAC and JOC displayed an immense vitality. They were never mass organizations. Statistics for both are very hard to come by, but at their peak in the early 1960s HOAC probably mustered about 12,000 active members, called militants, and about 20,000 other affiliates, while JOC had about 70,000 members and a generous fringe of active sympathizers.[19] These figures look small when set beside the many hundreds of thousands regularly claimed by Catholic Action as a whole, but have the advantage of actually meaning something. While involvement in Catholic Action often amounted to little more than occasional participation in some parish devotion, core membership of

[18] J. Castaño i Colomer, *Memòries sobre la JOC a Catalunya 1932–1970* (Barcelona, 1974), 42–78.
[19] Figures from G. Hermet, *Les catholiques dans l'Espagne franquiste*. 2 vols. (Paris, 1980, 1981), i, 213–14.

HOAC and JOC required regular attendance at meetings and in study sessions and campaigns. In addition to *Ecclesia*, published first fortnightly then weekly since 1941 as the organ of Catholic Action, a host of publications sprang up from the specialized branches. As early as 1949 HOAC's *¡Tú!* ran into trouble with the civil authorities, initiating a long series of skirmishes, while the Cardinal Primate, Pla y Deniel, also made the first of many interventions in defence of HOAC and JOC on the grounds that the state had no right to interfere in internal Church affairs. In 1955 JOC in Barcelona opened a publishing house, *Nova Terra*, and five years later the national organization founded another in Madrid, the *Editorial Popular*.

Political conditions helped Catholic workers' associations in the 1950s develop some muscle. In a dictatorial state with no political party except the official, bureaucratic Falange, and no labour organizations except the vertical state syndicates, the meetings and publications of Catholic groups were the only relatively safe channel for discussing labour issues and airing grievances. But internal factors made JOC and HOAC capable of filling this role far more effectively than most of the pre-war Catholic unions had been. Active members were 'militants', in the terminology adopted from Cardijn's work in Belgium, and JOC in Spain as elsewhere funded a number of full-time officials, 'liberated' from their normal jobs to pour all their energies into its ventures. The methodology perfected by Cardijn for JOC sessions fostered both realism and efficiency. It consisted of three stages: first the group tried to see the topic under discussion as clearly and with as much information as possible; then it judged what it saw; finally it decided upon specific remedial action. 'Seeing' might well involve, in a rural setting, a thorough questionnaire on schools provision, income levels, patterns of land ownership, vocational training, and social services in the local village; 'judging' would then try to discover, for example, why some labourers lived without land and on inadequate wages; and 'action' might initiate a planned campaign to effect change. This see–judge–act method could equally well be applied nationally on a particular issue, like working conditions. It could also enable a small group to take up the case of, for instance, a factory worker losing his part-time extra job—crucial to the family's survival—because of being put on to an evening shift, or a woman worker with a husband in prison who was being pestered by her male supervisor.[20] In a political regime that

[20] These examples are taken from a handbook, E. Miret Magdalena, *Método de formación y acción*. 2nd edn. (Madrid, 1963), 121–64.

encouraged people to see nothing, to have no independent judgement, and to remain isolated and passive, these processes were dangerously effective. It is not surprising that the Basque separatist ETA, whose first members had been trained in industrial and rural cells of JOC in Guipúzcoa and Vizcaya, retained the terminology of 'militants' and 'liberated' full-time activists, and the structure of the small, disciplined group. An ETA handbook issued in 1960, the *Libro Blanco*, proposed two useful models for revolutionary action—Leninist Communism and the JOC, this latter chosen because of its tight group structure, its leadership, its dynamism, and its refusal to separate thought from action.[21]

JOC and HOAC were not revolutionary organizations, but they were ever more openly and loudly reformist in a political and industrial regime where reform was not an acceptable concept, particularly if it were urged from below. Confrontation with the state was inevitable as JOC and HOAC became suspected of supporting illegal strike action in the 1950s. They criticized the harsh social effects of the Opus technocrats' economic measures. Speakers from both organizations were fined in Bilbao in 1959. In 1960 Syndicates Minister Solís Ruiz reacted with fury when leaders of JOC and HOAC male and female branches wrote to him complaining of corrupt practices in the syndical elections of that year. He was not appeased when Pla y Deniel intervened to argue that the state's relations with the Catholic workers' organizations were becoming perilous. Two years later, JOC and HOAC issued a declaration on labour conflicts in Asturias, which was seized by the government: since its authors refused to pay a fine, they were imprisoned. Various issues of Catholic worker publications were also seized, their authors tried, and the leadership in general accused of fomenting class struggle, while police cordons surrounded JOC and HOAC rallies.[22] From the government's point of view, these Catholic groups had strayed from religious into purely temporal and political domains, where they emphatically had no place.

Most of the pre-war predecessors of these groups had claimed to be syndicates or unions but in practice had rarely been what they claimed; JOC and HOAC, on the contrary, were officially religious associations of the Catholic laity but often acted as though they were labour unions. They were most buoyant not—like virtually all other Catholic insti-

[21] *ETA Documentos*, i (Donostia, 1979), 151–86.
[22] For a survey by one of the militants, see J. Castaño i Colomer, *La JOC en España (1946–1970)* (Salamanca, 1977).

tutions—where levels of religious practice were highest, but in industrial zones like Asturias, Catalonia, Bilbao, and an increasingly industrialized Madrid, where the Church's writ had not usually run. These arresting facts puzzled many of the bishops as much as they irritated successive governments full of ministers who also considered themselves good Catholics. As tension with the government increased, so the unease of some of the hierarchy became acute. Those who saw clear divisions between the religious and the secular, the spiritual and the temporal, lamented the inability of JOC and HOAC to see these divisions and observe them. Bishops also feared the radicalizing effect the workers' movements so obviously had on a whole generation of young priests who were their chaplains.[23] It proved to be the Church hierarchy, not the dictatorship, that in the late 1960s vitiated the specialized branches of Catholic Action until there was almost nothing left.

The crisis of 1966–9 has frequently been mourned by participants who suddenly discovered that their dream of a modern Spanish Catholicism, open to lay initiatives, congenial to the urban and rural working classes, and courageous in the fight for social justice, was unrealizable. In part their disillusion reflected an excessive earlier optimism that had not taken into account the very mixed motives of those who worked for JOC and HOAC because there was no other instrument of legal protest and militancy available—better take action under Church auspices, meeting in presbyteries and convents, than take no action at all. The Catholic workers' associations were superseded in their unofficial but real political and labour functions by clandestine groups without religious affiliation, though with many activists who had gained experience under the Catholic banner.[24] The Communist-led Workers Commissions (*Comisiones Obreras*) came in the last decade of the Franco regime to form an illegal but sometimes tolerated alternative to the moribund vertical syndicates. It is impossible to know whether they would have been any less successful had not their Catholic competitors so obligingly disintegrated. But what is certain is that JOC and HOAC were actually undermined, not by Communist rivalry nor by state oppression, but by episcopal hostility.

In 1966 the Spanish Episcopal Conference (CEE) was established, implementing the Vatican Council decision to give national hierarchies a 'collegial' or corporate structure. Henceforth it would be much easier

[23] See above, pp. 105–6.
[24] J. Maravall, *Dictatorship and Political Dissent. Workers and Students in Franco's Spain* (London, 1978), 73.

for Spanish bishops to ponder and decide together questions of interest in their country through regular meetings of the Conferences and its various committees. Although it was a conciliar creation, the Episcopal Conference did not produce a major document that reflected conciliar theology and pastoral attitudes until *The Church and the Political Community*, issued in 1973. Between 1964 and 1974 no fewer than fifty-three new bishops were consecrated—over twice as many as in the previous eleven years—reducing the average age from sixty-five to fifty-seven, and with these new appointments the balance within the Conference gradually altered to produce a clearly progressive majority.[25] But it was too late for the Catholic workers' movements. During the crisis of 1966–9 the majority of Spanish bishops remained wary of what they considered the excessive meddling in political and temporal matters by Catholic Action's specialized industrial and rural branches. Of the three bishops heading the CEE, Quiroga Palacios, president, was a moderate; Morcillo, vice-president, was a timorous conservative; Guerra Campos, secretary, was a determined Francoist and integrist, soon to become the regime's 'television bishop' propagandist and appointed to its undemocratic Cortes by Franco himself. Guerra Campos had become episcopal representative to Catholic Action in 1964, and in 1966 Morcillo replaced the sympathetic but now ancient Cardinal Primate, Pla y Deniel, as president of Catholic Action when he took up the presidency of the new episcopal committee for the lay apostolate. The secular officials and the chaplains of JOC and HOAC were therefore immediately responsible to Morcillo and Guerra Campos, and lacked any court of appeal beyond them since they also took two out of the three places at the head of the Episcopal Conference.

In 1966 Morcillo took the occasion of an address to a big national gathering of Catholic Action in the Valle de los Caídos to express reservations about the specialized branches and forbid any statement on temporal affairs.[26] The meeting's conclusions were then censured by the hierarchy, which also postponed indefinitely national meetings planned by the various movements within Catholic Action. So exercised were the bishops by the growing independence and range of lay initiatives that they admonished the 'apostolic minorities' in their extremely cautious *The Church and the Temporal Order in the Light of the Council*,

[25] *Iglesia y sociedad en España 1939–1975*, 131.
[26] The account that follows is based mainly on a chronological survey of the conflict in 'Jerarquía y apostolado seglar en España', *Pastoral Misionera* (1967), 75–84.

published the same, eventful year.[27] Amid ever more numerous signs of episcopal displeasure—including the sacking in September 1966 of seven national chaplains—and of bitter reactions from lay militants and priests, the CEE met in plenary session at the end of February 1967 to discuss new statutes for Catholic Action. It wanted a narrower definition of 'religious' and 'pastoral' activities than was current in progressive circles, tighter hierarchical control, and a return to the parochial and diocesan structures fundamental to Catholic Action before the 1959 approval of specialized branches that had tended to cut right across them.

The predictable reactions of anguish and anger followed one another in succeeding months as Catholic Action worker, student, youth, industrial and rural, male and female groups, and their chaplains, protested. Militant leaders resigned, while priests pleaded uselessly with CEE representatives for a more open pastoral style, and a disentangling of the hierarchy from the dictatorship. Even a lay apostolate congress in May without worker or youth representatives called for reform of legislation on civil rights including freedom of association, quoted Vatican Council documents against the hierarchy, and justified clear commitments on temporal questions as an essential part of Christian life. Undeterred, in November 1967 the sixth plenary session of the CEE approved the controversial new statutes, with only thirteen dissenting votes. In the course of 1968 the destruction of a Catholic Action that worked for social and political reform as an integral part of preaching the good news was virtually completed in a further flurry of sackings, resignations, and recriminations. A generation of very public lay leaders and clerics went private—sometimes leaving the Church altogether—and it was never replaced. It never could be replaced once the transition to democracy after Franco's death provided so many other legal channels for political participation and industrial and agrarian interest groups. But the great experiment had done something to erode working-class suspicion of the Church of the Crusade, and it had politically radicalized some energetic Catholics far beyond the bounds of the limited pluralism of the 1950s.

Ironically, hierarchical intransigence barely outlasted the crisis. In December 1968 Ramón Torrella, one of the chaplains sacked only two years earlier, was himself consecrated bishop. In January 1969 Enrique y Tarancón succeeded Pla y Deniel in the primatial see and then became

---

[27] Text in Iribarren, 370–403.

vice-president of the CEE. When Morcillo—now president—died in 1971, Tarancón took his place both in Madrid and as CEE president. A largely reconstituted bishops' committee on the lay apostolate (CEAS) did its belated best to accommodate JOC and HOAC, and in October 1970 itself complained to the government that the new Syndicates Law was insufficiently respectful of workers' rights to freedom and representation. As a JOC militant, José Castaño i Colomer, wryly noted; 'What it prohibited to the JOC in 1966, it now does itself'.[28] In August 1972 Guerra Campos was eventually ousted from authority over Catholic Action. Finally, in November 1972, the new majority on the Episcopal Conference published pastoral orientations for the lay apostolate that would have delighted militants if only they had appeared six years earlier.[29] By the time CEAS elaborated these into a document the length of a substantial book in 1974, few people cared any more.[30]

The specialized branches of Catholic Action were not the only postwar attempts to draw the Church and the working classes closer together. A very few of the diocesan clergy tried to create a new unity of the two in their own persons by becoming worker-priests, earning a living in manual work while trying out a pastoral role not in the conventional parish context, but in the factory. On the whole the experience was not encouraging since it often convinced those involved that—as a group of fifteen worker-priests of many years' standing explained in a letter to the Vatican Council—'the working class needs the Church neither as guide nor ally'. With their awareness of the anticlericalism and atheism of many labour militants, and their introduction to the reality of the class struggle in Franco's Spain, they pleaded for a greater shift of emphasis from personal morality and charity to an informed criticism of economic structures. They wanted a 'listening' Church that renounced its own power and might 'reveal the most profound significance of the values lived out by the working class'.[31] Such an aim was intangible and strangely reductionist. Had the one, holy, Catholic, Roman, and apostolic Church nothing to offer beyond a deepening and affirmation of proletarian values? This was precisely the fear felt by many observers, including bishops, about both worker-priests and the JOC and HOAC groups they were often in contact with:

[28] Castaño i Colomer, *La JOC en España*, 216, n. 19.
[29] Text in Iribarren, 493–520.
[30] CEAS, *El apostolado seglar en España* (Madrid, 1974), contains 415 pages.
[31] Text in J. Bertrán, *Los difíciles caminos de la misión obrera* (Barcelona, 1968), 233–47. Bertrán left the priesthood in 1970.

commitment to the social, economic, and political advancement of workers and their families seemed in many cases to leave little room for supernatural faith, prayer, and the sacraments. These fears were not allayed when radical priests became disillusioned and left the priesthood in the late 1960s, while some former priests and former militants left the Church altogether. Years later even militants sometimes decided that their enthusiasm for socio-political action had marginalized religious belief, practice, and symbolism.[32] Catholic renewal in the expanding industrial world of the 1950s and 1960s was a perilous enterprise.

One local venture which escaped these ambiguities because it was so concrete and practical was the extremely successful workers' co-operative established in the Basque village of Mondragón, thirty kilometres from Vitoria, in 1956. The initiative came from the young Basque priest José María Arizmendi-Arrieta, who was appointed assistant priest in Mondragón in 1941 and retained the position for his entire clerical career. Mondragón's recent industrial and political history had been tense. In October 1934 it was one of very few places outside Asturias and Catalonia to witness an attempted proletarian revolution. The chief victim was Marcelino Oreja, Carlist parliamentary deputy, leading Propagandist, and managing director of the local steel company, *Unión Cerrajera*, who was shot. When the civil war began two years later, there was no repetition of this brutality under a PNV mayor, and Mondragón remained loyal to the republic with joint Basque Nationalist and Socialist control. After conquest by insurgent troops as early as September 1936, forty-one people were executed, including three priests.[33] The young curate arriving in 1941—who had enrolled in the Basque army in 1936, been imprisoned after the fall of Bilbao, and then worked for the regime in Burgos—had a daunting task as he took up parochial duties which included being chaplain to Catholic Action.

Arizmendi-Arrieta's first achievement was to set up in 1943 the *Escuela profesional*, a centre for vocational studies that was open to everyone and always provided in-service as well as preparatory training. The anti-élitist spirit of the *Escuela* as of all that grew from it was quite intentional, owing something to its founder's sense of the possibilities

[32] 'Autocrítica de los movimientos renovadores', reprinted from a 1980 HOAC bulletin in R. Díaz Salazar, *Iglesia, dictadura y democracia* (Madrid, 1981), 487–90.
[33] This account is based on J. Larrañaga, *Don José María Arizmendi-Arrieta y la experiencia cooperativa de Mondragón* (San Sebastián, 1981). Jesús Larrañaga was one of the original five who founded the first co-operative, ULGOR, in 1956.

of communal co-operation in Basque culture and social structures, and something to papal teaching on social justice. Arizmendi-Arrieta was also interested in Mounier's writings in France that tried to find a Christian form of social organization which was neither capitalist nor communist. At the heart of Arizmendi-Arrieta's venture lay his conviction, 'in order to democratize power, socialize knowledge'.[34] In 1955 five former pupils of the *Escuela* worked together in Vitoria making domestic cookers, and a year later they returned to Mondragón, establishing there the first co-operative, ULGOR, an acronym from their names—Usatorre, Larrañaga, Gorroñogoitia, Ormaechea, Ortubay. ULGOR stimulated two additional co-operatives, an iron foundry and a machine engineering works, as it probed the new openings for gas and electric domestic appliances in a Spanish market now recovering from the austerity of the post-war years. These were followed by others, and when they ran into problems with finance capital, they created—at Arizmendi-Arrieta's suggestion—what was to become the keystone of their ambitious arch, their own bank, the *Caja Laboral Popular*. The system became self-funding, with a substantial proportion of profits reinvested in the bank. By 1973, sixty-three co-operatives in the Basque country were involved in the *Caja*, fifty-five in production, the others concerned with housing, services, and consumption. ULGOR alone employed over 3,000 people and was one of the hundred biggest enterprises in Spain. Where Mondragón had a population of under 9,000 in 1950, by 1973 it had reached 25,000. Over 700 workers attended in-service courses at the expanded and modernized *Escuela*.[35]

For Arizmendi-Arrieta, all of this began as an attempt to make Catholic Action real and dynamic in social and industrial relations. All of the founders were as interested in the social as in the economic results of the venture. Everyone paid the same entry fee that yielded no interest, and could then invest more that did earn interest; the highest paid never received more than three times the wage of the lowest; wages were rarely much more than those in capitalist industry; social security was a little better than that available elsewhere; there were no strikes. The co-operatives in Mondragón and elsewhere did not give spectacular remuneration, but they gave security and promoted solidarity instead

[34] Arizmendi-Arrieta's early ideas can be traced in a series of conferences he gave on, and usually to, Catholic Action in 1945–1955: *Escritos de Don José María Arizmendi-Arrieta*, i, *Conferencias apostolado social* (San Sebastián, 1978).

[35] Statistics from I. Gorroño, *Experiencias cooperativas en el país vasco* (Durango, 1975), 80–166.

of interest group conflict, the common good instead of profits for a tiny élite. Until his death in 1976 Arizmendi-Arrieta remained a crucial and practical adviser. It may be that Mondragón's success—unrivalled in western Europe—depended upon cultural structures peculiar to small Basque towns, and upon the unrepeatable opportunities of Spain's sudden leap into consumerism. It certainly owed its origins to the specifically Christian values of Arizmendi-Arrieta and the Basque laity he inspired to transform a pietistic notion of Catholic Action into a new form of industrial and social co-operation.

Alongside all the multifarious experiments with a renewed Catholic presence and mission among industrial and agricultural workers, new perspectives were also opening up for some sectors of the Catholic intellectual élite. As early as 1947 a group of Propagandists launched a yearly conference called International Conversations of San Sebastián, a title deliberately suggestive of informal, leisurely, discussions among Spaniards and participants from outside Spain. The organizer, Carlos Santamaría, drew Catholic lay intellectuals like José Luis Aranguren, and foreign theological luminaries like Yves Congar. Through the annual conference, and discussion documents circulated during the year, communication was established with progressive Catholic intellectual circles in France, Belgium, Holland, and Germany, which in the hermetic world of Crusade Catholicism was a remarkable innovation.

Originally as a domestic variant of these appeared the Conversations of Gredos in 1951, held annually until 1965 in a tourist *parador* in the Gredos hills south of Ávila, and then in other venues until they stopped in 1968. The central figure was former Propagandist Alfonso Querejazu, who convened the sessions of invited participants. Although a priest, his formation had been entirely untypical of the Spanish clergy. Born into a diplomatic family in Bolivia in 1900, his undergraduate education was received partly in Deusto, partly in England, and he studied for his doctorate in Germany. Before his ordination at the unusually mature age of forty-two, he had acquired both academic and diplomatic experience. He was well prepared to appreciate the emphases on international exchange, lay responsibility within the Church, and intellectual life that were characteristic of San Sebastián, and to create in Gredos a more intimate and spiritual, but still open and exploratory style. Regular participants in the Gredos Conversations and ancillary meetings during the year—and it is interesting to note that participants returned year after year—agree that the experience was immensely important, affording a precious opportunity to discuss topics like work, or the mission of seculars in the Church, or the components of Christian life, in an atmosphere of openness and tolerance far removed from the dogmatism and narrow orthodoxies of Crusade Catholicism.[36] A few priests formed part of this select group, but the great majority were laymen—the poets Luis Rosales and Luis Felipe Vivanco, many academics like Aranguren, Pedro Laín Entralgo, and Julián Marias, and some who would later play a significant political part in the transition from dictatorship to democracy such as Leopoldo Calvo Sotelo, Joaquín Ruiz Giménez, and Gregorio Peces Barba. Political topics were never introduced into their discussions, which concentrated rather on personal experience and spirituality. Nor could anyone claim that the harsh realities of social conflict intruded very far, and the group remained clearly highly élitist and entirely male. Yet the meetings of the first decade especially helped open the windows of a claustrophobic Church to the breezes of ecumenism, dialogue, and theological renewal that blew more freely elsewhere in Catholic Europe. San Sebastián and Gredos played a small but not negligible part in altering the mental world of some Catholic intellectuals in ways that gradually made first theological and then political pluralism easier to accommodate.

A few significant books and periodicals diffused new approaches more widely. In 1949 Pedro Laín Entralgo published a long and extremely controversial analysis of Spanish culture since the late nineteenth century, *Spain as a Problem*.[37] Profoundly out of sympathy with the coercive style of post-war national-Catholicism and its insistence that Spain had one, essential identity that was Catholic and anti-liberal, Laín pleaded instead for recognition of the enormous cultural contribution of free-thinkers in the period he was studying. Spain was a fusion of many traditions, not just one; its culture would be served by their integration, not the suppression of those regarded as heterodox by a vaunted orthodoxy. Only a decade after the end of a war fought—it was claimed—to establish the true Spain on the ruins of its false rivals, this was courageous. Soon afterwards, Laín was appointed Rector of the University of Madrid by Joaquín Ruiz-Giménez, who used his power as Minister of Education to try and liberalize the universities.

In 1952, Aranguren—central figure in the Gredos group—published a book with the challenging title *Catholicism and Protestantism as Ways*

[36] Various participants contributed to *Alfonso Querejazu. Conversaciones católicas de Gredos* (Madrid, 1977), on which this paragraph is based.
[37] For a discussion of the controversy over P. Laín Entralgo, *España como problema*, see E. Díaz, *Pensamiento español 1939–1973* (Madrid, 1974), 70–9.

*of Being.*³⁸ Many Catholics later claimed this book as an essential influence in their development. Deliberately eschewing orthodox apologetics, Aranguren adopted instead more historical and existential methods. Arguing that all Christians necessarily live an incomplete version of Christianity because it cannot be fully realized in any epoch or individual, he did not exempt Counter Reformation Catholicism from this incompleteness. In fact he traced the traditional division between Catholicism and Protestantism largely to particular historical situations and to differences of sensibility *(talante)*. Within this framework, Luther, Kierkegaard, and Unamuno had an authentic experience and insight to contribute to a Catholicism which might now benefit from comprehending ways of being, long rejected simply as 'non-Catholic'. It was at present excessively narrow, dogmatic, clericalist, and defensive. Writing as, at that time, a believing Catholic, Aranguren was chiefly interested in religious, and moral renewal, but his profound respect for different experiences and different styles in these spheres also presaged a later unease with authoritarian politics. His appointment as Professor of Ethics and Sociology in the Complutense University, Madrid, in 1955, ensured that Catholic students there heard religious and moral issues discussed in a new and disconcerting language. Ten years later, he was sacked for political reasons.

Both Laín and Aranguren gave expression in their controversial books to a more widespread critical appraisal among some Catholic writers and academics of contemporary Spanish Catholicism. Political, religious, and intellectual values are not always closely interdependent, but it is also rare for any one of them to be fully autonomous of the other two. Spanish integrist groups had frequently identified true religion with a particular political option, and Crusade Catholicism had recapitulated this tradition on a grand scale in its fusion of religion with social conservatism and authoritarian politics. In these circumstances, any major shift of religious sensibility, any severe questioning of intellectual presuppositions, was likely to modify the vocabulary and tone of political discussion, and ultimately to affect political values and expectations. It was hard to exalt the virtues of dialogue, accommodation, transigence, and respect for the individual in debates about faith, or national culture, without experiencing a consequent discomfort at their repudiation in politics and government. The gradual opening of Spanish administrative élites to democratic aspirations and con-

---

³⁸ J. L. Aranguren, *Catolicismo y protestantismo como formas de existencia* (Madrid, 1952).

victions in the 1960s and 1970s was an extremely complex and diverse phenomenon which included factors as different as increasing prosperity, self-interest, and a humanitarian distaste for military repression; but one stimulus was certainly that transformation of religious culture that began in some Catholic intellectual circles in the 1950s.

The political potency of this transformation was probably best seen in Ruiz Giménez's *Cuadernos para el Diálogo* (*Notes towards Dialogue*), a periodical founded in 1963 whose very title proclaimed its intentions neither to pontificate nor to proselytize, but 'to facilitate the communication of ideas and sentiments among people of different generations, beliefs and basic attitudes'.[39] This determined pluralism was to be the style of a publication dedicated to the study of contemporary religious, cultural, social, economic, and political problems. It would be hard to exaggerate the influence of *Cuadernos* in the remaining years of the Franco regime, since it acquired a formidable reputation for intellectual range and depth, courageously probed sensitive issues not easily discussed in print elsewhere in Spain, and managed to retain a genuine pluralism, notwithstanding Ruiz Giménez's own extremely well-known Christian Democrat stance. It helped create a new, democratic style which was also in itself a preparation for democratic politics. *Cuadernos* can stand as both example and symbol of a political diversification that owed much to changed cultural values in those sectors of the Catholic intelligentsia that learned in the 1950s to re-examine Crusade Catholicism and find it wanting, first on religious and intellectual grounds, and then on political.

Even a few of the bishops began in the 1950s to feel dissatisfaction with aspects of both the Church and the Catholic state. Spanish prelates participated at a very high level in government through two seats on the Council of State and more at Franco's nomination in the Cortes. They benefited enormously from the post-war reconstruction policy of Catholicism for all from cradle to grave, but they were also strategically placed to notice the limits of its efficacy. The ideological monopoly of national-Catholicism did not bring about either the universal fervour or universal conformity that might have been expected from the suppression of error. Bishop Jesús Enciso Viana authorized a survey of Mass attendance one Sunday in 1951 in his diocese of Ciudad Rodrigo. Although this rural diocese of Old Castile did not register the eloquently

---

[39] *Cuadernos para el diálogo*, no. 1 (1963), Introduction.

massive absences later tabulated for parts of Andalusia, a Sunday Mass attendance of 42% of men and 55% of women was not the harvest hoped for from the martyrs' blood shed in the Crusade. In 1951 and 1952 Casimiro Morcillo, first bishop of the new diocese of Bilbao, authorized similar surveys which disclosed that whereas in the Basque town of Guernica about 80% of the population attended Mass on Sundays and feast days, in the densely populated industrial area of Portugalete, on the outskirts of Bilbao, the equivalent figure was only around 30%. Since the market town boasted fewer than 20,000 inhabitants in comparison with Portugalete's more than 100,000, the nature of the pastoral challenge in the diocese was quite clear.[40]

At the same time, the man who would eventually succeed Morcillo in Madrid, Vicente Enrique y Tarancón, was also breaking new ground in the diagnosis of pastoral problems. In his Catalan see of Solsona, he wrote in 1950 a pastoral letter entitled *Our Daily Bread* which in both content and style abandoned the customary forms.[41] He forthrightly criticized irregularities in food rationing, pointed out political responsibilities for it, and commented that distrust of the state and its agencies was widespread. The letter was not well received by the majority of his episcopal colleagues. Undeterred—and perhaps encouraged by Pla y Deniel's support—Tarancón published in 1955 an equally controversial letter, this time a critique of Spanish Catholicism that castigated the hypocrisy and superficiality of a religious formalism without power to effect genuine conversion of life.

These three factors—the relative failure in statistical or sociological terms of the post-war revival, the plight of the poor and unprotected in this Catholic state, and the glaring lack of congruence between faith and life of many Catholics—emerged as warning signs to at least a minority of bishops that all was not well. One especially striking example of the new mentality was given in Seville. On Segura's death in 1957, his auxiliary automatically succeedèd him and immediately issued a brief and terse pastoral letter. Whereas Segura had been preoccupied about ecclesiastical rights and Church associations, Bueno Monreal urgently called attention to the lack of schools and the appalling living and working conditions of land workers and industrial labourers in Andalusia.[42] Some bishops in the 1950s assumed a critical stance

---

[40] The Ciudad Rodrigo and Bilbao surveys were reprinted in *Guía de la Iglesia en España* (1955) 153–7.
[41] An abbreviated version in Martín Descalzo, *Tarancón, el cardenal del cambio*, 281–7.
[42] *BEAS* (1 May 1957), 143–5.

against social and economic conditions without limiting themselves to proposing moral solutions at the level of individual conversion. They adopted a role described by Guy Hermet as that of tribune of the people, pleading for those with no voice in a political system bereft of representative institutions,[43] and described by those interested in biblical images and terminology as prophetic denunciation of injustice in the tradition of Isaiah and Amos. It is possible that the very experience of living in the ideal or 'thesis' situation of national Catholic unity vainly longed for by their predecessors itself stimulated new kinds of pastoral analysis.[44] Religious indifference and social injustice could no longer be blamed on liberal errors of foreign inspiration. If workers did not go to church and deeply resented the state and its institutions, the obvious targets for blame ten or twenty years after the end of the Crusade were no longer socialist or anarchist influences, or divisive party politics, but the confessional state and the Church along with it. Privilege necessarily eroded paranoia. It became possible—even necessary—to talk of reform in the Catholic Church and the Catholic state.

It is impossible to know how far these various reformist currents in minority sectors of Catholic Action, Catholic intellectuals, the clergy, and the hierarchy would have taken the Church if they had been left to run between the narrow banks of ecclesiastical and governmental conservatism. But one of those banks suddenly collapsed and the other one shuddered at the strain when Vatican policy in the 1960s radically changed. When Pope John XXIII announced in January 1959 the convocation of a Council of the Church, almost a hundred years after the premature dispersion of the first Vatican Council by the outbreak of the Franco-Prussian war in 1870, he thereby summoned the Spanish bishops to an intensive re-education whose effects on the Spanish Church are incalculable. The eighty or so Spanish bishops who attended the four sessions of the Second Vatican Council between 1962 and 1965 discovered with varying degrees of ease or anguish that on the whole they had more to learn than to teach. As they themselves admitted in their joint message to Spanish Catholics at the end of the Council, 'We have to confess that we have sometimes been lulled to sleep by confidence in our Catholic unity, backed by law and long traditions.'[45] Or, as Tarancón expressed it years later, 'The Council surprised every-

---

[43] G. Hermet, 'Les fonctions politiques des organisations religieuses dans les régimes à pluralisme limité', *Revue Française de Science politique*, xxiii (1973), no. 3.

[44] On the ideal 'thesis' see above, pp. 121–3.

[45] Iribarren, 369.

one. But for historical reasons and because of the social context in Spain, the surprise was much greater for us Spaniards.'[46] It is not true that there had been no inkling at all on the episcopal bench of what the Council might do. Bueno Moreal, for instance, wrote a very revealing pastoral instruction in September 1962, before the first session. Instead of discussing doctrine or liturgy, he surveyed the global problems of huge population expansion, the impact of new technology, and the political emergence of coloured races as the context for a new pastoral direction, a new 'awareness' he expected from the Council.[47] He was not to be disappointed. On the whole, however, Spanish bishops were unprepared for the way the Council deserted dogmatic abstractions in favour of language and methods derived from sources as diverse as modern biblical criticism, sociology, existentialism, humanism, economics, and movements for civil rights.

A foretaste of conciliar policies was afforded in 1961 when John XXIII published his encyclical letter *Mater et Magistra* to bring up to date the social teaching of *Rerum Novarum* (1891) and *Quadragesimo Anno* (1931). Paragraph 3 immediately stated the theme of this letter, its sequel on peace and justice, *Pacem in Terris* (1963), and the Council as a whole, when the pope argued that although the Church's main care was for souls 'she concerns herself too with the exigencies of man's daily life, with his livelihood and education, and his general, temporal welfare and prosperity'.[48] In addition to claiming for industrial and agricultural workers a just wage, humane conditions, and vocational training, Pope John insisted that they should have a say in the enterprises for which they worked, and furthermore 'be given the opportunity to exert their influence throughout the state, and not just within the limits of their own spheres of employment' (paragraph 97). He expressed 'heartfelt appreciation' of the International Labour Organization, called for a system of tax proportional to wealth, and the redistribution of wealth through social insurance (103, 132, 136). *Mater et Magistra* was received with understandable apprehension in managerial and governmental circles in Spain.

Pacem in Terris was more wide-ranging and more embarrassing.[49] Fraternally addressed to 'all men of good will', it provided a com-

[46] *RyF*, 935 (Dec. 1975), 351.
[47] *BEAS* (1 Sept. 1962), 277–80.
[48] From the English translation published by the Catholic Truth Society, John XXIII, *New Light on Social Problems* (London, 1961).
[49] The CTS published an English translation, John XXIII, *Peace on Earth* (London, 1963), used here.

prehensive defence of basic human rights, including the right of association, 'the right to take an active part in public affairs', and the right to freedom of worship in private and public (pp. 13, 14, 10), all of them denied in Franco's Spain. In statements soon to be known by heart and passionately quoted in the Basque country and Catalonia, the encyclical argued that ethnic minorities must be respected and their interests, including their language, promoted (pp. 24, 37). It also opened the way to Christian–Marxist dialogue by clearly distinguishing between 'false philosophical teachings' and the 'historical movements that have economic, social, cultural or political ends' that they inspired (p. 58). The pope stated very bluntly that any society 'established on relations of force must be regarded as inhuman' (p. 16), and made his antipathy to military dictatorship equally clear when pointing out that 'the doctrine which we have set forth is fully consonant with any truly democratic regime' (p. 23). Potentially revolutionary was the further comment that 'if any government does not acknowledge the rights of man or violates them, it not only fails in its duty, but its orders completely lack juridicial force' (p. 26). In this encyclical, John XXIII implicitly passed judgment on the Franco regime as, although confessional, insufficiently respectful of Catholic teaching. Henceforth reformist minorities in Catholic Action, the clergy, intellectual life, and on the bench of bishops, Christian Democrats and even Christian Socialists could and did argue that the Vatican was on their side.

The major documents of the Second Vatican Council continued along similar lines although, appropriately for the genre, with much more quoting of scripture and theology than in John's encyclicals. Human rights, justice, ecumenism, and dialogue reigned supreme. Since the central theme of the Council was the Church itself, and the Church's relationship to the modern world, a new ecclesiology was one of its most fundamental achievements.[50] Traditional models of the Church as a perfect society, or the sole guardian of truth and morality in an unsympathetic world were abandoned in favour of the more dynamic and populist biblical image of the people of God on pilgrimage. In *Gaudium et Spes* (on the Church in the world), the Council stressed the solidarity of Catholics with the whole human community, particularly the poor and afflicted: 'the Church, at once a visible organization and a spiritual community, travels the same journey as all mankind and

---

[50] See especially the documents *Lumen Gentium* and *Gaudium et Spes*; English translations in A. Flannery (ed.), *Vatican Council II. The Conciliar and Post Conciliar Documents* (Leominster, 1975).

Towards Modernity 249

shares the same earthly lot with the world' (section 40). It took up the themes of social justice and political participation already treated in *Mater et Magistra* and *Pacem in Terris*, but also dealt a great blow to the confessional state in Spain by assuming pluralistic societies as the norm and insisting that the Church 'is not identified with any political community nor bound by ties to any political system' (section 76).

If this humanist and pluralist orientation promised difficulties for the Franco regime, there were new questions also to be answered within the Spanish Church. Throughout the Council documents, and in a whole decree devoted to the topic, the apostolic role of lay people, their call to holiness and to full Christian responsibility recurred over and over again.[51] If it was the task of the laity to transform the temporal order, what exactly was the role of the priest in a Church now as interested, apparently, in social justice and human development as in prayer and the sacraments? What special role had religious when lay life in the world was clearly recognized as both missionary and sacred?[52] Since the Church was now poised to open a dialogue with other Christian denominations, other religions, and anyone else willing to take part, would not its own bishops also have to learn a less authoritarian style and enter into dialogue, in their turn, with priests and laity? *Aggiornamento* was as complex and problematic within the Church as it was in relationships between the Church and politics.

The Council that John XXIII opened and his successor Paul VI closed, stimulated both frenetic activity and crisis in the Spanish Church. A host of new publications and institutions appeared, dedicated to the exploration of conciliar teaching. As one of the most serious of the new Catholic periodicals, the theological journal *Iglesia Viva* pointed out in its first number in 1966, the renewal of biblical studies and theology and the openness to contemporary cultural trends that had prepared the way for the Council elsewhere 'had not penetrated deeply or widely enough among us to make possible a spontaneous and tranquil evolution'.[53] Inevitably, therefore, enthusiastic conciliar Catholics examined the Spanish Church in the new Roman light and found it wanting. In its early issues *Iglesia Viva* published articles with titles like 'On the movement from Catholic to Christian' by the socially radical Jesuit José

---
[51] See especially *Apostolicam actuositatem*, ibid.
[52] Many of the council fathers found it difficult to define a role for religious, and the document on religious life, *Perfectae caritatis* is widely regarded as one of the least satisfactory of the Council texts.
[53] *Iglesia Viva*, no. 1 (1966), 4. This publication is an excellent source for post-conciliar renewal in Spain.

María Llanos, or 'Evangelizing the poor, the Church's conversion' by Alfonso Carlos Comín who was a Catholic layman and also a Communist.[54] While the Council gave new hope to such innovators, it disconcerted many whose religious formation had not equipped them for the new vocabulary and values. When the hierarchy organized a massive joint conference with priests in 1971, for example, trying out new style consultation, it had the extremely difficult task of both convincing impatient radicals there was a place for them in the Church and reassuring those who felt quite unprepared for their new role in a 'modern' Church and society.[55]

Expectations often rose higher and quicker than the hierarchy's capacity for response, as the new prophets denounced both the confessional state and the Church's position of privilege within it. This was apparent in the sterile confrontation with the specialized branches of Catholic Action in 1966-9, and with a frustrated clergy, especially, though by no means only, in Catalonia and the Basque country. Catalan sensibilities were wounded by the Vatican itself when in February 1966 it named a conservative non-Catalan, Marcelo González Martín, coadjutor archbishop of Barcelona with right of succession. It was particularly unacceptable because the prelacies of two men sensitive to local aspirations and traditions and distanced from Crusade Catholicism—Ramón Masnou of Vich and Josep Pont i Gol of Segorbe-Castellón—had suggested a quite different policy. In 1967 González Martín gave permission for a police raid on a church in Sabadell during which workers sheltering there were arrested. Two years later a number of parishes in Barcelona and elsewhere were raided for 'subversive literature' under a state of emergency that the hierarchy had justified. Until González Martín was promoted out of harm's way to Toledo in 1971, Catholic opposition to the Franco regime's social and political measures in Catalonia was inextricably linked with lay and clerical antagonism to the most powerful member of the hierarchy there.[56]

In the Basque provinces, *Pacem in Terris* and the Council immeasurably strengthened the case of Catholic nationalists who argued that the military dictatorship violated papal teaching as well as human rights.

[54] Ibid., nos. 4 and 5 respectively.
[55] For the Asamblea Conjunta, see above, pp. 113-14.
[56] These conflicts are related blow by blow in *El vaticà i Catalunya* (Geneva, 1967). Its anonymous author, Josep Carreras de Nadal, was arrested on the Spain-France border in March 1968 with copies in his possession, and sentenced to a year's imprisonment for introducing them into Spain. The second edition (Paris, 1971) gives this information and continues the account of ecclesiastical tensions to 1971.

Many Basque priests considered it their duty as Christians and priests, as well as citizens, to take on the role of modern prophets and fearlessly denounce injustice and corruption.[57] Until 1968, this usually pitted them against their bishops as well as the government. Just before his death in that year, however, Bishop Lorenzo Bereciartua of San Sebastián gave the government a formidable demonstration of how dangerous a genuinely post-conciliar hierarchy could be when he issued an extremely outspoken pastoral letter defending priests who preached about social justice as well as individual virtue, repudiating violent methods by terrorists and public authorities alike, and emphasizing that 'in our days, dialogue is an essential (*insustituible*) means of good government'.[58] His example was followed by his successor, Jacinto Argaya Goicoechea, and the new bishop of Bilbao, José María Cirarda, whose courageous public analyses of the causes of acute political tension in their dioceses went a considerable way towards healing relations with their nationalist clergy while infuriating the government. The often explicit appeal to papal authority in their statements was a necessary safeguard against the angry disbelief of conservative Catholics. When Cirarda, for example, called in March 1969 for responsible government, clear legal principles, and popular elections, he did so in a long quotation from the Council document *Gaudium et Spes*.[59]

As the balance of opinion within the Episcopal Conference shifted decisively in the late 1960s and early 1970s, bishops moved closer to reformist groups in the Church and further away from the political regime. Conciliar teaching on religious liberty was incorporated into Spanish legislation in 1967; everything else was obviously problematic. In 1968 Paul VI requested Franco to relinquish the right of presentation to Spanish sees, but having failed, devised ways of appointing bishops without state vetting by first naming them auxiliary bishops or apostolic administrators, posts not covered by the 1953 concordat. Whereas a decade earlier, pastoral letters on socio-economic or political issues had been very rare, it was now almost commonplace to have an occasional Sunday Mass enlivened by a letter from the local bishop analysing the causes of violence or the statistics on salary and poverty levels, or the need for political participation or wealth redistribution or genuine trade unions.[60] An ever greater number of bishops considered all of these

[57] See above, pp. 107–13.
[58] *BEOSS*, no. 234 (15 Aug. 1968), 223–9.
[59] *BEOB*, no. 223 (Mar. 1969), 107–10.
[60] There is a useful collection in J. Angulo Uribarri, *Documentos socio-políticos de obispos españoles (1968–1972)* (Madrid, 1972).

subjects part of what *Mater et Magistra* had memorably described as the Church's concern for 'the exigencies of man's daily life, with his livelihood and education, and his general, temporal welfare and prosperity'. In this new development, bishops were seen to be in much closer sympathy than previously with priests all over the country who incurred governmental wrath and fines for preaching 'prophetic' sermons, allowing presbyteries to be used for clandestine meetings of dissidents, and generally disputing the regime's version of Catholic principles. To an affronted political establishment, it all seemed an entirely unwarranted incursion into politics that could only stir up opposition to the regime. It was all the more dangerous because the impact of the Council coincided with and legitimized a whole series of burgeoning discontents in Spain over regional policies, industrial relations, university education, and political repression. Conservative politicians in this confessional state came to regard both the pope in Rome and his bishops in Spain with profound suspicion tinged with fear and sometimes with contempt.

The inevitable crisis in Church–state relations has been chronicled many times. When fifteen defendants, including two priests, were tried in Burgos at the end of 1970 for terrorist offences related to the Basque separatist organization ETA, the CEE backed a petition by the bishops of Bilbao and San Sebastián that the hearing should be public and before a civilian rather than a military court, and that any death sentences should be commuted.[61] Ecclesiastical unease at the eventual trial of civilians by a military court was evident, and dozens of conciliar and episcopal statements as well as hundreds of Sunday homilies over preceding years had amply expressed Church disapproval of government policy and tactics—including torture—in the Basque provinces. To unsympathetic observers it seemed that the Church itself was in the dock, accused of encouraging and justifying terrorism, and undermining the authority of the state. (So insistent was this Right-wing criticism to prove, that eventually in 1979 the Basque bishops actually issued a catalogue of all the documents condemning terrorist violence they had published between 1969 and 1979.)[62]

In January 1973 the Episcopal Conference eventually produced a major statement on the Church and politics which reflected the views of its own, conciliar majority.[63] With a plethora of quotations from

[61] CEE statements on Burgos in Iribarren, 465–6.
[62] *BEOB*, no. 326 (Jan.–Feb. 1979), whole special issue.
[63] Text in Iribarren, 520–54.

Council texts, the bishops enunciated the Church's independence of the state, its prophetic mission (that is, its duty to review and judge temporal affairs in the light of Church doctrine), its political neutrality, and its respect for political pluralism. They recognized that the 1953 concordat was in urgent need of revision, and carefully avoided making any commitment to the preservation of the confessional state. They also declared their 'firm intention of renouncing any privilege granted by the state to ecclesiastical personnel or entities', including clergy exemptions from legal processes in civil courts, and the participation of bishops and priests in institutions of government. Where state funding of the clergy, Church buildings and Catholic education were concerned, however, the bishops were cautious, arguing that these were not privileges at all, but a proper payment for important services rendered dutifully and as of right. Privilege might give way to pluralism and prophecy, but in a new dispensation the Church would still expect the institutional underpinning it thought it needed and deserved in a country the vast majority of whose inhabitants called themselves Catholic. Surrendering the monopoly did not mean it expected to have to compete in an ideological free market. *The Church and the Political Community* formalized the Church's distancing of itself from the Franco regime, while also mapping out the territory it would undoubtedly claim in any new political world. Fifty-nine bishops voted for it, twenty against and four abstained: such was the arithmetic of political *aggiornamento* at the beginning of a decisive year.

Observers of the Spanish Church in the last few years of Franco's life offered many competing explanations for its disengagement from the regime it had helped him create. Liberal Christians hailed a wondrous, albeit delayed, demonstration of the Holy Spirit's transforming power; cynics preferred to talk about rats and sinking ships; Catholic reactionaries blamed communist infiltration and an unreliable hierarchy.[64] But the phenomenon so diversely explained was itself beyond question— the Catholic Church had become a dangerous enemy of the military dictatorship. In 1973, soon after the publication of *The Church and the Political Community*, a policeman died in street confrontations in Madrid on May Day. The extreme Right took to the streets in its turn with banners that clearly indicated those it held ultimately responsible:

[64] An excellent example of the last comes from a little later. José María Areilza relates in conversation that when he was Foreign Minister in Arias Navarro's government, he mentioned to Arias that he had just returned from Rome, where he had spoken with Pope Paul VI. Arias's reply was '*menudo rojo*' ('that Red').

'Tarancón to the firing squad, (*Tarancón al paredón*), and 'Justice for the red bishops'. In December, ETA terrorists assassinated Franco's most trusted colleague and recently named head of government, Admiral Carrero Blanco, by detonating an explosion under his car that sent it flying over a Jesuit residence in the narrow Claudio Coello Street in Madrid. Carrero was a devout Catholic, returning from his customary daily Mass when he was killed; but he was certainly not a conciliar Catholic, belonging instead to the ecclesiastical Right that deplored what Paul VI, Tarancón, and the CEE were doing to the Church.[65] More than any other politician, he was identified with the continuation of Francoism after Franco, and his death irremediably weakened the regime's possibilities of survival. At his funeral there was uproar against Tarancón.

On 12 February 1974 Carrero Blanco's successor, the cautious and indecisive Carlos Arias Navarro, provided an unexpected but brief hope of fundamental change when he promised a political 'opening' of the regime. Any such enterprise naturally had many powerful opponents, but Arias's capacity to deliver what he had promised was thrown open to doubt almost immediately by a dramatic and quite unnecessary confrontation with Bishop Añoveros of Bilbao. A group responsible for pastoral affairs in Bilbao diocese prepared and circulated under the authority of vicar-general José Angel Ubieta, four homilies on soteriology to be read instead of a sermon at Mass on four Sundays. The first sketched out the meaning of Christian salvation, and the second studied the Church as sign and sacrament of salvation. It was the third homily, read on Sunday 24 February, that angered a nervous government because its examination at a more practical level of how the Church could bear a message of salvation 'to the peoples' included a defence of the language, customs, and political rights of ethnic minorities.[66] It is easy to understand the government's indignation at this homily, only two months after Carrero's assassination by Basque terrorists, and Tarancón had advised Añoveros against the publication of what was obviously highly sensitive material. On the other hand, it was ludicrous for a Catholic head of government in a confessional state to protest at a homily squarely based throughout on papal and conciliar teaching. Arias was out of his depth. He made his own predicament worse by ordering Añoveros out of the country, since the bishop refused to go

---

[65] This was Tarancón's assessment of him; see Martín Descalzo, *Tarancón, el cardenal del cambio*, 191.
[66] *El cristianismo, mensaje de salvación para los pueblos* (Bilbao, 1974).

unless commanded by the pope, who remained silent. The government had to give way to an embarrassed but united hierarchy. No single incident better illustrated the end of the old Church–state alliance.

The bishops preached pluralism, even to the extent of preferring not to see the emergence of any new Catholic party identified with the Church, through which it might be politically compromised. It is not surprising, therefore, that the range of admitted political allegiances among Catholics was incomparably broader in the early 1970s than it had been twenty or even ten years before. Many, led by Franco and Carrero, and including a minority of bishops like Guerra Campos and Archbishop Cantero Cuadrado of Zaragoza, still found the integrist ideals of post-war national-Catholicism entirely satisfying. Some had distanced themselves from the regime, if not in overt and illegal dissent, at least in an internal semi-legal opposition. This was the case of individuals and tendencies as distinct as Manuel Fraga's reforming conservatism; the more and less radical versions of Christian Democracy represented by Ruiz Giménez and Gil Robles (never fully reconciled to or trusted by the Franco regime, and reincarnated politically through civil rights law work); and very recent democrats like the former Opus Dei apologist, Calvo Serer. It was also the case of a new group called *Tácito* that emerged from Propagandist circles in 1973, mainly incorporating a younger generation not directly involved in the civil war, and that studied how the discredited dictatorship might be legally and peacefully dismantled to make way for democracy after Franco died. *Tácito* was discouraged by the hierarchy from emphasizing its religious, Christian Democrat tendencies, in favour of a non-confessional stance, so as not to pre-empt or circumscribe Catholic loyalties.[67] To the left of all of these lay members of the Christians for Socialism group that produced its foundation manifesto at a meeting with 200 participants in Ávila in January 1973.[68]

Reforming conservatives, Christian Democrats, and Christian Marxists, and those holding innumerable positions around and between them all, disagreed not only on the future shape of Spanish politics but also on how that shape should be achieved. As there were monarchists and republicans, and among the monarchists adherents of Franco's

[67] For a detailed study of the origins, activities, and influence of the *Tácito* group, see the forthcoming doctoral thesis for Oxford University by Charles Powell, who kindly allowed me to read his manuscript.
[68] For articles on this movement by members, see *Iglesia Viva*, nos. 52–53 (1974), which also contains a useful critical commentary by the editors.

designated heir in Spain, Juan Carlos, and of his displaced father in Portugal, Don Juan, so there were advocates of a decisive break (*ruptura*) with the dictatorship, and those who wanted a more accommodating and piecemeal legal and constitutional transition. There is no doubt that as Franco neared death in 1974 and 1975, along the whole gamut of Spanish legal, barely legal, and illegal politics, Catholics were more prominent among the monarchists and gradualists than among the republicans and no-compromisers. At the time, oppositional purists—especially Socialists and Communists who had borne the bitter burden of exile or prolonged proscription and clandestinity—tended to treat the gradualists—most of whom had functioned successfully and some at a very high level under the dictatorship—as half-hearted and untrustworthy. But in fact, after Franco's death in November 1975, the desired transition to democracy was effected quickly, legally, and peacefully in 1976 and 1977 by gradualists who knew Francoist institutions from the inside. With King Juan Carlos's encouragement, Adolfo Suárez and his reforming government expertly untied the constitutional knots Franco had considered so secure. It is unlikely that this dissolution of the dictatorship from within could have been so rapid or so relatively lacking in conflict and anguish had not the Church earlier withdrawn its ideological validation.

By the mid-1970s, then, the definition of Catholic modernity, of *aggiornamento* in Spain was clear. It meant pluralism, human rights, and dialogue. When the first democratic general elections were held in Spain in June 1977, electoral surveys showed clear correlations between regular religious practice and a centrist or conservative vote on the one hand, and between religious indifference and a Socialist vote on the other. But the polarization between the two groups was not as clear as in the years of the Second Republic. Not only did Catholics vote heavily for Suárez's Centre Democratic Union—absolutely identified with the transition away from dictatorship—rather than for any party further to the Right, but over 10% voted Socialist, a result that would have been unimaginable at the last previous general elections back in 1936.[69] A strong Catholic vote for regional parties in the Basque provinces and Catalonia further diversified the electoral scene. Religious practice was not the almost infallible guide to political allegiance it had once been, but it was still a strong indicator of conservatism.

This became much more apparent in the late 1970s and the early

[69] Statistics from FOESSA, *Informe sociológico sobre el cambio político en España 1975–1981* (Madrid, 1981), 301.

1980s when the choice between democracy and dictatorship gave way to controversies over social and cultural policies, including the reform of Spanish education. *Aggiornamento* had never meant that the Church had entirely relinquished the distaste evinced by Pius IX back in 1864 for 'progress, liberalism, and modern civilization'. Many of the causes deemed progressive by campaigners on moral issues, particularly those concerning sexuality and the family, remained abhorrent in ecclesiastical circles. The liberalizing of views on the constitution did not imply new, relativistic approaches to abortion or—officially at least—even to birth control or sexual relations. The Church retained its own convictions on what modern civilization should be like, and wanted state support for the Catholic schools in which it would go on teaching them, even if it disclaimed any direct involvement in the modern state. It passionately defended human rights but did not define them in ways acceptable to, for example, feminists or secularists. Its commitment to political democracy would not prevent it demanding special treatment and institutional safeguards even from democratic parties whose constituency was largely uninterested in religion or even antagonistic. The identification of the Socialist Party with progressive causes and the Church against them established a new conservative Catholic politics, not tied now to dictatorship and property, but to moral and cultural traditionalism.

As the Church faced a democratic Spanish world, it could show very respectable, if somewhat recent, qualifications for entry. But it had never intended to become just one cultural institution among many competing for adherents there. Because it believed itself still the essential if not unique bearer of salvation, and an indispensable source, though not the only one, of Spanish cultural identity, it would not hesitate to use all the formidable means in its power to make a non-confessional, pluralistic democratic state protect its institutional interests and not only respect but embody its moral values. Modernity and pluralism would be expected to accommodate tradition and singularity.

Sources and Select Bibliography

A. PRIMARY SOURCES

The following sources are referred to as appropriate in the footnotes to the text: oral testimony; unpublished Archive materials; school textbooks; printed material issued locally by individual Catholic schools and other institutions.

1. Papal and Episcopal Documents

Pius IX: *Quanta Cura* (1864).
Leo XIII: *Aeterni Patris* (1879).
            Cum Multa (1882).
            Immortale Dei (1885).
            Libertas Praestantissimum (1888).
            Rerum Novarum (1891).
Pius X: *Inter Catholicos Hispaniae* (1906).
Pius XI: *Divinis Illius* (1929).
            Quadragesimo Anno (1931).
            Non abbiamo bisogno (1931).
            Dilectissima Nobis (1933).
            Mit brennender Sorge (1937).
            Divini Redemptoris (1937).
John XXIII: *Mater et Magistra* (1961).
            Pacem in Terris (1963).

The Documents of the Second Vatican Council.
Iribarren, J. (ed.), *Documentos colectivos del episcopado español 1870–1974* (Madrid, 1974).
Exhortación pastoral del obispo de Urgel sobre las actuales divisiones entre los católicos (Madrid, 1890).
Maura y Gelabert, J., *La cuestión social* (Madrid, 1902).
Guisasola Menéndez, V., *Justicia y caridad en la organización cristiana del trabajo* (Madrid, 1916).
——, *El peligro del laicismo y los deberes de los católicos* (Madrid, 1915).
Batllori, M., and Arbeloa, V. M. (eds.), *Arxiu Vidal i Barraquer: Església i estat durant la segona república espanyola 1931–1936*. 3 vols. (Montserrat, 1971–7).
Irurita, M., *Pastorales 1927–32* (Barcelona, 1932).
Gomá, I., *Por Dios y por España* (Barcelona, 1940).

Sources and Select Bibliography 259

Angulo Uribarri, J., *Documentos socio-políticos de obispos españoles (1968-1972)* (Madrid, 1972).
Conferencia Episcopal Española, *La iglesia y la educación en España, hoy* (Madrid, 1969).
Pastoral letters of individual bishops from the appropriate Diocesan Bulletins.

2. Official Publications of the Spanish State

Concordat (1851).
Constitution (1976).
Constitution (1931).
Convenio entre la Sante Sede y el Gobierno Español (June 1941, July 1946, Dec. 1946, Aug. 1950).
Concordat (1953).
Ministerio de Gobernación, *Apuntes para el estudio y la organización en España de las instituciones de beneficencia y de previsión*. 2 vols. (Madrid, 1909).
Diario de Sesiones de las Cortes Constituyentes de la República Española (1931-3).

3. Periodical Publications

Anuario Eclesiástico (Barcelona, 1915-36).
Boletín Eclesiástico del Arzobispado de Sevilla (1875-1975).
Boletín Eclesiástico del Obispado de Vitoria (1873-1937).
Boletín Eclesiástico del Obispado de Bilbao (1959-79).
Cruz y Raya (Madrid, 1933-6).
Guía de la Iglesia en España (Madrid, 1954-70).
Iglesia Viva (Valencia, 1966-80).
Mensajero del Corazón de Jesús y del Apostolado de la Oración (Bilbao, 1886-1931).
Razón y Fe (Madrid, 1901-75).

4. Books and Articles

Aguirre y Lecube, J. A., *Entre la libertad y la revolución 1930-1935*. 2nd edn. (Bilbao, 1976).
——, 'Discurso, Radio Euzkadi 22 diciembre 1936', *Obras completas*, i (Donostia, no date), 609-23.
Albó y Martí, R., *La caridad, su acción y organización en Barcelona* (Barcelona, 1901).
——, *Barcelona caritativa, benéfica y social*. 2 vols. (Barcelona, 1914).
Alfonso Querejazu. *Conversaciones católicas de Gredos* (Madrid, 1977).
Alonso, A., *Comunidades eclesiales de base* (Salamanca, 1970).
Aranguren, J. L., *Catolicismo y protestantismo como formas de existencia* (Madrid, 1952).
——, *Catolicismo día tras día* (Madrid, 1955).
——, *Moral y sociedad* (Madrid, 1965).
——, *El Marxismo como moral* (Madrid, 1968).

Aranguren, J. L., *El problema universitario* (Madrid, 1968).
——, *La crisis del catolicismo* (Madrid, 1969).
Arboleya Martínez, M., *Sermón perdido* (Madrid, 1930).
——, *La apostasía de las masas* (Barcelona, 1934).
Asamblea conjunta obispos-sacerdotes (Madrid, 1971).
Asamblea nacional de rectores. Seminarios menores (Madrid, 1968).
Aunós, E., *La reforma corporativa del estado* (Madrid, 1935).
Ayala, A., *Obras completas.* 2 vols. (Madrid, 1947).
Ayerra Redín, M., *No me avergoncé del evangelio.* 3rd edn. (Bilbao, 1978).
Azpiazu, J., 'La religiosidad del arciprestazgo de Portugalete', *Idearium,* ii (1935).
Barea, A., *The Forging of a Rebel* (London, 1972).
Barral, C., *Años de penitencia* (Madrid, 1975).
Bergamín, J., *Detrás de la cruz* (Mexico, 1941).
Bernanos, G., *Les Grands Cimetières sous la lune* (Paris, 1938).
Bertrán, J., *Los difíciles caminos de la misión obrera* (Barcelona, 1968).
Carbonell, A., *El colectivismo y la ortodoxia católica* (Barcelona, 1927).
Cardó, C., *Histoire spirituelle des Espagnes* (Paris, 1946).
——, *La moral de la derrota i altres assaigs* (Barcelona, 1959).
Carreras, L., *Grandeza cristiana de España* (Toulouse, 1938).
Castaño i Colomer, J., *Memòries sobre la JOC a Catalunya 1932–1970* (Barcelona, 1974).
——, *La JOC en España (1946–1970)* (Salamanca, 1977).
Castro Albarrán, A., *El derecho a la rebeldía* (Madrid, 1934).
Coloma, L., *Pequeñeces,* ed. R. Benítez (Madrid, 1975).
Comín, A. C., *España ¿país de misión?* (Barcelona, 1966).
——, *Fe en la tierra.* 3rd edn. (Bilbao, 1977).
——, *Cristianos en el partido, comunistas en la iglesia* (Barcelona, 1977).
Conversaciones con Monseñor Escrivá de Balaguer. 13th edn. (Madrid, 1980).
Diagnóstico sociológico de los conflictos sacerdotales en la diócesis de Bilbao (Bilbao, 1971).
Diez-Alegría, J. M., *¡Yo creo en la esperanza ...!* (Bilbao, 1973).
Echeandía, J., *La persecución roja en el país vasco* (Barcelona, 1945).
Escritos de Don José María Arizmendi-Arrieta, i, *Conferencias apostolado social* (San Sebastián, 1978).
Escrivá de Balaguer, J. M., *Camino* (Madrid, 1939).
La federació de jovens cristians de Catalunya. Contribució a la seva historia (Barcelona, 1972).
Fundación FOESSA, *Informe sociológico sobre la situación social de España. 1970* (Madrid, 1970).
——, *Estudios sociológicos sobre la situación social de España. 1975* (Madrid, 1976).
——, *Informe sociológico sobre el cambio político en España. 1975–1981* (Madrid, 1981).

——, *Informe sociológico sobre el cambio social en España. 1975–1983* (Madrid, 1983).
Gallegos Rocafull, J. M., *Una causa justa. Los obreros de los campos andaluces* (Córdoba, 1929).
——, *El orden social* (Madrid, 1935).
——, *Crusade or Class War? The Spanish Military Revolt* (London, 1937).
García Escudero, J. M., *Catolicismo de fronteras adentro* (Madrid, 1956).
Gil Robles, J. M., *No fue posible la paz* (Barcelona, 1978).
Giménez Caballero, E., *Genio de España* (Madrid, 1932).
——, *La nueva catolicidad. Teoría general sobre el fascismo en Europe; en España* (Madrid, 1933).
González Ruiz, J. M., *¡Ay de mí, si no evangelizaré!* 6th edn. (Bilbao, 1976).
Herrera Oria, A., *Obras selectas* (Madrid, 1963).
——, 'La Asociación Católica Nacional de Propagandistas en Loyola', *Estudios de Deusto*, xi (1919).
Iñigo, J., 'La situación religiosa en la zona minera vizcaína', *Idearium*, ii (1935).
ISPA, *La formación religiosa en los colegios de la iglesia* (Madrid, 1968).
Iturralde, J. de, *La guerra de Franco, Los vascos y la iglesia*. 2 vols. (San Sebastián, 1978).
Iztueta, P., *Sociología del fenómeno contestatorio del clero vasco 1940–75* (San Sebastián, 1981).
Jover Mira, M., *La España Inmortal* (Madrid, 1930).
Laín Entralgo, P., *España como problema* (Madrid, 1949).
Larrañaga, J., *Don José María Arizmendi-Arrieta y la experiencia cooperativa de Mondragón* (San Sebastián, 1981).
Larrañaga, P. de, *Contribución a la historia obrera de Euskalerría*. 2 vols. (San Sebastián, 1976, 1977).
——, *Emakume Abertzale Batza. La mujer en el nacionalismo vasco*. 3 vols. (Donostia, 1978).
Lizarza Iribarren, A., *Memorias de la conspiración. Cómo se preparó en Navarra la Cruzada 1931–36* (Pamplona, 1953).
López Rey, J., *Los estudiantes frente a la dictadura* (Madrid, 1930).
Llanos, J. M., *Creo . . .* 6th edn. (Bilbao, 1977).
——, *Evangelismo y talante burgués* (Madrid, 1972).
Maeztu, R. de, *Defensa de la hispanidad* (Madrid, 1934).
Maragall, J., 'L'església cremada', *La Veu de Catalunya* (18 Dec. 1909).
Márquez, G., *Explicación literal del catecismo de Ripalda, con una exposición y refutación de los errores modernos* (Madrid, 1929).
Mate, R., and others, *Herria-Eliza. Euskadi. pueblo-iglesia* (San Sebastián, 1978).
Maura, M., *Así cayó Alfonso XIII* (Mexico, 1962).
Maura Gamazo, G., *Recuerdos de mi vida* (Madrid, no date).
Mendizábal, A., *Aux origines d'une tragédie* (Paris, 1937).
Menéndez y Pelayo, M., *Historia de los Heterodoxos Españoles*. 8 vols. (Buenos Aires, 1945).

Miret Magdalena, E., 'Reflexiones sobre el hombre católico español de nuestros días', *Espiritualidad Seglar* nos. 27–8 (1955).
——, *Método de formación y acción*. 2nd edn. (Madrid, 1963).
——, *Los nuevos católicos* (Barcelona, 1966).
——, *Catolicismo para mañana* (Bilbao, 1974).
Monedero Martín, A., *La Confederación Nacional Católica-Agraria en 1920. Su espíritu, su organización, su porvenir* (Madrid, 1921).
——, *Siete años de propaganda para organizar la Federación Nacional Católica Agraria* (Madrid, 1921).
Monje y Bernal, J., *Acción Popular* (Madrid, 1936).
Mora, C. de la, *In Place of Spendour* (New York, 1939).
Moreno, M. A., *El Opus Dei. Anexo a una historia* (Barcelona, 1976).
——, *La otra cara del Opus Dei* (Barcelona, 1978).
Morote, L., *Los frailes en España* (Madrid, 1904).
Nelken, M., *La condición social de la mujer en España* (Barcelona, no date).
Onaindía, A. de, *Hombre de paz en la guerra* (Buenos Aires, 1973).
—— (ed.), *Ayer como hoy. Documentos del clero vasco* (St. Jean de Luz, 1975).
Ossorio y Gallardo, A., *Una política de derechas* (Madrid, 1921).
——, *Un libro del abate Sturzo* (Madrid, 1928).
——, *La España de mi vida* (Buenos Aires, 1941).
——, *La guerra de España y los católicos* (Buenos Aires, 1942).
——, *Mis memorias* (Madrid, 1975).
Peiró, F., *El problema religioso-social en España* (Madrid, 1936).
Pemán, J. M., *El hecho y la idea de la Unión Patriótica* (Madrid, 1929).
Rotllan, R. (ed.), *La ley llamada del 'candado' y la oposición católica en las Cortes* (Madrid, 1911).
Sáez Marín, J., *Datos sobre la iglesia española contemporánea 1768–1868* (Madrid, 1975).
Sáinz Rodríguez, P., *Testimonio y recuerdos* (Barcelona, 1978).
Sánchez de Toca, J. *Católicos y conservadores* (Madrid, 1885).
Sardá i Salvany, F., *El liberalismo es pecado* (Barcelona, 1884).
——, '¡Alta el fuego!', *Revista Popular* (11 June 1896).
Semprún y Gurrea, J. M., *República, libertad, estatismo* (Madrid, 1931).
Silió y Cortes, C., *La educación nacional* (Madrid, 1914).
Sínodo Diocesano de Sevilla, A multi-volume set of questionnaires and working papers prepared for the diocesan synod of 1973, by the Departmento de Investigación Socio-Religiosa (DIS) of Madrid. The papers cover all aspects of social, economic, and religious life in the archdiocese.
Tamayo-Acosta, J. J., *Un proyecto de iglesia para el futuro en España* (Madrid, 1978).
Tirado y Rojas, M., *León XIII y España* (Madrid, c. 1903).
Torras i Bages, J., *El clero en la vida social moderna* (Barcelona, 1888).
——, *La Tradició Catalana* (Barcelona, 1892).
Umbral, F., *Memorias de un niño de derechas* (Barcelona, 1976).

El Vaticà i Catalunya (Geneva, 1967).
Vicent, A., *Socialismo y anarquismo* (Valencia, 1893).
Vilar i Costa, J., *Glosas a la carta colectiva de los obispos españoles* (Barcelona, 1938).

B. SECONDARY SOURCES: BOOKS AND ARTICLES

Abad, P. M., *Vida de Doña Rafaela Ybarra de Vilallonga*. 2 vols. (Bilbao, 1919).
Alberdi, R., *La formación profesional en Barcelona* (Barcelona, 1980).
Albiach Martínez, A., *Religiosidad hispana y sociedad borbónica* (Burgos, 1969).
Aldea, Q., Marín, T., and Vives, J. (eds.), *Diccionario de Historia Eclesiástica de España*. 4 vols. (Madrid, 1972–5).
Alemany Briz, J., and Álvarez Bolado, A., 'Gabriel Palau S. J. y la Acción Social Popular: correspondencia inédita (1913–1916)', *Miscelánea Comillas*, 72 (1980).
Álvarez Bolado, A., *El experimento del nacional-catolicismo 1939–1975* (Madrid, 1976).
Álvarez Sierra, J., *El Padre Menni y su obra* (Barcelona, 1968).
Alzaga, O., *La primera democracia cristiana en España* (Madrid, 1973).
Andrés Gallego, J., *La política religiosa en España 1889–1913* (Madrid, 1975).
——, *Pensamiento y acción social de la iglesia en España* (Madrid, 1984).
Approximación a la historia social de la iglesia española contemporánea (Madrid, 1978).
Arbeloa, V. M., *Aquella España católica* (Salamanca, 1975).
——, *La semana trágica de la iglesia en España (octubre 1931)* (Barcelona, 1976).
Arrarás, J., *Historia de la Segunda República Española*. 4 vols. (Madrid, 1968).
Artigues, D., *El Opus Dei en España* (Paris, 1971).
'Autonomías e iglesia local', special issue of *Misión Abierta*, lxxiv (1981).
Aznar, S., *La revolución española y las vocaciones eclesiásticas* (Madrid, 1949).
Barberena, T. G., 'Las subvenciones económicas a la iglesia', in *Iglesia y comunidad política* (Salamanca, 1974).
Ben-Ami, S., *The Origins of the Second Republic in Spain* (Oxford, 1978).
——, *Fascism from Above* (Oxford, 1983).
Benavides Gómez, D., *El fracaso social del catolicismo español* (Barcelona, 1973).
——, *Democracia y cristianismo en la España de la Restauración 1875–1931* (Madrid, 1978).
Benítez, Claros, R., *Cruz y Raya (Madrid, 1933–1936)* (Madrid, 1947).
Blinkhorn, M., 'Ideology and Schism in Spanish Traditionalism 1876–1931', *Iberian Studies*, i (1972).
——, *Carlism and Crisis in Spain 1931–1939* (Cambridge, 1975).
Bonet i Baltá, J., 'Eclesiàstics de Barcelona enaltits en el consistori papal de

1899: Vives i Tutó—Morgades—Torras i Bages', *Analecta Sacra Tarraconensia*, xxxvii (1964).
Brenan, G., *The Spanish Labyrinth*. 2nd edn. (Cambridge, 1950).
——, *South from Granada* (London, 1974).
Buitrago y Hernández, J., *Las órdenes religiosas y los religiosos—estudio jurídico sobre su existencia legal y capacidad civil en España* (Madrid, 1901).
Cacho Viu, V., *La Institución Libre de Enseñanza* (Madrid, 1962).
Callahan, W. J., *Church, Politics, and Society in Spain, 1750–1874* (Harvard, 1984).
——, 'Was Spain Catholic?', *Revista Canadiense de Estudios Hispánicos*, viii (1984).
Cambio social y religión en España (Barcelona, 1975).
Carballo, F., and Magariños, A., *La iglesia en la Galicia contemporánea* (Madrid, 1978).
Cárcel Ortí, V. (ed.), *Historia de la Iglesia en España*, v (Madrid, 1979).
——, *Tercera época del seminario conciliar de Valencia (1896–1936)*. 2 vols. (Valencia, 1970).
Carr, R., *Spain 1808–1975*. 2nd edn. (Oxford, 1982).
Carrasco, S., 'Los superiores domínicos ante el 'catolicismo social' y la incapacidad de los sindicalistas católicos para lograr formulas de inteligencia', *Escritos de Vedat* iv (1974).
——, 'El padre Gerard, fundador y propagandista del sindicalismo católico-libre 1911–1919; ocho años de lucha con la incomprensión de los suyos', *Communio*, viii (1975).
Castells, J. M., *Las asociaciones religiosas en la España contemporánea* (Madrid, 1973).
Castillo, J. J., *El sindicalismo amarillo en España* (Madrid, 1977).
——, *Propietarios muy pobres: sobre la subordinación política del pequeño campesino* (Madrid, 1979).
Cervera, F., *Ángel Ayala* (Madrid, 1975).
Chao Rego, J., *La iglesia en el franquismo* (Madrid, 1976).
Christian, W. A., *Person and God in a Spanish Valley* (New York and London, 1972).
Comás, R., *Isidro Gomá. Francesc Vidal i Barraquer* (Salamanca, 1977).
Cooper, N., 'The Church: From Crusade to Christianity', in P. Preston (ed.), *Spain in Crisis* (London, 1976).
Coverdale, J. F., *The Basque Phase of Spain's First Carlist War* (Princeton, 1984).
Cuenca Toribio, J. M., *Sociología de una élite de poder de España e Hispanoamérica contemporáneas: La jerarquía eclesiástica (1789–1965)* (Córdoba, 1976).
Cuesta, J., *Sindicalismo católico agrario en España (1917–1919)* (Madrid, 1978).
Díaz, E., *Pensamiento español 1939–1973* (Madrid, 1974).
Díaz del Moral, J., *Historia de las agitaciones campesinas andaluzas* (Madrid, 1977).
Díaz Mozaz, J. M., *La iglesia de España en la encrucijada* (Madrid, 1973).
Díaz Salazar, R., *Iglesia, dictadura y democracia* (Madrid, 1981).

Sources and Select Bibliography   265

Don Bosco. Cien años en España (Madrid, 1980).
Duocastella, R., Mataró 1955. Estudio de sociología religiosa sobre una ciudad industrial española (Madrid, 1961).
Duocastella, R., Lorca, J., and Misser, S., Sociología y pastoral. Estudio de sociología religiosa de la diócesis de Vitoria (Barcelona, 1965).
Duocastella, R., Marcos, J., and Díaz-Mózaz, J. M., Análisis sociológico del catolicismo español (Barcelona, 1967).
Ellwood, S., Prietas las filas. Historia de Falange Española 1933–1983 (Barcelona, 1984).
Estudios históricos sobre la iglesia española contemporánea (El Escorial, 1979).
Fernández-Areal, M., La política católica en España (Madrid, 1970).
Fontán, A., Los católicos en la universidad española actual (Madrid, 1961).
Fraser, R., Blood of Spain (London, 1979).
Freeman, S. T., Neighbours. The Social Contract in a Castilian Hamlet (Chicago, 1970).
——, 'Faith and Fashion in Spanish Religion: Notes in the Observation of Observance', Peasant Studies vii (1978).
Frías, L., La provincia de Castilla de la Compañía de Jesús. 2 vols. (Bilbao, 1915).
Fusi, J. P., Política obrera en el país vasco 1880–1923 (Madrid, 1975).
——, El problema vasco en la II República (Madrid, 1979).
Gabriel, C., La obra Lasaliana en España (Madrid, no date).
Galino, A., 'Pedro Póveda—una pedagogía para nuestro tiempo', in Textos pedagógicos hispanoamericanos (Madrid, 1968).
Gallego, S., Sembraron con amor (San Sebastian, 1978).
García Cortázar, F., 'La iglesia en la crisis del estado (1898–1923)', in VIII Coloquio de Pau.
——, 'Análisis sociológico del episcopado español de la Restauración', Revista Internacional de Sociología (1976).
——, 'La iglesia española de la restauración: definición de objetivos y práctica religiosa', Letras de Deusto viii (1978).
——, 'La iglesia española de 1900: política e económia', Letras de Deusto x (1980).
García de la Torre, F., Estudio histórico-artístico de la Hermandad del gremio de Toneleros de Sevilla (Seville, 1979).
García Nieto, J. N., El sindicalismo cristiano en España (Bilbao, 1960).
García Venero, M., Historia del nacionalismo vasco (Madrid, 1968).
Garriga, R., El Cardenal Segura y el nacional-catolicismo (Barcelona, 1977).
Génesis e historia de la fundación católica de escuelas y patronato de San Vicente de Paúl de Bilbao (Bilbao, 1952).
Gil Cremades, J. J., El reformismo español. Krausismo, escuela histórica, neotomismo (Barcelona, 1969).
Gil Delgado, F., Conflicto Iglesia-Estado (1808–1975) (Madrid, 1975).
Gómez Molleda, M. D., Los reformadores de la españa contemporánea (Madrid, 1966).

Gómez Pérez, R., *Política y religión en el régimen de Franco* (Barcelona, 1976).
González-Anleo, J., *Catolicismo nacional: nostalgia y crisis* (Madrid, 1975).
Gorroño, I., *Experiencias cooperativas en el país vasco* (Durango, 1975).
Hermet, G., 'Les fonctions politiques des organisations religieuses dans les régimes à pluralisme limité', *Revue Française de Science Politique*, xxiii (1973).
——, *Les Catholiques dans l'Espagne franquiste*. 2 vols. (Paris, 1980, 1981).
Herr, R., 'El significado de la desamortización en España', *Moneda y Crédito*, 131 (1974).
Ibarruri, D., *They Shall Not Pass* (London, 1966).
Iglesia y sociedad en España 1939–1975 (Madrid, 1977).
Infante-Galán, J., *Rocío, la devoción mariana de Andalucía* (Seville, 1971).
'Jerarquía y apostolado seglar en España', *Pastoral Misionera* (1967).
Jobit, P., *L'Eglise d'Espagne à l'heure du Concile* (Paris, 1965).
Lannon, F., 'A Basque challenge to the pre-civil war Spanish Church', *European Studies Review*, ix (1979).
——, 'The Socio-Political role of the Spanish Church—A Case Study', *Journal of Contemporary History*, xiv (1979).
——, 'Modern Spain: the Project of a National Catholicism', in S. Mews (ed.), *Religion and National Identity* (Oxford, 1982).
——, 'The Church's crusade against the Republic', in P. Preston (ed.), *Revolution and War in Spain 1931–1939* (London, 1984).
Las fuentes ideológicas de un régimen (España 1939–1945) (Zaragoza, 1978).
Lisón-Tolosana, C., *Belmonte de los Caballeros* (Oxford, 1966).
Llabres i Martorell, P., 'Cursets de Cristiandat: un moviment apostòlic mallorquí pels quatre vents del mon', *Questions de vida cristiana*, 75–6 (1975).
Llorens, M., 'El P. Vicent S.J.', *Estudios de Historia Moderna*, iv (1954).
López-Morillas, J., *The Krausist Movement and Ideological Change in Spain 1854–1874* (Cambridge, 1981).
Los Hermanos de las Escuelas Cristianas en España. Su labor educadora durante medio siglo 1878–1928 (Madrid, 1928).
Luzuriaga, L., *La Institución Libre de Enseñanza y la educación en españa* (Buenos Aires, 1957).
Manent i Segimón, A., and Raventos i Giralt, J., *L'església clandestina a Catalunya durant la guerra civil (1936–1939)* (Montserrat, 1984).
Mantilla, S., *Un jesuita en las minas. El P. Juan Manuel Obeso en la zona minera de Vizcaya* (Valladolid, no date).
Maravall, J., *Dictatorship and Political Dissent. Workers and Students in Franco's Spain* (London, 1978).
Marquina Barrio, A., *La diplomacia vaticana y la España de Franco (1936–1945)* (Madrid, 1983).
Martín, I., and González Ruiz, N., *Seglares en la historia del catolicismo español* (Madrid, 1968).
Martín Descalzo, J. L., *Dios es alegre—antología del humor español posconciliar* (Madrid, 1971).

———, *Tarancón, el cardenal del cambio* (Barcelona, 1982).
Martín Gonzalez, A., *Los Salesianos de Utrera en España* (Sevilla, 1981).
Martín-Sánchez Julía, F., *Ideas claras* (Madrid, 1960).
Massot i Muntaner, J., *Aproximació a la historia religiosa de la Catalunya contemporánea* (Montserrat, 1973).
———, *L'església catalana al segle XX* (Barcelona, 1975).
———, *Església i societat a la Mallorca del segle XX* (Barcelona, 1977).
———, *L'església catalana entre la guerra i la postguerra* (Barcelona, 1978).
———, 'El Vaticà i Catalunya', *Questions de vida cristiana*, cix (Montserrat, 1981).
Mintz, J. R., *The Anarchists of Casas Viejas* (Chicago, 1982).
Montero, J. R., *La CEDA. El catolicismo social político en la II Republica*. 2 vols. (Madrid, 1977).
Montero Moreno, A., *Historia de la persecución religiosa en España 1936-1939* (Madrid, 1961).
Montoya, P. de, *La intervención del clero vasco en las contiendas civiles (1820-1823)* (San Sebastián, 1971).
Moriones, I., *Euzkadi y el Vaticano 1935-1936* (Rome, 1976).
Muntanyola, R., *Vidal i Barraquer, Cardenal de la Pau* (Montserrat, 1976).
Núñez Muñoz, M. F., *La iglesia y la restauración 1875-1881* (Tenerife, 1976).
Olabarri Gortezar, I., *Relaciones laborales en Vizcaya 1890-1936* (Durango, 1978).
Ollero Tassara, A., *Universidad y política. Tradición y secularización en el siglo XIX* (Madrid, 1972).
Orcasitas, M. A., *Unión de los Agustinos españoles (1893). Conflicto iglesia-estado en la restauración* (Valladolid, 1981).
Ordóñez Márquez, J., *La apostasía de las masas y la persecución religiosa en la provincia de Huelva 1931-6* (Madrid, 1968).
Oresanz, A. L., *Religiosidad popular española (1940-1965)* (Madrid, 1974).
Pabón, J., *España y la cuestión Romana* (Madrid, 1972).
Palacio Atard, V., *Cinco historias de la República y de la guerra* (Madrid, 1973).
Payne, S. G., *Falange: A History of Spanish Fascism* (Stanford, 1961).
———, *The Spanish Revolution* (London, 1970).
———, *Basque Nationalism* (London, 1975).
Petschen, S., *Iglesia-estado. Un cambio político. Las constituyentes de 1869* (Madrid, 1974).
Pitt-Rivers, J., *The People of the Sierra*. 2nd edn. (Chicago, 1971).
Portero, J. A., *Púlpito e ideología en la España del siglo XIX* (Zaragoza, 1978).
Prat, R., 'La crisi vocacions—Seminari a Barcelona (1960-71)', in 'Correspondència de diàleg sacerdotal', no. 100 (Dec. 1971), cyclostyled.
Preston, P., 'Alfonsist Monarchism and the Coming of the Spanish Civil War', *Journal of Contemporary History*, vii (1972).
———, 'El accidentalismo de la CEDA: aceptación o sabotage de la República?', *Cuadernos de Ruedo Ibérico*, nos. 41-2 (1973).

Preston, P., 'The "Moderate" Right and the Undermining of the Second Spanish Republic, 1931–1933', *European Studies Review*, iii (1973).
—— (ed.), *Spain in Crisis* (London, 1976).
——, *The Coming of the Spanish Civil War* (London, 1978).
—— (ed.), *Revolution and War in Spain 1931–1939* (London, 1984).
Puelles Benítez, M. de, *Educación e ideología en la España contemporánea* (Barcelona, 1980).
Raguer, H., *La Unió Democràtica de Catalunya i el seu temps (1931–1939)* (Montserrat, 1976).
——, *La espada y la cruz* (Barcelona, 1977).
——, *Divendres de passió. Vida i mort de Manuel Carrasco i Formiguera* (Montserrat, 1984).
——, 'La Iglesia española en la II República', *Arbor*, cix (1981).
Raguer, H., Estrade, M., and Massot, J., *La integració de les religioses a Catalunya* (Montserrat, 1977).
Rodríguez Aisa, M. L., *El Cardenal Gomá y la guerra de España* (Madrid, 1981).
Romero Maura, J., *La rosa de fuego: el obrerismo barcelonés de 1889 a 1909* (Barcelona, 1975).
RR. del Sagrado Corazón, *Cien años de educación cristiana* (Zaragoza, 1946).
Ruiz Rico, J. J., *El papel político de la Iglesia Católica en la España de Franco* (Madrid, 1977).
Sáenz de Santa María, C., *Historia de la universidad de Deusto (1886–1961)* (Bilbao, 1962).
Sáez Alba, A., *La ACNdeP. La otra 'cosa nostra'* (Paris, 1974).
Salaberri, K., *El proceso de Euskadi en Burgos* (Paris, 1971).
Samaniego Boneu, M., *La política educativa de la segunda república* (Madrid, 1977).
Schumacher, J. N., 'Integrism: a study in nineteenth century Spanish politico-religious thought', *The Catholic Historical Review*, xlviii (1962).
Simón Segura, F., *La desamortización española del siglo XIX* (Madrid, 1973).
Southworth, H. R., *El mito de la cruzada de Franco* (Paris, 1963).
——, *Guernica! Guernica! A Study of Journalism, Diplomacy, Propaganda and History* (Berkeley, 1977).
Steer, G. L., *Tree of Gernika* (London, 1938).
Tello, J. A., *Ideología y política. La iglesia católica española (1936–1959)* (Zaragoza, 1984).
Turin, Y., *Education et l'école en Espagne* (Paris, 1959).
Tusell, J., *Historia de la democracia cristiana en España*. 2 vols. (Madrid, 1974).
Ullman, J. C., *The Tragic Week: A Study of Anticlericalism in Spain, 1875–1912* (Harvard, 1968).
Vázquez, J. M., Medín, F., and Méndez, L., *La iglesia española contemporánea* (Madrid, 1973).
Viñayo, A., *El seminario de Oviedo* (Oviedo, 1955).
Winston, C. M., *Workers and the Right in Spain, 1900–1936* (Princeton, 1985).

Index

Acción Española 188-9, 197, 221
Acción Social Popular 157-9, 161
Adoratrices 202
aggiornamento 46, 58, 88, 224-5, 249, 256, 257
Aguirre, Cardinal Gregorio 130
Aguirre y Lecube, José Antonio 69, 194, 213-14
Agustín, Brother Antonio 66
Ajurias y Magunas 108
Alarcón, Julio 126, 139
Álava 12-13, 143
Albacete 169
Albareda, José María 222, 227
Alberca Montoya 183-4
Albó y Martí, Ramón 73 n. 31, 162, 171
Alcalá-Zamora, Niceto 184-5, 195, 196
Alfonso XII 1, 119, 121-2
Alfonso XIII 1, 30, 122, 172, 176, 177, 178, 179
Alfonsism 198, 199, 201, 215, 218, 222
Alicante 207
Almaraz, Cardinal Enrique 162
Almería 22, 169
Almonte 24-5
Álvarez Bolado, Alfonso 49
Amargos, Vicente 105
Amuriza, Javier 111
anarchism 14, 15, 30, 32, 68, 102, 145, 149, 166, 173, 178, 193, 195, 199, 201, 202; Catholic attitudes to 95, 151, 153, 154, 157
Andalusia 10, 13-16, 22, 24-8, 92, 100, 102, 168, 169, 182, 193, 201, 245
Ángela de la Cruz 68
Añoveros, Bishop Antonio 254
anti-clerical violence (1834-5) 2; (1909) 20, 165; (1931) 181; (1936-9) 77, 102-3, 201-2, 205, 210
Antoniutti, Monsignor Hildebrando 207
Aragón 13, 19, 24, 152
Arana y Goiri, Sabino 142
Aranguren, General 213
Aranguren, José Luis 46, 241, 242-3
Arboleya Martínez, Maximiliano 17, 102,

152-3, 154, 157, 162, 165, 167, 170, 179, 180, 182, 212
Areilza, José María 253 n. 64
Arenal, Concepción 40
Argaya Goicoechea, Bishop Jacinto 251
Arias Navarro, Carlos 253 n. 64, 254
Aristizábal, José Manuel de 174
Arizmendi-Arrieta, José María 239-41
Ariztimuño, José de 103
Armentia, David 108
Asamblea conjunta obispos-sacerdotes 47, 86, 113-14, 250
Asociación Católica Nacional de Propagandistas (ACNP) 52, 54, 134, 144, 163-5, 167, 174, 189, 190, 221, 227, 241, 255
Astorga 168
Asturias 16, 100, 102, 105, 154, 157, 190, 196, 234, 235
Atxa, Joseba 112
Augustinians 66, 81, 154, 175, 178, 184, 185 n. 41
Aunós, Eduardo 173, 197
Ávila 122, 255
Ayala, Ángel 52, 54, 163, 227
Azaña, Manuel 81, 184, 185, 199, 200, 222
Azcue, Resurección María 142
Aznar, Admiral 178
Aznar, Severino 154, 161, 162, 167, 171
Azpeitia 64
Azpiazu, J. 17 n. 14, 19

Badajoz 201, 209
Barandiarán, José Miguel 142-3
Barbastro 202
Barbera, Bishop Ramón 168
Barcelona 49, 100, 160-1, 162; Catholicism in 20, 46, 50, 51, 92, 102, 106, 107, 157-9, 165, 187, 202, 210, 228, 232, 250; religious communities in 68, 73-4, 76
Barea, Arturo 98-9
Baroja, Pío 43
Barrachina, Francisco 144

Index

Barriobera 183
Bases of Manresa 139, 140
Basque nationalism 56, 87, 100, 102–3, 107–13, 125, 142–3, 145, 159, 176, 205; see also Partido Nacionalista Vasca
Basque provinces 10, 12–13, 30, 56, 92, 100, 106, 107–13, 124–5, 129, 205, 213, 250–1, 252, 256
Basterra, Ángel 51–2
Batet, General 213
Bayle, Constantino 42
Benedictines 66
Bereciartua, Bishop Lorenzo 109, 251
Berenguer, General Damaso 177, 178
Bergamín, José 43, 183, 196, 211, 212
Bernanos, Georges 209 n. 28
Besteiro, Julian 40
Beunza 87
Bienvenido, Archbishop 133
Bilbao 143, 214; Catholicism in 16, 30–1, 51–2, 67, 129, 159, 232, 234, 235, 245, 252, 254; religious communities in 68–72, 79
Bilbao Atxikallende, Patxi 108
bishops 23, 50, 56, 57, 58, 86, 105, 106, 107, 113, 114, 136, 148–9, 156, 157, 164, 168, 170–1, 228, 229, 235, 244–7; appointment of 119, 121–2, 140–1, 146, 176, 236, 250, 251; killed in civil war 201; and politics 32, 112, 119, 120–3, 127–8, 130–2, 137, 139, 143, 176–7, 179, 187, 193, 202–7, 222, 251–5; see also pastoral letters, Spanish Episcopal Conference
Boix y Lluch, Joaquin 106
Bonet, Albert 210, 231
Bonet i Baltá, Joan 124 n. 11, 125 n. 12
Borrás, Bishop 202
Bosco, Don 68
Brenan, Gerald 22 n. 28, 98
Brothers of the Christian Schools (de La Salle) 65–6, 70–1, 79, 82, 83, 185 n. 41
Brothers of St. John of God 74, 77
Bueno Monreal, Archbishop José María 245
Burgos 31, 130, 147, 151, 168, 172, 191; Franco's government in 207, 208
Burgos trial (1969–70) 111–12

Cabanellas, General 32, 205
Cacho Viu, Vicente 142
Cádiz 16, 21–2, 98

Calvo Serer, Rafael 227, 230, 255
Calvo Sotelo, José 197
Calvo Sotelo, Leopoldo 242
Calzada, Luciano de la 190
Cambó, Francisco 140
Camino 226
Canalejas, José 77, 129, 136, 137–8
Cánovas del Castillo, Antonio 1, 3, 120, 122, 133, 136
Cantero Cuadrado, Archbishop 255
Carbonell, Ángel 100, 182, 210
Cardijn, Joseph 231, 233
Cardó, Carles 36, 182, 196, 210–11, 212
Carlism 1, 99, 120, 121–8, 133, 134, 145, 147, 160–1, 188, 198, 201, 215, 218, 222
Carlos, Don 124, 127
Carner, Josep 141
Carrasco i Formiguera, Manuel 80, 183, 195, 213
Carreras, Lluis 210
Carrero Blanco, Admiral 230, 254, 255
Casañas, Cardinal Salvador 125, 128
Casares Quiroga, Santiago 199
Casa Ulloa, Marquis of 67
Casas Souto, Bishop 128
Casas Viejas 98
Cascajares, Bishop Antonio María de 135–6
Castaño i Colomer, José 238
Castile 36, 174
Castro, Fernando de 40 n. 10
Castro Albarrán, Aniceto 188
Catalan nationalism 87, 100, 125, 139–42, 145, 176–7
Catalonia 178, 193, 205; Catholicism in 17, 23, 24, 34, 36, 77, 158, 231, 235, 256; priests in 100, 106, 124–5, 126, 128, 250
Catholic Action, pre-civil war 134, 146–9, 157, 163, 166, 169, 171, 172, 179, 180, 196; post-civil war 92, 218, 219, 221, 232, 240–1; see also Catholic workers' associations
Catholic agrarian associations 163, 164, 166–9, 174, 179, 196; see also Juventud Agraria Rural Católica
Catholic Congresses 147–9, 151, 172
Catholic Crusade (1936–9) 56, 203, 205, 207, 209–12, 214, 222, 230
Catholic Union 132–4
Catholic workers' associations, pre-civil war 148, 150, 151–61, 162, 164, 168,

172, 173-4, 179; *see also* Consejo Nacional de Corporaciones Católicas Obreras; post-civil war 56-7, 105-6, 107, 148, 218, 232-8; *see also* Hermandades Obreras de Acción Católica, Juventud Obrera Católica.
Cerro de los Angeles 30
Chopitea, Dorotea de 68
Christian, William 20, 28
Christian Democrat Group 161-2, 163, 164, 167, 171
Cicognani, Monsignor Gaetano 207
Cirarda, Bishop José María 96, 110-11, 112 n. 61, 251
Ciudad Real 202
Ciudad Rodrigo 10-11, 168, 244
Civil war (1936-9) 5, 28, 32-3, 45, 77, 83-4, 101-3, 104, 114, 198-215
Claretians 79, 202
Clemente (anti-Pope Gregory XVII) 29
Coloma, Luis 44, 50, 126
Comillas, Claudio Lopez Bru, Marquis of 31, 147, 148, 151, 152, 154, 155, 157, 158, 161, 162, 165, 171, 172
Comillas seminary 9, 106, 172
Comín, Alfonso Carlos 49, 250
comités paritarios 173-4
comunidades de base 58
communism 19, 199, 256; Catholic attitudes to 44, 203-4, 208, 212, 248; Catholic involvement with 49, 111, 213
concordat (1851) 60, 119, 124, 207, 215
concordat (1953) 110, 215, 251, 253
Confederación Española de Derechas Autónomas (CEDA) 163, 169, 174, 189-96, 198, 221
Confederación Nacional Católica Agraria (CNCA) 166-9, 174, 191
Confederación Nacional de Sindicatos Obreros Católicos (CNSOC) 153, 156-7, 160
Confederación Nacional del Trabajo (CNT) 68, 158, 161
Congar, Yves 241
Consejo Nacional de Corporaciones Católicas Obreras (CNCCO) 152-3, 155, 156, 157, 166
Consejo Superior de Investigaciones Científicas (CSIC) 222, 226-7
Conservative Party 133, 134, 136, 138, 139
Córdoba 16, 68, 102, 152, 182
Coria 172

Coripe 15
Cortina, Count of 68
Costa, Joaquín 40
Covadonga 56
Cruz y Raya 36, 43-4
Cursillos de Cristiandad 230-1

Daughters of Charity of St. Vincent de Paul 60, 66, 74
Daughters of the Cross, 67, 71
Dávila, General 214
Derio seminary 96, 110
desamortización 2-3, 59-60, 133
divorce 5, 6, 35, 57, 181, 189, 192, 215
Domingo, Marcelino 78
Dominicans 154-7
Duocastella, Rogelio, 10, 17
Durán i Bas, Manuel 122, 140

Echevarría, F. 126
education, state provision of 73, 78, 79, 80, 85, 86, 136-7, 175, 181, 203, 218, 221, 253; church provision of 5, 6, 18-19, 38, 50-1, 57, 62, 68-72, 74, 76-86, 175-6, 192, 221; *see also* universities
El Berrocal 14-15
El Ciervo 46
El Debate 70, 101, 163, 164, 167, 169, 174, 180, 196
El Rosal de la Frontera 13
El Siglo Futuro 124, 127, 171, 189
Emakumes 56
Enciso Viana, Bishop Jesús 231, 244
Enrique y Tarancón, Archbishop Vicente 228-9, 237-8, 245, 246-7, 254
Escolapios 60, 66, 79, 80
Escorial 81, 175-6, 190
Escrivá de Balaguer, José María 225, 226, 227
Espiritualidad Seglar 46, 51
ETA 109, 234, 252, 254
Etxabe, Jon 111, 112
Etxebarria, Mikel 112
Etxebarrieta Ortiz, Xabier 109
Extremadura 10, 168, 169, 172

fascism 178, 199, 200-1, 208, 211, 216
Falange 55, 199, 200-1, 215, 216-18, 221, 222
Falla, Manuel de 45
Federació de Jovens Cristians 231-2
Fernández Alia, Felipe 105

Fraga, Manuel 255
Franco, General Francisco 191, 217, 254, 255, 256; and the Spanish civil war 84, 202, 203, 204, 207–9, 213, 215; dictatorship of 5, 19, 21, 107–8, 171, 206, 215, 217, 222, 224–57
Freeman, Susan Tax 20
Fuente, Vicente de la 133
Fuenteovejuna 201

Gabacacogeascoa, Albert 108, 109, 111
Gaceta Regional 163
Gafo, José 154, 156, 160, 161, 162, 177, 197, 202
Galicia 168–9
Gallegos Rocafull, José Manuel 102, 182, 211, 212
Gamero, Pedro 216
Gamo, Mariano 111
García Escudero, José María 46
García Gallega, Jerónimo 101
García Hernández 195
García Morente, Manuel 220–1
García Prieto, M. 137
García Romero, José 126
García Salve, Francisco 111
Gaudí, Antoní 45
Gerard, Pedro 154–6, 158, 159, 160, 162
Gil Robles, José María 80, 134, 174, 190–1, 196, 197, 198, 255
Giménez Caballero, Ernesto 200–1
Giménez Fernández, Manuel 191
Giner de los Ríos, Francisco 40, 41, 43
Gomá, Bishop Isidro, and the Second Republic 179, 180, 187, 188; archbishop of Toledo 191–2, 193, 199, 201; and the Spanish civil war 202–5, 208–9, 211, 213; and the Franco regime 215–16, 220; obituary 42
Goñí, Blas 161
González, Archbishop Ceferino 41, 131
González Álvarez, Ángel 227
González de Cardedal, Olegario 49
González Martín, Archbishop Marcelo 106, 228, 250
González Ruiz, José María 47–8
Granada 40, 101, 133, 175
Grazalema 21–2, 29
Great Social Campaign 164–5
Gredos, Conversations of 241–2
Group at the Service of the Republic 178
Guernica 108, 214, 245
Guerra Campos, Bishop José 236, 238, 255

Guipúzcoa 101, 107, 125, 143, 194, 214, 234
Guisasola Menéndez, Archbishop Victoriano 131, 162, 167
Gúrpide, Bishop Pablo 96, 110

Hermandades Obreras de Acción Católica 105, 108, 232–6, 238
Hermet, Guy 246, 247
Hernández, Miguel 43, 44–5
Herrera, Ángel 129; and the ACNP 70, 134, 163, 164, 174, 195; and the CNCA 167, 169; and accidentalism 189–90, 207, 220; head of Catholic Action 196; bishop of Málaga 48
Herria-Eliza 112
Hervás i Benet, Bishop Joan 230
Hospital Sisters of the Sacred Heart 74
Huelva 13–14, 16, 24–5
Hurtado, Amadeo 183

Ibáñez Martín, José 221–2
Ibarra, Fernando de 70, 71
Ibarra, Gabriel María de 70
Ibarra de Vilallonga, Rafaela 72, 75
Ibarruri, Dolores 31
Ibeas, Bruno 154, 161, 162
Icaza, Pedro de 69
Iglesia Viva 249–50
Ilundain, Cardinal Eustaquio 13–16, 25, 193
Iñigo, J. 17
Institución Libre de Enseñanza (ILE) 38–42, 43, 69
Institute of the Guardian Angels 72
Integrism 99, 121, 122, 124–30, 142, 145, 147
integrist Catholicism 29, 42–3, 44, 46, 142, 161, 171–2, 220, 243, 255
Irastorza Loinaz, Francisco Javier 204
Irujo, Manuel 215
Irurita, Bishop Manuel 187
Isabel II 1, 82
Iturriza, Casilda 70

Jerez 154–6
Jesuits 61, 62, 66, 80, 93; and ACNP 163; and colleges at Deusto 68–70, 81, 175–6, 178, 183; and devotion to the Sacred Heart 29–31, 149; dissolution by Second Republic 181, 182, 184, 185, 192; and ILE 41–2; and Integrism 125–6, 129; and Marian congregations 51–2; and

Opus Dei 227, 228; restored by Franco 215; and Social Catholicism 154, 155, 157, 158, 162, 172, 232; see also, *Messenger of the Sacred Heart, Razón y Fe*
Jiménez, Inocencio 144, 145, 154, 162, 171
Jiménez de Asua, Luis 81, 184
Jobit, Pierre, 146
John XXIII, Pope 46, 88, 108, 224, 246-8; *Mater et Magistra* 247; *Pacem in Terris* 57, 247-8, 250
John Paul II, Pope 229
Juan de Borbón, 222, 256
Juan Carlos I 5, 256
Juventudes de Acción Popular (JAP) 190, 201
Juventud Agraria Rural Católica (JARC) 108, 109, 110
Juventud Obrera Católica (JOC) 105, 231-6, 238

Kalzada, Julen 111, 112
Krause, Karl Christian Friedrich 39

La Ciencia Tomista 156
Laín Entralgo, Pedro 45-6, 242
Lamamie de Clairac, José María 80, 187, 191
La Muela 15
Largo Caballero, Francisco 198
Larrañaga, Policarpo de 56 n. 49, 100, 159 n. 22
La Salle, de *see* Brothers of the Christian Schools
La Tour du Pin 173
Lecuona, Martín 103
Ledechowski, Fr. 208
Leo XIII, Pope 44, 85, 94, 122-3, 125, 128, 139, 144, 149, 155, 189, 191
León 166, 167, 168
Lérida 176, 202, 207, 230
Levant 152, 168
liberalism, Catholic attitudes to 29, 31, 37-8, 42, 45-6, 63, 81, 82, 83, 99, 100, 120, 122-30, 131, 133, 147, 150-1, 160, 162, 173, 187, 189, 224
Liberal Party 1, 136-9; and the religious congregations 62, 77-8; Catholic views on 81, 129
Lisón-Tolosana, C. 19, 22
Llanas, E. 128
Llanos, José María 49, 250
Lliga Regionalista 139-40

Llopis, Rodolfo 78
Llorens i Ventura, Josep María 102
Lobo, Leocadio 102
Logroño 168
López-Doriga Meseguer, Luis 101
López-Rodó, Laureano 229
Luca de Tena, Juan Ignacio 181
Lucia, Luis 194

Machado, Antonio 40
Maciá 179
Madariaga, Dimas de 80
Madrid 40, 106, 174, 175, 253-4; Catholicism in 16-17, 20, 36, 49, 92, 98, 102, 111, 137, 155, 156, 163, 167, 172, 180-1, 202, 203, 207, 228, 230, 235; religious communities in 67, 74, 75, 77, 80
Maeztu, Ramiro de 189, 197, 220
Málaga 16, 47-8, 49
Mallorca 209 n. 28, 230-1
Manterola, Ander 107 n. 45, 109
Manzanas, Melitón 109, 112
Maragall, Joan 165, 212
Marañón, Gregorio 178
María Luisa Fernanda, Infanta 68
Marian lay congregations 51-2, 163
Marias, Julian 43, 242
Marist Brothers 66, 79
Maritain, Jacques 43, 44, 210
Martín Álvarez, Carlos 152
Martínez, Bishop Zacarías 176
Martínez Anido, General 161
Martínez Campos, General 1
Mataró 17-18
Masnou, Bishop Ramón 250
Mass attendance 10-22, 34, 35
Maura, Antonio 80, 136, 139, 150
Maura, Gabriel 80
Maura, Miguel 195
Maura y Gelabert, Bishop Juan 150
Menaca 108
Mendicute, Alejandro 103
Mendizábal, Alfredo 196, 210, 212
Menéndez y Pelayo, Marcelino 9, 37-8, 40, 41, 45, 173, 220
Menéndez Pidal, Ramón 175
Menesianos 79
Menni, Ángel 74
Merry del Val, Cardinal 130, 155
Messenger of the Sacred Heart 29-31, 33, 41, 44, 126, 129
Miaja, General 32, 213

Millán Astray, General 84
Minguijón, Salvador 144, 162
Minteguiaga, Venancio María 129
Mintz, J. R. 98
Miret Magdalena, Enrique 51
Mola, General 198, 199, 203
Monasterio, Fermín 112
Mondragón 109, 239–41
Monedero, Antonio 166, 167–9
Montseny, Fedérica 56
Montserrat 23
Mora, Constancia de la 80
Morán, Francisco 162, 167, 171
Morcillo, Bishop Casimiro 105, 236, 238, 245
Moreno, Archbishop Juan 120, 133, 134, 147
Moreno Zulueta, Francisco 69
Moret, Segismundo 40
Morgades, Bishop José 140, 141
Múgica, Bishop Mateo 107, 143, 187, 195, 204–5, 206, 207
Murcia 221

National Assembly (of Primo de Rivera) 177
National Block 197, 199
national-Catholicism 33, 173, 220–1
Navarre 10, 92, 124–5, 143, 168, 188, 198, 203, 205, 206–7
Navarro Rubio, Mariano 229
Naverán, Jesús 111
Nelken, Margarita 56, 75, 80
Neva 13
Nevares, Sisinio 153, 167, 169, 172
Nocedal, Candido 124, 126, 127
Nocedal, Ramón 124, 126, 127
Noguer, Fr. 154

Olabarria, José Manuel 108
Olaechea, Bishop Marcelino 205, 206–7
Old Castile 10, 92, 152, 166–8, 200, 244
Onaindía, Celestino de 103
Opus Dei 52, 54, 114, 134, 221, 222, 225–30, 234
Orbe, Martín 112
Oreja, Marcelino 239
Oreja, Ricardo 144
Orgaz, Count of 133
Orihuela 121, 150, 204
Orovio, M. 39, 40, 124
Ortega y Gasset, José 40, 41–2, 43, 178

Ortí y Lara, Juan Manuel 40–1, 133–4
Ortiz, Luis María 31
Ossorio y Gallardo, Ángel 144, 145, 170, 181, 195, 196, 211, 212
Oviedo 31, 162, 175, 196

Pacelli, Cardinal Eugene *see* Pius XII
Palmar de Troya 29
Palos 13
Palau, Gabriel 157–9, 161
Palencia 166, 167, 168, 169
Pamplona 10, 92, 153, 155, 205, 226
Pardo Bazán, Emilia 40, 44
Partido Nacionalista Vasco (PNV) 102, 125, 142, 143, 145, 194–5, 204–5, 207, 213–14
Partido Social Popular (PSP) 143–5, 174
pastoral letters 50, 54, 130–1, 136, 141, 149 n. 5, 150, 162, 164, 170–1, 178–9, 186, 192–3, 202–6, 211–12, 214, 245, 251
Pastrana, Duke of 67
Patriotic Union 144, 173, 174, 177, 178
Paul VI, Pope 57, 110, 228, 249, 251, 253 n. 64, 254
Peces Barba, Gregorio 242
Peiró, Joan 202
Peiró, Francisco 16–17, 20
Pemán, José María 173, 177, 197, 220, 221
Pemartín, José 173, 220
Perancho, Tomás 156, 157
Pérez Galdós, Benito 40, 41, 62
Pidal i Mon, Alejandro 132, 134, 147
Pildain, Antonio 80, 101, 187
pilgrimages 23, 31, 34, 219
Pitt-Rivers, Julian 21–2
Pius IX, Pope 39, 120, 122, 257; *Syllabus of Errors* 122, 130, 131
Pius X, Pope 129
Pius XI, Pope 207–8, 214
Pius XII, Pope 108, 192, 206, 207–8, 211
Pla y Deniel, Archbishop Enrique 202, 208, 233, 234, 236, 245
Pont i Gol, Bishop 228, 250
Popular Action 134, 163, 174, 189–90, 191
popular piety 22–35
Prat de la Riba, 139, 140
priests (diocesan) 14–16, 142–3, 168, 182, 217; and celibacy 97–9, 114; in constituent Cortes (1931–3) 101; education of 47, 48, 54, 92–6, 113; funding

of 2–3, 5, 14–15, 104, 119, 171, 179, 181, 185, 192, 215, 253; killed in civil war (1936–9) 102–3, 201, 202, 205, 214; numbers of 2, 62, 89–90; and politics 99–103, 105–14, 123, 125, 132, 195, 206, 209, 252; and popular piety 23–9; recruitment of 90–3, 193; worker-priests 238–9
Primo de Rivera, José Antonio 200, 217
Primo de Rivera, Miguel, dictatorship of 4, 131, 142, 143, 144, 145, 161, 170–9, 188, 220
processions 24–8, 30–1, 34, 154, 196, 219
Professional Unions 158, 159
Propagandists *see* Asociación Católica Nacional de Propagandistas

Queipo de Llano, General Gonzalo 28, 83
Querejazu, Alfonso 241
Quiroga Palacios, Bishop Fernando 236

Ragonesi, Monsignor 155, 162
Razón y Fe 36, 41–2, 44, 46, 52–3, 129, 139, 180, 208
Reig, Archbishop Enrique 156, 162, 170, 171, 172
religious communities, finances of 2, 67–8; members killed in civil war 77, 201–2; legal restrictions on 137–9; numbers in 2, 60–2, 137; political values of 81–4, 179, 183; recruitment to 65–7; in Second Republic 181–6, 189, 192–3; schools and colleges of 62, 68–72, 76, 77–86, 182, 184–6; suppression of (1837) 59–60; welfare establishments of 73–7, 183, 184
religious liberty 2, 123, 180, 251
Republicans 129, 182, 188, 190, 194
Remesal, J. M. 82, 126
Revista Popular 126, 128
Revista Social 158
Ridruejo, Dionisio 222
Río, Cirilo del 81, 183
Ríos, Fernando de los 78, 175, 185
Ripalda catechism 81
Rodríguez Sampedro, Count 172, 178
Rojo, General 213
Romanones, Count 73, 77–8, 137
Romero Robledo, F. 140
Rosales, Luis 242
Ruiz, Agustín 153
Ruiz Amado, Ramón 38, 41

Ruiz Giménez, Joaquín 242, 244, 255
Rutten, Fr. 155

Sacred Heart, devotion to the 29–34, 62, 68, 149, 198, 219
SADEL 185 n. 41
Sáinz Rodríguez, Pedro 197, 207, 221, 222
Salamanca 10–11, 46, 80, 163, 175, 187, 188, 202
Sales, Ramón 200
Salesians 66, 68, 76, 80, 185 n. 41
Samblancat, 183
Sancha, Archbishop Ciriaco María 147, 152
Sánchez Carrasco, Bishop Pedro 122
Sánchez Mazas, Rafael 43, 200, 201
San Sebastián 109, 111, 232, 251, 252; Conversations of 46, 241, 242
Santamaría, Carlos 241
Santander 20, 28–9
Santiago 175, 219, 230
Sanz del Río, Julián 39–41
Sardá y Salvany, Félix 99, 126, 127, 128, 138
Sarrabia, Ramón 12
Second Republic 4, 24, 28, 32, 101, 142, 163, 169, 179–97; and the religious congregations 62, 75, 78, 80–2
Second Vatican Council 21, 36–7, 46, 48, 57, 64, 90, 97, 105, 224, 228, 237, 246–7, 248–9, 251, 252
Segorbe-Castellón 250
Segovia 101
Segura, Archbishop Pedro 47, 162, 171–3, 178–9, 180, 181, 186–7, 188, 192, 193, 195, 216–18, 228, 245
separation of Church and state 138, 181, 185, 192
Serra, Bishop 128, 133
Serrano Suñer, Ramón 190
Seville 10, 13–16, 47, 67, 68, 83–4, 92, 102, 121, 175, 193, 216–18, 245; Holy Week processions and brotherhoods in 25–8, 54
sex, Catholic attitudes to 35, 49–53, 55, 175, 226, 257
Silvela, Francisco 136
Sindicatos, Independientes 157, 165
Sindicatos Libres (of Barcelona) 160–1, 178, 200
Sindicatos Libres (Católicos) 155–7, 159, 165, 174, 178
Slaves of the Sacred Heart 80

socialism 70, 149, 166, 177, 181, 195, 198, 199, 200, 256; Catholic attitudes to 42, 95, 100, 114, 130, 131, 144, 145, 150, 153, 157, 159, 162, 163, 165, 169, 174, 189, 190, 194, 223, 224; Catholic involvement with 101, 213, 255, 256; and the Church 14, 15, 30, 31, 182, 257
Society of the Sacred Heart 66, 67, 83–4
Society of St. Vincent de Paul (SVP) 70
Solidaridad de Obreros Vascos (SOV) 143, 159, 160, 194
Solis Ruiz, José 234
Solsona 245
Sotomayor, Duke of 152
Spanish constitution (of 1876) 3, 119–24, 126, 127, 130, 132, 137, 170; (of 1931) 4, 14, 181–6, 190; (of 1978) 9
Spanish Episcopal Conference (CEE) 105, 110, 112, 228, 235–8, 251, 252–3, 254
Spanish Sacerdotal Brotherhood 114–15
Spínola, Archbishop Marcelo 102
Sturzo, Luigi 43, 144, 170
Suárez, Adolfo 256

Tácito group 255
Tarancón *see* Enrique y Tarancón
Tarazona 179
Tarragona 33, 148, 176, 204, 228
Tedeschini, Monsignor Federico 179, 191–2, 207
Tellería, Nicolás 111
Teresian Institute 55–6
Thomism 44, 94
Tibidabo 68
Toledo 34, 148, 171, 188, 193, 202, 228
Toniolo 155
Torras i Bages, Bishop José 122, 128, 140–1
Torrella, Ramón 105, 237
Torres, Humberto 183
Tortosa 176
Traditionalism 122, 123–5, 128, 133, 134, 138–9, 144, 145, 147, 160, 187, 188, 197, 199
'tragic week' (1909) 20, 100, 165
Tribujena 15

Ubieta, José Ángel 112 n. 61, 254
Ullastres, Alberto 229, 230
Unamuno, Miguel de 42, 43, 62, 175
Unión General de Trabajadores (UGT) 158, 159, 166, 173
universities 39–40, 69, 93, 175–6, 221–2
Uriarte, Eduardo 112
Urquijo y Ibarra, José María 129
Urquijo y Ibarra, Luisa 72
Ursulines 66
Utrera 68

Valdemora 20, 98
Valencia 10–11, 16, 31, 89, 94, 95, 106, 151, 232
Valencian Regional Right 194
Valencina y Castilleja de Guzmán 25
Valladolid 133, 135, 153, 168, 169, 172, 174, 175, 190, 191
Vallellano, Count 144
Valverde del Camino 16
Verdeguer, Jacint 44
Vicent, Antonio 150–3, 166, 167
Vich 122, 230, 250
Vidal i Barraquer, Cardinal Francesc 33, 141, 171, 176, 179, 180, 186, 188, 191–3, 202, 204, 205–6, 207
Vigón, General 32
Vilar i Costa, J. 211–13
Vilariño, Remigio 30, 126
Villada, Fr. 154, 162
Virgin Mary 22–9, 30–1, 34, 51, 53, 55, 83, 151, 154, 209
Vitoria 12–13, 176, 187, 204, 240; seminary 95, 106
Vivanco, Luis Felipe 242
Vives i Tutó, Cardinal 129
Vizcaya 17, 24, 79, 107, 113, 125, 143, 194, 214, 234

welfare, religious congregations and 73–7; state provision of 73–5
women, Catholic attitudes to 50, 53–8

Xirinacs, Luis María 107

Yegen 98

Zamora prison 109–11
Zaragoza 22, 144, 155, 190, 219, 255

Ch. 2, excellent for gender & sexuality issues

Printed in the United Kingdom
by Lightning Source UK Ltd.
1717